D1547434

THE DYING OF THE LIGHT

By the same author

THE DYING
OF THE LIGHT

A Searching Look at America Today

by ARNOLD A. ROGOW

G. P. Putnam's Sons, New York

Copyright © 1975 by Arnold A. Rogow

The lines from the poem "Expecting the Barbarians"
in *The Complete Poems of Cavafy* translated by Rae
Dalven are quoted by permission of Harcourt Brace
Jovanovich, Inc.

Quotations from "Do Not Go Gentle into That Good
Night" in *The Poems of Dylan Thomas*. Copyright 1952
by Dylan Thomas. Reprinted by permission of New
Directions Publishing Corporation.

SBN: 399-11509-9

Library of Congress Cataloging in Publication Data
Rogow, Arnold A
    The dying of the light.
    Bibliography: p. 359
    Includes index.
    1. United States—Social Conditions—1960-
2 Social problems.   I. Title.
HN65.R595 1975   309.1'73'092   75-15762

To
Bu, Jenny, Sarah
and
Ethan, Mark, Tina, Scott

Contents

An element of realism is needed in all morality; pure virtue is murderous . . . and an element of morality is needed in all realism; cynicism is murderous.

—CAMUS

Normal people do not know that everything is possible. . . . Only the inmates know.

—DAVID ROUSSET
VETERAN OF AUSCHWITZ

Preface

The supreme difficulty facing any interpreter of life in America is that almost any statement he wishes to make about the United States he can show to be at least half true. Thus he could say of most major problems, whether of poverty, racism, urban decay, or the spoilation of the environment, that the situation is improving, and indeed there is no lack of facts and figures to support such a statement. But with equal plausibility he could argue with reference to these and other problems that the situation is worsening, and this argument, too, can be buttressed with an impressive amount of data. No wonder that Americans of all ages, whatever their qualifications as trained scholars or informed laymen, are confused about the condition of the country on the eve of the national bicentennial. And if Americans are confused about the state of the union, how much more confused must be the rest of the world?

Until recently I had thought that our contemporary bewilderment about the nation's present and future was a relatively new development, that in the past there was less uncertainty about the meaning of the American experience and the direction in which the country was moving. But I discovered there were always two ways, at least, of viewing American society, and I concluded that much depends on whether the expectations one brings to the subject are fulfilled or disappointed. Thus not long after Tocqueville visited the United States and wrote his generally favorable *Democracy in America* (1835), Charles Dickens spent six months in America and was bitterly disillusioned by what he found. He had been prepared to encounter, in 1842, an orderly democratic country

11

that was well governed and free of class distinctions; instead he found "a body without a head," political oppression, coarseness, "the most pitiful, mean, malicious, creeping, crawling, sneaking party spirit," and a variety of other "follies, vices, grievous disappointments." Dickens returned to England with no doubt that "the heaviest blow ever dealt at Liberty's head, will be dealt by this nation in its ultimate failure of its example to the Earth."[1] Unlike Tocqueville, who as a liberal aristocrat entertained modest expectations of American democracy, Dickens, who was a self-styled "Lover of Freedom," expected too much.

As someone who is also a "Lover of Freedom" and whose political coming-of-age coincided with the years of the New Deal and World War II, I, too, perhaps expected too much of American politics during the decades that followed the death in 1945 of Franklin D. Roosevelt. Certainly the Roosevelt years, years of depression, fascism, unprecedented death, and war, were bleak enough, and I do not mean to romanticize them. Nor would I relive them if I could.[2] But I do not remember feeling at any time between 1933 and 1945 what I now feel, namely, that the United States would probably fail to resolve its most urgent internal problems, or that the quality of life, especially urban life, was steadily deteriorating, or that the political leadership in large measure was incompetent or corrupt (and sometimes both). I never believed that World War II was unnecessary and a tragic mistake, as I now believe the Korean War and even more the Vietnam War were unnecessary and tragic mistakes—indeed I am convinced that World War II was the last 'good' war the West will ever fight. Finally, I did not anticipate after World War II that the United States would seek to promote in almost every part of the world not freedom and equality, but its own economic and strategic interests. The confident expectations I nourished between 1933 and 1945, I now see, were naïve, given the balance of forces within the country and the world, but whether they were totally unrealistic I leave to the reader to determine.

Perhaps the present condition of the United States would have developed in the same way had Roosevelt and John F. Kennedy lived longer and had Nixon been defeated in 1968 or 1972. Not all problems, as the book tries to make clear, reflect a lack of political leadership, although there are many difficulties, in my view, that result from an absence of suitable moral models in social and political life. A major obstacle in this study and any study of the

United States is the need to distinguish between marginal and central tendencies and between those aspects of national life that are temporary or short run and those that are likely to prove permanent. Above all, no one who writes about life in America can avoid making an effort to determine which trends can be changed or reversed and which cannot.

In the category of centrality, permanence, and nonreversibility I would place the decline of the superego and the continuing loss of affect (or the capacity to feel and to respond to others), a further expansion of permissive sexual culture (more popularly known as the 'sexual revolution') and decline of the family, diminishing ethnic and cultural diversity (and the eventual dominance in the world of a universal mass or 'pop' culture of which the leading characteristics are American), increasing conflict between hedonistic consumption and resource scarcity, and a movement away from traditional individual and personal freedoms. These projections, all of which are discussed in the following chapters, are contingent on the world being able to avoid a third world war and the United States not becoming involved in a major war anywhere. I also am assuming that the system of government is more or less maintained in its present form. It is needless to make the point that another world war or a radical change in the form of government, neither of which can be entirely ruled out, could change and even completely reverse what formerly had been regarded as permanent.

Of all these developments that I regard, with the qualifications noted, as nonreversible, I view the decline of the superego and the conflict between hedonism and scarcity as the most threatening to the future of Western civilization. I am aware, of course, that probably no contemporary subculture or counterculture, unless it be psychotic, is without some type of superego, that is, some kind of moral code and value system. To go further at the risk of anticipating some later chapters: I doubt that middle-aged, middle-class Americans have anything to teach the youth culture about morals or ethics.* The old saw that there is honor among thieves probably applies more to the corporation than the com-

---

*Indeed certain attitudinal and behavioral changes in recent years that I most welcome are more evident among young people than among adults. I refer to attitudes toward blacks making possible relaxed social relationships and greater acceptance of sexuality and therefore less need for repression. Both developments owe much to the youth culture.

mune; perhaps the more apt saying, in terms of recent American experience, is that there is no dearth of thieves among those in positions of honor.

But in any case, the superego to which I refer is not that of the small social group of Western society as a whole, or at least that part of it that historically is identified with the Judaic-Christian tradition. In this context, the term "superego," to which here I am giving a different meaning from that assigned to it by psychoanalysts, should be broadly understood as the *conscience and sensibility* of the Western mind, a conscience and sensibility that place a supreme value on human life and dignity, that attach importance to the intelligence of man and its ability to reason through to a right conclusion, that accept the inevitability of self-denial and frustration in private and social life, and that encourage in everyone respect for others and an awareness of the things that are *not* done. If, as I suspect, this conscience and sensibility are in decline, then the prospect that the United States will take positive action to end world poverty by curtailing its demand for scarce resources and by reducing consumption, or that white Americans will undertake to share their wealth with black Americans, is not very great.

For I submit that middle-class America's most appropriate response to the revolution of rising expectations in Africa, Asia, and Latin America and among its own poor against the background of scarcity would be to initiate a domestic revolution of falling expectations. Nothing less, in my view, can avert catastrophe abroad and further deterioration at home, a deterioration that sooner or later will lead to repression and the beginnings of a garrison state. But for a variety of reasons, any revolution of falling expectations would encounter formidable counterrevolutionary obstacles. To begin with, such a revolution would require fundamental changes in the corporate enterprise system, changes that those who profit most from the system will not willingly permit and even those who profit least do not want. To the extent the system provides for the poor, which is to a very little extent, it does so out of growth and expansion in the economy; the operating principle, someone once said, is that you fed the sparrows by feeding the horses. If there is little or no growth and expansion, poverty programs and social services can be provided only by shifting resources from the private sector to the public sector or by sharply reducing military expenditures. Since there is no popular demand that these shifts be made, and since, further, they are opposed by powerful interests, the likelihood is that the poor will remain poor and continue to filch what they can from the horses.

Would a charismatic leader in the White House who was also a superego figure make a difference? One reads in almost all newspapers and magazines that the nation is willing to make sacrifices in behalf of peace and 'cries out' for courageous leadership. Perhaps both statements are true, but I am forced to question not merely whether such leadership exists in the ranks of either party but whether, if it did exist, Americans could be led in a direction significantly different from the direction currently being taken. The charismatic superego heroes have long since been replaced, in the public mind, by apostles of hedonism in one form or another; Jesus and Freud have given way to Norman Vincent Peale and Hugh Hefner. No political figure would survive in politics if he declared himself opposed to affluence and rising levels of consumption. Certainly he would be a very nearsighted politician if he failed to notice the American taste for luxury that leads all classes to "build their plans, the rich to spend more and save less, and the poor to spend more and work less."[3] If he campaigned against those "plans," he would be a defeated politician as well.

Because the problems often seem insurmountable, I sometimes am tempted to "powerfully assume," with Franz Kafka, "the negativity of my times." How long, I wonder, will the blacks, the unemployed, the alienated, and the rootless tolerate an existence "in which," to quote from Matthew Arnold, "suffering finds no vent in action; in which a continual state of mental distress is prolonged, unrelieved by incident, hope, or resistance; in which there is everything to be endured, nothing to be done." Men will endure a good deal, to be sure, if the suffering is equally shared and if the social contract binds races and classes in society as well as generations in what Edmund Burke termed "a partnership not only between those who are living, but between those who are living, those who are dead, and those who are to be born." Unfortunately, in the United States neither races nor classes nor generations have felt themselves to be bound by anything more than a minimal agreement in recent years, with the result, on the eve of the bicentennial, that little remains of the spirit of American "partnership."

But while I regard the light that once blazed so brightly, that once was hailed as a beacon to the world, as a dying light, I do not think of it as dead. Not yet. In the chapters of this book I have tried to suggest what could be done to promote integration, eliminate poverty, restore the cities, improve the quality of everyday life, and reduce the chances of war. America and the world have trembled before on the edge of the void and on each occasion have managed to pull back in time. Thus mankind has averted, until now, nuclear war, global totalitarianism, the starvation of entire populations, and actions that would render the earth itself unfit for human life. I therefore am not willing to rule out the possibility that we shall extricate ourselves from the morass and find solutions to seemingly insoluble problems. Still much of our history and psychology, most of our rules and arrangements, many of our habits and customs point us away from rather than toward such solutions. But so long as there is life and hope and the slightest chance, let us "Rage, rage against the dying of the light."[4]

THE DYING OF THE LIGHT

1

When the Saints Went Marching In

In the American beginning it was not enough to be what the Puritans called a "civil man," that is, someone "outwardly just, temperate, chaste, carefull to follow his worldly business, will not hurt so much as his neighbours dog, payes every man his owne, and lives of his owne; no drunkard, adulterer, or quareller; loves to live peaceably and quietly among his neighbours." It was not enough, thundered the Reverend Thomas Shepard from his pulpit at Cambridge, because "though thy outside, thy sepulcher, be painted," there was little but rottenness and sin within. Good citizens, therefore, no matter how they "comfort themselves in their smooth, honest, civil life," are nevertheless guilty of "heart whoredom, heart sodomy, heart blasphemy, heart drunkenness, heart buggery, heart oppression, heart idolatry." And since God looks to the heart, the Reverend Shepard assured his listeners, even good citizens could be certain that hell loomed ahead because their sins of the heart were those "that terribly provoke the wrath of Almighty God against thee."[1]

No doubt an impressive number of Americans still believe, with Shepard, that if they have any "good thing" in them, "it is but a drop of rosewater in a bowl of poison," but they are likely to be either psychiatric patients or communicants in a fundamentalist religious order. For the most part Shepard's fulminations, which in his time were capable of making strong men weep and women faint, now occasion only amusement and perhaps some speculation about the nature of that worthy's dreams and fantasies. But before dismissing them as outpourings of a typical seventeenth-century Puritan mind, we would do well to ponder certain implications of the Puritan belief that it is faith, not good works, that leads to salvation. For by sharply distinguishing between "smooth, honest, civil life" and the "sins of the heart," Shepard was making virtue and the reward of heaven dependent not on everyday acts and appearances, but on the nature of one's innermost wishes and desires. In declaring that the bad thought counted for much more than the good deed and that, in particular, secret lusts and lewdness weighed more heavily than civic virtue, Shepard and other Puritan divines were driving a moral wedge into the depths of the national conscience, the effect of which was to create a fateful division in the American mind between private and public morals. The frequent spector in America of scandals perpetrated by men whose private lives are as exemplary as their public lives are corrupt, and whose humility before God is equaled only by their arrogance and contempt in the presence of their fellowmen, owes a good deal to Shepard's implicit assumption that the Almighty cares more about the transgressions of the bedroom than those of the boardroom and that He will forgive much evildoing if only it is accompanied by appropriate expressions of God-fearing piety. The ease with which the public has always accommodated itself to evidence of dishonesty in high places and the eager welcome the churches have always provided for men of great wealth and little rectitude are other legacies of Shepard and his fellow Puritans.

Still his metaphor of the "painted sepulcher" is not altogether misleading once it is freed of the connection with sex and blasphemy. While the metaphor no longer serves to call attention to the alleged sinful side of the American psyche, it has a certain relevance to American society itself, which some Americans in recent years have come to view as a kind of "painted sepulcher" concealing not only the dead and dying victims of American firepower abroad and at home but all manner of sin and villainy. Shepard's metaphor, indeed, is an apt one insofar as it reminds us, in the midst of an anniversary celebration, that there is a dark side to the American experience which no amount of paint can entirely cover over, a side of violence and primitive passion, of ruthless greed and unprincipled ambition, that would risk all and stop at nothing to advance itself. In the awareness of some Americans the dark side began to emerge with the assassination of John F. Kennedy and to mature with the turmoil of the Vietnam War and the successive crises of the Presidency. In the perception of others the dark side was always there, rooted in the ancestral European past with its interminable wars and revolutions and raised to brute strength by the perils of immigrant crossings and the struggle to survive in isolated frontier settlements and friendless cities. But whatever the source and history of the dark side, there was little doubt in the minds of many thoughtful Americans that it could not be disregarded in any estimate of the nation's present or future prospects. There was little doubt and, as the following chapters attempt to demonstrate, much evidence, as America prepared to enter its third century, that after 200 years the paint on the sepulcher had begun to wear thin.

Perhaps, however, it was never very thick. Certainly every generation is tempted to regard its own time as the best or the worst or both, and it is reassuring to discover that as early as 1679, according to the late Harvard scholar Perry Miller, the New England colonists were inquiring into the civic health of the nation, some of them with a concern that is almost modern in its intensity. Then, too, there was anxiety about the institution of marriage and family life, the quality of education and the attitudes of the young, even the crime rate; in 1643 no one was charged with murder or manslaughter in ten Massachusetts Bay Colony towns containing some 6,000 persons, but there were 8 cases of robbery including breaking and entering, 10 cases of assault, 7 of drunkenness, 6 of sexual crimes such as prostitution and illegitimacy, and 7 of extortion which included the practice of weighting short.[2]

By the standards of today, of course, the incidence of serious crime, was negligible, but this does not mean that there were no problems or that those early migrants to America were saints and supermen. To begin with, the migration was relatively small during the first 100 years, and not many of those who braved the terrors of the Atlantic were what was then referred to as "quality." The great majority of the 70,000 people who left England for the New World were from the ordinary class of citizens and, while the numbers are not certain, included a good many failed tradesmen and farmers evicted by enclosures, agricultural laborers, bankrupts, younger sons victimized by primogeniture, servants, beggars, orphans, criminals, women of uncertain status, and even some prisoners of war (mainly from among those captured by

Cromwell's forces).* The Spanish and French immigrants were of similar social origin, but the colonies of Spain also attracted the poorer nobility and those who were seeking both fortune and adventure. Of the English migrants, moreover, about half went to the West Indies—leading some Puritans to wonder whether Massachusetts would not become a way station en route to the West Indian islands—and another 12,000 settled in Virginia, Maryland, and Bermuda. No more than 18,000 English immigrants had made their homes in New England by 1640, of whom 14,000 were living in the Puritan heartland of Massachusetts Bay Colony.

While it is conventional historical wisdom to regard religious motives, chiefly the experience of persecution in Europe or a certain zealotry, and economic factors as the principal causes of the seventeenth-century migration, these motivations were by no means equal in strength. Except for the Puritans and, to a much lesser extent, the Quakers and a few small sects favoring esoteric religious practices or political reforms, the migrants to the New World "were, in general, those who were most acutely discontented with their status in European society and who had the least hope of being able to improve it . . . the majority expected to improve their economic condition."[3] Nor were those who migrated later different in this respect. Unlike the Philadelphia Quakers, of whom it was said that they came over to do good and ended by doing well, almost all of the 60,000,000 Europeans who arrived in the United States during the first 300 years of its history came over to do well, and a very large proportion of them ended by doing well, or at least better than they would have done had they remained in Europe.† A large number of the early English mi-

---

*Some idea of the social-class distribution among the English migrants can be gained from records referring to paying passengers aboard ships as "Eighteen men of quality and eighty-seven others," "Seven men of quality and sixty-four others," and "a Score of quality, one hundred and four others." (M. Campbell, "Social Origins of Some Early Americans," in P. Goodman, ed., *Essays in American Colonial History* [New York: Holt, Rinehart and Winston, 1967], p. 204.) One estimate is that only 12 of 2,000 immigrants in 1630 were freedmen or stockholders in the settlement company. (H. Hockett, *Political and Social Growth of the American People* [New York: Macmillan, 1940], p. 36.)

†Unfortunately, one must emphasize that the migrants referred to do not include the estimated 5,000,000 to 10,000,000 Africans who were brought over as slaves, most of them to the West Indies, and the unknown number of Chinese,

grants, for example, came from economically depressed and over-populated areas of England such as East Anglia and the Midlands, and it is a commonplace that the later movement to America of the Irish, Italians, and Scandinavians derived its energy from prolonged economic slumps and repeated crop failures. No doubt it was a rare European emigrant to America who did not have lodged in his memory, even after he had settled there, the old-world experience of civil war or invasion, pestilence, oppression, hunger approaching famine, and, above all, no hope of any substantial improvement for either himself or his children.

But in a special sense those who came to America were no commonplace human beings driven to leave Europe by poverty and the lack of opportunity. For not everyone, as historian Henry Bamford Parkes has suggested, who was underprivileged or harshly treated chose to migrate. Perhaps it is reasonable to suppose that most of those who left their homes for an unknown country were to some degree self-selected and possessed certain qualities lacking in those who remained behind, qualities of courage and enterprise that made them different from the others and, in the course of time, became the basis for the American character itself. It is in this sense, Parkes comments, "that America was from the beginning a state of mind and not merely a place."[4]

Within this state of mind the desire for material improvement was so strong and the expectation of it so confident that all religion and morality inevitably were to bow to it, although some religions not without a struggle. As Michael Walzer and other historians have demonstrated, Puritanism was in part a response to the gradual transformation of England from a medieval to a modern society, a transformation to which the Puritans were opposed. Liking little that they saw around them, either in England or Holland, they hoped to establish in the New World a theocratic society that would somehow hold back the movement of moderniza-

---

Mexicans, and persons of Hispanic origin who came to the United States as contract laborers or, not to put too fine a point on it, peons. To go further: not until well into this century was the term "American," as popularly used, understood to include nonwhites; and even now it cannot be said that the black American has fully entered upon the stage of our history. In this sense the black effort to move upward in American society can be viewed as one of the most important migrations in history and the millions of blacks attempting it as constituting the last of the large immigrant groups to arrive in the United States.

tion and its attendant secular impulses. The main thrust of Puritanism was, in a word, reactionary, and while ultimately the Puritans, too, failed as counterrevolutionaries, they left a heritage of values, attitudes, and dispositions that includes much more than the Reverend Shepard's obsessive fear of "atheism, sodomy, blasphemy, murder, whoredom, adultery, witchcraft, buggery . . . all these things stirring within thee . . . like a nest of snakes. . . ."[5]

The Puritan view of life, to begin with, was a harsh and pessimistic one which deeply stained the character and institutions of America. Placing the emphasis on work and prayer, the Puritans proscribed pursuits which today are regarded as essential to culture and happiness, pursuits such as the theater and most forms of art and literature that were not of a religious nature. As the British historian Macaulay later commented, "The Puritan hated bearbaiting, not because it gave pain to the bear, but because it gave pleasure to the spectators," and there was also a good bit of truth in the definition of Puritanism as "the haunting fear that someone, somewhere may be happy." The God of the Puritans was, after all, a vengeful Old Testament God who was worse, even, than the God of the ancient Hebrews and who held out little promise of contentment either in this world or in the next. Given the ubiquity of sin, most men were damned from the start, and especially damned were those who enjoyed life and who were relatively free of guilt—those, in short, whom we would today describe as well adjusted.*

The Puritan work ethic, of course, was well suited to the American environment, and in general Puritanism stressed virtues which, whether or not they were Christian ones, were certainly the virtues necessary for the country's economic development, namely, thrift, frugality, sobriety, and above all a diligent application to the work at hand. The physical austerity of early New England life was entirely compatible with the Puritan life-style, and

---

*It was not long ago that this influence was manifest and in some parts of the country still is manifest in so-called Blue Laws preserving Sunday as a day of rest and therefore requiring that stores, cinemas, and other recreation centers be closed. Of course the Puritans were not the only ones who believed that Adam and Eve were actual people and who promoted temperance, but laws banning the teaching of evolution in the schools and the "dry" laws in various states are consistent with Puritanism.

the raw conditions of existence, the need to clear land and establish settlements, demanded unremitting hard work and sobriety. No wonder that waste, ostentation, and idleness were frowned upon and greed and avarice condemned; in an economy dominated by scarcities, some restrictions of consumption and regulation of wages, prices, and profits were also necessary.

In a setting that abounded with natural resources and opportunities to develop them, the qualities extolled by the Puritans were inevitably those that made some men rich. Wealth in the early period was regarded almost as a trust from God because it was evidence of God's blessing. As Calvin had put it: "Though some seem to enrich themselves by diligence, it is nevertheless God who blesses and cares for them. Though others are rich before they are born and their fathers have acquired great possessions, this is nevertheless not by accident but the providence of God rules over it." From this point of view, the man of wealth was a steward or trustee for his wealth and as such expected to live unobtrusively and to perform good works. Certainly he was not free to exploit this evidence of God's favor and do with his property whatever he wished.

But it was not long before the Puritans, like other religious sects, were forced to make their peace with mammon and ultimately to abandon the idea that frugality and simplicity were essential aspects of a Christian life. The shift was gradual, to be sure; not until two centuries later was Protestant Episcopal Bishop William Lawrence of Massachusetts able to declare without any apology that "Godliness is in league with riches."[6] The concept of wealth as conferring a stewardship remained, but the emphasis on obligation and responsibility was reduced. Wealth, no matter how obtained and used, was still evidence of God's favor, and it is a matter of record that none of the robber barons, not even the worst of them, ever departed this world without the accompaniment of fulsome praise from the minister to whose church he had, in life and sometimes in death, contributed handsomely. Thus a Presbyterian doctor of divinity, over the casket of one of the most corrupt political figures in Pennsylvania history, declared the deceased to have been "always on the right side of every moral question." A distinguished Methodist minister who later became a bishop, when called upon to officiate at the funeral of a Western railroad millionaire known for his ruthlessness, compared the man's youth to the boyhood of Christ, while a Unitarian clergy-man, delivering a funeral oration in the United States Senate in behalf of a Senator who had obtained his office through bribery and had boasted that he carried "the larger business methods" into politics, eulogized "this whole-souled child of God who believed in success and knew how to succeed by using the infinite powers."

Not surprisingly, the corollary principle that the poor are poor in accordance with divine intention gained ground, thereby making it possible to countenance the most extreme forms of poverty without a twinge of guilt, much less the desire to remedy the situation. Even the Reverend Lyman Abbott, an enlightened clergy-man, was not entirely opposed to the "gospel of wealth," as he demonstrated in 1896 by declaring: "The Old Testament declares that it is God who bestowes wealth as a reward for virtue so that it becomes, though by no means an infallible sign, yet a sign of holiness and divine favor." Abbott also reminded his listeners that "there is as little authority in the New Testament as in the Old for the indiscriminate condemnation of private property. . . . In his teaching Christ never condemns private property; he impliedly approves it . . . and in the day of reckoning the only one who is condemned is he who has done nothing to increase the store entrusted to him. . . . It is indeed a truism that there can be no distribution, no beneficence without acquisition, no giving without something first obtained which may be given."[7] In many a city toward the end of the nineteenth century few clergymen could be found to support measures limiting child labor or reducing the number of hours worked, and there was even less support for union-organizing efforts and minimum-wage laws. Clearly Horace Greeley was not wrong to observe in 1867 that "Religion would seem often a part of the subordinate machinery of police, having for its main object the instilling of proper humility into the abject, of contentment into the breasts of the downtrodden, and of endowing with a certain reverence for property those who have no personal reason to think well of the sharp distinction between Mine and Thine."[8]

Greeley's point, however, was generally lost; few ministers observed that there was one morality for the rich and another for the poor. Indeed, the churches of America have always been skilled in accommodating scruples to the needs of the time and the exigencies of life. Thus the Quakers, whose principles precluded their bearing arms and subscribing to war loans and requisitions, made substantial gifts of money to the British Crown during the French and Indian Wars, and although teetotalers, some of them had no difficulty supplying the British, French, and Indians with liquor as well as guns. Under the Puritan moral code, you could not dig up Indian graves and desecrate their burial grounds, but you could kill Indians for the flimsiest of reasons, as Miles Standish did in 1623.* Prior to and during the Civil War the churches of the South had no trouble reconciling slavery with a devout belief in the fatherhood of God and brotherhood of man, just as those in the abolitionist strongholds of the North had no trouble demonstrating that God was on the side of the One and Inseparable Union; it was, perhaps, to this talent in reconciling principles and realities that Lincoln referred when he commended the Methodists, who were more numerous than other sects, for sending "more soldiers to the field, more nurses to the hospital, and more prayers to Heaven than any! God bless the Methodist Church. Bless all the churches, and blessed be God, who, in this our great trial, giveth us the churches." The discovery by *Everybody's* magazine in 1908 that the Trinity Corporation, a church body in New York, owned several flourishing brothels and housing "not fit for the habitation of animals" tended to show that even Shepard's inspired proscription of "heart whoredom" had significantly weakened, at least so far as it related to activities in which religious institutions were not directly involved and from which they could derive important material benefits.†

---

*Standish and six other men, according to Massachusetts historian Thomas Boyston Adams, lured a number of Indians into a stockade near Boston under the pretext of trade. Suddenly closing the gates behind them, "they stabbed and murdered two chief warriors, hung another with rope and shot or hacked to death three more. . . . The alleged reason for the massacre was a plot suspected against the settlement of Plymouth." Adams notes, however, that the "Wessagusset Affair," as it was called, was by far the worst crime that could be charged against the Pilgrims, who were "decidedly tolerant, almost gentle," compared with John Winthrop and settlers of Boston Bay. (New York *Times*, November 25, 1971.)

†Lincoln's commendation appears in J. G. Nicolay and John Hay, eds., *Complete Works of Abraham Lincoln* (New York: Century, 1894), Vol. 2, p. 522. In today's America the "rendering unto Caesar," for a profit, is more likely to take the form of church investments in corporations active in arms production. In 1972 it

With the secularization of religion, which was well under way by 1865, the churches gradually ceased to have much influence on either morals or manners outside of rural America, and their religious influence was likely to manifest itself in crusades against "sin," mainly involving sex and drinking, and the banning of certain school textbooks. The pleasures of the flesh remained the enemy, and in fact only recently, when church basements are given over to encounter groups and Masters and Johnson-type sexual-therapy clinics, can it be said that the ghosts of the Puritan fathers have finally been banished from the land. Marginally, perhaps, the churches are more relevant to problems of social welfare and civic responsibility than they were in earlier times, but it is fair to comment that the average minister in the average churcl on an average Sunday is unlikely to say anything that would ruffle either the conscience or the digestion of those who occupy the front pews.[9]

The decline of religious orthodoxy was paralleled by the democratization of politics, and this, too, was not achieved without bitter struggle. The Puritans, of course, could not conceive of a society in which church and state were separate, and they did not hesitate to use the powers of the state to enforce their position. Civil laws were brought to bear on all who violated the sabbath, and church attendance was compulsory, as was taxation to support the churches. The worst penalties of all were reserved for those deemed to be heretics or thought to be practicing witchcraft; the choice in most cases was death or exile, and even such a

---

was revealed that 10 major Protestant denominations owned stock in 29 of the top 60 defense contractors including United Aircraft Corporation, Litton Industries, Lockheed, TRW Inc., Texas Instruments, and ITT. By value of stocks owned, the leading church investor was the United Methodist Church, with investments in 23 companies worth almost $60 million, followed by the United Presbyterian Church, with holdings in 18 companies worth $58 million. The total investment for the 10 denominations was estimated at $1.5 billion. Of the 29 defense contractors, one, Lockheed, was engaged in military production to the extent of 73 percent of total sales, and another, United Aircraft, was engaged to the extent of 37.5 percent of total sales. The defense business of 5 companies, Litton, Honeywell, Texas Instruments, Olin, and Sperry Rand, accounted for between 20 and 30 percent of total sales. ("Church Investments, Technological Warfare and the Military-Industrial Complex," report of the Corporate Information Center, National Council of Churches, as summarized in the New York *Times*, January 5, 1972).

mild dissenter as Roger Williams, who tried to distinguish between what was spiritual and what was temporal, was banished.
The idea, said John Cotton, that civil magistrates should confine
their attention to laws based on the last six commandments and
exclude from their jurisdiction those based on the first four was
"carnal philosophy." God, he insisted, does not hesitate to use
"legal terror to prepare hard and stout souls for conversion."

In Puritan strongholds only church members could become
freemen with the right to vote. Not until 1692 in Massachusetts
were property qualifications substituted for church membership
as the basis of the franchise. One estimate is that only a fifth or so
of adult men were freemen. Cotton himself regarded democracy,
or rule by many, as the worst form of government, and when he
rejected the establishment of a government based on aristocracy,
as he did in a letter of 1636 to Lord Say and Seale, he did so not
because he was opposed to the principle of minority rule, but because such a government would involve the abandonment of
church membership as a requirement for the suffrage. Puritans
willingly acknowledge, he wrote, two distinct ranks in society, the
first consisting of nobles, elders, and gentlemen, the second of the
people, with only the former entitled to hereditary honors and
privileges.

The democratic features of Puritanism are essentially peripheral to the main body of Puritan thought, and democratic government, in general, draws little inspiration from any system of religious belief. In the idea that man can face his Maker in direct con-
frontation rather than through the intermediary of a priest or
other go-between there is, of course, an important kernel of what
later became the democratic belief in the capacity of every man
for self-government. It may also be said that the compact or contract, of which the Mayflower Compact was an example, used by
the Pilgrims, Puritans, and others as a means of organizing their
settlements in accordance with certain laws and customs is an important early expression of the social-contract theory upon which
was constructed, in 1787, the foundation of the Constitution of
the United States. Nor need there be a quibble about the Puritan
and Quaker emphasis on local government—the form of government in those days could hardly have been anything but local—or
on the importance of participation in community affairs, or on
those qualities of mind and outlook, tangible and intangible, that

two centuries afterward and well into our own time were to be celebrated as essential components of American character. The Puritan elders, were they to return to America today, would not like very much what they saw around them, but they could hardly deny some responsibility for what they saw, whether they approved or disapproved.

Religious questions aside, the Founding Fathers with a few exceptions were hardly less conservative than the Puritan fathers in their attitude toward most questions of the day including, until the very last years of the colonial period, the question of American independence. As late as 1774 John Adams could describe independence as "a Hobgoblin of so frightful mien, that it would throw a delicate person into fits to look it in the face."*[10] Again and again the sober men of the period cautioned both sides, the British and their fellow Americans, against intemperate action as they groped for a compromise that would give the colonies a substantial measure of self-government within the framework of the British Empire. Some of them, Franklin in particular, urged on the British plans of government that anticipated what much later became the British Commonwealth of Nations, plans that envisaged a type of dominion status for the American colonies. But even Franklin despaired of what he termed "a sufficient quantity of wisdom" on the part of London, and it was a despair that contained more than a trace of personal sorrow and regret. "Upon the whole," he wrote Lord Kames in 1767, "I have lived so great a part of my life in Britain, and have formed so many friendships in it, that I love it, and sincerely wish it prosperity; and therefore wish to see that union, on which alone I think it can be secured and established. As to America, the advantages of such a union to her are not so apparent. . . . America, an immense territory, favored by nature with all advantages of climate, soils, great navigable rivers, etc., must become a great country, populous and mighty; and will, in a less time than is generally conceived, be able to shake off any shackles that may be imposed upon her, and perhaps place them on the imposers. In the mean time every act of oppression will sour their tempers, lessen greatly, if not annihi-

---

*By the end of his life Adams had reached a somewhat different conclusion. The "true history of the American Revolution," he commented in 1818, could not be recovered because the "revolution was effected before the war commenced. The revolution was in the minds and hearts of the people."

late, the profits of your commerce with them, and hasten their final revolt; for the seeds of liberty are universally found there, and nothing can eradicate them."

The Revolution, whether viewed as "Hobgoblin" or as seedbed of liberty, could not be contained and perhaps would have been inevitable in the course of time no matter what transpired in English corridors of power. The provocations, Americans believed, were numerous, although they were not notably different from those inflicted upon the other British colonies. In those days *all* colonies were taxed without representation, had their trade and commercial affairs regulated, and occasionally were forced to meet requirements of men and money for imperial wars by their mother countries. Indeed, British rule in North America was, if anything, more humane and permissive than British rule elsewhere, partly because the rulers much of the time had their attention distracted to other parts of their empire. The American colonists were generally prosperous, and had it not been for the taxation issue that was raised by the financially hard-pressed British in 1763 after the Seven Years War, certainly the momentum of the Revolution would have been a good deal slower.

Nevertheless, Franklin in his letter to Kames had found the fatal weakness in even the best of arguments against independence. The future of America, he saw clearly, was as a "great country, populous and mighty"; as Thomas Paine remarked at the time, it was essentially "absurd for an island to permanently govern a continent." Unlike other colonial peoples, Americans could not be tamed into thinking themselves inferior to their foreign governors, and even less could they be persuaded that they were unfit for self-government. On the contrary, visitors to Europe, such as Franklin and Jefferson, had no doubt that the most miserable American was incomparably better off than all but a few Europeans. "Of twenty millions of people supposed to be in France," Jefferson observed in 1785, "I am of opinion there are nineteen millions more wretched, more accursed in every circumstance of human existence than the most conspicuously wretched individual of the whole United States. . . ." Franklin in 1770, following a tour of the British Isles, did not hesitate to assert that compared with ordinary Englishmen, "every Indian is a gentleman in the possession and enjoyment of the various comforts of life. . . ."[11] Franklin exaggerated, but allowing for this, he was expressing a view that most Americans, then and since, have tended to share. For with respect to material circumstances, America was a success even before there was a United States.

It was also a melting pot long before the expression became current. Ties to England of blood and culture were already diluted before the Revolution, so much so that French traveler and agriculturalist Crèvecoeur could raise the question in 1780: "What is the American, this new man?" In America, he wrote after an extended visit of fifteen years, "individuals of all nations are melted into a new race of men. . . . I could point out to you a family whose grandfather was an Englishman, whose wife was Dutch, whose son married a French wife, and whose present four sons now have wives of different nations." But he was not referring only to that "strange mixture of blood, which you will find in no other country." Crèvecoeur noted that the European who came to America had left behind the prejudices and manners of his ancestors and had taken up "new ones from the new mode of life he has embraced, the new government he obeys, and the new rank he holds."[12]

Yet there was more than a trace of English restraint and civility in the American Revolution. Indeed its link with the British political tradition was such that the great conservative Edmund Burke could regard it as almost an extension of England's Glorious Revolution of 1688 and take pains to distinguish it from the French Revolution, which he thought of as destructive to civilization itself. There were excesses, to be sure, especially on the battlefield; the American soldiers at the battles of Concord and Lexington were accused of scalping dead and wounded British soldiers, and the British were charged with murdering innocent women and children, among other atrocities.[13] But there were relatively few deaths among either soldiers or civilians and nothing corresponding to the violence and savagery usually associated with revolutions.* Those on the losing side were deprived of their property

*According to the Veterans Administration, among the 290,000 participants there were 4,000 service deaths during the Revolutionary years 1775–1784, or about 1 death for every 70 soldiers. This would make the Revolutionary War the second least costly war in our history, in terms of lives lost, ranking behind the War of 1812 with a death rate of 1 soldier in every 143. By contrast, the Civil War death toll was 1 in every 6, and in both world wars roughly 1 soldier died for every 48 who were in service.

in many cases, but apparently no one who remained loyal to the British was required to forfeit his life. Certainly the American Revolution was unique among revolutions in that "there were no revolutionary tribunals dispensing 'revolutionary justice'; there was no reign of terror; there were no bloodthirsty proclamations by the Continental Congress. . . . As Tocqueville later remarked, with only a little exaggeration, the Revolution 'contracted no alliance with the turbulent passions of anarchy, but its course was marked, on the contrary, by a love of order and law.'"[14]

The American Revolution, then, was a humane revolution, and ever since 1776 humanity everywhere has been stirred by its affirmation that "all men are created equal" and enjoy the right to "life, liberty and the pursuit of happiness." But these evocative phrases, like the Revolution itself, can be understood only within the context of the times, not in the setting that developed later with the rise of democracy and the implementation of basic rights. Not in 1776 or, for that matter, 1976 were "all men created equal" unless it be in some metaspiritual sense, and in 1776 even the expression "men" did not mean all males, let alone females. In addition to women, slaves and Indians were without political rights, and in most of the colonies that later became states, indigents, paupers, and persons who owned little or no property could not vote. In Massachusetts, Maryland, and South Carolina those elected governors after 1783 were required to possess substantial freehold property, ranging from a value of at least £1,000 in Massachusetts to £10,000 in South Carolina. Six states made it mandatory that officeholders be Protestant,* two states insisted that they be Christian,† and five states required that members of the legislature declare themselves to be Protestants.** Only four states, Virginia, Delaware, New York, and Rhode Island, imposed no religious test whatever for any office. In other words, the inalienable rights referred to in the Declaration of Independence were those of a white, male, property-owning, and mainly Protestant group in the population.

*New Hampshire, New Jersey, North Carolina, South Carolina, Pennsylvania, and Georgia.

†Massachusetts, Maryland. Massachusetts also required voters to be church members.

**Georgia, New Hampshire, New Jersey, North Carolina, and South Carolina.

There were other themes in the Revolution that, while innocent at the time, reflected attitudes that much later were to provide twentieth-century America with some sources of its discontent. The first gathering of the men who eventually signed the Declaration of Independence called itself, prophetically, the Continental Congress, although the colonies in 1774 were far from constituting any geographical entity that corresponded to a continent. The term was, in effect, implicitly expansionist and to that extent foreshadowed that reckless urge and ambition in national policy that ultimately would carry American power through Indian lands to the Pacific and beyond. Nor did any colony or state, North or South, prohibit slavery. In the rhetoric of revolution and the state constitutions that followed it, much was said about the rights of individuals and the limitations placed upon government. Little attention was paid to the obligations of individuals and the rights of society. The political thought of the Revolution was vague about such matters, and American political thought to this day remains more or less silent about the duties individuals owe to society and to each other.

Partly for this reason, the revolutionaries were more successful in overthrowing a government than they were in creating one. The political system that emerged between the Revolution and the Constitutional Convention in 1787 was weak at the center, so weak, in fact, that it was confidently predicted abroad that the new government would soon petition for a return of British authority. Congress under the Articles of Confederation could not enforce its decisions even to the extent of requiring the states to pay requisitions levied upon them in connection with the cost of the Revolutionary War. A good many soldiers were either not paid off when the war was over or paid in depreciated currency; some of then upon returning home found their mortgaged farms had been foreclosed during their absence. As the debtor class grew, there were increasing demands that interest rates be reduced and loan payments deferred, demands that made themselves felt in "cheap money" bills passed by a number of state legislatures. The resulting epidemic of paper money further undermined the credit of the struggling nation, and it was among those most adversely affected, the bankers and merchants, the wealthier farmers and plantation owners, the creditors and property interests in general that the movement for a new constitution originated.

Had the movement failed, the future of the United States might have been similar to that of Britain under the monarchy or France under Bonaparte. According to De Witt Clinton and James Madison, both politically active at the time, there was talk of a military coup in the early 1780's, and it is established that several officers who had served in the Revolution urged Washington to take command of the faltering government. Perhaps the opinion of historian Charles A. Beard is extreme, but certainly there are grounds for his view that "besides the radicals and conservatives there was an influential group on the extreme right of the conservatives—a group that was ripe and ready for a resort to the sword, especially after Daniel Shays and his followers in Massachusetts had taken up arms against the grinding creditors and the bigots who would yield nothing. Had the movement for forming a new Constitution by peaceful processes failed, there is no doubt in my mind that the men of the sword would have made a desperate effort to set up a dictatorship by arms."*

The "men of the sword," in any event, never had their chance, although there were those who were certain that the Constitution would work no better than the Articles of Confederation. By 1802 Alexander Hamilton, who earlier had favored a monarchical form of government modeled after that of the British, was describing the Constitution as a "weak and worthless fabric," and he was by no means alone in this judgment. But for everyone who thought that the Constitution did not go far enough, there were several who believed that it went too far in the direction of what Richard Henry Lee and others opposed to its ratification called "consolidated government." Had some of those opponents and critics of the Constitution, who were prominent in the state ratifying conventions, attended the deliberations in Philadelphia, the

*Shays' Rebellion in the summer of 1786 was named for Captain Daniel Shays, a hero of Bunker Hill and other engagements. Leading 2,000 farmers, many of them Revolutionary War veterans, in an attack on the state court in Springfield, Shays forced the court to adjourn, thereby preventing further foreclosures and actions against delinquent tax accounts. The Massachusetts legislature's upper house was then controlled by creditor interests, and it was the intention of Shays and his followers to force a change of policy. Shays and some of his men were arrested by the state militia, but freed a few months later by the legislature. Probably the chief consequence of the rebellion, which inspired fear among conservatives, was to generate further support for the forthcoming Constitutional Convention.

Constitution might have emerged a somewhat different document. Sam Adams, the Massachusetts firebrand, was not there, and Patrick Henry refused to attend, saying he "smelled a rat." Jefferson, who made it clear in letters that he had reservations, especially about the omission of a bill of rights, was in France, and also abroad representing American interests were John Adams and John Jay. More than fifteen of the fifty-five delegates who appeared in Philadelphia, including two of the three New Yorkers and such luminaries as Luther Martin of Maryland and Edmund Randolph and George Mason of Virginia, were dissatisfied enough with the proceedings to leave before the conclusion of the convention or refused to sign the document. In the end, of the seventy-four delegates appointed by the states to attend the meeting, only thirty-nine attached their signatures to the Constitution of the United States.

The achievement of the convention, which labored from May 25 to September 17, 1787, is unparalleled in the political history of mankind. No written constitution has lasted as long as the American Constitution, and no other constitution has required as little formal revision over a comparable period of time. Yet the Constitution was designed for an eighteenth-century society that was, in major respects, more similar to seventeenth-century England than to late-nineteenth-century America, much less the America of our own time. In 1789, when Washington became the first President, the entire population of the country was smaller than the population today of any of our largest cities, and the entire national income could be measured in millions of dollars. As late as Jefferson's inaugural in 1801, about 2,000 people worked for the federal government. The vast changes in the nation and the world since those early days are obvious enough, but these changes have not made the Constitution obsolete or even created much interest in the possibility of another Constitutional Convention. Truly the Founding Fathers built better than the most confident among them knew or the most hopeful could imagine.*

---

*No one can doubt that the durability of the Constitution also owes much to the willingness of the Supreme Court to give it flexibility by interpreting it liberally. Thus when the needs of the times have necessitated government action in behalf of economic stability, the Constitution has usually been construed to permit such action, although not always immediately; and on some occasions, in accordance with the moods of the Supreme Court or the country, the Constitution

Indeed, the accomplishment of the Founders was such that it is easy to overlook the fact that the passage and ratification of the Constitution was a very near thing. More than once a crucial decision on the convention floor was decided by one state delegation's vote and a willingness to compromise at the last possible moment. There was an occasion when the small states were imminently prepared to leave the convention, and several times it was predicted that the state ratifying conventions would not give their approval to the document. In the event, there was no contest in New Jersey, Delaware, and Georgia and not much difficulty in Pennsylvania, Connecticut, and South Carolina. But the key states of New York, Virginia, and Massachusetts were another matter. In New York it required the brilliant maneuvering of Alexander Hamilton and the persuasive arguments of *The Federalist,* written by Hamilton, Madison, and Jay, for the Constitution to triumph by the close vote of 30 to 27. The Massachusetts result was a narrow 187 to 168 margin of victory, and in Virginia, despite all the influence of Washington, who agreed to become the first President, and the conversion of the influential Edmund Randolph, the vote was 89 to 79. In other words, a shift of only two pro-Constitution votes in New York and six in Virginia would have seen the Constitution rejected in those states, and without New York and Virginia the United States of America could not long have survived.

The arguments against the Constitution mustered by the opposition—generally known as Antifederalists—were formidable. There was the fear, first of all, that the central government would be too powerful and that ultimately it would be able to swallow up the states. It seemed to many Antifederalists that too much influence in government was given to men of property and to the upper classes in general and that the Constitution was essentially designed to protect and further the interests of the wealthy. Above all, the opposition complained that the Constitution was lacking in democratic features, and it was apprehensive about the omission of a bill of rights. As Rufus King of Massachusetts, who favored

---

through the justices has come down on one side of civil liberties and civil rights questions while at other times it has taken a quite different position. This flexibility has always bothered constitutional purists and strict constructionists who do not understand that if the Constitution were not periodically amended by the Supreme Court, it would long since have been discarded.

ratification, put it to James Madison in a letter of January, 1788, the belief "that the liberties of the peoople are in danger, and a distrust of men of property and education have a more powerful effect upon the minds of our opponents than any specific objections against the Constitution."[15]

Amendments protecting basic civil rights and liberties, strongly advocated by Jefferson and other moderates and assented to by Madison and most of the Federalists, were quickly enacted by Congress in September, 1789, and a little more than two years later ratified by the required three-fourths of the states. The conservatives, in short, were farsighted and flexible enough to realize that the Bill of Rights would not materially affect the substance of power since the outcome of any clash between individual rights and government authority would be decided by courts that in the main represented the more sober elements in the community. Realizing this, the wisest among them were willing to concede what there was no good reason to withhold, and it is not anticipating too much to say that this lesson in wise, timely, and essentially harmless concession was not lost on later generations of sophisticated conservatives.

Still, while the Founders succeeded in creating a new American government in much less time than it takes to create a new American, they succeeded not so much because of themselves as in spite of themselves. To begin with, they were fortunate in that the most influential men of the time were in favor of the Constitution rather than opposed to it. Their allies included most of the community leaders, clergymen, those who were well-to-do, and the majority of publishers and educated persons, many of whom were able public speakers. There was no foreign intervention or effort abroad to subvert the American Republic through financial manipulations. Nor, on either side, was there anyone dedicated to subversion or counterrevolution, and if Burr comes to mind, remember that it was not until much later that questions of that nature arose about Burr.

The Founders were also fortunate in that their antidemocratic sentiments, fully and often passionately expressed on the convention floor, were not reported outside or easily traced in the Constitution itself. For there was much truth in the suspicion that the Philadelphia delegates were hostile to democratic principles and favorable to property rights; indeed, they regarded democracy as incompatible with property. As Richard Hofstadter has observed, it is "ironical that the Constitution, which Americans venerate so deeply, is based upon a political theory that at one crucial point stands in direct antithesis to the main stream of the American democratic faith. Modern American folklore assumes that democracy and liberty are all but identical. . . . But the Founding Fathers thought that the liberty with which they were most concerned was menaced by democracy. In their minds liberty was linked not to democracy but to property."[16]

The Founders' fear of democracy was reinforced by their assumptions regarding human nature, about which most of them were deeply pessimistic. "What is government itself," Madison asked in *Federalist* 51, "but the greatest of all reflections on human nature?" If it be asked, "Why has government been instituted at all?" wrote Hamilton in *Federalist* 15, the answer must be, "Because the passions of men will not conform to the dictates of reason and justice, without constraint." Again and again the view is expressed, both in the Constitutional Convention and in the *Federalist*, that human nature is characterized by "caprice" and "wickedness," "folly" and "depravity," and that "men are ambitious, vindicative, and rapacious." "Have we not already seen enough," Hamilton rhetorically asked in *Federalist* 6, "of the fallacy and extravagance of those idle theories which have amused us with promises of an exemption from the imperfections, weaknesses, and evils incident to society in every shape? Is it not time to awake from the deceitful dream of a golden age . . . ?"[17]

If the Founders followed the misanthropic Thomas Hobbes and the Reverend Shepard on human nature, they followed the great English Whig philosopher John Locke on property or, rather, a blend of Locke and Malthus. In his *Of Civil Government* a century earlier, Locke had anchored property rights in natural law and had made the protection of property the chief end of government.[18] Certainly the Founders, being themselves men of property or entertaining reasonable hopes of acquiring property, could not disagree with this view, but they were concerned about the future when most of the population neither owned property nor had any expectation of significantly improving their material condition. Madison repeatedly warned his fellow delegates that "in future time, a great majority of the people will not only be without land, but any other sort of property. When that happens, these [the majority] will either combine under the influence of their common situation—in which case the rights of property and public liberty will not be secure—or what is more probable, they will become tools of opulence and ambitions, in which case there will be equal danger on the other side." And again: "the landed interest at present is prevalent, but in the process of time . . . when the number of landholders shall be comparatively small . . . will not the landed interest be overbalanced in future elections? And unless wisely provided against, what will become of our governments?" The solution, he thought, was for the government "to secure the permanent interests of the country against innovation. Landholders ought to have a share in the government, to support these invaluable interests, and to balance and check the other. They ought to be so constituted as to protect the minority of the opulent against the majority."

Hamilton went even further in stating that private property was "the great and fundamental distinction" of civil society. "All communities," he told the Constitutional Convention, "divide themselves into the few and the many. The first are the rich and the wellborn, the other the mass of the people. The voice of the people has been said to be the voice of God; and, however generally this maxim has been quoted and believed, it is not true to fact. The people are turbulent and changing; they seldom judge and determine right. Give, therefore, to the first class a distinct, permanent share in the government. They will check the unsteadiness of the second. . . ." If the executive could not serve for life, a tenure he favored, then it was even more important that the propertied aristocracy "be so circumstanced that they have no interest in change" and the government as a whole enabled to resist "the sudden breeze of passion."*

*Unlike Thomas Paine, of whom it could be said that he failed at everything he tried except the Revolution, Hamilton succeeded at everything he attempted except the Constitution, his plan for which was not accepted by the delegates. Hamilton in his message on the public credit and the better-known *Report on Manufactures* expressed the psychology of industrial capitalism at its worst 100 years before it had formally crystallized in urging as one of its benefits "the employment of persons who would otherwise be idle . . . [and] a burden on the community . . . women and children are rendered more useful, and the latter more early useful. . . . Of the number of persons employed in the cotton manufactures of Great Britain, it is computed that four-sevenths are women and children; of whom the greatest proportion are children, and many of them of a ten-

It is tempting to characterize these views as those of upper-class Marxists, for many of the Founders believed no less than Karl Marx himself that in the course of time the poor would become poorer and more numerous, and the rich, richer and fewer. But unlike Marxists, they took their stand with those who would become richer and fewer, and perhaps it is not carrying the comparison too far to suggest a certain resemblance between the Founders' view of what the government should be and the Marxist version of what the government, in fact, had to become under capitalism. For the Founders, especially Hamilton and the Federalists, intended that the government should protect and advance the property interest and that its principal functions should be entrusted to men of wealth, by which they meant the landowners, bankers, merchants, and manufacturers. They were promulgating a constitutional theory that in its basic assumptions about the relationship between economics and politics was not dissimilar to certain assumptions of Marxist political theory; in arguing that "the rich and the wellborn," in Hamilton's words, should secure "a distinct, permanent share of power," they were advocating that

----

der age." Yet it is unfair to say of Hamilton, as did Woodrow Wilson, that "he was a great man, but not a great American." Like many another immigrant—Hamilton came from the West Indies—who started life poor but who was ambitious, hardworking, and careful not to miss a main chance, Hamilton in his rise to wealth and prominence was quintessentially American. Apparently the ambition was always there. He was only a teenager in 1774 when he wrote a friend: "To confess my weakness . . . my ambition is prevalent, so that I condemn the groveling condition of a clerk or the like to which my fortune, etc. condemns me, and would willingly risk my life though not my character to exalt my station. . . . My folly makes me ashamed and I beg you'll conceal it; yet . . . we have seen such schemes successful when the projector is constant. I shall conclude saying, I wish there was a war." Perhaps ambition was responsible for Hamilton's somewhat hysterical response to imaginary or exaggerated plots and conspiracies aimed at the government, a response not unlike that later associated with Senator Joseph R. McCarthy. When Hamilton voluntarily joined, in 1794, an expedition of militia to western Pennsylvania to put down the so-called Whiskey Rebellion—of which there was no trace when the militia arrived—he characterized the handful of farmers who were protesting a tax on whiskey as "banditti," "rioters," and "delinquents" bent on overthrowing the Republic. He was so convincing he almost persuaded Washington that civil war was imminent. There was also a trace of dementia in his relentless pursuit of Burr to the point of no return for them both, a dementia not too different from the obsessional paranoia of certain Watergate persons that led them, in the end, to the point of no return.

the government constitute itself what the Marxists later were to call "the Executive Committee of the bourgeoisie."

Fortunately for the future of the country as well as the Constitution, the Founders were as wrong as the Marxists about the eventual distribution of wealth. Thus far in our history, wealth has increased faster than population, with the result that while the rich have become richer, most of the poor have also become richer. In the United States, unlike in Europe and the rest of the world, the economic gains of one class or section of the population have not been at the expense of another, and because of the relative lack of conflict between classes and sections, business interests and the rich, with few exceptions, have not turned politically to the extreme right, nor have the workers and the poor, again with few exceptions, turned politically to the left, as has happened elsewhere. Because of our natural wealth and, until recently in our history, immunity from the worst horrors and costs of wars, invasions, and occupations, most Americans most of the time have experienced an improvement in their living standards or have anticipated such improvement. Put simply, there has almost always been enough to go around.[19]

As a result, practically the entire period from 1787 to the present has been marked by the ascendancy and supremacy of the business class and the values associated with it. Except for the South, by 1825 there was little left of the power and influence of those whose wealth was based on land ownership exclusively, and the Southern aristocracy, or what remained of it after the Civil War, was never able to mount an effective challenge to industrialism. The South, and occasionally the Midwest and West, have been capable of sectional politics, but the political battles of regions and sections have not for the most part been class struggles or even conflicts about fundamental economic issues. Broadly speaking, there has never been a major challenge to the free-enterprise system or any serious proposal that those who own and operate it should be dispossessed of their wealth and forced to step down in favor of public managers. Indeed, were such proposals to be put forward, the nonowners and workers, especially those belonging to trade unions, would be among the most impassioned objectors.

Because there has been enough to go around, the need for a politics of scarcity, as envisaged by the Founders, never developed. In the early nineteenth century the expansion of the suffrage did not produce that leveling of property that was so fearfully anticipated by the Constitution-makers of 1787, and toward the later part of the century the millions of European poor who entered the country did not, contrary to some expectations, strike the Red Flag. Those who were disenchanted, unemployed, destitute on farms, or hungry in cities were offered a variety of panaceas and cure-alls: communism, socialism, syndicalism, anarchism, the single-tax movement, and a good many other nostrums. But neither then or at any time since have any large number of Americans, however desperate their condition, abandoned the faith of the Fathers.

Indeed, it is conservative politics, not liberal politics, that constitutes the mainstream of American political history. In the sixty-seven years between the end of the Civil War and the election of Franklin D. Roosevelt in 1932, there were only two reform Presidents, one of whom, the Republican Theodore Roosevelt, became President in 1901 as the result of an assassination, and the other of whom, the Democrat Woodrow Wilson, was first elected in 1912 as the consequence of Republican vote-splitting between William Howard Taft and Theodore Roosevelt. Of the four reform Presidents, all Democrats, since 1932, one, Franklin D. Roosevelt, owed his first electoral victory to a major depression that was blamed on his predecessor, and two others, Truman and Johnson, were put in the White House by the deaths of the incumbent Presidents Roosevelt and Kennedy.

A total of six reform Presidents, in other words, who collectively served for forty-four years, have held the nation's highest office since 1865, which means that reformers have been President about 40 percent of the time since the assassination of Lincoln. Five of these six Presidents, moreover, could be regarded in some sense as "accidents," "accidents" because it was an exceptional or extreme circumstance rather than a "normal" electoral contest and conventional conditions that were responsible for their first term as President; three of the five, in fact, reached the White House through direct succession as Vice President. These three, to be sure, were elected to second terms, but it is a political fact that incumbent Presidents who seek to be reelected have a significant advantage over challengers irrespective of party affiliation or position on issues, and since 1865 almost all of them have been elected to second terms.* In 110 years the only "normal" or straight electoral contest won by a liberal who was not already President or Vice President, at a time when there was neither war nor depression, was in 1960, when John F. Kennedy defeated Nixon by the small margin of 120,000 votes.

Conservatives, nevertheless, have frequently behaved as if the country were on the verge of a red revolution. When state legislatures toward the end of the nineteenth century took hesitant steps toward minimal regulation of corporations, there were cries of anarchism and socialism in business circles and appeals to the courts to intervene. There were also efforts, many of them successful, to bribe legislators and judges, for when its basic interests are at stake, business has rarely hesitated to buy influence and in other ways corrupt the democratic process. When, much later, businessmen found it increasingly difficult to purchase legislatures and courts, and there was talk on the hustings of trust-busting, ten-hour-day laws, minimum-wage standards, recognition of unions, and other measures regarded by business as "socialistic," the emphasis shifted to mass opinion and ways of promoting a favorable public view of the so-called free-enterprise system. This remains a major emphasis, in accordance with the assumption that the decisive battles over property rights are won or lost at the polling place, where voters ultimately must decide between New Deals and Fair Deals, on the one hand, and the economic status quo, on the other. But the war is fought on many fronts, not least among them congressional committees and regulatory agencies, and many a battle has been lost on Election Day by a corporation or trade association, only to be won a month later in the form of an administrative decision.

As some of the following chapters try to show, the business community, despite an occasional setback, has never lost the war itself or even been seriously threatened with defeat. Judged by its nervous reaction to the elections of Roosevelt, Truman, and Kennedy, all of them enlightened conservatives who were regarded by the propertied class as radical innovators, business frequently

---

*The exceptions are Grover Cleveland, who lost to Benjamin Harrison in 1888, although Harrison had almost 100,000 fewer popular votes; Harrison, who lost to Cleveland in 1892 at least partly because of a third-party candidate who received more than 1,000,000 votes; and Herbert Hoover in 1932.

runs scared, but it nevertheless does run the country. It does so, moreover, with relatively little interference from any quarter, and short of a prolonged economic collapse on a scale far greater than that of the 1930's Depression or defeat in another world war, business is not likely to face any significant political challenge to its commanding position. It is possible, of course, that worldwide pressures on resources may reduce business profitability and require some movement toward a managed economy, but these changes will affect corporate power only marginally, if at all.

The challenge to business, like the challenge to other American institutions, comes not from ideology but from the immense number of problems for which, thus far, there appears to be no solution we can base upon past experience or any formula for the present that is acceptable to a majority of the country. These problems, many of them discussed in the following pages, were not anticipated by the Founding Fathers, and they were beyond the imaginative reach even of the best minds of the nineteenth century. In dealing with them we cannot consult the constitutional blueprint that was drawn up almost 200 years ago in Philadelphia, much less look for guidance in the works of Plato and Aristotle or Hobbes and Locke. Indeed, much literature of this century, including most of the "must reading" and "important" books of twenty and thirty years ago, seems almost as irrelevant to the present American condition as the writings of John C. Calhoun in 1850 defending the right of secession.

In confronting such problems as the breakdown in America of the traditional value system, the increasing withdrawal from affective involvement with others and the manipulation of interpersonal relations, the deliberate confinement of the blacks, the poor, the aged, and other helpless minorities to material and spiritual impoverishment, the decay of cities and the decline in the quality of urban and suburban life, the erosion of standards and taste, the recourse to violence and indulgence in "endless wars to end war," the multiple corruptions and failures of leadership—in confronting these and other developments we confront the most formidable challenge yet to American civilization. This is not to minimize the worldwide crisis of resources and the consequences for the United States of scarcity, much less to dismiss the possibility of a war between the Great Powers that would effectively terminate all hopes for the future and not just American hopes. But all human experience, including the history of nations, seems to demonstrate that enemies within are more difficult to conquer than enemies without, and when there is ultimate defeat, it is usually the enemies within that have forced capitulation.

Yet the American condition, two centuries after 1776, while bleak, is not hopeless. If the chapters of this book have any single thesis, it is that the future of American democracy depends upon our willingness to settle for less—less influence in world affairs, less independence in managing our personal lives, less consumption and reckless allocation of resources. Given such willingness, and the vast social invention and reconstruction it would make possible, we may again, as in the early years of our history, be able to offer ourselves as a worthy example to other nations. Of course, we shall never regain the innocence that has been lost, and it may be, given the problems existing elsewhere, that from time to time we shall have to deal with new Hitlers and Stalins, new pogroms and genocides, new wars and famines. Perhaps no country in the twentieth century, great or small, can look forward to long periods of peace and contentment. But surely it would contribute to peace and contentment everywhere if America endeavored not to remain the world's most powerful and richest nation, but to become the world's foremost egalitarian multiracial society, in other words, the world's most successful free society. For the problems of inequality and race have been resolved, to the extent they have been resolved anywhere, not by democratic governments, but by authoritarian regimes. The urgent question for the future is whether freedom and decency, inseparably linked in all democratic theory and aspiration, can be joined together in the reality of social experience.

In seeking to answer that question affirmatively, we would do well to recall Benjamin Franklin's description of the United States six years after the Declaration of Independence. In his *Information to Those Who Would Remove to America* (1782), Franklin commented that there were among his countrymen "few people so miserable as the poor of Europe," and "very few that in Europe could be called rich. . . . It is rather a general happy mediocrity that prevails."[20] Assuming that by "mediocrity" Franklin meant a relative equality of condition, we would confer honor upon ourselves and contentment upon our posterity by choosing Franklin's America as a model for the future.

2

The Decline of the Superego

"**H**ey, Janis is Feeling Great," was the story caption in the *Rolling Stone* of May 28, 1970. Rock star Janis Joplin, dead less than two years later from an overdose of heroin, had put together a new band, and she was very pleased. "Man," she told the *Stone* reporter, "I feel so fucking great that I thought I'd put a flower around my wrist." So she had gone to a tattoo parlor near the Greyhound bus station in San Francisco and come away with a "baroque bracelet hearts and flowers" and "a little heart placed near Janis' own." Janis confided, "A lot of my Capricorn girl friends have tattoos. It's fuckin' beautiful." Delighted with the new ensemble that had replaced the old one, known as Main Squeeze, Janis exclaimed, "They're fuckin' professionals. . . . I'm super-gassed. . . . I've got my head back."

Seeking a similar type of euphoria, thousands of persons in the early 1970's were attending sensitivity training centers modeled after the Esalen Institute in Big Sur, California. Esalen itself began in 1962 as a weekend seminar center housed in a few ramshackle buildings grouped around a hot springs. Ten years later, with a full-scale residential program and an affiliation with several colleges, Esalen was offering thousands of people each year programs designed, in its own words, "to explore those trends in education, religion, philosophy and the physical and behavioral sciences which emphasize the potentialities and values of human existence." But some of the seminars, at least, bore Joplinesque titles: "You Don't Have to Suffer to Feel Good; Divorce: A Creative Experience; Play, Touch and Talk: Aboard the SS Vallejo [a houseboat in Sausalito]; Gay and Glad; Come Out, Come Out, Whoever You Are; and Knots Are From Nots."*

Other thousands of Americans, mostly male, were patronizing the pornographic theaters and bookstores in America's larger cities, and millions of Americans, male and female, were enjoying the careful cinema depictions of murder and torture that are a conspicuous feature of *The Godfather, The French Connection,* and *The Exorcist. The Godfather* quickly set a record for gross box-office receipts. Meanwhile, in London, Germaine Greer, sometime lecturer in English literature at Warwick University and author of *The Female Eunuch,* was describing a movie in which she plays the sister of a hippie girl. "George wants to fuck her. She says no. Peace, flowers, love. He asks her for some head. She says no. Well, the whole thing is unreal. She should plate him in the middle of the scene." When someone tells Germaine that the vice-chancellor of her university is "very big on you," she laughs and says: "He's been trying to fuck me for a year. I've got him with a cleft stick, don't I?" Later, at the zoo, she observes of a rude attendant: "I bet he hasn't gotten his rocks off in months. What if I went down on him?"†

At Will Rogers State Beach in Southern California, a substantial number of people, young and old, were spending most or all of their time surfing, beachcombing, playing volleyball, jogging, and people watching. Many of them, Steven V. Roberts suggested in the New York *Times,* are refugees from everyday life, for whom the beach is "like a siren, enticing men and women away from the burdens of responsibility. . . . The [volleyball] courts are littered

---

*From a recent Esalen catalogue. The catalogue, which in size equals forty regular-size foolscap pages, also features workshops and seminars dealing with massage, Zen, I-Ching, Yoga, dance, and "Soma, the Sacred Mushroom." Insofar as Esalen, which is host to a variety of approaches, is based on any theory, the theory is gestalt psychology as developed and practiced by the late Frederick S. Perls. Esalen seminars also reflect the humanistic psychology of Abraham Maslow and Carl Rogers.

†*Rolling Stone,* January 7, 1971. The story about Germaine Greer was titled, "A Groupie in Women's Lib." Ms. Greer was on her way to New York to promote her book, where she would stay at the Chelsea Hotel rather than the Algonquin because "they won't let me fuck my friends in the Algonquin." According to her, "Ernest Hemingway, when his cock wouldn't stand up, he blew his head off. He sold himself a line of bullshit and bought it." One can hardly wait for Ms. Greer to publish her English-literature lectures.

with failed stockbrokers and lawyers." "It doesn't matter how great your wife is," observed medical student Wayne Freeman, "you come down here and you always see someone better looking." Scott Allen, a newcomer to beach life, was hoping for a cloudy day so he could get something done. "There have been two warrants out for my arrest for over a year," he told Roberts, "vehicle checks or something like that, but I still haven't gotten the car fixed. I feel guilty about things like that—for about ten minutes."[1]

On Eighth Street in New York's Greenwich Village, along Telegraph Avenue in Berkeley and in Old Town on Chicago's near North Side, in every American city there were small gatherings of young people aged anywhere between fifteen and thirty who could be described, in Christopher Lasch's words, as "precocious fugitives from respectability, prematurely hardened tramps and migrants. . . . Long hair, ragged clothing, rock, drugs . . . are one characteristic."[2]

Another was language. One of these lumpen adolescents, formerly known as a flower child, is talking: "Mop's old man just got busted for beating up this biker who burnt him with bad meth . . . and they were all on 700 mikes of acid when it happened—and, wow, what a bad trip, like it was very freaky, see, because the cops got this guy to sing who had been crashing with them on Avenue B, but this cat was making it with Melissa and laying a lot of grass on them, but Mop got bad vibrations from him and tried to get Melissa to go back with Kenny, who was her previous old man, but Kenny had split after he got busted, and besides he was very paranoid and like a drag . . . so they're all pretty uptight at the moment, and Mop thinks she might be knocked up but she doesn't know if it's Grok or some spade dealer she made it with over on 3rd Street . . . so they threw an I-Ching this morning and it read changes and maybe they should split to Berkeley and get away from the bad vibrations in New York, but nobody has any bread, so Melissa wants to deal meth but Mop thinks it's a bad scene, especially with all those down vibrations and the I-Ching reading changes, so they thought they'd try to find Fang, who's this cat who's splitting to the coast on a big Harley. . . ."[3]

Janis Joplin, Esalen, Germaine Greer, the beach people, and the lumpen adolescent essentially are speaking a common language, and that language, to borrow a useful psychoanalytic term, is closely associated with primary process. By "primary process" psychoanalysts mean thought and behavior that is dominated by instinctual drives. Emotions, wishes, and desires, relatively free of rational thought processes and controls, are allowed free play: essentially one talks and acts according to impulse. The emphasis is on immediate pleasurable feeling and gratification as opposed to reason and self-denial. Hence an individual who characteristically acts in accordance with primary-process imperatives has not advanced much beyond or has regressed to stages of infantile and early-childhood behavior.*

Western culture, on the other hand, traditionally has been based on secondary-process thought and behavior, or thought and behavior that is related to reason, memory, judgment, and one's perception of the real situation. Whereas primary-process behavior is dominated by the id or instinctual drives, secondary-process behavior is significantly influenced by the superego, which, broadly speaking, corresponds to conscience. From Moses to Freud, a long line of thinkers, in one fashion or another, have insisted that the superego or something very much like it is an indispensable foundation of civilization. Is it possible that they were wrong?

Before dealing with this question, it would be well to dispel some popular confusions. Contrary to a widely held impression, Freud was no more in favor of a harsh, punitive superego than he was in favor of pornocracy. He was well aware that the repressive moral climate of Vienna in his day was apt to foster a tyrannical superego quite capable of overwhelming the personality system with guilt, anxiety, and hysteria. The task of psychoanalysis, as he saw it, was not to position itself on the side of such a superego,

---

*Such regression is a staple of innumerable films, such as those of Sam Peckinpah, and novels where primary process has taken the place of plot and action and the emphasis is on "the happening" rather than any story line. In effect, the fantasies of the viewer or reader, usually of an erotic-sadistic sort, are enacted for him. While the traditional novel may not be dead, its intricacies of narrative and characterization have given way to shock effects that usually make their appearance as early as the first chapter or even the first few pages. Nor are our best writers immune from the need to "capture" the reader's interest almost as soon as he opens the book, as witness the novels of John Updike and Philip Roth. Proust, Henry James, Edith Wharton did not enjoy immediate success, but one wonders whether, today, they would be able to find publishers for their slow-moving novels with little plot or "action."

much less to join forces with the rapacious id, but to lend support to the ego itself in its efforts to master the conflicting forces within the self. "Where id was," began the statement that was to become famous, "there ego shall be," and by "ego" Freud meant something more than the English "I" or the German *Ich*. Certainly the ego in Freud's usage encompassed secondary-process thought and the reality principle, but above all the ego and the superego together were the repository of culture and tradition. For Freud as for most humanists, the quality that finally distinguishes man's nature from animal nature is not superior intelligence or skill but his commitment to the values associated with civilized life.

Whether for most people such a commitment is possible in the absence of sanctions and some system of rewards and punishments need not concern us here; up to the present, there is no instance in recorded history of men living peaceably in groups without enforceable laws, rules, and customs. In the West morality has been based mainly on Judaic-Christian religion, and this morality, at least in ideal circumstances, forms the nexus of the superego. To be sure, much of the superego is unconscious, and it may well be, as Freud suspected, that the unconscious component is less compromising and more strict than that part of which we are conscious. In any event, the superego, both conscious and unconscious, incorporates the prescriptions and prohibitions of the society in which we live.

Above all, it incorporates the definitions of good and bad that early in life were established by parents or their equivalents. According to the psychoanalytic model of superego development, now widely accepted, the child as early as one year of age, and certainly by the time he is two, becomes aware of his parents' approval or disapproval of his behavior. Much of this awareness is in connection with such enterprises as eating, sleeping, and toilet training, and as the child becomes more active and his world larger, the parental exhortations and admonitions grow more numerous. By the time he is three or four the normal child has a fairly clear idea what behavior elicits approval from his parents and what behavior arouses their displeasure. But for the most part, the child's own sense of right and wrong is not yet strong enough to operate in the absence of parents; the father or mother must be present to enforce the rules. When the child is five or six, however, many of the rules become internalized and no longer wholly dependent on enforcement from the outside. The child, in effect, has learned to say "Yes" and "No" to himself.

One can sometimes observe this process of moral development in a youngster. He will have been told, for example, not to play with a glass ashtray on the coffee table or a cigarette lighter or whatever. While he is still a toddler, the little boy occasionally will approach the coffee table and pick up the ashtray, meanwhile keeping a wary eye on mother or father. He knows that he will be scolded, perhaps even punished, for his transgression, and yet he persists. To some extent he is testing the environment: are they watching? Do they really mean it? On the other hand, he does not know why he should not touch the ashtray, and the prohibitions have not yet become part of himself. Because the child of this age quite literally does not know the limits, much less the dangers, of his environment, he needs and depends on parental guidance however much he may chafe under restrictions. A few years later, however, the prohibition has become a part of himself. Alone in the room, he may approach the forbidden object, but he will stop before touching it, perhaps pointing an accusing finger at it while shaking his head vigorously in the negative.

With puberty, it is possible to speak of a relatively well-developed moral sense that has become internalized, or, in other words, a superego. While there is increasing evidence that the superego may become modified during adolescence and adult life, for most individuals the likelihood of major change later in life is remote. If by the time he is twelve or thirteen the individual wholly or partially lacks a moral sense, if, that is to say, he is uncertain what constitutes wrongdoing and is little or not at all troubled by conscience in the face of it, if, further, he customarily acts on impulse or whim, alert only to his own desires and indifferent if not contemptuous of the needs and wishes of others, we may speak of a severe impairment of superego functioning. Such impairment may not interfere with everyday life; indeed, as we shall see later, a healthy superego may be superfluous in large areas of American society. But in extreme cases of impairment, the result often is sociopathic (antisocial acts such as crime and delinquency) or psychopathic (gross immorality, sadism, and the like) behavior.

Where the superego develops in a normal way, identification with parents and surrogates comes to replace the earlier submission to parents. Psychoanalysts believe that the first object of the child's instinctual drives is his parents, that he will, in general, wish to possess sexually the parent of the opposite sex and, by way of gratifying this desire, wish to eliminate the parent of the same sex. This mixture of incestuous and aggressive impulses, commonly known as the Oedipus complex, arouses guilt and anxiety in the child because he somehow knows that these impulses are not merely forbidden but dangerous. The boy child, according to psychoanalysis, fears that if he is found out, he will lose his penis, i.e., be castrated. The girl child faces an even more difficult situation. Initially she, like the little boy, may want to possess her mother; for her, too, mother is the first and most important love object in her life. Lacking a penis, she cannot entertain this fantasy for long and, blaming mother for her condition, she may transfer her affections to father, in which case her wish, too, cannot be gratified, with the result that the child must either become reconciled to her feminine state—hence the expression "anatomy is destiny"—or continue her angry and desperate search for the missing penis throughout her life.

Assuming that the Oedipal period is relatively free of traumas and extremes, the boy is likely to resolve his Oedipal complex in favor of father: abandoning his illicit desires for mother, he will love father and want to be like him. In the case of the girl, the successful resolution of the Oedipus complex requires her to give up her incestuous wish to possess her father and return to the side of her mother. In both instances the earlier feelings about parents, ranging from incestuous love to murderous aggression, have been replaced by identifications. It is by means of these identifications that the parents' values, attitudes, standards, and moral perspectives become internalized, forming the basis of the superego. The approving, rewarding aspects of parental behavior that the child has experienced form in the superego what Freud called the ego ideal. The ego ideal, however, does not always reflect actuality in the parent-child relationship; the important point is that it represents an idealized version of the parent, whether or not based on reality, that eventually comes to serve as a model for oneself. If the parents have communicated love and respect for the child, which is not the same thing as being permissive and indulgent, the ego model will incorporate their ideals as well, not merely the child's images of their day-to-day behavior.

But not just the parents. In adolescence and even later the ego ideal can be influenced by identifications with persons in public life, historical figures, characters in novels, artists, musicians, and athletes, heroes in general. More will be said about this later; for the moment let us note that while the parents' role in superego formation is the crucial one, their influence is not the only one at work.

Of course, all this is highly simplified. Not everyone would accept the Freudian model in its entirety, especially that aspect of it that argues the ubiquity in girls of penis envy. Many would argue that the role of castration anxiety has been exaggerated in psychoanalytic circles. Nothing has been said here that would account for the severity of a particular superego. Freud himself believed that such a punitive quality owed less to strict or even cruel parents than to the strength of the original incestuous and aggressive wishes; his theory was that the energy attached to these wishes was transferred, as it were, to the superego upon its formation. Hence a child whose incestuous or aggressive impulses toward his parents were particularly strong would suffer as an adult more guilt and anxiety than one whose prohibited impulses were less forceful.

But however one views the superego, it can hardly be questioned that its role in contemporary America, indeed its very existence, is in doubt. To be sure, few have gone so far as to proclaim the death of the superego, but some have come close. "Reason, though dead," says Leslie Fiedler, "holds us with an embrace that looks like a lover's embrace, but turns out to be rigor mortis. Unless we are necrophiles, we'd better let go. Where Ego has so unsatisfactorily displaced Id, Id shall flourish once again."[4]

Intellect and reason are also the targets of Julian Beck, director of the Living Theater. According to him, the traditional theater is a "theater of lies," of which the foremost example is Shakespeare "with his Anglo-Saxon heroes, those model heroes with all the wrong values, who rationalize and reason. We don't need Shakespeare's objective reason. His ignorance of collective joy makes him useless to our time. In fact, the whole theater of the intellect will go. . . . One leaves the theater of our time and goes and thinks. But our thinking, conditioned by our already conditioned minds, is so corrupt that it is not to be trusted."[5]

Peter Schrag writes that the "book enslaves, entraps, deludes, equivocates," whereas "human beings feel." Presumably this is what the college student has in mind when he says to his professor, " 'I don't want to read Augustine because I don't like Augustine.' The youngster is a feeler, he already knows. History is a copout. The liberal arts are dead or dying because we have begun to lose faith in relational possibilities."[6]

Apparently the liberal arts have come back from the grave; in 1974 there were almost 10,000,000 college and university students, and while there was a shift toward courses with vocational value, enrollments in psychology, fine arts, and social-science courses remained high. But it probably is true that the intellectual demands made by such courses have diminished. Between 1963 and 1973 average Scholastic Aptitude Test scores of high school graduates dropped more than thirty points on the verbal scale and more than twenty points on the mathematical aptitude test, perhaps because of a decline in the quality of high school education.[7] Since most high school graduates go on to college, one would accept that more were flunking out as a result of inadequate preparation for college, but apparently this is not the case. In a majority of schools, grade-point averages have been rising, and it is far from unknown for colleges and universities to graduate students who can barely express their own thoughts in simple English, much less deal with the complexities of Shakespeare's plays or the Supreme Court's decision in *Brown* v. *Topeka Board of Education.** Not all schools lowered their standards in response to student pressures during the turbulent sixties, but the abandonment or curtailment in many institutions of required-reading lists or of any book list at all, the introduction of the pass-fail grading system, the substitution of elective and student-designed courses for those formerly regarded as essential—these and other developments suggest that higher learning in America is now less oriented toward Learning and more toward Life than once was the

---

*The novelist Anthony Burgess, visiting professor of English at New York's City College in 1972–73, has written amusingly of his difficulties in grading papers that describe Shakespeare's Cressida as "kind of a C.T." and Ophelia as "going crazy because of her dad's being wiped out." What does one do, Burgess asks, with "Lady Mackbet says she had a kid not in so many words but she says she remembers what it was like when a kid sucked her tit so I reckon she was a mother some time and the kid must have died but we don't hear no more about it . . ."? (*New York Times Magazine,* November 19, 1972.)

case. In many classrooms what passes for education is little more than an endless dialogue in which it is impossible to tell the teacher from the students.

Moreover, even those students pursuing traditional goals in the traditional manner evidence a fundamental change in their attitudes and life-styles. It was not long ago that widespread drug usage was confined to the ghetto, dropout communities and a few of the nation's urban college campuses, among which Berkeley and New York colleges and universities were conspicuous.[8] But in recent years heroin has become a problem in some suburban middle-class schools, and cadets have been expelled from the service academies for recourse to marijuana, LSD, mescaline, and cocaine. Estimates of heroin addiction in the Army during the Vietnam War ranged as high as 25 percent.* According to the New York Chamber of Commerce, drug use by employees of business firms is "almost as serious as the alcoholism problem."[9]

The flight from the superego and breakdown of social controls also is apparent in other sectors. No one familiar with corporative history or crime in America, both of which are discussed in later chapters, will regard the "rip-off" as entirely a new phenomenon; if Balzac had lived in the United States, he might have been tempted to write that behind every large business lies a crime. What is new is the institutionalization of the "rip-off" as a wholly justified form of behavior. Much of this behavior is unrelated to poverty or need, and in fact, if the target is Bell Telephone or the electric utility or the bus company, stealing is regarded as a game or sports activity in which it is fun to match wits with the ticket seller or the company's computerized billing system. Hence the growing popularity of shoplifting, with losses estimated at $5 billion per year, much of it carried out by adolescents and middle-class housewives, and the increasing incidence of thefts by employees. According to the National Retail Merchants Association, internal

*In August, 1972, John Eric Engstrom, a former Army captain and Vietnam veteran, told the New York *Times* that a classified 1971 Army report had established heroin addiction among lower-ranking enlisted men in Vietnam at 25 percent. According to Engstrom, the report, which had been based on a two-day drug-rehabilitation workshop sponsored by the Army, was replaced by "a watered-down" version more acceptable to the United States command. The report had shown that in two Army units, the 23rd and 25th divisions, heroin use ranged from 10 to 44 percent. The Defense Department, citing urinalysis studies, has fixed heroin usage at 5.54 percent. (New York *Times*, August 16, 1972.)

theft accounts for 75 percent of all losses from shoplifting, the total of which is more than 2 percent of sales.* Book thefts from university libraries and campus bookstores have become serious problems. Apart from the fact that such thefts usually lead to the installation of expensive electronic checkout systems, many books are irreplaceable. In 1971 the Princeton University Store, hardly comparable in size or sales to Macy's, lost the considerable sum of $83,000 in stolen merchandise; the store did not attempt to distribute the responsibility between its affluent customers and its largely middle-class employees. Three months after the John F. Kennedy Center for the Performing Arts opened in Washington, a member of its board of trustees reported that "virtually everything reachable and detachable" had been removed, including parts of crystal chandeliers, swatches of rugs and curtains, faucets, costumes and sections of stage sets, brass covers on electrical outlets, plants, paintings, all the ashtrays and salt and pepper shakers, and "much china, glassware, and linens." In return the 500,000 visitors to the center had left behind numerous cigarette burns on carpets and smears of candy and chewing gum in the theaters. It was not clear from the report, which asked Congress for an "emergency" grant of $1,500,000 to maintain the center, how much of the mischief was attributable to theft, how much to souvenir-hunting, and how much to vandalism.[10]

The looting of public utilities, stores, libraries, and other establishments was memorialized in 1971 by the publication of Abbie Hoffman's *Steal This Book,* enthusiastically reviewed by Dotson Rader in the *New York Times Book Review* of July 18, 1971. The central theme of *Steal This Book,* which, despite its title, sold for $1.95—one wonders how Hoffman would have reacted had all copies of his book been stolen—was, in Rader's words, "how to live for free and survive." Living free included nonpayment for

*New York *Times,* December 24, 1974. In April, 1971, New York State Attorney General Louis J. Lefkowitz sued the Waldorf-Astoria Hotel for $452,000 on the grounds that the hotel had padded guests' bills to the extent of $113,212.83 between December, 1969, and May, 1970. Mr. Lefkowitz charged that the padded amount was 2 percent of total charges and that the action against the Waldorf was not an "isolated" case. Presumably the hotel might have replied, "Doesn't everybody?" or it might have been expected that the Waldorf, in keeping with the times, would defend itself in terms of the thefts by guests of hotel towels, blankets, and other sundries, but it did not. (New York *Times,* April 15, 1971.)

"food, clothes, housing, transportation, medical care, even money and dope" and therefore necessarily required knowledge of "the newest techniques in the art of shoplifting or 'inventory shrinkage' as it is referred to in the trade." It is also useful to know "how to sell your hungry body to several universities at the same time" and how "you can acquire cheap guns and ammunition by starting a National Rifle Association Gun Club in your parents' basement." Whatever the purpose of the guns and ammunition, Dotson strongly urged that the book "be read by the young, for it will help them to make it through life in hip America with their mind and body relatively intact."*

If, in principle, shoplifting and related activities irrespective of need provide nourishment for mind and body, it follows that crime directly or indirectly related to poverty and discrimination becomes subject to redefinition. Of course, theft is an old, established method of evening economic scores, and if the thief is hungry and poor, it is almost impossible to feel outraged by his actions unless his victim is also hungry and poor or is physically injured. But in certain circles the defense of black crime in particular has taken a different direction. The argument is that the black robber or mugger is simply getting back his own; "Whitey," after all, has been stealing from *him* for generations and even centuries. It little matters that the "Whitey" who has been robbed or mugged is not the employer who exploits black labor or the tenement owner who has let the rats and cockroaches take over. The assumption appears to be that just as the white American is guilty because he is white and better off, the black American because he is black and a ghetto resident is not responsible for his acts and therefore should not be punished. This argument, frequently heard in the case of crime related drug addiction, in effect holds that society itself is the criminal, not the thief, and to be sure, there is much truth in this. But in either instance, whether the thief is seen as a modern Robin Hood or as the helpless victim of circumstances, the effect is

---

*Hoffman, whose New Left charisma had largely faded by 1973 when he was arrested on a charge of attempting to sell three pounds of cocaine to an undercover narcotics agent, apparently practiced what he preached about "nonpayment." In 1971 a "People's Tribunal" sponsored by the Youth International Party accused him of refusing to pay collaborators on *Steal This Book*. In 1972 he and Jerry Rubin, author of *Do It!* and other works, were expelled from YIP for not sharing lecture fees with the organization.

to deny individual responsibility and, perhaps, what is more important, in some instances establish the criminal as a heroic type.*

It may also be true that in each stalwart American, that is, in each of us, there is something of the delinquent and that this may explain, at least in part, the public's considerable tolerance for certain types of crime.† The frequency of movies and ads making use of "Godfather" types could suggest that an identification with Mafia figures was not confined to a population minority; perhaps for millions of Americans images of the Mafia center not on the ugly reality but on one person, voice, and manner of actors chosen to play Mafia roles in movies.** In a similar way we may find it impossible to believe that Americans committed war crimes in Vietnam because the faces we associate with such acts are the faces of the young man down the block who was a Navy pilot or the son of a coworker who was drafted into the Army, in short, our own faces. It is conceivable that those Americans who remained loyal to Nixon through the entire Watergate scandal did so because they simply could not believe that some of the most respected Republican Party officials in and out of the White House, persons very much like them, were guilty of felonies. When it comes to

*For a fuller discussion of this issue and the crime problem in general, see Chapter 6. Nothing said here is intended to minimize the fact that black and brown Americans have been brutalized for more than 300 years by the white majority, who, for that reason alone, have much to feel guilty about. Nor is there any implication that all crimes, however defined, should be punished with prison. Still there are such things as murder, assault, armed robbery, and rape, and not all of them are the result of sociological determinism.

†Bank robbers, for example, are often viewed as Robin Hoods, and not just in films starring Alec Guinness. In 1971 thousands of T-shirts were sold inscribed "D. B. Cooper," the name used by a man who successfully hijacked a Northwest Orient Airlines 707 from which he parachuted with $2,000,000 in ransom money. Possibly the only criminal acts about which the public feels strongly are murder, mugging, rape, home burglary, and automobile theft.

**One such advertisement features a tough-looking character complete with cigar, felt hat, and striped shirt, sitting in front of an electric calculator. The caption: "The Casio 122 can do wonders for your business no matter what business you're in." Marlon Brando, who scored a striking success in *The Godfather*, probably has had more influence on youthful attitudes and behavior than any other Hollywood figure. In *The Young Lions* he managed to make a Nazi officer somewhat appealing, and in *The Wild One* he inaugurated the cult of the leather-jacketed motorcyclist that some years later matured in the form of Hell's Angels. If and when he plays Adolf Hitler or Joseph Stalin . . . ? A significant number of young Americans who idolize Brando know very little about Hitler or Stalin.

atrocity stories involving their own kind, Americans almost always maintain that where there is smoke, there is not, indeed there cannot be, any fire.

The increasing acceptance of crime, violence, and delinquency on and off stage, the popularity of what Pauline Kael has called "cinema fascism,"[11] signifies not merely the demise of moral indignation but a shift of the entire culture toward primary-process behavior. Whether one looks to the literary and theater worlds in which pornographic sadism is regarded as an art form or to the social leaders and celebrities, many of whom, in a manner of speaking, have become themselves exemplars and "pushers" of drugs and delinquency, or to everyday life, in which it is no longer clear what the rules are or to whom they apply, one can hardly avoid the conclusion that a great many Americans, reversing Descartes and the whole thrust of the Western tradition, operate on the principle: I do, therefore I am. Such fantasy-oriented behavior, termed "acting out" by psychoanalysts,* whatever form it takes, is unconsciously designed to avoid or bypass an unpleasant reality within the psychic system. To that extent, acting out is a defense mechanism not in the service of the ego but in the service of the id. Such behavior functions, so to speak, at the expense of or in the absence of the superego, but if it results in more rather than less suffering, it also functions at great cost to the ego. In extreme cases, of course, acting out can become threatening to others, in which event it invites punishment and even greater suffering for the ego.

In contemporary America much acting out is designed to avert anxiety, and there can be little doubt that anxiety stemming from external and internal sources has been the American condition throughout most of this century. An American born in 1930 has lived through one major depression and several recessions and has survived three wars, one of them a world war that took an estimated 35,000,000 lives; he can hardly recall a time when there was no threat of war with American involvement. He has witnessed the Nazi holocaust, the worst years of the Stalin era, and the first use of the atomic bomb. During his lifetime two Presi-

---

*In the analytic situation, "acting out" usually refers to actions or words based on unconscious attitudes and conflicts involving parents or early-childhood experiences. Here I am using the term in a broader sense.

dents have died in office, one through assassination, while a third President, widely distrusted, was more or less forced to retire from office and a fourth, threatened by almost certain impeachment, to resign in midterm. The American born in 1930, if a capitalist, has seen private property abolished or curtailed in many parts of the world; if a workingman, he has seen his job abolished or threatened—the "seen" here is used both subjectively and objectively—by economic slumps, automation, blacks, women's liberation, and other developments. If the American is a woman, she probably has experienced some confusion of roles due to changing mores or some personal event in her life, such as divorce, and she almost certainly has had more trouble with her adolescent children than her own mother, as she remembers the situation, had with her; whether she lives in a city or a suburb, she has seen the neighborhood "change" for the worse.

We have been talking about Americans in their forties, but it is important to note that an American born in 1940, who is now in his thirties, has experienced everything but the Depression, and as a result of World War II he may have been deprived of his father during the crucial first five years of his life or, as a consequence of the Korean War, deprived of him during the almost equally crucial early-adolescent years. An American born in 1950 arrived too late for the Depression, Hitler, World War II, and the dropping of the atomic bomb, but the impact of some of these events is a continuing one, and in any case, the American who now is in his twenties was very much on time for the turmoil of the Kennedy-Johnson-Nixon years. Even the American born in 1960, who is now a teenager, can hardly point to an untroubled childhood, including as it does the Vietnam War, the death of John F. Kennedy, and the assassinations of Martin Luther King and Robert F. Kennedy, the turmoil of the late sixties, Watergate, the resignation of President Nixon, and the genocidal struggles in Asia and Africa. Above all, Americans of every age have lived through or, more accurately, have lived *in* the very center of an age of violence.

While it is well known that violence generates anxiety, it is less known that much of this anxiety comes from within. We are anxious in part because we are reminded of our own aggressive impulses, and we fear giving in to them. To be sure, we realistically may feel threatened by the violence around us; wars and muggings are genuine possibilities. But the root of the fear lies in our awareness that all the ways of curbing violence have failed or are failing. We perceive that the traditional restraints are no longer working, that society can no longer protect us in our homes or on the streets. This somewhat exaggerated awareness that social institutions cannot be depended on reminds us, in effect, that we ourselves are endangered by our own aggressive impulses, and since aggression invites punishment and death, our anxiety is all the greater.

In America the escape from aggression and anxiety takes many forms. As the Calley case demonstrated, an insistence on the innocence of the aggressor or the repeated assertion that the murder of unarmed women, children, and babies was a necessary measure serves to reassure ourselves that we, too, are guiltless; in denying Lieutenant Calley's responsibility for My Lai and, subsequently, in supporting the acquittal of the other officers involved, we deny our own murderous aggressive and sadistic impulses.*

Most drugs popular with the young suppress aggression and reverse or alleviate other unwanted states of feeling such as depression and loneliness. It is noteworthy, as a number of observers have pointed out, that the fantasy or illusion produced by LSD and other hallucinogenic compounds is that of a symbiotic union with others similar in feeling to that between mother and child. Indeed, a major thrust of the youth counterculture is, symbolically, toward a return to the breast, in which state, of course, one is untroubled by anxiety, loneliness, frustration, and the fear of aging and death. No longer believing that, in the normal course, paradise can be gained in heaven or on earth, we seek and to some

---

*Whether or not such a motive was present in the actions of President Nixon, transferring Calley three days after his conviction from the Fort Benning stockade to private quarters where he was under house arrest, his intervention in the case was characterized by the prosecutor, Captain Aubrey M. Daniels, as extremely damaging to the military judicial system. "Totally shocked and dismayed at the reaction of many people across the country," Captain Daniels wrote the President, "how much more appalling it is to see the moral issue or, having seen it, to compromise it for political motive. . . ." (New York *Times*, April 7, 1971.) As Commander in Chief of the Armed Services and the man directly responsible for the intensified bombing of North and South Vietnam in 1969–72, Nixon would have had more reason than Calley and the public for failing "to see the moral issue. . . ." The Vietnam War is dealt with at length in Chapter 9.

extent find a substitute bliss in the psychedelic experience, the religious cult, the commune, the organic farm, the Zen colony, and what William Schutz of Esalen has called the "joy workshop." Hence the back-to-nature movement with its emphasis on organic food, Indian lore, homespun and handicrafts, nudity, and freedom of bodily movement.* Hence, too, the number of folk-rock songs seeking to drive away the clouds (depression) and bring on the sunshine (euphoria).

Of course, there are countercultures and countercultures, and in some of them the values associated with the superego and with morality in general, although they may be expressed in unconventional forms, are far from dead. As René Dubos has suggested, throughout history countercultures have appeared irrational to outsiders, but in fact many of them have been motivated "by a higher kind of rationality than that of the Establishment. . . .They represent a soul-searching in quest of values which once gave zest to living and which are being lost—such as direct experience of nature, intimacy, uniqueness and even eccentricity."[12] Dubos sees modern countercultures as protests against technology, gadgets, "plastic knicknacks," materialism in general. Certainly no one can deny the appeal of back-to-nature or take issue with a lifestyle that is opposed to violence, the spoilation of the natural environment, gluttony, hypocrisy, sensory deprivation, and the consumption ethic. America is, after all, the only country in the world where prostitutes are arrested in front of pornographic theaters and restaurants advertise "all you can eat for $5.00."

But not all aspects of the counterculture are benign and rational. Whether or not Charles Manson became, in one students' words, a "Big Man on Campus" in 1972 in the sense that many students "are now quoting with approval" his ideas,[13] the Manson colony of runaway schizophrenic girls, borderline dropouts, and psychotic hangers-on was also a counterculture, albeit one based on violence and racism. The frequency with which counterculture types find their way to hard drugs and/or mental hospitals reminds us that however much their way of life appeals to those of

---

*Is it fair to speculate that the current interest in ethology owes something to the nature movement? Certainly the behavior of primates and other creatures was studied and written about a long time before it became the subject of popular books in the late sixties.

all ages who are having second thoughts about the "rat race," it appeals as well to those who are disturbed in mind to one degree or another.* For the counterculture is based not merely on a rejection of mindless consumption and stultifying convention but on an intolerance of life's great or small frustrations and on insistence on immediate, satisfying experience. Whatever the citizen of counterculture may want by way of alleviating his loneliness and sense of futility, he wants it *now*—and he is not always understanding or nonviolent with those who stand in the way of *now*. In fact, since the counterculture, like most cultures, provides ample opportunities for projection of internal conflicts onto the external world, it is not unusual to find in counterculture literature a dislike verging on contempt for older generations, as in Jerry Rubin's *Do It!*, unless they become, in effect, camp followers. Even a respected counterculture scholar like Theodore Roszak is not above writing: "For we are young. And they are old. Strange, is it not? How they keep growing older and older and older . . . while we . . . grow younger . . . and younger. . . ." (Ellipses by Roszak.) He notes, in a similar vein, that the counterculture revolution will succeed because it stands for "beauty—the beauty of human souls reclaimed and illuminated. . . . A beautiful politics. Despite the bastards."[14]

Of course, it is only fair to add that many, perhaps even most adults regard counterculture youth with equal suspicion. Just as the youthful revolt against authority can be symptomatic of rebellion against the superego or the failure to internalize it, so the adult dislike of hippies and preoccupation with law and order can indicate that inner conflicts have been dealt with through projection and displacement. By such mechanisms the sexual and aggressive components of the id can be projected onto countercul-

---

*Evidence for this may be found in the pages of some underground press publications in which the emphasis is on drugs, violence, sadism, and pornography. Charles Manson and his "Family," for example, were eulogized in the Los Angeles *Free Press*, *Tuesday's Child*, the *Berkeley Barb*, and other underground newspapers. Weathermen leader Bernadine Dohrn is quoted by the *The Guardian*, a New Left publication, as saying of the Manson "Family": "Dig it, first they killed the pigs, then they ate dinner in the same room with them, then they even shoved a fork into a victim's stomach! Wild!" (Irving Howe, "Political Terrorism: Hysteria on the Left," *New York Times Magazine*, April 12, 1970.)

ture youth, with the punitive superego assigned, as it were, to the police, courts, university administrators, and so forth. Those adults who are most obsessed by the long hair, alleged promiscuity, and relaxed life-style of many young people are invariably those who feel most threatened by counterculture values, seeing in them a reflection of their own forbidden selves.* For such adults the Kent State shooting of four students and other violent confrontations between youth and authority perform a function of relief: the regret, often, is that more students were not killed, beaten, or maced. As one father, a physician, wrote his son who was about to attend Tulane University, following the deaths of the four students: "the sweet little girl in Kent . . . was helping contest the ground with duly constituted United States authorities. In this case, I back the United States. I think it rather remarkable that they didn't shoot 200 more. In this case, the girl was a revolutionary and she got exactly what a revolutionary should expect. The same, Snap, would be true of you. . . . If you take part in something like this and get shot, Mama and I will still back the United States. . . . Now use your head, son. Remember this country is getting tired of student demonstrations which lead to revolution. The National Guard can shove in a couple of clips and clean Tulane. I think they ought to when students disturb the peace and destroy property."[15]

One consequence of such views is the fiscal attrition of some universities due to a shrinkage of financial support by alumni and state legislatures. By withholding funds from those thought to have failed in the role of *loco parentis*, the alumni and legislators were doing more than punishing school administrators for their alleged permissiveness toward student activism. They were also avoiding certain questions about themselves as parents and citizens and their society. "Perhaps we should be asking," wrote another physician, Harvard psychiatrist Leon Eisenberg, in 1970, "not why there is student unrest, but why there is no *adult* unrest, except in response to students. Why are we content to tolerate an immoral and futile war? Why do we as physicians permit health

*A joke, current at the time, was about an old man who was asked his opinion about the counterculture. "I'm agin it for three reasons," he replied, "one, it's illegal, two, it's immoral, and three, I ain't gettin' any of it."

services to be cut back while $100,000,000 each day is committed to the war in Vietnam? Is it perhaps because we have been complacent that the young are frantic?"[16]

But not all of Roszak's "bastards" are complacent or opposed to "the beauty of human souls reclaimed and illuminated." While no one has counted the number of middle-aged Americans whose life-styles mimic those of their counterculture children, the total probably is not inconsiderable. Anyone who lives in a major city in the East or West or who teaches in a university knows people aged between forty and sixty who have let their hair (and beards) grow to an impressive length and who turn on, swim nude, dispense with bras, frequently dress in blue jeans, wear Indian-style jewelry, and listen to rock. A recent advertisement for Talon zippers features a teenage boy in dark blue suit, conservative shoes, shirt buttoned at the collar, and necktie, standing next to his long-haired and mustached father, who is wearing a flaming red shirt open halfway to his navel, striped pants, sandals, a beaded necklace, and a large peace symbol medallion.

Equally impressive is the facility with which parents have adapted to jive talk and counterculture language, for example: pig (usually a reference to husbands or other men rather than policemen, as in the expression "male chauvinist pig"), far out, heavy, trip, mind-blowing, downer, bummer and bum-out, split, to lay something on someone, etc. Many of these parents subscribe to *Time* or *Newsweek* and *Saturday Review World*, but they also are readers of *Rolling Stone* and occasionally see *Mad* and the *National Lampoon*.

Some of the most fervent literary celebrators of the youth counterculture are well into middle age, and there are even a few who have entered the Social Security years. Is it an accident that several of these articulate spokesmen for counterculture values are homosexual? To view their books about the counterculture as a form of sublimated pederasty probably is unfair, but it remains true that overt and latent-homosexual preferences blend well with the polymorphous perversity of the youth counterculture.[17]

The major role of the "bastards," of course, has not been that of aging hippies but of parents who have been too remote, too indulgent, or too confused to take much part in their children's everyday activities, much less to exert a positive influence on their unconscious mental life. Many parents in our affluent society see no need to establish a close relationship with their children, but, instead, to be by turns permissive and evasive in dealing with the young. In effect, they find it easier to achieve conformity by the use of bribery than by facing the emotional turmoil of suppressing the child's demands and of giving genuine and intense love as a reward for the renunciation of unacceptable forms of behavior. Because this renunciation is neither properly timed in terms of the child's development nor combined with love, the child as he grows into adolescence and adulthood may continue to pursue gratifications with no firmly organized self system that identifies with the traditions and values of the larger society. The bribery that affluence makes possible is itself a mode of gratification, not a method by which frustration becomes bearable because in return for love the completion of disapproved acts is relinquished. Bribery at most can achieve only short-term and superficial results; it cannot promote the incorporation of moral models and the approved value system.*

According to a number of studies, the closest relationship of student activists through the adolescent and college years is with their mother or another maternal figure, whereas the runaway or delinquent is likely to have had a poor relationship with both parents or no relationship at all.[18] But in a majority of all such cases, although the social consequences are different, the father was either absent a good deal of the time or cold and punitive during the crucial years of childhood and adolescence. Most of the fathers, off in the Army or occupied with work and career, presumably were home only occasionally during these years whatever their relationship with their children. But it is a fact of considerable importance that, in America, a very large number of homes are fatherless homes as a consequence of either death, desertion, or divorce. An estimated one-sixth of the nation's children or more than 11,000,000 youngsters, live with one parent, usually the mother, as a result of divorce, or with none.

Boys who remain too attached to their mothers and distant

---

*It is probably for this reason that all modernizing societies begin to experience difficulties with their youth as they become more affluent. In the Arab countries and Israel, for example, the shift from discipline combined with love to bribery by means of monetary rewards or their equivalents has resulted in increasing delinquency and alienation among young people.

from their fathers may have a desperate time establishing themselves as young men; the defense against their own femininity and passivity may take an ultramasculine form that requires, among other things, the maximum physical and moral distance between their world and that of their parents. Girls unable or unwilling to rediscover their mothers and give up their fathers may fantasize themselves as men and reject the roles that marriage and motherhood require. The boy whose parents are college graduates may give up college altogether; if he has experienced his professional or businessman father as a weak, ineffectual man, he may choose to pump gas or wait on tables for a living. Boys and girls, if they are estranged from parents or cannot accept the separation from parents that is inevitable in growing up, may seek to relieve their inner anguish with drugs or communality or substitute parental figures of whatever age. It is no accident that young couples in the counterculture often refer to each other as "my old lady," "my old man."

Ways of handling loneliness and despair are infinitely varied. One young man grew up in a home that was dominated by his mother. Mother, however, was a woman given to posturing and pretenses; in particular, she presented herself as a devoted mother, whereas in reality she neglected her son, for example, by forgetting his dental appointments and losing his school report cards. Late in his adolescence the boy began to hero-worship Robert Kennedy. He hung pictures of Kennedy in his room, collected his speeches, and eventually attached himself to Kennedy's campaign for the Presidency in 1968. He was not far from the Senator when the latter was shot in Los Angeles' Ambassador Hotel. Following a period of severe depression the boy turned savagely against "the system," holding it responsible for Kennedy's death. He joined the Weathermen and took part in a bomb plot. He also became a dealer in marijuana. After a time he was arrested by the police and referred for consultation to a psychiatrist . Consistently suspicious and hostile, he became very angry when the psychiatrist suggested that his substantial income from dealing was incompatible with his extreme anticapitalist views. Accusing the therapist of being part of the system, he finally broke off treatment. His parting "gift" to the psychiatrist was a paper bag containing Acapulco Gold.

Much has been written about the extent to which the student activists of the late sixties shared their parents' generally liberal political outlook or took up positions to the left of it, however much their life-styles may have differed from those of their parents. In some instances, apparently, young revolutionaries are motivated by their parents' unspoken and perhaps even unconscious assumptions about the United States that, in effect, deny the utility of liberal reforms. One such case involved a girl whose parents had been members of the Communist Party during the Depression. Since that time her father had achieved a good deal of success, financial and otherwise, and while he had long since left the party, he remained convinced that American society was too corrupt to be changed by peaceful gradual means. This attitude was not verbally communicated to his daughter, but she, like her father, eventually came to believe that the only possible solution for society's ills was revolutionary violence and that, in any event, American capitalism was sufficiently rotten to merit overthrow. But unlike her father, who had never broken the law, she acted upon these assumptions, and following an unsuccessful kidnapping attempt designed to raise money for a revolutionary movement, she was placed on the "most wanted" list of the Federal Bureau of Investigation. Instead of introjecting her parents' superego, which in turn reflected most of the rules of society, including the rule of law, she introjected the aggressive and destructive components of her father's id. Had she been estranged from her parents, either rejecting them or being rejected by them, her life probably would have taken a wholly delinquent direction.

If, as these cases illustrate, a parental superego model is missing from the childhood scene, there can be no more than a faulty or partial identification with the moral standards and values of which the parents are the first exemplars. Nor can children identify with parents if the parents themselves devote a good deal of time to identifying with their children, as in some examples cited earlier. Indeed, the confusion about norms and values can only become worse if an older generation, perhaps for the first time in history, takes its cues on how to behave, how to enjoy life, how to *live*, not from its own parents and the past, but from its children. Children who look to their parents for guidance and example and see only images of themselves, albeit slightly older images, are hardly likely to respect and emulate what they see.*

In the absence of a mother or father who can serve as an ego-ideal representation, the child and adolescent may turn to parental surrogates or other models in the culture. Even a child without parents, if he is raised in a culture that is anchored firmly in religion or secular piety or whose institutions reflect a continuity of tradition, is likely to internalize the accepted code of behavior. But suppose the parental surrogates and models are lacking or are themselves given to primary process and acting out and there are few if any cultural anchors and traditions? Most persons who reach adulthood in a society without clearly defined heroes and traditions, if they are not enthusiasts of one or another deviant sect, will feel lost and bewildered as they endeavor to locate themselves in a landscape that has no fixed boundaries or contours. Nor is it just individual behavior that is confused. The government and politics of that society, its art, music, and theater, the whole range of its esthetic life ranging from architecture to fiction, inevitably will display an equal confusion.†

In contemporary America the droppings of confusion are found almost everywhere. Perhaps the last ten years can be viewed as a decade during which the ego ideal in the home and elsewhere was replaced by a variety of heroes who were, in the main, amoral or sinister or corrupt or violent. No doubt the replacement process was significantly aided by a dearth of conven-

---

*The extreme point in this direction was reached in 1974 when it was disclosed that a hot line in Greenwich, Connecticut, established to help teenagers in trouble, was being extensively used by adults. Drawing 40 percent of its callers from those over thirty years of age, the hot line, staffed mainly by trained high school and college volunteers, was dealing with such "adult" problems as sex, family relationships, divorce, and alcoholism. (New York *Times*, June 21, 1974.)

†A culture in which an Andy Warhol painting of a soup can is valued at more than $15,000 and an Yves Klein canvas painted a uniform green is priced at $6,000 is revealing something more than esthetic confusion; it is displaying a fundamental ambivalence about art altogether. Such a culture is not likely to care much when the countryside is raped by bulldozers in behalf of a shopping center or a historic and beautiful brownstone of perfect proportions is replaced by a concrete tower. It may be, as Erich Kahler has suggested, that much modern art and literature reflect a serious and perhaps fatal fragmentation or split in the heart of the Western humanist tradition. See his *The Tower and the Abyss* (New York: Braziller, 1957).

tional heroes and the assassinations of John F. and Robert F. Kennedy, Martin Luther King, and Malcolm X; those scarred by violence, as in the example of the boy who became a Weatherman, often turn to violence. But the decade was also marked by a massive failure on the part of the nation's leaders and celebrities. Forgetting that the morale of society, especially the morale of the youth, is sapped by widespread evidence of dishonesty, hypocrisy, bad taste, and lawbreaking in high places, the nation's rulers behaved much of the time like the English upper class toward the end of the nineteenth century, if we can believe Henry James. That class, he wrote in a letter, "seems to me to be in many ways very much the same rotten and *collapsible* one as the French aristocracy before the revolution—minus the cleverness and conversation. . . ."[19] The English upper class survived, of course, but in those days only insiders like James were aware of the rot; there was only a minuscule popular press and no gossip columns or television. As there was little voyeurism on the part of the public, partly for technological reasons, so apparently was there little exhibitionism among those eminent in British society.

The same cannot be said of the American upper class, the members of which are only too willing to expose themselves on television panel shows or in the profile pages of magazines. Thanks to *Playboy* interviews, the assorted adulteries, fornications, and masturbations of several hundred prominent persons have moved from the bedroom to the coffee table. Thanks to the business acumen of the nation's astronauts, those modern Magellans and Drakes who were almost every boy's heroes, one can obtain, at a price, canceled envelopes, signed postcards, stamps, coins, wristwatches, autographs, clothing, and other paraphernalia that accompanied the astronauts to the moon and back.* Some of those who were prisoners of war in Hanoi, it was recently disclosed, were also thinking of the main chance while still prisoners; in 1973 the Pentagon confirmed that a group of senior American

*In 1972 a coin that had been aboard the Gemini 7 spacecraft in 1965 was sold for $15,000 by William Ulrich, a coin dealer. It was not clear how Ulrich had obtained the coin, a 1973 penny, which had been placed in the spacecraft by a NASA flight surgeon. According to Ulrich, who regretted the sale, the coin was worth at least $100,000. Following disclosures that the astronauts were doubling as salesmen, NASA limited to twelve the number of items astronauts may carry into space! (New York *Times*, October 5, 1972.)

pilots captured by the North Vietnamese had agreed to establish a
corporation that would manage "their income from publishing,
speech-making and other public appearances."[20] In recent years
reputable publishers have advanced substantial sums for "authorized" biographies that turned out to be complete fabrications,
while in other biographical books by respected authors happen-
ings were reported that proved ultimately to be inventions.[21] The
Metropolitan Museum of Art, it was alleged by the New York
Times, contrary to agreements with former owners of paintings in
its possession and its own established rules, sold a number of these
important paintings, some publicly and others secretly, not to other museums but to commercial galleries and private collectors. An
opening at the Museum of Modern Art was hailed by an art critic
in a magazine as "fascinating and illuminating" not only before
the opening took place but before the art being shown had been
fully installed. Meanwhile Army generals in Vietnam were found
to be falsifying not only atrocity and bombing reports but citations
of themselves that led to decorations for valor. Perhaps if one had
to choose one expression, and one only, by which to categorize the
Johnson-Nixon era, it would not be the word "war" or "unrest" or
"alienation" or "drugs" or even "Watergate." It would be the expression "rip-off."

No doubt the social leaders of society, sometimes known as the
beautiful people, cannot be held to the same standards as ordinary Americans. Richer than others and therefore able to buy sur-
pluses of time and opportunity, beautiful people can hardly be
blamed for wanting—and getting—most of what there is to get,
whether it be possessions, sex, or simply kicks. Still, they have
some influence on the nation's morals, manners, and tastes, and
that influence is hardly in the direction of traditional behavior. In
effect, beautiful people represent another kind of counterculture
and one also given to primary process and acting out. Moreover,
beautiful people live well in addition to living free of conventional
restraints, and living well has always been the ultimate American
dream. For this reason they exert an appeal far greater than that
of the youth counterculture with its relatively austere and primitive life-style, and it therefore is possible for many older Americans who disapprove of drugs, communes, and the so-called sexual revolution to overlook the fact that the beautiful people counterculture and the youth counterculture have much in common.

Just how much begins to emerge from even a cursory study of

recent changes of sexual mores. It was not hippies and activists or simply advances in birth-control technology that overturned the older traditions of premarital chastity and monogamous marriage, but the beautiful people with their multiple affairs and extramarital relationships, some of them blessed by children, fully publicized in certain popular magazines.* When we think of the drug pusher as a shady character on a city street or in the schoolyard, we overlook those who have promoted drug usage through books, articles, or personal example, such as Timothy Leary and Ken Kesey, not to mention the rock stars. Most Americans associate the amphetamine known as speed with dropout adolescents and delinquents, forgetting that in 1972 a prominent physician who regularly used speed in treating many of his patients revealed that the more prominent of these patients included President and Mrs. Kennedy, Tennessee Williams, Truman Capote, Eddie Fisher, Congressman Claude Pepper, Otto Preminger, Anthony Quinn, and Alan Jay Lerner.[22] Although the possession of LSD is illegal, eminent persons in many different professions have admitted using the drug; in the theater world, apparently, it is as *infra dig* not to have tried LSD as it is gauche in rock circles not to have injected heroin. The widespread acceptability of drugs is underlined by the 1972 popular song hit "The Candy Man," played by disc jockeys with tongue-in-cheek amusement since, in knowledgeable circles, "candy" is a slang term for cocaine.

There was a time, to be sure, when music groups such as the Beatles were thought to possess a charming innocence and wholesomeness that was not much less attractive to parents than to their teenage children. Parents and their offspring who saw the movie *Help!* or listened to *Rubber Soul* could hardly be blamed for regarding John, Paul, George, and Ringo with some affection. When it became evident that the Beatles, like other folk-rock bands, were not immune to drugs, groupies, violence, prejudice, and exploitation, parental attitudes if not those of their children changed, but it remained for one of the Beatles, and the best-known one at that, to reveal that the image and the reality, even in the early years, had never been in accord. "The Beatles tours,"

*The point is not whether the sexual revolution is or is not desirable, in whole or in part, but that it was the beautiful people, in the main, who first took to the barricades. For a fuller discussion of recent changes in sexual behavior see below, Chapter 4, "Phallic Culture."

John Lennon tells us, "were like the Fellini film *Satyricon*. We had that image, man, our tours were like something else. . . . Wherever we went, there was always a whole scene going, we had our four separate bedrooms. We tried to keep them out of our room. . . . [The] rooms were always full of junk and whores and the who-the-fuck-knows-what, and policemen with it. Satyricon! We had to do something. What do you do when the pill doesn't wear off and it's time to go? I used to be up all night . . . whether there was anybody there or not, I could never sleep, such a heavy scene it was. They didn't call them groupies then, they called it something else and if we couldn't get groupies, we would have whores and everything, whatever was going."*

When Lennon remarked, at the height of the Beatles' fame, that "kids are more influenced by us than by Jesus," he was not exaggerating much. But whatever he was saying about the kids, he was saying something more about their parents and the society in which they live. For in a society characterized by weak family ties, faltering leadership, and institutional collapse, the younger generation will tend to seek its heroes outside the mainstream of the society and even among its enemies. As Freud and others have suggested, a loss of faith in leaders and institutions can create a sense of panic, and perhaps it is a feeling very much like panic that in recent years has led many of the young to embrace a miscellaneous assortment of revolutionaries, apostles of violence, criminals, and antiheroes. Others, less attracted to the Maos and the Che Guevaras, have sought reassurance through identifications with swingers and playboy athletes, while still others have left the real world altogether, in a sense, for the solace of a guru or mystic.† In effect, the introjection of parents as behavioral models has given way to an introjection of corrupt ego ideals, and this development, in turn, has had far-reaching and largely nega-

---

*Interview in *Rolling Stone*, January 7, 1971. According to Lennon, some of the Beatles songs were inspired by LSD, and he himself was on "pills . . . bigger drugs than pot" during the making of *A Hard Day's Night*. After "a thousand trips" he gave up LSD only to start again. "I was reading that stupid book of Leary's. . . ."

†There is much evidence that the spiritual cults, in particular, function as ego and superego supports for many young people whose sense of themselves is weak or fragmented and who lack effective impulse controls. The insistence, in some cases, upon vegetarian diets, sexual abstinence, and strict obedience to the rules laid down by the "perfect master" can be viewed as an expression of puni-

tive consequences for the maintenance of the traditional Western value system.*

Among these consequences is an indifference to ugliness, cruelty, and wrongdoing, much of it attributed to the nightly portrayals on television of the horrors of war somewhere in the world and to the insensitizing effects of television in general. There is truth in this indictment of television, as witness the ease with which Americans move from an atrocity depicted on the tube to the dinner table and back again; in many homes dinner is customarily eaten in front of or near the set. But another explanation concerns the possible blunting of fantasy that may be a consequence of television and the movies. If, from an early age or over the course of many years, the work of fantasy is done, not in the mind, where it makes use of imagination and the unconscious, but on a screen, the probable result is a loss of capacity to fantasize and to dream. Since fantasy is related to empathy or the ability to imagine oneself in someone else's situation, the impoverishment of fantasy may be responsible for decline of feeling and caring. To the extent that the decline is experienced as deadening, the individual may resort to extremes of behavior to recapture the sense of feeling, and he may also seek more vivid, "realistic" fantasy portrayals on television and in the theater. In short, television and the movies may explain in part the increasing frequency of primary-process behavior and the growth of indifference.

But even if there were no television or movies, the conditions of modern urban life make survival dependent upon an ability *not* to know, *not* to see, *not* to smell, an ability, in other words, to "turn off" and stay turned off. It is not only that in many cities, as a result of overbuilding, population, congestion, and filth, the average citizen exists in a state of sensory deprivation;† in many parts

---

tive superego demands that have become externalized. It is no accident that a large number of those attracted to the Maharaj Ji and the Hare Krishna movement, among others, have a history of drug experiences and sexual promiscuity or deviation.

*I am indebted to Samuel Atkin, MD, for the phrase "introjection of a corrupt ego ideal."

†In most urban areas it is difficult if not impossible for the majority of citizens to witness a sunrise or sunset, breathe fresh air, listen to a bird sing, walk in the moonlight, lie under a tree, or eat anything that has fallen on the ground. Some of these experiences are available, of course, but only to the citizen who likes to live dangerously.

of the United States the ordinary person can avoid intolerable anxiety only by staying uninvolved, that is, by *not* noticing that someone down the street is being molested, or that his next-door neighbor has not been seen for several days, or that a thief is breaking into a parked car out front. Living in an age of massive death and violence, he knows beyond any doubt that life is cheap, his own life no less than the lives of others, and at some point he has probably weighed the benefits and risks of civic responsibility. Having weighed them, he knows that the risks are far heavier in the scales. Indeed, all the risks of city life increase with each passing day, while the benefits decline.*

The expression "conscience dictates," in other words, may be as passé as "God bless you" on parting or "Your obedient servant" at the end of a letter. Even the citadels of law and order, although theoretically committed to the superego, have contributed to the undermining of conscience and the sense of personal responsibility.[23] Thus the courts have refused to affirm the right to remain silent when asked for the names of friends and associates involved in an action deemed to be unlawful. The status of conscientious objectors also is in doubt since the Supreme Court ruling of March, 1971, that such status would be upheld only if the individual involved objected to all wars and not only the "unjust war" in Vietnam. Speaking for the Court's 8-to-1 majority, Justice Thurgood Marshall declared that the claims of conscience with reference to any war regarded as "unjust" by a prospective draftee were overcome by "the Government's interest in procuring the manpower necessary for military purposes." Only Justice William O. Douglas, the lone dissenter, argued for the principle that the protection afforded by the First Amendment extended to a conscience founded on "travail, meditation, or sudden revelation related to a moral comprehension of the dimensions of a problem" (i.e., the Vietnam War).

In general, "a moral comprehension of the dimensions of a problem," *any* problem, does not appear to be a foremost American characteristic as the nation approaches its two hundredth an-

*Even in Princeton, New Jersey, where civic-conscious citizens abound, it is not always easy to find responsible persons. Following a collision between the local shuttle train, or "Dinky," and a car, in which two women were killed, the police reported that all of the six or seven passengers on the train "disappeared without a trace." (Princeton *Packet*, March 10, 1971.)

niversary. In the face of a rapidly increasing rate of juvenile delinquency and schoolroom violence, the New York City Board of Education in 1970 issued a lengthy school-behavior code detailing the rights and obligations of high school students. There is no way of knowing students' reactions to such statements as "Students have the right to determine their own dress, except where such dress is clearly dangerous . . ." and "No student has the right to interfere with the education of his fellow student . . ." but the disruption by students of two separate public hearings held by the board provides a clue. In a similar vein, the reactions of many Italian-Americans to the existence of the Mafia is not to take action against it but to seek to eradicate the words "Mafia" and "Cosa Nostra" from the vocabulary of news media and establish the Italian-American Civil Rights League under the direction of reputed Mafia chieftain Joseph Colombo. Shortly before he was shot at a league rally, Colombo boasted that the league had 45,000 dues-paying members and 2,000 "captains," 200 of whom were Jewish and 90 of whom were blacks.*

Instead of reacting sympathetically if guardedly to consumerism—businessmen, after all, are also consumers whose cars break down and whose wives use detergents—many business leaders accuse the movement of dealing with minor problems and making matters worse. Government officials and consumer activists, one businessman complained, "act on the basis of emotion and prejudice. . . . Costly government bureaus have been created. . . . Much of what government consumer protectors do is the result of the politics of the problem, not the problem itself."[24]

The gay liberation movement, rather than confine itself to establishing equal rights and an atmosphere of public acceptance for homosexuals, takes the extreme view that homosexuals are "probably the most harassed, persecuted minority group in history. . . ." Not to be outdone, one of the leading theoreticians of

---

*As for the Mafia: "What's the Mafia?" Colombo asked in an interview. "There is not a Mafia. Am I head of a family? Yes. My wife and four sons and a daughter. That's my family. . . .What gives the Government the right to label anybody? What are we, in Nazi Germany?" (New York *Times,* April 4, 1971.) The league later took credit for the fact that the word "Mafia" is nowhere mentioned in *The Godfather* film. In 1971 Colombo was named "Man of the Year" by the *Tri-Boro Post,* a weekly newspaper that circulates in the New York boroughs of Queens, Brooklyn, and Staten Island.

women's liberation insists that "the prostitute is the only honest woman left in America . . . honest . . . because [prostitutes] charge for their services, rather than submitting to a marriage contract which forces them to work for life without pay."[25]

"Pay" in one form or another is what matters, says a man of God delivering the invocation at a Florida banquet. "Almighty God," he begins, "we thank Thee for a free land where private property is a sacred reality. For millions it is not. Among us, Lord, are millions who own no home, no land, and no business. Owning nothing, they demand everything from a paternal government. Dear Lord, we fear they are potential victims for the panacea of Socialism. . . . Bless all among us who work, produce, save, and invest, creating real wealth for our well-being."[26]

That all this betokens massive confusion and the loss of a sense of direction is easily apparent. Less apparent is any answer to the question whether the confusion can be dissipated and a sense of direction regained. But perhaps there is a hint of an answer, though not a very satisfactory answer, in the recent history of a society that is America's foremost competitor in many areas and, in the eyes of some, foremost threat. Between the years 1860 and 1870, runs a memoir of the time, "all the educated classes of Russian society were occupied exclusively with one question—the family discord between the old and the young. Ask about whatever noble family you would at that time, you always heard one and the same thing—the parents had quarreled with the children. And the quarrels had not arisen from any substantial material causes, but simply upon questions of a purely theoretical, abstract character. 'They could not agree about their convictions!' It was only that, but this 'only' sufficed to make children abandon their parents and parents disown their children."[27]

One hundred years later in Russia socialization processes were no longer left to chance. A distinguished American sociologist, comparing these processes in the United States and the Soviet Union, found much to praise in Soviet child-rearing practices. "The one thing a Russian child can never feel," Urie Bronfenbrenner reported, "is that he isn't loved." In addition to spending more time with their children than Americans do, the Russians emphasize the importance of sharing and collective responsibility, according to Bronfenbrenner, and place the stress on working toward group goals. The childhood and early-adolescent years of Russians are, in effect, planned and oriented toward the values and goals of Soviet society, whereas in the United States the "planning" consists of the haphazard influences, for good or ill, of home, school, friends, and an estimated 12,000 to 15,000 hours of television. No one in Russia speaks of superego development, and it therefore is all the more fascinating to learn that "American children were more likely, and Russian children less likely, to engage in dishonest or antisocial behavior if other children were going to know what they had done."[28]

The behavior of the American children would seem to support Freud's view advanced more than forty years ago and somewhat eerily bears out his pronouncement about the state of American civilization. In his *Civilization and Its Discontents* of 1930, Freud wrote: "we are imminently threatened with . . . [what] one may call 'la misère psychologique' of groups. This danger is most menacing where the social forces of cohesion consist predominately of identifications of the individuals in the group with one another, whilst leading personalities fail to acquire the significance that should fall to them in the process of group formation. The state of civilization in America at the present day offers a good opportunity for studying this injurious effect of civilization which we have reason to dread."[29]

Clearly some of the problems dealt with in this chapter have been germinating for a considerable time, and since America has survived at least four decades of *la misère psychologique*, one probably exaggerates too much in saying that those who value a civilized way of life must ultimately choose between the superego and the superstate. Certainly neither Russians nor Americans would agree with such a statement, the former because their value system is relatively intact and they have not experienced the loss of a sense of community, and the latter because they believe that the difficulties are temporary and do not call for new social institutions that can generate support for ethical and moral behavior. But it is far from clear that a society increasingly given to primary-process behavior, acting out, and the ever more frenzied pursuit of hedonistic gratification can remain cohesive enough to function, let alone solve urgent problems. Perhaps America will continue to survive, even flourish, with little or no superego restraints; perhaps the operating principle need only be, as on a current bumper sticker, "If it's fun, do it!" But surely it would be ironic if the Soviet Union, and ultimately China, became the last refuge of the Western conscience.

3

Political Economy and Other Cruelties

Perhaps sex was once a dirty secret, to use the famous phrase of D. H. Lawrence, but that was some time ago. Relatives, friends, and business associates, even strangers met casually in public places, will talk openly and willingly about their sexual lives, and some will not scruple at confessions of shocking practices accompanied by all kinds of forbidden fantasies. But there is one topic universally avoided by almost everyone, including, as psychoanalysts know, patients all too eager to talk about everything else, and that topic is money. People who have been intimate for a long time, such as parents and children, husbands and wives, and close friends, may exchange much information about themselves over the years, but as a rule they know little or nothing about each other's income and net worth. Money, in short, has become the last of the dirty secrets.*

The secret is especially well kept in the higher echelons of American business, where the making and keeping of large amounts of money, legally and illegally, is hidden from the public

---

*The term "dirty" is well advised, in this context, since it reminds us that money, like sex, has some relationship to excrement. In dreams and associations money is frequently equated with feces, although not exclusively, and it is a commonplace in psychoanalytic experience to find that a patient's characteristic parsimony or avaricious behavior can be traced back to an anal-stage fixation. Many persons regard the giving and receiving of money as acts of love, and inasmuch as they unconsciously identify money with the libido, they are apt to experience an impoverishment in one as an impoverishment in the other. Thus depressed patients are apt to feel that they are practically destitute even if the truth is otherwise. Perhaps this tendency is especially pronounced in America.

view so far as possible. Hence when it is discovered that the profits of major oil companies increased by 50 percent and more during the so-called energy crisis in 1973–1974, or that the International Telephone and Telegraph Corporation in an effort to safeguard its investments offered the White House and Central Intelligence Agency a million-dollar contribution toward the prevention of Chilean President Salvador Allende's election in 1970, there is a sense of shock in the public press and elsewhere. But in such instances the shock is usually of short duration, and rarely is it followed by sustained outrage. For Americans have come to know, somewhere in their minds, that money and business are, mainly, what America has always been about and, God willing, always will be about. "Business," an immigrant wrote home in 1836, "is the very soul of an American. He pursues it, not as a means of providing for himself and his family, but as the fountain of all human felicity. It is as if all America were but one gigantic workshop, over the entrance of which there is the blazing inscription: 'No admission here, except on business.' "[1]

The relationship between economic self-interest and the American "soul," however, did not originate with Jacksonian democracy. As Charles A. Beard demonstrated in 1913, although he weakened his case by overstating it, the "overwhelming majority of [Founding Fathers], at least five-sixths, were immediately, directly, and personally interested in the outcome of their labors at Philadelphia, and were to a greater or lesser extent economic beneficiaries from the adoption of the Constitution."[2] And what the Founders left undone, either intentionally or inadvertently, by way of ensuring that the Constitution, in Beard's words, "was essentially an economic document based upon the concept that the fundamental private rights of property are anterior to government and morally beyond the reach of popular majorities,"[3] was rendered complete a century later by Supreme Court interpretations and congressional enactments. "Documents like the Constitution," South Dakota Senator R. F. Pettigrew sadly observed after two terms in the Senate toward the end of the nineteenth century, "which I, as a child, had been taught to regard as almost divine in their origin, stood before me for what they were —plans prepared by businessmen to stabilize interests."[4] Seventy years after Pettigrew the only important change in the Constitution-government-business ecosystem was the extension of the stabilization concept to the far reaches of the globe. Confessing his "shock," in 1973, at the economic decline of the United States, Japanese Minister of International Trade and Industry Yasuhiro Nakasone lamented "the inability of [the United States] Government to regulate behavior of America's multinational corporations."[5] Had he approached the subject from the opposite point of view, that is, the extent to which the multinational corporations were able to regulate the behavior of the government, Minister Nakasone's shock would have been all the greater.

He was assuming, of course, that the multinational corporations are purely business entities rather than political-economic states, each with its own civil service, foreign policy, diplomatic staff, intelligence network, financial reserves, and above all the power to enforce decisions and coerce governments as well as other multinational corporations. In 1972 the sales income of General Motors exceeded $30.435 billion, and its net profit was well over $2 billion. Only 14 countries of the world, excluding the communist bloc, had gross national products, or GNPs (the total value of all goods and services produced), greater than General Motors' sales income, and only 68 countries, or half the UN membership, had GNPs larger than General Motors' net profit. The combined net profit of two oil companies, Exxon and Texaco, exceeded the GNPs of all but 47 countries of the world. At the other end of the scale Varian Associates, which ranked five hundredth and last in *Fortune* magazine's list of top 500 corporations, had a sales income greater than that of Botswana, Gambia, Guinea, Laos, Lesotho, Swaziland, and Yemen.* No wonder, then, that the multinational corporation is more and more beyond the reach of controls operated by governmental agencies and increasingly able to dictate the terms upon which it operates.

*"As a group, the multinationals now have a GNP of $450 billion, or 15 percent of world Gross National Product." (Physicist John P. Holdren in *Bulletin of the Atomic Scientists*, January, 1975.) Even the major food companies are wealthier than some of the developing countries, according to *Medical Tribune* publisher Arthur M. Sackler, MD. Ranking food companies and countries in terms of their 1969 (in two cases 1967 and in one case 1963) sales or GNPs, Sackler's list in descending order of wealth was as follows: Swift, Morocco, Algeria, Kraftco, Iraq, Armour, Nestlé, Borden, Ethiopia, Sudan, Foremost-McKesson, Ecuador, Consolidated Foods, Ralston Purina, and Coca-Cola. (*Medical Tribune*, April 25, 1973.)

But the power over government exercised by corporations is not automatic, and only rarely is it the result of a conspiracy. In the United States corporate regulation of government does not usually involve methods as crude as those of the dairy cooperatives in 1971 which contributed $422,000 to the Nixon reelection campaign in return for a large increase in the government's support price for milk. In fact, only infrequently is it necessary to bribe anyone in government to assure a meeting of minds between the corporate managers and their government counterparts. By and large the key posts in government are filled by individuals who either have corporate careers behind them or who come from social and educational backgrounds similar to those of the business leaders.* Thus between 1940 and 1967, 70 of the 91 men holding the very top jobs in national security and defense agencies—that is, the secretaries of the State and Defense departments, the three service secretaries, the chairmen of the Atomic Energy Commission, the directors of the CIA—were either investment bankers, businessmen, or lawyers for business.[6] In 1972, when the F-111 airframe contract was awarded to General Dynamics instead of the Boeing Company, the preference of military consultants, by Secretary of Defense Robert S. McNamara, two of his top advisers who participated in the decision had close ties to General Dynamics.† In tax and regulatory matters government policies toward the oil industry have always been friendly and cooperative, not least because an impressive number of past and present top officials of the State and Defense departments for-

---

*Military officers would appear to be an exception, but since in a great many instances they have business careers ahead of them and usually by the time of retirement have had extensive contacts with the business community, the effect is the same.

†The advisers were Roswell G. Gilpatric, Deputy Secretary of Defense and former senior policy adviser to General Dynamics, and Secretary of the Navy Fred J. Korth, who had been executive vice-president and president of a Fort Worth bank with which General Dynamics was connected. The F-111 fighter-bomber, which was built in Fort Worth, ultimately cost the government $7.8 billion for a total of 500 planes; the contract was described by the Senate Permanent Subcommittee on Investigations as a "fiscal blunder of the worst magnitude." (New York Times, December 19, 1970.) For a detailed account of the F-111 fiasco see Robert J. Art, The TFX Decision: McNamara and the Military (Boston: Little, Brown, 1968).

merly were employed in some capacity by oil companies or law firms servicing these companies,* and while the United States obviously cannot afford to disregard the interests and views of the oil-producing countries, strategic concerns alone do not account for decisions such as the one taken in 1954, by Secretary of State John Foster Dulles, restricting the smaller independent oil companies to no more than a 5 percent interest in the consortium that was to develop Iran's oil resources. Nor do strategic American interests satisfactorily explain secret agreements negotiated by the State Department in 1950 enabling oil companies "to abruptly reduce the taxes paid by the companies to the United States Treasury while dramatically increasing the tax revenues accruing to the oil-producing governments."[7]

As the history of the regulatory commissions testifies, corporate manipulation of government in behalf of corporate interests is not new. The Interstate Commerce Commission, for example, was no sooner created in 1887 than it became the instrument of the very railroads it was designed to regulate, and this with the blessing of the then Attorney General Richard Olney. Cautioning the president of the Chicago, Burlington and Quincy Railroad against efforts to have the ICC abolished, Olney pointed out that the "Commission, as its functions have now been limited by the courts, is, or can be made, of great use to the railroads. It satisfies the popular clamor for a government supervision of railroads, at the same time that the supervision is almost entirely nominal. Furthermore, the older such a Commission gets to be, the more inclined it will be to take the business and railroad view of things. It becomes a sort of barrier between the business corporations and the people and a sort of protection against hasty and crude legisla-

---

*The list includes secretaries of State Acheson and Dulles and secretaries of Defense Forrestal, Lovett, and Clifford. The industry connections of CIA directors perhaps make that agency particularly sensitive to the treatment of American corporations by foreign governments. John A. McCone, CIA head between 1961 and 1965, was in charge of the agency when it became involved in the 1964 Chilean election contest between Eduardo Frei Montalva and Allende. In 1970, when the International Telephone and Telegraph Corporation and the CIA spent large sums of money in another effort to defeat Allende, McCone was an ITT board member. Clearly the relationship between the CIA and ITT in Chile, and no doubt elsewhere as well, was an intimate one.

tion hostile to railroad interests. . . . The part of wisdom is not to destroy the Commission but to utilize it."[8]

The "utilization" of the independent regulatory commissions is equivalent to ensuring that the commissions are neither independent nor regulatory.* The first requirement of utilization is that the law creating the commission be written in such a way as to permit, if not to require, that the commission see itself as the agent of the special interests it is supposed to regulate. Congress, for example, in creating the Federal Maritime Commission made it more or less mandatory for the commission to grant exemptions from antitrust laws; and in other cases the intent of Congress, at least as understood by the commissions, was to favor the industry involved at the expense of its competitors and even to the detriment of its customers.[9] In accordance with this interpretation, the Federal Communications Commission has restricted the number of television channels, and although it is authorized to cancel licenses for a variety of reasons, in its entire history it has revoked only thirty-three radio and television licenses or permits.† The Civil Aeronautics Board has raised air fares between 30 and 80 percent above competitive levels; there are few instances of its intervening to lower fares deemed desirable by the airlines.

Even where the legislation establishing the commission is forthright and unambiguous in its definition of regulation, the intent

---

*"Utilization," in the words of Federal Trade Commission Chairman Lewis A. Engman, has made it possible for "most regulated industries [to] become Federal protectorates, living in a world of cost-plus, safely protected from the ugly spectors of competition, efficiency and innovation." (New York *Times*, October 8, 1974.)

†Reasons for license or permit revocation include technical violations, discrimination in employment, fraudulent billing, questions relating to the so-called fairness doctrine, and misrepresentations to the commission. In January, 1974, a total of 8,400 radio and television stations licensed by the FCC were on the air, or, in other words, only 1 station in every 225 has ever lost its license or permit to broadcast. Nevertheless, in 1974 the principal industry lobby, the National Association of Broadcasters, sponsored a further effort to weaken regulation. A bill before Congress that was supported by the NAB extended the life of TV licenses from three to five years and made it more difficult for outsiders, such as consumer-protection groups, to challenge the issue and renewal of licenses. On October 8, 1974, the bill, in the form of an amendment to a general FCC enabling measure, was approved by the Senate (it had passed the House previously).

can be vitiated by inadequate staffing and funding of commission functions. In 1971 the budgets of the two most important agencies charged with antitrust enforcement, consumer protections, and other key regulatory tasks, the Federal Trade Commission and the Antitrust Division of the Justice Department, totaled approximately $33,000,000 or about $1,000,000 *less* than the original estimated cost of three F-14 Navy fighters (by 1974 the cost had risen to almost $18,000,000 per airplane). The FTC budget, which was $22,000,000, represented a little more than half the cost of one B-1 bomber and a third of the cost of a C-5A (cargo) aircraft.[10] The $22,000,000, moreover, was the budget for the entire FTC, not just its subdivisions that deal with business practices. One result was an FTC announcement in December, 1971, that its investigation of American Telephone and Telegraph long-distance telephone rates, which was supposed to have begun six years earlier in 1965, "never really got off the ground" because of inadequate staff and money and therefore was being officially terminated. The uproar that followed, in and out of Congress, led to the resumption of the investigation a month later and effort in Congress to increase substantially the appropriation for the FTC. But there was never a satisfactory explanation for the repeated failure of the FTC to request more money from Congress for business regulation.

The FTC is by no means unique. In the Food and Drug Administration, which is responsible for the processing of most of the food Americans consume, among other functions, 212 inspectors are assumed to be sufficient for the supervision of 60,000 food plants.[11] Enforcement of antipollution regulations in the automobile industry, a regulatory function affecting the millions of domestic and foreign cars sold each year in the United States, is a task of the Environmental Protection Agency, in which it is entrusted to ten employees. In these and other instances, if the industry concerned does not regulate itself or at least make some effort to do so, there is no regulation at all.

If self-regulation worked, there would be less reason for concern, but here, again, the evidence is not reassuring. A revealing example not of self-regulation but of resistance to regulation was the crash near Paris in March, 1974, the worst in commercial air history, of one of McDonnell Douglas' DC-10 jumbo jets, taking the lives of 346 persons. The investigation of the near crash in

1972 of another DC-10 had revealed flaws in the locking mechanism of a rear cargo door that were responsible for the loss of the door in flight. In the fatal Paris crash the inadequately secured rear cargo door had literally blown out of the big jet, thereby damaging the plane's central cables and causing the pilot to lose control. In short, the flaws discovered following the earlier near-fatal incident had not been corrected, and although McDonnell Douglas initially denied any responsibility for the accident, it became clear that the company, in what amounted to collusion with the Federal Aviation Administration, had refused to make the changes that the earlier incident had indicated were necessary.

Subsequent investigation of the fatal Turkish Airlines crash near Paris revealed that two years earlier the FAA, in response to pressure from the company, did not issue the only one of four types of "airworthiness directive" that has the force of law. In fact, the FAA made use of its least urgent and most routine "standard" service bulletin rather than its campaign wire or "ALERT" notice, the latter confined to matters affecting aircraft safety. The "standard" service bulletin sent to McDonnell Douglas left it to the manufacturer and airlines using the aircraft whether or not to revise the cargo door's locking mechanism, although the FAA's Los Angeles office had sought to issue an "ALERT" notice following the 1972 near disaster. The Los Angeles FAA office, however, was overruled by then FAA Administrator John H. Shaffer, who, according to newspaper accounts, accepted an "oral agreement" with McDonnell Douglas to the effect that the locking mechanism would be corrected. Unfortunately for the 346 passengers who were aboard the doomed DC-10, the aircraft manufacturer also refused the FAA recommendation that it redesign the plane's floor, urging instead that the FAA finance a study of the problem "because of the magnitude of the effort required." Meanwhile, its letter to the agency concluded, six days before the Paris disaster, "we will not plan any further action . . . until we hear from you."*

*New York *Times*, March 23, 1974; March 28, 1974; April 1, 1974. On March 25, 1974, a subcommittee of the House Commerce Committee reported that of the thirty-nine DC-10 aircraft in operation at the time of the 1972 near crash, only five were modified within ninety days of the "standard" service bulletin issued July 3, 1972, and eighteen were not modified until 1973, some of them not until June of that year, or eleven months later. One DC-10 was not modified un-

The DC-10 crash, like those mine disasters that are also caused by inadequate inspections and faulty safety devices, reminds us of the frequency with which "business-as-usual considerations" and the "magnitude of the effort required" weigh more heavily in the balance than the risk to human life. "There's been a certain degree of complacency in the agency in the last five years," said a "top official" of the FAA in late March, 1974, and he anticipated a change as the result of the tragedy.* What he was really saying, in essence, was that the risk to the lives of passengers was deemed worth taking. After all, nothing had happened since the near disaster in 1972, and on that occasion the pilot had somehow managed to land the plane although the floor had collapsed into the hold, rupturing or damaging the control cables, and the tail engine was not working.

Complacency in business and government gives way only when the body count—and not always then—has reached an impressive figure. Hence the cargo door lock change in the DC-10 is now mandatory, and in this respect the case of the faulty cargo door lock is not much different from the history of other life-protecting changes in industrial environments. As many small towns in America have learned to their sorrow, the railroad is not likely to install a warning device at a grade crossing until there has been an accident involving death or injury. Indeed it is difficult to think of

til after the fatal crash on March 3, 1974. (New York *Times,* March 28, 1974.) Whatever McDonnell Douglas could have meant by "magnitude of the effort required," it could not have been referring to costs so great as to threaten the firm with bankruptcy. In 1972 McDonnell Douglas, the thirty-second largest industrial corporation in the United States, had sales totaling $2.7 billion and net profits of $112,000,000.

*This was one of the year's prize understatements. In April, 1974, the FAA's own inquiry board charged the agency with "questionable" actions and "ineffectiveness" in certifying the DC-10. Later that year it was revealed that the FAA, despite a number of landing accidents, still was not requiring the installation of cockpit warning devices to signal dangerously low landing approaches; the FAA had been urged for at least four years to make such devices mandatory by the National Transportation Safety Board. Early in January, 1975, the Transportation Department announced that it was taking an "in-depth look at the agency's operations." (New York *Times,* December 12, 1974; December 27, 1974; January 7, 1975.)

any industrial improvement in any area that was in force before rather than after one or more fatal accidents.*

Who were the FAA employees, one wonders, who sought to issue an "ALERT" notice in 1972 but were overruled by the head of the agency? Did they seek to appeal the decision to some higher authority—for example, by writing to members of the congressional committees that oversee the FAA? Were there McDonnell Douglas officials who favored immediate remedial action?† Or did they all conclude, in the usual American fashion, that "you win some, you lose some," as if nothing more than the outcome of a baseball game were at stake? Perhaps it is even true that a majority of businessmen agree with Leo Durocher that "nice guys finish last." A 1961 *Harvard Business Review* survey revealed that four of seven businessmen in a sample of 1,700 believe that businessmen "would violate a code of ethics whenever they thought they could avoid detection." One-half of the group agreed that "the American business executive tends to ignore the great ethical laws as they apply immediately to his work. He is preoccupied chiefly with gain." Four-fifths responded affirmatively to the question: "In your industry are there any [accepted business] practices which you regard as unethical?"[13] A later survey of 1973 suggests that a majority of businessmen often or occasionally have to sacrifice personal ethics and morality in order to stay in business. According to the American Management Associations' study, "About 70 percent of the businessmen . . . admit they have been expected, frequently or on occasion, to compromise personal principles in order to conform either to organizational standards or to standards established by their corporate superiors."[14]

---

*It was only after March, 1972, that a protective device at a railroad grade crossing was finally installed in the village of Congers, New York. Unfortunately, it was installed too late to save the lives of five high school students who were killed on March 24, 1972, in a collision between their school bus and a train.

†According to trial testimony related to damage suits arising out of the Turkish Airlines crash, a General Dynamics engineer engaged in subcontract work on the DC-10 had earlier warned his company that a crash "was close to 'inevitable'" if the cabin floor was not redesigned. The warning was not transmitted to McDonnell Douglas because it might have been interpreted "as a 'tacit admission' by General Dynamics that its original concurrence in the design was 'in error'" and therefore might involve it in liability. (New York *Times*, March 12, 1975.)

In such self-justification it is easy to identify the time-honored mechanisms of "pass the buck" and "I was only following orders," but much less easy to identify the *to whom* and *from whom*. Certainly it is difficult in most organizations to distinguish the personnel from something called "organizational standards," or to explain how it is that the morality of "corporate superiors" is less refined than that of other organization men. Indeed, there are as many cases of corporate superiors claiming that they are innocent of the wrongdoing of underlings about which they were never informed, as witness President Nixon's efforts to separate himself from Watergate, as there are cases of the opposite. Surely it is more realistic to suppose that the morals of business are the morals of businessmen and that, as a good many studies have demonstrated, the only important difference between corporation crime and other types of crime is that crime in behalf of the corporation is seldom punished in the same way that murder and theft are punished.

Edwin H. Sutherland's classic work *White Collar Crime,* published in 1949, revealed that 70 of the nation's largest corporations had been convicted an average of 14 times each of violations of law, most of which "may properly be defined as crimes." Twelve corporations averaged between 25 and 50 decisions each and 13 between 1 and 5 decisions. Sixty corporations had been convicted of restraint of trade, 53 of patent infringement, 44 of unfair labor practices, 28 of advertising misrepresentation, and 26 of rebates. The penalties for such violations were usually court orders prohibiting the continuation of the illegal practice and/or fines; almost none of the businessmen involved were sentenced to jail.[15]

Given this history, it is not difficult to understand those recent episodes in corporate behavior which Robert Heilbroner has termed "like My Lai . . . atrocities."[16] Thus the Penn Central debacle is not very different from those earlier railroad scandals which led railroad attorney Charles Francis Adams to lament, in 1916, "the covetousness, want of good faith, low moral tone of railway managers . . . complete absence of any high standard of commercial honesty,"* or one railroad president in 1890 to say to

---

*Those who lived by the business ethic, Adams further noted, were as vulgar as they were corrupt. "I have known, and known tolerably well," he wrote in his

sixteen others, "I have the utmost respect for you gentlemen individually, but as railroad presidents, I wouldn't trust you with my watch out of sight."[17] The 1961 conspiracy in electrical manufacturing, involving almost every firm in the industry, the plundering of Investors Overseas Services by Robert Vesco in 1970–1972, the uncovering in 1973 of the Equity Funding Corporation fraud, perhaps the biggest swindle in business history,* the successive efforts to monopolize or restrict production and fix prices in pharmaceuticals, oil, plumbing fixtures, automobile tires, lumber, chemicals, and other industries testify to the fact that while the technology of business enterprise has wholly changed in the last hundred years, the morality of business has remained essentially the same.

Nor is there evidence, despite the impassioned rhetoric at annual meetings of stockholders, that the investing public welcomes the corporation's assumption of social responsibility or that corporate gestures in that direction are much more than public-relations maneuvers designed to placate the minority that is critical of business and demands more effective regulation. Perhaps nothing conveys the realities so well as the collapse in 1974 of a short-lived mutual fund specializing in shares of corporations whose policies reflected a sense of social responsibility; few investors bought shares in the fund which invested in such established oil compa-

---

Autobiography, "a good many 'successful' men, 'big' financially, men famous during the last half-century; and a less interesting crowd I do not care to encounter. Not one that I have ever known would I care to meet again, either in this world or the next; nor is one of them associated in my mind with ideas of humor, thought, or refinement." (*Autobiography* [Boston: Houghton Mifflin, 1916], p. 190.)

*According to Ronald L. Soble and Robert E. Dallos, the Equity Funding Corporation swindle involved counterfeiting, computer rigging, forgery, and falsification of financial data, among other deceptions. To demonstrate growth, the company's officers manufactured 56,000 fictitious life-insurance policies worth $2 billion, and an imaginary $25,000,000 blue-chip bond portfolio. Leading accountant firms could find nothing wrong with the firm's bookkeeping, and by November, 1973, when twenty-two Equity officers and employees had been indicted in Los Angeles, a consortium led by the First National City Bank had loaned the firm more than $50,000,000. See Soble and Dallos, *The Impossible Dream: The Equity Funding Story* (New York: Putnam, 1974). On October 8, 1974, the former president and chairman of Equity pleaded guilty to five counts of conspiracy and fraud. The IOS-Vesco history is recounted in Robert A. Hutchison, *Vesco* (New York: Praeger, 1974).

nies as Atlantic Richfield and in corporations as respectable as Weyerhaeuser.* Although industry accounts for at least half of all air and water pollution, its "war on pollution" largely takes place on the advertising pages of magazines and in televison commercials. On the real battlefields, which are mainly legislative and regulatory bodies, business is more often found in opposition to antipollution measures.† As late as 1974 the employment policies of more than a third of the twenty largest corporations were still discriminating against blacks and women, and despite conclusive evidence that cigarette smoking is positively related to lung cancer, the tobacco industry continues to oppose advertising bans and efforts in the schools and elsewhere to discourage smoking; apparently some firms require senior executives to smoke. Indeed all this is so familiar that were Steffens, Tarbell, and other muckrakers alive today, they might have difficulty coming to terms with the sexual revolution and women's liberation but no difficulty whatever comprehending the rise of Ralph Nader.

Nader, of course, is not simply the current version of Upton Sinclair, nor is he a Marxist or, as hinted by *Fortune* magazine and other business periodicals, a paranoid who "has visited his own suspicions and fears upon a whole society. . . . "[18] Nader is best understood not as a business scandalmonger but as a crusader with a touch of the fanatic; indeed, he is reminiscent much more of Martin Luther and other religious zealots than of those who have periodically inveighed against the trusts and the robber barons. In Luther's time the dedicated reformer struck at the influence and decadence of the church, and since Luther the focus has

---

*New York *Times*, June 11, 1974. It is arguable that the First Spectrum Fund, Inc., failed because it was launched at a time "of deteriorating markets and investor disillusionment with mutual funds." On the other hand, mutual funds with a different base survived, and it is also true that there were no efforts prior to the First Spectrum Fund designed to link the corporate-responsibility concept with investment strategy.

†In December, 1970, it was reported that "air and water pollution boards in 35 states [are] dotted with industrial, agricultural, municipal and county representatives whose own organizations or spheres of activity are in many cases in the forefront of pollution. The roster of big corporations with employees on such boards reads like an abbreviated blue book of American industry, particularly the most pollution-troubled segments of industry." (Gladwin Hill in New York *Times*, December 7, 1970.)

been largely on the state and the military establishment. The Luthers of our day, recognizing that the large coprporation is the single most powerful institution of modern life, have sought to scourge it into exercising responsibility and accountability to the public interest.*

There, however, the resemblance between Luther and Nader ends. The sought-for reforms in the conduct of modern American business do not constitute a Reformation, and consumerism, successful or not in achieving its limited objectives, is hardly the equivalent of Protestantism. Nader's personality aside, the function he serves is essentially one that the independent regulatory commissions and the antitrust agencies were intended to perform, but which, as all the evidence makes clear, they have failed to carry out. Had there been no Richard Olneys in regulatory history, there would have been no Ralph Naders demanding safe cars, clean air and water, uncontaminated food, and decent nursing homes, and while the Naders of modern America are more limited than the official regulators because they are on the outside and possess no legal authority, they also can be effective because they at least, unlike the regulators, cannot be bought.

But while the influence of Naderism is not unimportant, it is mainly corrective and in the direction of promoting improvements in the existing system. The reforms it effects are not designed to change the essential nature and shape of the private-enterprise economy. Naderism, in short, is not socialism, and it would be exaggerating a good deal to say that it implicitly or explicitly constitutes a fundamental critique of the values of our acquisitive society. Neither Nader nor his most extreme supporters advocate the socialization of production, and they do not seek to redistribute wealth. No doubt there are elements of "consumer socialism" in Nader's efforts to improve conditions in nursing homes and food-processing plants, but the elimination of abuses in private pension programs, for example, is hardly equivalent to the elimination of poverty or even unemployment. From this

---

*Even Nader's life-style, which according to all accounts is austere and somewhat monkish, reminds us of the great religious reformers of the past. All the resources of General Motors, which in 1965 hired private detectives to spy on Nader in the hope of discovering some "dirt" with which to discredit him, were unable to find anything other than the fact that he had a sweet tooth.

point of view, Naderism, which many businessmen view as a threat to their existence, is to the right of the British Labor Party and most of the socialist parties of Europe.

In fact, Naderism and consumer socialism in general are largely rooted in middle-class aspirations and conceptions of the good life. Nader-style liberalism, like the liberalism of the magazine *Consumer Reports,* is oriented toward those who are employed long enough to afford a bewildering display of consumer goods and who also can manage to live long enough to retire. To the millions of Americans who are chronically poor, most of whom have never owned a Corvair or ridden as passengers in a DC-10, forms and varieties of Naderism must seem as remote as Hare Krishna.

Yet the cruelties of poverty are more "like My Lai . . . atrocities" than even the worst examples of corporate irresponsibility. For in the world's richest country, where nothing is sought so avidly as money and no people are envied so much as the rich, the condition of being poor has special significance. Most of the world, to be sure, is poor, and poverty everywhere is mean and dehumanizing, but where poverty is the common misfortune, as it is in most of Asia, Africa, and Latin America, it is not usually regarded as a disgrace. In the countries of Western Europe, moreover, the poor are provided with services and amenities that make their lives, if not comfortable in the material sense, at least tolerable. In a number of countries they receive free medical care of a quality far superior, in the view of most students of the subject, to that provided for poor Americans. The aged, the handicapped, and mothers with dependent children, in addition to the ill, apparently fare better in Britain, West Germany, Belgium, the Netherlands, Austria, and the Scandinavian countries than they do in the United States.

But perhaps the major difference between Europe's poor and the poor in the United States is that the latter are economically no better off than they were at the end of World War II. In 1947, for example, the bottom 20 percent of all American families had 5.1 percent of the nation's income, and the top 20 percent 43.3 percent. Twenty-five years later, in 1972, the poorest one-fifth of families had almost the same share of income, 5.4 percent, and the richest one-fifth enjoyed 41.4 percent. Since 1967, in fact, the richest families have improved their position in terms of income shares. In 1967, the top 20 percent received 40.4 percent, or 1 percent *less* than the amount received in 1972, while the top 5 percent of families increased their share of income from 15.2 percent in 1967 to 15.9 percent in 1972.

According to some standards and measures, the poorest individuals and families in the United States were worse off in 1972 than they were in earlier years. In 1959 families defined as "poor" by the federal government had an income about half as much as the typical family; by 1972 the income of these poor families was only slightly more than a third that of typical families.[19] Between 1958 and 1972 the share of aggregate wage and salary income earned by the lowest fifth of male workers declined from 5.10 percent to 4.60 percent, whereas the share of the top fifth rose from 38.15 percent to 40.55 percent.[20] In recent years, these figures seem to suggest, the nation's rich have become richer, and the nation's poor poorer, despite a variety of federal, state, and local poverty programs designed to reduce income inequalities.

The poor have also become, in a sense, more numerous, although not in the same sense that Marx meant when he asserted the inevitability of increasing poverty under capitalism. It is conventional, of course, to point out that the number of very low-income families has been declining for decades and that, as a consequence, there are fewer poor people than ever before. But what is forgotten is that substantial numbers of so-called intermediate and even middle-income families are experiencing lower living standards as a consequence of long-term inflation and, to a lesser extent, diminishing employment opportunities. For a variety of reasons, some of them technical and having to do with complexities in determining wage, price, and cost-of-living relationships over a long period of time, government statistics considerably understate the amount of income needed for the adequate support of a typical family of four persons.

Thus as late as 1971 the officially defined "poverty level" income for an urban family of four (the rural "poverty level" was a good deal less) was $4,137.* So defined—and it will be clear shortly how unrealistic bordering on fantasy such a figure was—13 percent of all families, or approximately 25.6 million persons, were at or below the poverty line. In other words, about one of every

---

*Despite the "double-digit" inflation of 1973–1974, the "poverty level" had risen to only $4,550 by May, 1974.

eight Americans in 1971 was a member of an urban family unit subsisting on roughly $80 or less a week. If these were the only poor people in the United States, the situation would be bad enough, but by any reasonable standard the number of poor was far greater. Indeed, if we more than double the "poverty level" income by increasing it to $10,971 for 1971, we still are dealing with a living standard that falls very much below the level of affluence. And in 1971 more than 50 percent of families had incomes lower than $10,971.

For that amount of money in 1971 an urban family of four would have been able to manage, according to the Bureau of Labor Statistics, an "intermediate" living standard based on a budget of $50 per week for food. The cost of housing, including utilities, maintenance, and replacements for furniture and other household equipment, was estimated at about $219 per month. Transportation expenses were to account for approximately $80 per month, which would have made it difficult to support even one car unless insurance was waived, repairs neglected, and parking space free. A total of $612 was allocated for the entire year's medical and dental bills, including health insurance, and $1,196 for clothing, cosmetics, and personal care. Union dues, gifts, Christmas presents, life insurance, and charitable contributions could amount to $653 annually. All other consumption, including entertainment, vacations, radio and television-set purchases, hi-fi equipment and records, school supplies, pets, toys, movies, sports events, and reading material including newspapers, was not supposed to exceed $684 for the year, or $57 per month.*

The "intermediate" budget can be regarded as affluent only by comparison with the much lower "poverty level" figure, and yet it envisages a living standard that remains considerably beyond the reach of most Americans. Since 1971, moreover, living standards in general have been eroded further by an inflation that has effectively wiped out the real-income gains of millions of workers, not

---

*As usual, there is a minimal curtsy in the direction of culture and its pursuit. The "intermediate" budget allows $80 per year for all reading. At the rate of a little over $1.50 each week, the family might have afforded one daily paper but not two, and for its other reading in an average week, it would have had to choose between a low-priced paperback and a magazine.

to mention those living on fixed or marginally elastic incomes and salaries.* In 1973–1974 the real-income loss for a typical production worker was 4 percent, and the rise in per capita income of 9.5 percent, a rise accounted for, in part, by increased total employment, is largely a fictitious one if notice is taken of the 12 percent increase in the price level. In terms of real weekly earnings after taxes and Social Security payments, between August, 1971, and July, 1974, the weekly pay of the average worker with three dependents *declined* from $92.62 to $91.04, according to the Bureau of Labor Statistics. Inflation, in other words, is accomplishing what American capitalism has so far failed to accomplish, that is, to make the poor poorer and more numerous.†

The rich, on the other hand, irrespective of whether they work or do not work for a living, are better able to cope with inflation. Until August 31, 1973, for instance, a corporation could grant its executives salary increases well above the 5.5 percent limit

---

*Notwithstanding, labor costs in the United States have risen less than costs in any other country with the exception of Canada. In 1973, unit labor costs in manufacturing increased 3.1 percent (the difference between productivity and hourly wage increase) as compared with 17.8 percent in Japan, 22.6 percent in France, 14.2 percent in Sweden, and 6.1 percent in Britain. In other words, the gap between productivity and wage increases was less in the United States than almost anywhere else.

†As already implied, much depends on definitions of "poor" and "intermediate" budgets or living standards, and here the ingenuity of government statisticians in manipulating statistics should not be underestimated. The "intermediate" urban family budget of $10,971 in 1971 was only $1,780 more than the "intermediate" amount of $9,191 the government estimated was required by the same family in 1966. But by 1971 the consumer price index had increased by approximately 25 percent since 1966, suggesting that the typical "intermediate" urban family in 1971 would have needed almost $2,300 more to maintain the 1966 living standard. If, furthermore, the typical "intermediate" family is not arrived at by averaging "intermediate" living costs in both large and small cities (the latter including Lancaster, Pennsylvania, and Orlando, Florida) but in the larger cities only, such as New York, Chicago, and Los Angeles, the "intermediate" budget in urban areas increases an additional 2 to 11 percent. In 1966, for example, it cost about 11 percent more to live in the New York metropolitan area than the $9,191 average for cities, and other cities above the average included Boston, San Francisco–Oakland, Buffalo, Milwaukee, Chicago–Northwestern (Indiana), Minneapolis, Washington, D.C., and Cleveland, in addition to Chicago and Los Angeles.

imposed by the Cost of Living Council by including these executives in employee groups containing all corporation employees.
Thus executives could be granted increases of 20 percent while
assembly-line workers received 3 percent pay raises.[21] Partly as a
result, the total compensation of top executives in all industries in
1972 rose by an average of 13.5 percent, or more than enough to
offset inflation.[22] In 1973 the cash remuneration including salary
and bonuses of a group of top executives whose names appeared
in the New York *Times* increased a further 11.8 percent.[23] The
two chief executives of the Chrysler Corporation led the field with
increases in cash remuneration of 26.5 and 40.9 percent, respectively.*

The rich also are more skilled in coping with taxes, or, to put it
more accurately, the rich know how to benefit from tax laws
which, for the most part, are written in their favor. Through a
variety of devices, including mineral-depletion allowances,
write-offs, and investing in so-called tax shelters such as state and
municipal bonds, a significant proportion of the income of the
rich is tax-exempt. According to the Internal Revenue Service,
thousands of Americans with substantial incomes pay no income
taxes at all or no more taxes than are paid by low-income workers.
Several hundred persons with annual incomes of $100,000 or
more apparently pay no taxes whatever, while many thousands of
wealthy individuals pay taxes at the same rates that are levied on
incomes of $6,000 a year. Even the wealthiest taxpayers, that is,
persons with incomes over $1,000,000 annually, pay taxes averag-
ing no more than 46.4 percent of their adjusted gross income,
which is usually much less than actual income since it excludes interest on government bonds and certain other securities, depletion and other allowances, and half of long-term capital gains.[24]
In 1971 persons with an adjusted gross income of between
$100,000 and $200,000 paid an average tax of only $47,066. The
effective tax rate in the first illustration may be little more than
that of a married taxpayer filing a joint return whose taxable in-

---

*By contrast, the minimum wage for most workers is scheduled to rise from
$2.00 per hour in 1974 to $2.30 in 1976, an increase of 15 percent. By that date
the minimum wage, which was $1.60 per hour in 1966, will have increased a total
of 44 percent, or much less than the cost of living during the same period of
time, assuming a continuing high level of inflation.

come is $42,000 and in the second instance probably is a good deal less.*

Hence it is hardly surprising to discover that with the exception of the very rich and the very poor, almost all American families pay roughly the same percentage of their incomes in taxes. A study published by the Brookings Institution in 1974 showed that 1966 taxes of all kinds took from 20 to 25 percent of family income, unless the family's income was in the top 3 percent or the bottom 10 percent. Since most tax changes since 1966 have been regressive, it is likely that the distribution of taxes between rich and poor has changed very little, if at all. Sales taxes, of course, discriminate against low incomes, and recent changes in the financing of Social Security benefits represent a dramatic shift of the cost burden of Social Security to low- and moderate-income wage earners.Because all incomes are taxed at the same rate for Social Security purposes, the low-income worker, in effect, is partially subsidizing the retirement of those in the work force who are better off, and unlike them, he is doing so at the expense of his current living standards.

Given these inequities and a continuing reluctance to take action against the causes and sources of poverty, most of the poor are likely to remain poor or even to become poorer. Nor is it, as many better-off Americans like to think, only a matter of living standards, with the poor owning fewer material comforts than others, that is, fewer cars, television sets, and household appliances. Perhaps the perfect analogy for the condition of the poor in the United States is the condition of the prisoner, for there are striking similarities between poverty and imprisonment. The cruelties of the latter, Gresham Sykes demonstrated some years ago, are not confined to the loss of liberty for a specified period of

*Because the rich pay less than their fair share of taxes, poor and middle-income families pay more. Some indication of how much more is found in the fact that the lower capital-gains tax in 1972 cost the government an estimated $7.6 billion in needed revenue. Tax-exempt interest on government bonds amounted to $2.9 billion and depletion allowances $1.7 billion. Wealthy corporations fare even better than wealthy individuals. In 1973, according to Ohio Congressman Charles A. Vanik, ten corporations with total profits of $976,000,000 paid no federal corporate income tax, and another twenty corporations with profits of more than $5 billion paid an effective federal tax of between 1 and 10 percent. See Representative Vanik's statement in *Congressional Record* (93rd Congress), No. 178, Part II, December 18, 1974.

time, but go on to include a variety of punishments and indignities inflicted daily. To the fact of the prison sentence is added a
long list of deprivations, ranging from the loss of sexual companionship to restrictions in the number of visitors, letters, phone
calls, and cigarettes one may have.[25]

Poverty, it could be said in a similar vein, also involves a sentence, and the sentence refers to something more than the loss of
liberty to spend money how and where one chooses. In the United
States poverty means not only that one is condemned to live in
substandard housing but that one is condemned to live less long
than other people as well as less well. Strong evidence suggests
that the poor, irrespective of race, are sicker more often and have
a shorter life expectancy than people of higher economic status
and that the black poor have the highest disease rate and the lowest life expectancy of all. Infant- and maternal-mortality rates appear to be higher in poor families; indeed, fluctuations in the infant-mortality rate in the United States as compared with several
Western European countries have been associated with economic
instability, with higher mortality rates linked to job and income
loss.[26] The connection between poor health and poverty has also
been demonstrated in the tendency of cardiovascular and kidney
diseases to increase a few years after periods of high unemployment. A study of chronic disorders in a New York City population
found that prevalence rates for such diseases as heart disorders,
high blood pressure, diabetes, peptic ulcer, arthritis and rheuma-
tism, asthma, hay fever, and chronic bronchitis were 414.6 per
1,000 persons whose family income was less than $4,000 annually,
221.1 for those with a $4,000–7,499 family income, and 218.6 for
those with family incomes of $7,500 and over.[27] The death rate
from cirrhosis of the liver, a disease often caused by alcoholism,
also increases several years after a job loss, while admissions to
mental hospitals rise within months following a time of economic
instability.[28] And when the sick poor are hospitalized, the death
rate among them is often high as a result of delays in admission
and subsequent lack of proper care.*

---

*In 1970 an estimated 1,000 Chicago citizens, mainly poor ones, died because
of health-care neglect, according to an official report. A total of 18,000 persons
were refused "private health service," of whom 50 subsequently died. The other
deaths were attributed to failure to admit sick patients into hospitals, delays in
treatment, inadequate prenatal care, and a shortage of doctors. (New York

The high prenatal- and infant-mortality rate, and perhaps mortality rates in general, among the poor are to some degree a reflection of poor nutrition, but the reference is not simply to unbalanced diets. It has been estimated that at least half of the poor are hungry all or most of the time despite the food stamp program and other measures designed to eliminate malnutrition.[29] Moreover, they have grown hungrier since 1970, according to food experts testifying before a Senate committee, as a result of increasing food costs, with some needy families subsisting almost exclusively on dog food, chocolate bars, Wonder bread, and hog jowls. A National Nutrition Survey reported to Congress, based on a sample of 13,373 persons in Louisiana and Texas, established the existence of two or more nutritional deficiencies in 48.5 percent of children aged one to nine, 39.5 percent in children aged between ten and twelve, and 54.5 percent in children aged thirteen to sixteen; in Texas eight of every ten preschool children examined were deficient in vitamin A.[30]

Poor health, listlessness, and lack of energy, failure or an inability to keep up at school are only some of the effects of prolonged hunger. The most serious far-reaching consequence of all may be a kind of brain damage, for there is increasing evidence that the infant who is malnourished may never achieve his full brain growth even if, after infancy, he is well fed. A study of Chilean children has established that hunger when it is experienced by the fetus, as is the case when the mother is underfed, prevents the growth of a certain number of brain cells and structures, thus dooming the child and later adult "to stunted brain development and therefore to considerably diminished mental capacity *for the rest of his life.*"[31] It may also be true that the brain damage is irreversible or at least not subject to correction for several generations. In an experiment with rats the mating of an underfed female rat with a well-fed male produced offspring with clear signs of brain malnutrition even though they were fed a normal diet

Times, June 21, 1973.) In New York in 1970 a group of 2,000 city-hospital interns and resident physicians announced plans to start an "abuse registry" that would document evidence of patient deaths caused by lacks of nurses, equipment, or facilities in city hospitals. (New York *Times,* October 16, 1970.) New York municipal hospitals were reported to have fewer than 40 percent of the nursing staff authorized in their budgets.

from birth. This second generation, in turn, eventually gave birth to infants whose brain growth was similarly retarded.* In short; the experiment seemed to demonstrate that once the brain fails to develop in the normal way as a result of malnutrition, the consequences are passed on from generation to generation.[32]

Whether or not such research has a bearing on the controversy regarding IQ comparisons between blacks and whites,[†] it is clear that a society that permits millions of its citizens to go without essential foods may be depriving them of the intelligence needed for coping with modern technology and the complexities of urban life. Such inferiority is not necessarily remedied by improving educational opportunities and access to better jobs, as important as these may be, nor can even the most imaginative poverty programs totally succeed if they neglect nutritional needs. But the consequences of undernourishment may extend beyond considerations of skill and performance. Certainly questions must be raised about the implications for democracy and a peaceful world order of prolonged hunger in a given population. Is there a possible relationship, one wonders, between the near-famine conditions that existed in Germany and other parts of Europe after World War I and the political instability that culminated in Nazism and World War II? Specifically, to what extent did the infants born to underfed mothers during the earlier period, compared with those born to mothers whose diets were adequate, grow up to become eager recruits to the Hitler Youth and other Nazi organizations? While it is difficult if not impossible at this late date to obtain reliable answers to a question of this type, it is suggestive that German infants who were born during the near-

---

*According to Dr. Myron Winick of Columbia University's Institute of Human Nutrition, rats malnourished during gestation "had 15 percent fewer brain cells than did normal rats. The same was true—a 15 percent reduction—for rats underfed immediately after birth. But the rats who were malnourished both during gestation and after birth had 60 percent fewer brain cells than normal rats." (New York Times, April 2, 1973.) Whatever this may imply for human beings, it is hardly encouraging that the incidence of low birth weight increased from 7 percent in 1970 to 10 percent in 1974. While most of this increase was due to poverty, some of it, in the view of some physicians, was the result of diet fads and the "irrational, unscientific nutritional guidance" given pregnant women by their gynecologists, a phenomenon referred to as "iatrogenic [physician-induced] starvation" by Dr. Tom Brewer in Medical Tribune, July 10, 1974.

†See below, p. 216 ff.

famine years 1916–1919 and who survived were adolescents when Hitler came to power in 1933, and it was with this age group that Hitler was extremely popular well into the war period.*

The most disadvantaged infants, of course, do not survive in any society, and whether that society be Germany or the United States, perhaps it is just as well. For if they manage to live beyond middle age and become what is euphemistically and somewhat deceitfully referred to as "senior citizens," they are apt to conclude, with Rousseau in another context, that their birth was the first of their misfortunes. But birth is not the worst misfortune of many of those born poor to whom, so long as they remain youthful and in relative good health, some measure of pleasure and small modicum of happiness is not denied. Moreover, there is always the hope, if not always the possibility, that by a combination of hard work and luck, poverty will be left behind. The elderly poor, however, have no such hope, and they are not only old and impoverished. They are very likely to be ill all or a good part of the time and to be failing in mind as well as body. They eat less food than the other poor, and the quality is apt to be even more inferior. If they live alone in a city, their housing probably is among the worst available, and invariably it is located in the most dangerous neighborhoods. Because it is assumed implicitly or explicitly that the poor, as the phrase goes, have all the time in the world (it is only those with good incomes who say, "My time is valuable"), they are forced to wait hours and even days for the free or low-cost health and legal services they may urgently need, and many of those the elderly poor must deal with treat them with respect so little as to amount to contempt. If they survive all this, and millions somehow manage to survive into old age, they may want to challenge the popular view that the course of humankind has been from the primitive conditions of jungle to the niceties of civilization. The life histories of a very large number of the elderly poor have been

---

*An estimated 750,000 Germans died of starvation between 1914 and 1918. There was a sharp fall in the birth rate and a precipitous rise in the infant- and child-mortality rates. Rickets, tuberculosis, and parasites were widespread among children, and the weight of those in their third year was up to 2.2 pounds lighter than normal body weight by 1917. Cf. Peter Loewenberg, "The Psychohistorical Origins of the Nazi Youth Cohort," American Historical Review, Vol. 76, No. 5 (December, 1971), pp. 1457–1502.

a retrogression from civilization to a jungle where life itself is "solitary, poor, nasty, brutish" but, alas, not as short as some of them would wish.[33]

In effect, the gerontophobia of society ensures that the aged are given no more than a subsistence allowance that enables most of them to stay alive, but hardly more than that.* Over half the aged in 1972, before the rampant inflation of the later years, had an income less than the $3,000 per year that was needed for bare necessities, and half of those who lived alone received less than $1,000.[34] In the course of the following two years food prices increased almost 40 percent, rent 18 percent, and medical care—the aged occupy 25 percent of hospital beds—rose 22.5 percent in cost. Yet the average monthly Social Security check was $186, and public-assistance offices throughout the country reported that the fastest-growing welfare case load consisted of nonwelfare elderly people seeking food help. In New York City more and more aged persons were resorting to shoplifting of such items as tuna fish, milk, and meat packets.[35]

The worst off are those who live by themselves in decaying hotels and rooming houses, for in addition to the enervations of poverty there are the depressions of loneliness and physical helplessness. The aged are particularly vulnerable to burglaries and street crimes. One survey of almost 200 elderly people living in the Bronx, 71 percent of whom had annual incomes below $3,500 in 1974, found that more than a third had been mugged "in their later years" and 59 robbed or mugged more than once.[36] A so-called welfare hotel in Manhattan during a period of ten months

---

*Gerontophobia, that is, an aversion to those who are old, manifests itself in social attitudes toward the physical and behavioral side of aging. Many people find the sagging physiques and bodily deterioration of the aged rather repulsive, and the sexual activity of the aged is, of course, a stock subject for television and movie humor. Since in those who are old we see our own inevitable futures culminating in death, it is probable that gerontophobia is a derivative of necrophobia, but it is far from clear why this is more pronounced in some societies than in others. Americans, for example, may feel and express more gerontophobia than the British, French, and Italians and, conversely, be more oriented toward youth than the citizens of other Western countries. Perhaps it is partly for this reason and not simply economics that each month almost 300,000 Social Security checks are sent overseas to Americans retired abroad. A society that lacks a past, i.e., that possesses a relatively short history, tends not to respect both the living and inanimate reminders of the past.

in 1972 was the scene of 89 arrests for a variety of crimes ranging from narcotics to homicide; burglaries and robberies accounted for 29 offenses, criminal trespass for 8, felonious assault for 6, and attempted murder for 3. "My God," a nearby shopkeeper exclaimed of the hotel on Broadway between Seventy-fifth and Seventy-sixth streets, "this place is unbelievable. The prostitutes come out and solicit on the corner, the dope addicts come here to get their needles. . . . They throw garbage out the window all the time . . . bottles, bricks, one time a fire extinguisher. . . . And that's not all—they throw dogs out, and people too." Perhaps he was referring to two persons who jumped, fell, or were thrown to their deaths during one three-month period.[37]

Old age, Anatole France said, "is a shipwreck," but perhaps the metaphor is too benign.[38] Even the aged who are not poor cannot escape the cruelties and indignities that an indifferent society permits to be inflicted upon them. Those who have worked steadily until retirement may find, despite the pension-reform legislation of 1974,* that the pension they had been led to expect does not exist; a Nader report estimate, prior to the pension act, that at least half of all those covered by private pension plans will never receive a cent of their anticipated pension probably is still valid.[39] The elderly who can afford nursing homes may find that the quality of the food, accommodations, and care they receive, and for which a respectable amount of money is being paid, is inferior to what they once were able to provide for their household pets.[40] Even the aged who can afford to live decently in their own homes may find, if they are disabled, that they cannot cope with stairs and doorways; it would require only about five cents more per

---

*The pension act, like most social-welfare legislation, promises more than it delivers. For the estimated 23,000,000 workers covered by private, nongovernmental pension plans and those already retired, the act provides full pension rights only if they remain with the same employer for a minimum of between ten and fifteen years, depending on the type of plan chosen by their employer. If, however, the worker leaves his job before that time, his pension rights diminish to almost nothing. As New York *Times* columnist William V. Shannon has pointed-ed out, a typical $10,000-a-year white-collar employee who leaves his job after five years would have a vested right to an annual pension at age sixty-five of $187.50; because of differences in calculating pensions for wage workers, the blue-collar employee would receive even less in most cases. Hence the most that can be said for the pension act is that it is a belated and timid step in the right direction or, as one cynical observer put it, a case of "too little, too late, too bad."

door to make a bathroom entrance in an apartment house large
enough for a wheelchair, but most of them continue to be smaller
than the required thirty-two-inch width.[41]

A simple matter, one would think, to enlarge the width of a
door, requiring only the assent of the architects. Perhaps it *is* a
simple matter, as, no doubt, are other problems in society that do
not call for elaborate and complicated solutions. Decent Americans like to believe that where there is enough money, there will
also be enough determination, given a certain degree of public
enlightenment, to correct such evils as the conditions under which
migrant workers live and work or the treatment accorded inmates
of prisons and mental hospitals. They no more believe that society
condones these evils than they believe that society condones such
cruelties and grotesqueries as the so-called Tuskegee Study sponsored by the United States Public Health Service, under which
some 600 black men were used as guinea pigs in an investigation
of the effects of syphilis; 400 of these men were deliberately un-
treated for periods of up to forty years.[42] It defies the imagination, they would argue, to hold that citizens of Ohio are somehow
responsible for the physical and sexual abuse of patients by thirty-
one employees of its Lima State Hospital for the Criminally
Insane[43] or that the citizens of North Carolina, by permitting the
mummified body of an Italian carnival worker, nicknamed
"Spaghetti" by local residents, to be displayed in a glass coffin, are
expressing a certain attitude toward the death of those whose lives
are deemed to be of no importance.[44] These are the actions, many
would maintain, not of the normal people who constitute the
great majority of Americans, but of a few disturbed or borderline
types.*

Their point is well taken but perhaps it neglects an essential

---

*The term "borderline" as used in mental-health circles refers to conditions
which have both neurotic and psychotic features. The behavior of borderline
types functions as a defense against primitive impulses, and hence "superficial
adaptation to the environment and the ability to maintain object relations may be
relatively intact. . . . Yet there is a weakness in the defenses against primitive
instinctual impulses and interference with the overall evaluation of reality. . . . Under stress the psychotic aspects may come to the fore, since the flexibility and adaptability of these patients are reduced." *A Glossary of Psychoanalytic
Terms and Concepts* (Burness E. Moore and Bernard D. Fine, eds., 2nd ed. [New
York: American Psychoanalytic Association, 1968]).

fact, namely, that the atrocities mentioned were not isolated in time or place or known only to a few. The Tuskegee Study, which began in 1932, almost surely involved many hundreds of government employees and medical personnel and hundreds of thousands of dollars. The employees of the Lima State Hospital—and other investigations at other state hospitals have revealed similar practices—charged with lewdness, assault, torture, and sodomy, included the director of personnel and a deputy county sheriff who was a former employee; other hospital workers, angered by the charges and arrests, wore black ribbons to work as an expression of sympathy with the accused. The mummified body of the carnival worker no doubt had been seen by a large number of people even assuming it was not on display during the entire sixty-one years since his death in 1911. These and similar incidents, the number of which can hardly be counted as they are reported daily in the newspapers and on television news programs, may suggest not only that borderline behavior has become increasingly accepted as normal social behavior but that in many, if not most, Americans there is at least a trace, and perhaps something more than a trace, of the borderline type.

At the same time, there is, to vary an old expression, a method or meaning in much of society's madness. Elsewhere it will be shown that the condition of blacks and the prevalence of war have important positive functions for American society, indeed, that from certain points of view the positive functions outweigh the negative ones. Perhaps it is also true that many Americans are more comfortable with inequality than with equality, quite apart from racial or ethnic considerations. This would explain, at least to some extent, the outcry in recent years over moves to raise income and property taxes in certain states and the tendency of many cities to reduce taxes rather than increase spending on welfare programs under the federal revenue-sharing program. The failure of social-justice movements and poverty programs, past and present, may also owe a good deal to the fact that in the United States the view that "all men are created equal" has never been, in reality, widely accepted, much less "self-evident."

Viewed superficially, the movement toward social equality would appear to have deep roots in the ideological and institutional past. The egalitarian theme, so regarded, permeates Jeffersonian and Jacksonian democracy, the abolition of slavery, the rise of trade unionism, and modern reformist politics. The claim that the American tradition is based on the principle of equality has seemingly provided premise and goal for efforts to extend the suffrage, emancipate blacks, develop a system of mass education, and promote equal economic opportunity. The American creed, Gunnar Myrdal and others have observed, "not merely espouses equality but has lodged it so firmly in the national conscience that discriminatory treatment of blacks and other minorities gives rise to profound guilt feelings."[45]

But even in the early days there were important ambiguities and inhibitions in our pursuit of equality, and they have become more pronounced in recent years. Alexis de Tocqueville in 1835 declared that he knew "of no country, indeed, where the love of money has taken stronger hold on the affections of men, and where a profounder contempt is expressed for the theory of the permanent equality of property."[46] Whatever his politics, the typical American has never regarded the possession of wealth as inherently immoral, and even the poorest of Americans have never sought to reduce the wealthy to their own economic and social position. Depressions, financial panics, recessions, and the prevalence of poverty amidst plenty have never undermined the faith in America as the land of individual opportunity.

By and large, the rich have been more imitated than envied and more envied than disliked. But in essence they have been imitated and envied not merely because they were rich but because they were richer *than*. In America as an acquisitive society the envy of the rich has been, at least in part, an envy of the select status and prestige of the rich, apart from envy of their material possessions. In seeking wealth for himself, the American has sought the status and prestige that go with wealth. Put another way, he has tended to think in terms of advancement not as part of an advancing class or group, but of individual advancement *relative to the condition of the mass of citizens.*

The economic system, however, is vitally dependent upon a continuing general improvement of conditions, that is, dependent upon rising levels of mass consumption, which increasingly transform the so-called luxury goods into mass-produced and consumed commodities. The reason is not merely that high levels of employment and wages create demand for higher-priced goods, although these are important factors in the transformation. The producers of such goods are both tempted and forced to increase their output, both as a way of making maximum use of capital investment (and reinvestment) and as a way of maximizing profits. Furthermore, in certain cases (e.g., automobiles, boats, household furnishings, home entertainment, sporting goods, etc.) the "luxury market" is fairly easily and quickly supplied, and in such instances the market must be expanded if current output is to be maintained. Hence the luxury market must be steadily transformed into a mass market, through advertising, through the broadening of installment-buying plans and personal loans, through a wide distribution of credit cards, and, occasionally, through price reductions. In this fashion the luxury goods of fifty years ago became the mass necessities of our time. Ultimately, if the economy is to continue to function at a high level, and assuming that the raw materials remain available, everything must be sold to everyone.*

But if economic gains and an unprecedented expansion of credit make this possible, then some things, at least, tend to diminish in value. In a society whose supreme value is individual success in terms of money, no one gains if everyone gains, because in that event no one is left behind. One's allegedly no-account neighbors in the slum become one's apparently equal neighbors in the suburbs, reducing the sense of personal achievement and mastery. (Some part of the satisfaction of Cadillac ownership is denied when it is observed that blacks, Puerto Ricans, and Mexicans are driving Cadillacs.) The anticipated pleasure of the resort or the "night out" evaporates rapidly when it is discovered that the hitherto-favored hotel or restaurant no longer caters to a "select clientele."

While one important consequence of the conflicting drives toward equality and inequality is an increasing resistance toward efforts to abolish poverty, another is the obsessive concern with ever more conspicuous, wasteful, expensive, and initially confined modes of consumption. There is apparel snobbery, reflected in

*The probability that the era of unlimited consumption is drawing to a close and some implications of that development are discussed in the final chapter. For the moment let the point be made that in the future, assuming increasing tension between population and resources, "'everything" will not be manufactured, much less sold, to everyone.

the greater demand for more expensive types of clothing; gourmet snobbery, expressed in the quest for ever more exotic recipes and methods of cooking and serving food; and decorator snobbery, manifested in the preference for unusual furnishings and rare materials.* There is the "luxury cruise" and "red carpet" airline service, the "exclusive" vacation spot, the sofa trimmed with mink, and the $2,500 collection of pipes. In New York in 1973 someone purchased a pair of matching 1966 Rolls-Royce James Young Phantom limousines for $250,000; in San Francisco a sterling-silver lunch box was sold for $575.† At Neiman-Marcus of Dallas one could purchase a forty-skin "Kojah" mink coat for $150,000 in 1969 and in New York have no hesitation about feeding the dog "two medium-rare lamb chops," steaks, caviar, fresh strawberries, and other varieties of dog food. La Banque, a Fifth Avenue branch of the Franklin National Bank, required a minimum deposit of $25,000 to open a checking account.[47]

But the dilemma remains. The free-enterprise economy can function at a high level only if more and more of everything is sold to more and more people, but anything that can be acquired by everyone tends to lose value. The ideal solution, of course, would be a situation where everything was manufactured and sold in great numbers, but not everything was bought and consumed; unfortunately only the defense sector of the economy, where much costly production becomes obsolete even before it comes off the assembly line or is destroyed in war, approximates the ideal. But economics aside, social equality and a fairer distribution of resources cannot be rejected as goals unless democracy itself is renounced in favor of a political system based on rigid stratification

*Since high-rise office towers inevitably tend to look alike, corporate efforts to be "different" may go to elaborate lengths on the inside of buildings. The Shell Oil building in Houston was furnished with "enough primavera mahogany from Guatemala and Honduras to deplete the supply for some time. Persian walnut burl from Iran that may not be available again for 20 years. Real leather for the elevators, unseamed, requiring nine-foot cows. . . ." (Ada Louise Huxtable in New York *Times*, July, 1972.) To establish itself as the tallest building in San Francisco, the Transamerica Pyramid is topped by a 212-foot spire.

†Perhaps it was bought for a blue-collar worker who has everything. An inquiry to Carriage House Motor Ltd., which advertised the Rolls-Royces in a full page of the New York *Times*, Arpil 8, 1973, elicited the reply that the cars had been sold but that a 1961 James Young Phantom V was available at $65,000.

and segregation, in other words, enforced *in*equality. Within the framework of a democratic society there is no alternative to a continued movement toward equality, although ways will always be found, by those who dislike equality, of establishing social distance between themselves and the rest.

4

Phallic Culture

"There may be some things better than sex," W. C. Fields once observed, "and some things worse. But there is nothing exactly like it." Sex, he might also have added, is extremely controversial, at least in America, where there has never been general agreement on what constitutes a good sex life. Above all, sex is unique not only in its physiological aspect but in the way it relates to so many individual and social facets of behavior. Although a private activity for the most part, sex is endlessly debated in public, legislated about, written up in the newspapers and magazines, and discussed at length in hundreds of published books each year, some of them best sellers. It is related to religion, morality in general, law, education, crime, and mental health, not to mention marriage and the birth rate, and there are those who believe with George Orwell that sex is not innocent of a connection with war and totalitarianism.*[1]

Implicit in the Orwellian view is the notion that there is good sex and bad sex, and that, of course, is what the argument is usually about. Few desire to exclude it altogether from human relations—but it should be underlined that the availability of sex in any society varies according to law, class and income, occupation and geographical location, age, health, and physical appearance as well as other factors—and few have taken the position that all forms of sex are equally good and socially desirable. In America,

*Some of the material in this chapter is based on research undertaken in collaboration with Harold D. Lasswell.

112

in particular, a variety of so-called unnatural acts has always been punishable on the statute books if not also in the courts, and the moralizing agencies have always disapproved of sexual activity outside of marriage. Most of them, in fact, still do disapprove, although the evidence is overwhelming that Puritan standards no longer apply. Presidents of the United States, ministers, service-club leaders, judges, parents who have daughters, "Dear Abby," and countless others apparently agree that sexual intercourse is permissible only if (1) a man and a woman are involved and (2) they are married to each other.

The actual practices, however, are something else, reflecting once again the extent to which, in America, the sacred tends to lose out to the profane. Perhaps what is sacred survives only if the sexual distribution is roughly equal or, if unequal, the men outnumber the women in a given population; presumably this latter factor, by permitting women to set the standards, promotes morality in addition to chivalry and courtly manners. But where women outnumber men, tipping the balance of choice toward the male side, morals and manners are apt to decline, and a little-noted but significant fact is that the number of women in the United States is increasing faster than the number of men. Prior to 1950 there were more men than women in the population as far back as there are census records of sex ratios, which is back to 1820. In 1910, for example, there were 106 men for every 100 women. But in 1950, for the first time in our history, there were 99 men for every 100 women, and this downward trend for males has continued. Thus in 1960 there were 97 men per 100 women, and in 1970 the number of men had declined to 95. It is also relevant here that in 1970 there were 60 divorced women for every 35 divorced men and, as of March, 1971, almost five times as many widows as widowers.

The increased competition for men, in other words, may not only account for much of the change in America's sexual culture but for the particular character of that change, the nature of which is the principal subject of this chapter. But whatever the cause or causes of the change, no one can doubt that there has been a significant alteration in at least the externals of sexual behavior during the past two decades. The widespread acceptance of nonmarital sexual intercourse, accompanied by an increased availability to the young of contraceptives, the legalization of abortion, the spread of nudity to public beaches and the freer use of dirty words, the rise of gay liberation and greater public tolerance, if not understanding, of homosexuality, the migration of pornography from the back alleys to Main Street—these and other developments suggest that the volume and variety, although not necessarily the quality or enjoyment, of sexual acts engaged in by many Americans have experienced remarkable growth in recent years. Does it follow that American sexual behavior is no longer characterized by, in psychiatrist Harry Stack Sullivan's phrase, a "lurid twilight" generated by a culture of unrestricted stimulation conflicting with a morality of restricted response?*

There is much evidence that we are not so far removed from the "lurid twilight" as we sometimes like to believe. Quantitatively speaking, more Americans of all ages are probably more involved in sexual activities of all sorts than ever before, but they pursue these activities with anxiety, guilt, and more than a little frustration. This accounts in part for the popularity of the "sane sex life" and "how to do it" books, a vast literature that in recent years has been augmented by catalogues of explicit pictorial representations.† While it has always been the function of psychiatrists to re-

---

*Sullivan commented in 1947: "We still try to discourage premarital sexual performance; hold that abstinence is the moral course before marriage. And we discourage early marriage; in fact, progressively widen the gap between the adolescent awakening of lust and the proper circumstances for marriage. These two factors work through many cultural conventions to make us the most sex-ridden people of whom I have any knowledge." (*Conceptions of Modern Psychiatry* [Washington: William Alanson White Psychiatric Foundation, 1947], p. 29.)

†An important confusion of our time is the belief that almost anybody can be an authority on almost anything, hence the emergence in many areas of the amateur as expert. The favored fields for such expertise are ethology and anthropology; apparently anyone who owns animals or who has spent a year in the bush can become, by writing a book, an authority on the similarities between human and animal behavior or on the origins of civilization. But with regard to sex, *no* knowledge or experience whatever is required. Thus experts on the subject include priests, rabbis, novelists, actresses, professors, entomologists, the never married and the much married. A case in point is Norman Mailer, who has advised against any form of contraception on a variety of grounds, the most original of which is his belief that to use a contraceptive is to "scalp" a woman. The choice of verb is unfortunate since it implies either that women have contraception forced upon them or that the Indians welcomed being scalped. In this area as in others related to sex, Mailer's views bring to mind the occasion when a lady

lieve their patients of anxiety and guilt arising from their sexual behavior, psychiatrists lately have been hearing from men and women married many years nervous questions about what constitutes a "normal" sex life. The circulation in the millions of Playboy-type magazines* and the estimated billion dollars spent each year on pornographic books and films suggest at the very least that here, too, the ability to fantasize has become increasingly dependent upon external sources of stimulation. Pornography, after all, is nothing more than the playback by words or pictures of one's own sexual fantasies.

Insofar as these fantasies can serve to intensify a shared sensual experience, there is much to be said for them; in Japan and elsewhere in the Far East it is not unusual for a lovemaking couple to peruse a pornographic text. But in America sexual fantasies tend to remain unshared and private, with the frequent result that they deplete rather than enhance the act of love. The problem is not just that one's mind is elsewhere or that one's husband does not resemble Robert Redford or one's wife the current centerfold girl, but that the reality experience necessarily falls short of the fantasy. In sex as in politics, to vary an expression from Edmund Burke, the fantasied best is the enemy of the actual good.

Given the ubiquity of sexual themes in American society, for example, the endless parade before us of inviting and, at least in imagination, available women (or men), it is not to be wondered that an increasing number of Americans are less and less willing to make do with one wife (or husband), inviting or not. If one consequence is a soaring divorce rate, not that all divorces begin in someone else's bed, another is the rising incidence of extramarital sexual experience, notably adultery, group sex involv-

---

addressed the Duke of Wellington as "Mr. Brown, I believe." "Madame," said the duke, "if you believe that, you'll believe anything."

*To be sure, Playboy itself publishes the best fiction of any American magazine, but it is unlikely that the millions of men who buy Playboy each month buy it for that reason. Certainly the centerfold and related features have helped to establish Hugh Hefner as a foremost rival of King Midas. When Playboy went public in 1971, it was revealed that Hefner owned shares worth $170,000,000 and paying some $800,000 in dividends, in addition to receiving an annual remuneration of $303,847. (Authors Guild Bulletin, October–November, 1971.)

ing married couples, so-called wife- (or husband-) swapping arrangements, and *ménages à trois*. Some studies of American sexual behavior also report that the most fantasy-oriented sexual act of all, masturbation, increases sharply in frequency after the first sex years of marriage, and apparently it is also the case that more marriages of long duration have been ending in divorce than ever before.*

But perhaps the psychological consequences of the "lurid twilight" are greatest of all for the unmarried young; for them, with exceptions, there is neither the best nor the good. Boys and girls have fewer rationalizations and defenses for masturbation and more fears and anxieties related to homosexuality than their elders. Although there has been some liberalization of parental attitudes, teenagers have less access to contraceptives and hence run greater risks if they indulge in sexual intercourse.† They also have less opportunity to relieve sex-related tensions through the use of

---

*Until 1960 the divorce rate was fairly stable. Since then it has increased from 35 divorced persons for every 1,000 married persons living with their spouses to the 1974 rate of 63 divorced persons for every 1,000 persons. While the median duration of marriages has not changed much since 1960, a more significant fact is the breakup of many marriages that have lasted for fifteen or more years. In 1965, for example, almost one-fourth of persons filing for divorce had been married for fifteen years or longer. Another 12 percent of men and 14 percent of women were demonstrating "the triumph of hope over experience," that is, had been married twice, and 563,000 men and 706,000 women, who had been married at least three times, had gone beyond both hope and experience.

†A study in 1971 at Johns Hopkins University showed that about three of every ten teenagers who have premarital intercourse become pregnant and that a third of them marry before their babies are born. Only 14 percent of the pregnant girls had used any form of contraception, and it was estimated that less than half of all unmarried adolescent girls who are active sexually use contraceptives. According to Professor John F. Kantner of Johns Hopkins, "The probability of a girl currently aged 15 having intercourse is three to four times greater than the probability that a girl now aged 19 had intercourse when she was 15." (*Medical Tribune*, August 28, 1974.) Despite such figures and a sharp rise in venereal-disease rates among teenagers, magazines and newspapers are still reluctant to accept ads for condoms, the most popular form of contraception among young people. In 1970 only two of nineteen major magazines, *Playboy* and *Ebony,* would accept condom advertising, and all but two newspapers in the top ten market areas, the San Francisco *Chronicle* and the Des Moines *Register*, rejected ads. By the mid-seventies other magazines, such as *Ms.,* were accepting condom ads, but still few newspapers.

alcohoi and tranquilizers. If they are caught violating the conventional mores, they may find themselves in legal trouble, expelled from school, and severely punished by their parents. Adult violators, by contrast, run none of these risks. As a rule, they have only to face their consciences and deceived wife or husband—assuming the marriage relationship has not reached the point at which adultery is taken for granted.

Someone has aptly said that much juvenile delinquency can be traced to juvenile adults or adult delinquents. Surely insofar as adults are responsible for the sexual double binds in which the young find themselves, adults *are* responsible in some degree for those aspects of teenage behavior they find reprehensible. It is, after all, adults who edit the magazines, write the books, and produce the movies that stimulate the sexual proclivities of adolescents, and it is also adults who originate and enforce the prohibitions that characterize the laws and mores. The resulting double standard, however, does not escape the notice of the children, and because children are quick to detect hypocrisy where it exists, they frequently become—from their parents' point of view—rude and unmanageable, in short, behavior problems.

As an earlier chapter tried to make clear, youthful rebellion is not primarily a consequence of the "lurid twilight," but many phases of it may relate to sexual tensions. In their seminal work *Frustration and Aggression* John Dollard and his collaborators cite a number of studies that suggest a close connection between the onset of puberty and aggressive behavior.[2] It has been widely observed, Dollard remarks, that adolescent behavior is typified by "impatience with restriction, independence of action, gregariousness, restlessness, irritability, day-dreaming, and the more serious forms of behavior found in some individuals such as running away and actual delinquency." Although the evidence is not conclusive, certain studies cited by Dollard support the contention that frustration and aggression in adolescents correlate with the physiological changes associated with pubescence.*

*Also relevant is the statement by John W. M. Whiting that "there seems to be some support for the hypothesis that societies inducing high sex anxiety and sex inhibition are likely to permit and even to ritually require a high degree of cruelty and sadism in the treatment of prisoners of war." John W. M. Whiting, "The Place of Aggression in Social Interaction," in James F. Short, Jr., and Marvin E. Wolfgang, eds. *Collective Violence* (Chicago: Aldine-Atherton, 1972), p. 196.

The turmoil of adolescent sexual awakening is inevitably intensified by the subtle and overt sexual excitation that exists in the teenager's world. His younger siblings may be playing with the sexually seductive "Barbie" and "Ken" dolls, dolls described by Suzanne K. Langer as "pernicious." These new dolls, she argues persuasively, "are not little girls for little mothers to dress and wheel and bring up, but teenaged puppets. . . . If you look at the dolls you see the epitome of vulgar feeling; a smart and smirking high school boy in tapered pants, and an incredibly provocative girl with a wardrobe chiefly of bathing suits, underwear, high-heeled shoes, and similar items. . . ."[3] Perhaps older sisters and brothers are wearing clothes that draw attention to crotch, breasts, and buttocks. For both boys and girls there is the local drugstore with its shelf upon shelf of paperback and magazine erotica and the records with their suggestive lyrics and dust covers, not to mention the films and television programs referred to in newspaper publicity as "bold" or "for mature audiences only." Add to all this the summer exhibitions of seminude male and female bodies at the beach or pool—or at some beaches totally nude bodies—and it is small wonder that many adolescents experience puberty as a form of torture.

Indeed, the miracle is that more of them do not strike out violently at the sources and symbols of their torment, namely, parents, principals, teachers, policemen, adults in general. Much has been written about the increasing rates of juvenile crime and drug-taking, but from the point of view expressed here the miracle is that most adolescents suffer in silence. Of course, many teenagers are ingenious in finding ways to circumvent the rules and regulations; the teenage gangs and get-togethers, even the Boy Scout and Girl Scout troops, provide opportunities for sexual experiments however insistent the claims to respectability. These departures from convention, on the other hand, are often accompanied by severe guilt feelings and anxiety.

But many adults, too, are hardly free from sexual tensions and conflicts. The boy or girl "in trouble" has a good deal to lose, but the adult may have a great deal more. Children who engage in sex play may be forgiven—certainly there will be little or no problem if their parents have read Spock or Gesell—but adults who engage in sex play outside of marriage may find themselves, if not in legal trouble, at least suffering from certain discriminations and censure.* And it is moot whether the girl who faces an abortion or is forced into marriage as a result of pregnancy suffers more than the couple in the divorce court who are there because of adultery. In one respect, the unmarried mother holds a distinct disadvantage: she cannot very well pretend she is married and that the child has a father. The married woman who has a child by someone other than her husband can and often does pretend that the child is not merely in the marriage but of it. On the other hand, the single person with a venereal disease can conceal it more easily than a husband or wife.

The point, however, is not that single people have fewer sex-related problems than married people or that adolescents have more problems than adults. The point is that the "lurid twilight" casts its flickering luminescence on almost everyone without regard to age or marital status. Some, to be sure, suffer from sexual conflicts and frustrations more than others, and some suffer little or not at all, but one can hardly avoid the conclusion that the more time and energy Americans give to the pursuit of sex, the more it eludes them, and that in this respect, sex, like the Bomb, race, and pollution, is one of the great unresolved problems of America.

All this might suggest that if sex is sought everywhere, it is found nowhere, and indeed there are good reasons to think that while Americans may be copulating more than ever before, they are enjoying it less. If the reports of psychotherapists are any guide, the sexual malfunctions of impotence, frigidity, and premature ejaculation have been increasing, and even more striking is evidence that many young men in their twenties, to all appearances healthy and normal, are finding themselves invariably or frequently impotent. Psychiatrists are not certain how general this phenomenon is or what the causes may be, but one explanation, according to Dr. George L. Ginsberg of the New York University School of Medicine, is that the "average expectable sexual behav-

---

*A case in point is the 1972 ruling of a New York family court judge that a divorced woman "must not expose [her] child" to the man with whom she lives because to do so would be to acquaint the child with "low moral standards." As a consequence, the child's mother, forbidden to have her child in her own home, where the child might possibly meet the man described by the judge as her "paramour," must see her child at the home of the grandparents. (New York *Times*, February 23, 1972.)

ior" of young women, having ceased to be inhibited or passive, is experienced by their male partners as "threatening." Where once women were sexually undemanding and indifferent to their lack of response, says Dr. Ginsberg, they now insist on "sexual performance" from their boyfriends, thereby making them anxious and impotent.*

But why should a young man feel threatened by his girlfriend's demanding sexual satisfaction? One possible reason is the emergence in America of phallic culture, by which is meant a culture whose sexual ethic regards women and men as primarily outlets for gratification.† The emphasis of such a culture is less on the mutuality of sexual pleasure than on self-satisfaction, and even when "performance" is valued, it is valued not because it enables one's sexual partner to experience orgasm but because of the associated narcissism and opportunities for exhibitionism. The entire body, being viewed and treated as essentially a phallus, is endlessly anointed, stroked, groomed, and decorated; the cathexis of the body as phallus is the main reason for the proliferation of body-conditioning centers and spas, where the body is reverentially treated and massage, the bath, and exercise take on some of the aura of religious rituals.

Sex in the phallic culture is, therefore, somewhat impersonal and promiscuous; as in the movie *Carnal Knowledge,* which could well serve as a documentary study of phallic culture, "scoring" becomes an end in itself, whether or not one keeps a record on slides of the body count. Since the dimensions of the sexual organs are of particular importance, great value is attached to being "well en-

---

*Formerly, Dr. Ginsberg reported, "patients with impotence were, for the most part, married men who gradually began to abandon sexual activity with their wives after a period of more successful functioning. They complained that the excitement had passed, and that their wives no longer provided the variety of sexual practices they craved. Impotence was accompanied by minimal anxiety; they usually had conscious fantasies about the secretary at work, the girl next door, etc., and felt confident that novel objects or practices could revive their interest." (New York *Times,* March 15, 1972.)

†The term "phallic" is borrowed from psychoanalytic usage, but is not here being used in precisely the same way. In psychoanalysis phallic refers to the stage of psychosexual development that follows the anal phase. It is characterized by a heightened awareness of and interest in the penis or phallus of the male child (usually at ages of three to five) and the clitoris of the female. Masturbation is common, as are pleasurable sensations associated with urination.

dowed" or "well hung." Nor are sexual tastes and preferences unaffected. With the erotic focus on the self, foreplay, oral-genital-anal contacts, and mutual masturbation are increasingly substituted for intercourse as primary sources of gratification, and because there is a strong sadistic and masochistic component, painful sensations are not infrequently associated with pleasure. The paraphernalia of sex in phallic culture abounds with gadgets and devices designed to ward off the always present threat of impotence and frigidity: mirrors, vibrators, special lotions and ointments, aphrodisiacs, pot.

Even if all goes well, the experience of orgasm in phallic culture is often a disappointing one, and here again it is instructive to hear from psychiatrists that many of their male and female patients complain of feeling "let down" or unsatisfied after intercourse. Apparently many men who are disappointed in this fashion experience some degree of anxiety or depression, and there is often irritability and restlessness as well. As a consequence, not long after intercourse there may be resort to masturbation, but this may only add a feeling of guilt to the existing anxiety or depression. In effect, so male and female patients report, that deep, satisfying orgasmic experience, about which they have read and heard so much and which some individuals seem easily to experience, has eluded them.

We find it easy to dismiss this as the result of having seen too many movies in which the hero and heroine thrash around ecstatically in the throes of orgasm.* Yet the truth is, in phallic culture, that whole books and numerous magazine articles stress the full and complete importance of orgasm without always making it clear that there are many varieties of orgasm and that all persons are not equal in orgasm capacity. Perhaps because it is erroneously assumed that ejaculation and orgasm are identical, the question

---

*I am speaking of mass-audience movies, not pornographic fare, in which, as in the love scene between Karen Black and Jack Nicholson in *Five Easy Pieces,* the moment of climax is marked by visual and sound effects as dramatic as those that accompany depictions of battle scenes. The fantasy elements in cinema orgasms have been too little noted by critics and viewers. Novelists, too, have been prone to this kind of exaggeration. In J. P. Donleavy's *The Onion Eater* (Baltimore: Penguin, 1972), for example, one of the female characters achieves orgasm simply by being touched on the inside of her arm "by the elbow." The hero has three testicles, while in Donleavy's *A Singular Man* (Baltimore: Penguin, 1966), the central figure's penis is unusually large.

of male orgasm has received much less attention than the question of female orgasm.

In the germinal sense, phallic culture began when sexual intercourse became freed of any necessary connection with marriage and procreation, or, to put it another way, phallic culture originated with the discovery that sexual pleasure was an end in itself and not merely a means to an end. But in its mature form phallic culture is founded on the peculiarly American tendency to treat sex as totally separate from personality, that is, from affective involvement. As psychologist Rollo May, in positing a "new Puritanism," has suggested, the typical sexual relationship in America is characterized by a "separation of emotion from reason, and use of the body as a machine." Doubting that there is any less guilt, loneliness, and frustration in contemporary America than there was at an earlier time, May argues that we have simply reversed the Victorians, who "sought to have love without falling into sex; the modern person seeks to have sex without falling into love."[4] May, like theologian Harvey Cox and other critics of the sexual values espoused by *Playboy, Penthouse, Playgirl,* and other magazines, regards much of the sexual revolution as, in essence, antisexual because of the treatment of sex as a consumer-goods commodity that is promoted and sold much like any other consumption product. From Cox's point of view, a *Playboy* cartoon in which the young man, as he is about to have intercourse with a girl, asks: "How can you speak of love at a time like this!" must be regarded as more an expression of reaction than revolution.*

While the divorce of sex from personality can be observed in many areas of social life, perhaps nowhere is it more perfectly expressed than in the Miss America contests that began in 1921. Designed to promote Atlantic City, New Jersey, as a resort, the Miss America competition, by its success, has spawned not only the

---

*And perhaps also an expression of sexism since, in a magazine like *Playgirl,* it would be the girl who made the remark. *Playgirl,* with its nude male centerfold, achieved a circulation of 1,700,000 in not much more than a year. According to advertising promotion material, 52 percent of its estimated 14,000,000 readers in 1974 were women, most of whom were married, with a median age of almost thirty. In another magazine aimed at women, *Viva,* several nude males have been photographed with semierect penises; perhaps they point the way, so to speak, toward the future.

Miss Universe, Miss U.S.A., and Miss Black America contests but also the assorted queens of businessmen's conventions and football bowl games. Contestants are said to be of "good moral character," and sponsors, sensitive to certain criticisms, have alleged that the girls must demonstrate a skill or talent. Apparently this requirement is satisfied by demonstrating an ability to sew clothes or play "Abide with Me" on the piano. But the winners are usually described only in terms of 36-24-35 or thereabouts. Rarely is the public supplied with anything more than the names, ages, hometowns, and measurements of the rivals.

The numerous sex manuals and guides, by focusing on the purely physical aspects of sexual behavior, also contribute to the tendency to detach sex from any affective involvement. Beginning with the Kinsey reports of 1948 and 1953,[5] the behavioral scientists, in particular, have been guilty of depersonalizing sex by treating it as almost entirely a stimulus-response phenomenon. Kinsey himself, in tabulating the frequency of orgasms no matter how achieved, was inclined to regard all "outlets"—a remarkable expression in itself—as essentially equal, thereby implying that there were no important differences between sexual intercourse and masturbation in terms of sexual satisfaction.*

In the more recent investigations of William H. Masters and Virginia E. Johnson the Kinsey tradition continues, but the Masters-Johnson approach to sexual behavior is even more impersonal and detached. Whereas Kinsey based his findings on what was reported by volunteer respondents, Masters-Johnson have devised

---

*Nothing said here is intended to minimize the fact that the Kinsey studies were a significant pioneering contribution to knowledge. The point being made is that they did not deal with aspects of sexual behavior other than the physical, thus denying, in effect, their importance. Hence it was not altogether unfair to describe both Kinsey and Masters-Johnson as proving, in the words of one sardonic reviewer, "that sexual intercourse is no substitute for masturbation." Indeed, this is the point of view, advanced in all seriousness, by artist Betty Dodson in *Liberating Masturbation: A Meditation on Self Love Dedicated to Women* (New York: Bodysex Designs, 1974). "I would like to point out," she argues, "that in addition to heterosexuality, homosexuality, bisexuality, and group sexuality, that self sexuality as a total sex life is absolutely valid. . . . Masturbation is our primary sex life. It is our sexual base. . . . Under ideal circumstances, there would be no set or prescribed way in which we would sexualize" (p. 55).

elaborate techniques for measuring orgasm response in a variety of situations. In their first book, *Human Sexual Response,* the result of an eleven-year inquiry into the anatomy and physiology of sexual response, Masters-Johnson and their associates reported in detail the orgasm experience of 382 women and 312 men, mostly between the ages of twenty-one and fifty, almost all of whom were paid volunteers.[6] The total of more than 10,000 orgasms, of which three-quarters were experienced by females, were recorded by camera, electrocardiographs, electroencephalographs, and other devices while the volunteer subjects were engaging in coition and masturbation. The conclusions of *Human Sexual Response,* tending to confirm what had long been known about physiological aspects of sexual experience, nevertheless were given extensive coverage in every major newspaper, and the book itself was widely reviewed; the New York *Times,* for example, devoted forty-one column inches to the book, including a two-column article about it on the front page of the second section, April 18, 1966.*

Unlike Kinsey, Masters-Johnson have long been interested in sexual malfunctions such as impotence, premature ejaculation and inability to ejaculate, frigidity, vaginismus (involuntary spasm of the muscles at the entrance to the vagina, thus preventing entrance of the penis), and painful intercourse. In *Human Sexual Inadequacy,* their second book, published in 1970, they reported the results of eleven years of work on these problems, during which they treated 510 married couples and 57 single persons, all but three of whom were men.[7] The immediate and five-year follow-up results were impressive: the overall success rate was a striking 80 percent, with primary impotence (men who have never experienced intercourse) accounting for the highest failure rate of 40.6 percent and premature ejaculation the lowest, at 2.7 percent. Failure was defined as the inability to achieve orgasm during the

---

*Despite the statement by the book's publisher that it would be of interest primarily to physicians, the book was on the New York *Times* best-seller list for thirty-two consecutive weeks following publication. It was also known that the two Kinsey reports had been best sellers, although they, too, had been billed as of interest primarily to physicians and marriage counselors. Since publishers are not known for their naïveté, the initial statement deceived no one.

two-week treatment period or as a return to the sexual malfunction within a period of five years after treatment.

Certainly these results are impressive, but again note should be taken that until recently the Masters-Johnson approach to sex was to treat it as almost entirely a physiological and nonaffective response to a variety of stimuli. This emphasis was reflected even in the clinical setting; since they were unwilling to administer sexual therapy to persons without partners, "carefully screened female volunteers" were selected to work with the single men. Couples saw the therapists one hour or more each day, seven days each week for two weeks, during which the emphasis was on uninhibited communication and mutual participation. In keeping with the assumption that sexual satisfaction is always a stimulus-response outcome unless there is blocking, inhibition, anxiety, separately or in combination at some point in the sequence, the couple was gradually led to maximize their "sensate pleasure" in each other's bodies through tactile explorations. Toward this end the entire sensory apparatus of touching, feeling, hearing, tasting, and smelling was enlisted, and only when the therapists were convinced of the probability of successful intercourse was the couple permitted to make the attempt.

As might be expected, the sexual-therapy techniques of the Masters-Johnson Reproductive Biology Research Foundation have been widely copied and almost as widely distorted. In 1974 there were more than 3,500 sex-therapy clinics charging up to $4,000 for a course of treatment, of which an estimated 100 were run by trained professionals; some of them were offering, as one informed article put it, "little more enlightenment than a weekend of dirty movies."* Thus there are nude encounter groups specializing in massage and other kinds of body exploration and

*Constance Holden in *Science*, October 25, 1974. She describes a number of sex-therapy approaches, including that of a West Coast clinic that features films, hypnosis, and a "sexological" examination in which a couple is given a guided tour of each other's bodies. At another center, also on the West Coast, "Every possible sex practice—including bestiality, sadism, masturbation, and practices of other cultures—is depicted and discussed at length. That is 'desensitization.' . . . They come back for 'resensitization' the next day, where with more movies and talks they find out how good and normal sexual expression is" (pp. 330–34).

clinics where the "therapy" is supplied by surrogate sexual partners. Whether or not many such clinics are hardly more than dis-
guised houses of prostitution, frequently the surrogate partners
are former prostitutes who are paid well for their services. In at
least one New York sex-therapy center the therapists themselves,
who mainly are psychiatrists or psychologists, function as surrogate partners, while in other centers therapists and their patients
are encouraged to observe each other performing sexual acts.

In effect, the sex-therapy centers and phallic culture in general
tend to eliminate distinctions between what is public and what is
private, just as they make it difficult to determine which behavior
falls on the side of exhibitionism and which on the side of voyeurism. In the name of sexual liberation from inhibition and repression, all sexuality is deemed to be of public interest, and all citizens
are at once both participants and observers, exhibitionists and
voyeurs. Thus in phallic culture no biography, even of the most
scholarly type, will be regarded as complete or "thorough" unless
the author has discussed in detail the sexual life of his subject or,
if factual information is lacking, has speculated at length about it.
A female anthropologist who has done a study of aboriginal culture will be shown in a provocative pose on the book's dust jacket;
the jacket photo of a young and pretty ethologist will display her
in shorts and a halter. Advertisements for novels increasingly will
feature photos of authors made to look as sexually enticing as possible, if they are women, or, if they are men, as rugged and hand-
some as the photographer's art will permit. In phallic culture everyone is or must appear to be an object of sexual desire.*

Since celebrities, almost by definition, thrive on exposure and a
willingness to exhibit themselves, they usually offer no objection
to having their sexual lives become public property; perhaps this
is particularly the case if they are persons of uncertain achieve-

---

*While it is conventional practice for paperbacks and record albums to fea-
ture nude female models on their covers, a recent innovation in the record field
is the nude appearance of the performing artist. Outstanding examples include
front views of John and Yoko Lennon on an album released in Britain, although
not in the United States, and a back view of Joni Mitchell on the inside cover of
her album *For the Roses*. The dust jackets of at least two books by Mickey Spillane
feature photographs of his wife in the nude.

ment whose celebrity status derives not from any accomplishment but from the space accorded them in the mass media. Prior to the emergence of phallic culture there were relatively few magazines publishing intimate information about the private lives of well-known individuals. The most successful ones, such as *Confidential,* based themselves on the formula that in every celebrity's life there is a secret vice, aberration, weakness, or departure from the moral norm about which many people would like to know, presumably because such knowledge satisfies the desire to see the famous, powerful, and rich reduced to the common condition of mankind and also provides vicarious relief for lives that are drab and mediocre. Thus one could read articles in the so-called scandal magazines about the alleged adulteries, promiscuities, alcoholism, homosexuality, and illegitimate children of a large number of Hollywood personalities.

In recent years the *Confidential* formula has been adapted to general-circulation magazines and newspapers, in which, in the guise of a "profile" or "close-up," the private lives of celebrities is written about at length. For example, the profiles in the drama section of the Sunday New York *Times* invariably discuss the marital, drug, and drinking problems, if any, and the current sexual liaisons of profile subjects. Magazines such as *Good Housekeeping, Ladies' Home Journal, Esquire, McCall's,* and *People* regularly publish articles or short pieces about the private lives of the Leonard Bernsteins, the Nelson Rockefellers, Princess Margaret and Lord Snowden, and the Shah of Iran, in addition to stories about leading actors and actresses. John J. Miller, a widely read syndicated newspaper columnist, has made a career of reporting the fistfights, "emergency operations" (usually abortions), and underworld connections of celebrities, in addition to their extramarital affairs, paternity suits, drunken episodes, etc.*

*Techniques of snooping and spying have been transformed in recent years by the revolution in electronic gadgetry that has effectively destroyed what remained of privacy in and out of the bedroom. No doubt most of the eavesdropping devices—the microphone hidden in the martini olive, the concealed tape recorder in the attaché case, and so forth—are used for purposes of business espionage, but it is probable that these and other devices are coming into extensive use for personal and social entertainment. Magazines such as *Esquire* have advertised "The Snooper—World's Only Private Listening Device," guaranteed to

For the most part, these stories are rarely challenged in the courts, and when they are, it is rare for the courts to rule in favor of the plaintiff. In a case brought against now-defunct *Look* magazine in 1957, Frank Sinatra, at that time the leading *persona* of many profiles and close-up articles, disputed "the right of the press to report publicly the personal or private lives of celebrities, as distinguished from their professional activity." *Look* "welcomed" the challenge as an "ideal test . . . if the press is to be restricted as to facts it can publish about such a public personality, it is important that the limits be clearly defined."[8]

Sinatra's suit was settled out of court, but by now it is clear that *Look*'s position, implying that "public personalities" are entitled to much less privacy than ordinary citizens, has been accepted by most courts and, needless to say, almost all magazine editors. But, quite apart from the legal issues, it could hardly be otherwise in phallic culture, considering the supreme importance the culture accords to sexual performance. Indeed, the impact of the sexual revolution is such that what used to be regarded as loose and promiscuous behavior is now viewed as sexual emancipation or enlightenment, and those once stigmatized as tarts and gigolos are now admiringly referred to as "swingers." It follows that the male and female sex symbols in society must be capable or appear to be capable of outstanding sexual achievement, and this in turn requires open and frequent evidence in the mass media that they are "making out." Hence subsequent articles about Sinatra, depicting at length his numerous romances with leading actresses, did not occasion response from the singer other than satisfaction, with the result that by 1970 he had been accorded the supreme accolade of phallic culture. He had become not merely the chief male celebrity, or the leading "swinger," but, as the New York *Post* put it, a "happening."

The Sinatras of real life have their counterparts in the popular novels, and here, too, the isolation of sex from other personality

---

pick up normal conversations at a distance of 500 feet. A New York firm specializes in bedroom and bathroom mirrors that can be seen through from one side and wall-attachment listening gadgets that can pick up whispered conversations in the next apartment. The 1974 popular film *The Conversation,* starring Gene Hackman, was the first full-length movie about "bugging," but undoubtedly it will not be the last.

components that is the central feature of phallic culture can be seen in the treatment of love. Prior to World War II love in the best-selling novels was usually depicted in romantic terms, which is to say that the lovers in these novels were drawn to each other by something more than the purely physical, clinical aspects of sex. Frequently the occurrence of the sexual act itself was hinted at rather than made explicit, and when the sexual relationship was described, as in *For Whom the Bell Tolls* or *Anthony Adverse*, it was done with tenderness and romantic feeling.*

The clear tendency of much current fiction is to treat sex in purely clinical terms and to emphasize deviant practices such as rape, incest, and homosexuality. Even in the work of distinguished writers, such as Mary McCarthy, the reader is better informed about the sexual experiences of the leading characters than about any other aspect of their lives or personalities. In McCarthy's *The Group,* to take one instance, there are episodes of defloration and lesbianism, and although the people in the novel live together in and out of wedlock, marry and divorce, bear children, have jobs, even commit suicide, what is most vivid is their sexual behavior. In *The Group* as in other novels any emotion corresponding to love or affection, respect, and tenderness is subsidiary to sexual desire or absent altogether.

But sexual desire itself may be muted, as in the novels of John O'Hara, in which sexual intercourse is without passion and sometimes almost as if the couple were bored by the whole business. Much of the copulation in contemporary fiction is casual and totally lacking in commitment, the result of chance encounters in bars, hotels, offices, planes, ships. What seems to matter is the sexual act itself reduced to its simplest fundamentals, namely, the achievement of orgasm, or "climax." Frequently a relationship

---

*It is arguable that the character of hard-core pornography has also changed with the emergence of phallic culture. For example, in *Fanny Hill*, first published in 1748, the kindness and thoughtfulness that Fanny's successive lovers display for her sensibilities as well as for her erogenous zones almost justify characterizing the book as a novel of manners and courtly behavior. From *Fanny Hill* to today's movies depicting women as "whores, quasi-whores, jilted mistresses, emotional cripples, drunks, daffy ingenues, Lolitas, kooks, sex-starved spinsters, psychotics, icebergs, zombies" is a very long way, indeed. Cf. Molly Haskell, *From Reverence to Rape: The Treatment of Women in the Movies* (New York: Holt, 1974).

proceeds to this as expeditiously as possible, with a minimum of characterization and description of setting and scenery. We hear only of the physical and/or sexual attributes of the couple as they proceed to an orgasm free of psychological or emotional nuances. In O'Hara novels, which express a literary mastery of this orgasmic style, even conversation is reduced to the barest essentials.

Perhaps the popularity of some recent fiction by women writers owes something to their tendency to focus on the physical aspects of sex and play down or eliminate altogether the emotional overtones. In novels such as Erica Jong's *Fear of Flying* and several others that have appeared in recent years, sexual encounters are not only depicted at length and in detail, but depicted from a female point of view that probably all readers, but male readers especially, find particularly stimulating. While sexual fantasies are aroused by third-person narratives of erotic experiences, they are much more exciting when the narrator is a participant and in the case of men even more so if the narrator is a woman. The enormous success of *The Happy Hooker* and *Inside Linda Lovelace,* the former of which has already sold 9,000,000 copies in paperback, not to mention *Deep Throat* and *Behind the Green Door,* derives from the capacity of men to fantasize themselves as the stud males portrayed in the books and films, that is, to imagine that they are the objects of intense overpowering female desire. Whatever their physical condition and however weak or uncertain their sexual drive, the fantasy they are enabled to indulge is that it is their penis that is being caressed and stroked to orgasm by Xaviera Hollander, their penis that has entered the mouth, vagina, or anus of Linda Lovelace, their penis that is responsible for the ecstasy of Marilyn Chambers. Even if the woman is taken by force—one has the impression that the incidence of rape in movies of all types is increasing—the fantasy remains essentially the same: no matter how much she initially resists, in the end she, too, carried away by pleasure, is sucking and fucking away. But in most erotic books and films, as in phallic culture in general, it is the sexually voracious female demanding satisfaction, who has only to see a man to become aroused, who initiates the encounter.

Given this emphasis of phallic culture, one begins to think of one's own autobiography as a sex drama that can be performed in front of a live audience; a husband's depiction of his wife's orgasm becomes simply another instance of life imitating not so much art as living theater.* The popular books and movies, such as *Last Tango in Paris,* starring Marlon Brando, begin to resemble pornography, and pornographic works to take on some of the attributes of an art form. Hence the necessity to make further distinctions, as between "hard-core" and "soft-core" pornography, and between X- and R-rated movies. What was formerly pornographic in the art world and bought and sold behind the scenes is now relabeled erotic and becomes a legitimate subject for gallery exhibitions. The off-Broadway theater simulations of sex acts and the nude shows presented in cellar cabarets to select audiences now move to the big midtown playhouses and ultimately are performed nationwide by touring companies; *Deep Throat* is shown in Princeton, New Jersey. Phallic culture, in other words, inevitably gives rise to pornographic imperialism, the expansion of which is marked by a horizontal movement toward the mass audience and an upward thrust toward acceptance as a genuine esthetic experience.

But if phallic culture is, in this sense, democratic, it is far from egalitarian because not everyone, after all, benefits from the largesse. Not everyone capable of sex is capable of experiencing, in Anatole Broyard's words, that "incredible complex of emotions, history, misconceptions, fears, hopes, defenses, risks, threats, promises and God knows what else" that goes into a single act of love.[9] An important and conspicuous failure of the so-called sexual revolution is that it makes no provision for those who cannot form a loving relationship and who, for one reason or another, are unable to find sexual partners without resort to bribery or force. These millions include the maimed, the deformed, the crippled, and the hideously ugly, for whom any voluntary sexual rela-

---

*In an article about his release from prison after having served an eight-month sentence, *Eros* publisher Ralph Ginzburg writes of his reunion with his wife: "Wordlessly, we undressed. . . . I was overwhelmed by the lush revelation of things about her that are precious to me: a certain look in her eyes, the conformation of her hands, the smell of her hair, the curve of her hip. . . . Lost to all reason and restraint, we made love. The force of our orgasm shattered the damming walls of anxiety . . . at the moment when the tidal wave of my wife's sexual passion burst through, all her other passions flooded close behind." (*New York Times Magazine,* December 3, 1972.)

tionship may be out of the question. There are also the elderly, especially elderly women, and the widows and widowers, most of whom are destined to spend the remainder of their lives in sexual want.* Additional unfortunates are the prisoners and the inmates of mental hospitals and other incarcerates who are denied sexual relationships, not to mention the feebleminded and those suffering from mental retardation. There are those who are too poor to afford sex—too poor to marry or even indulge in the social preliminaries that customarily precede a sexual liaison or who lack the means to purchase even the cheapest contraceptives. Finally, there are those whose sexual needs and proclivities are such that few if any suppliers can be found, except for money. Many of these unfortunates haunt the seedy peep shows and bookstores on the meanest streets of American cities, and their existence is testimony to the fact that for them the rewards of phallic culture are far from evenly distributed. For this legion of the sexually damned the sexual revolution is itself a fantasy.

If this were not the case, the sexual revolution would be less oriented toward the values of youth, beauty, and affluence and more insistent that all citizens, regardless of age, physical condition, and financial status, have a right to sexual satisfaction. A sexual revolution less oriented toward the already privileged sexual classes would provide sexual opportunities not only for men who desire women but for women who desire men, for homosexuals and lesbians, and for deviants of all sorts. It would create more means than now exist by which discreet introductions could be arranged between persons of similar tastes or dispositions and also establish a larger network of theaters, libraries, and low-cost therapy cen-

---

*Even a woman as appealing as Simone de Beauvoir, approaching her fifty-fifth birthday, can lament the end of sexual life at an age that marks the end of neither sexual interest nor capacity. In her *Force of Circumstances* (New York: Putnam, 1964) and *The Coming of Age* (New York: Putnam, 1972) the cruelties of aging and the sexual deprivations inflicted on the aged are movingly portrayed. Certainly men suffer less than women from age and sexual want. Despite increasing sophistication at all levels of society, it takes more courage by far for an older woman to have an affair with or marry a much younger man than for an older man to have an affair with or marry a much younger woman. Indeed, the older man will be given credit for his success with women and presumptive virility, whereas many will think that the older woman is neurotic or is driven by a frustrated maternal instinct and mothering complex.

ters designed to make the sexual experience more available as well as more satisfactory at both psychic and physical levels.*

Such steps would not in and of themselves remove all sexual inequalities, to be sure, but they would go far to equalize opportunities for sexual enjoyment. In sex as in other areas of life those who are young, beautiful, and rich can generally create their own opportunities, and everyone knows that any and all manner of sexual tastes are widely indulged at the more expensive resorts, spas, and watering places in America and abroad. The hotels of Las Vegas, Miami Beach, Scottsdale, and Palm Springs and the "islands in the sun" already cater to every kind of sexual fantasy; given the desirability of sexual equality, there is no good reason why the privileges of the few should not become the rights of the many.

The sexual revolution also carries with it implications for marriage that have not yet been fully articulated. Historically the case for marriage—and still the case against divorce, although the divorce rate is less and less affected by it—was the preservation of the species, specifically, the conviction that the necessary social function of child-rearing is best carried on in a family setting. From the dawn of the Christian era to very recently in the Western world sex was justified only in terms of procreation, and even procreation Augustine regarded as sinful. Pauline Christianity held and still holds that the sexual act *per se* is base, although inevitable in the nature of man, from which it followed that the only available options were to marry or to burn.

The modern experience, however, is that marriage and all types of self-immolation are far from incompatible. The divorce rate is such that today's adults can well reflect that divorce is to

---

*If, as seems to be the case, prostitution, massage parlors, peep shows, and pornography are becoming an accepted part of the folk culture, it is futile to pretend they do not exist and dishonest to refuse them legal supervision and recognition. Certainly the citizens of Iowa, Kansas, Colorado, and other states where in 1974 prostitution, pornography, masturbation for hire, and other sex-related activities were tolerated should be able to visit their local massage parlors and other establishments without fear of disease, blackmail, or violence. In this respect as in others, American cities could do worse than to follow the examples of Amsterdam and Copenhagen, where entire quarters are given over to "red light" enterprises and where there is licensing, inspection, safety, and, significantly, large numbers of curious American tourists.

their generation what the Depression was to the generation of their parents. Probably many of tomorrow's adults will not marry at all, or if they do marry, they will insist that marriage as a way of life undergo a major transformation. Few experts on children believe any longer that the family setting always provides the best environment for them; while all the evidence is not yet in, there are reasons to believe that children may be raised satisfactorily in nurseries, such as those maintained in the *kibbutzim*. What is important is that the child be loved—it hardly matters by whom—and love, apparently, is precisely what is missing in a great many family settings. In fact, physical mistreatment of children is increasing, as measured by reports from medical personnel of rising injuries, fractures, and beatings experienced by children at the hands of their parents. Nor does evidence exist that the psychological abuse of children has become less a problem in recent years. And even where there is on the part of parents genuine love for children, there remains what Bernard Bergonzi has termed "one of the cruelest of modern American dilemmas: a great devotion to children combined with a conviction of the infinite dissolubility of marriage."[10]

One does not need great courage to suggest that marriage and the family structure itself may be dying institutions. With the traditional functions of the family passing increasingly to other organizations—child-raising and education to nurseries and schools, work to factories and offices, recreation to clubs and leisure centers, and sex to an unlimited variety of settings—what becomes increasingly clear is that the family, functionally viewed, is no longer a necessary social arrangement.

What, if anything, is likely to replace marriage and the family? One possibility suggested by Margaret Mead is a contractual relationship entered into for set periods of time, with options to renew and with provision made for children that might result from such a relationship. Another possible replacement for marriage is a noncontractual relationship freely entered into and terminated, with the children provided for in community or state nurseries. Still another possibility, and one that has already emerged in certain subcultures, is the extended family structure comprising several or even a fairly large number of adults living together in a communitarian fashion and sharing responsibility for the children, who are viewed as the offspring of all the adult members.

The "ideal type" of extended family could broaden and deepen affective relationships by reducing the excessively demanding and frequently selfish two-person dependencies that marital partners often find stultifying. Divisions of household labor more satisfying to individual skills and interests would be possible, with some adults, male and female, cast as breadwinners and careerists and others, male and female, performing as child-tenders, cooks, handicrafters (the revival of home arts and crafts as central concerns and not mere hobbies would be an important gain), and homemakers. Under present arrangements many wives are poor or indifferent mothers and housekeepers but are unable to change to other more congenial roles, while many husbands would much prefer to be home making furniture or ceramics or woven fabrics than to be commuting to office jobs in big cities. A further benefit of the extended family in "ideal type" terms would be that all children and not just one's own would be loved and cared for. The prevailing cultural condition under which parents rarely love any children but their own—and often not even their own—would be transformed into one in which children were assured love and care regardless of origins and attributes. The status of orphan, foundling, or legal ward would be abolished.

Note that the discussion is about an "ideal type" of extended family, not about any heterogeneous collection of adults and children thrown together in a subculture of drugs or psychedelic experience. The psychic requirements of the extended family have nothing at all to do with LSD or marijuana, but a very great deal to do with the ability to give and receive affection, to feel, to empathize, and to care *without the interventions* of drugs. Reference is to an environment in which people seek not to be "turned on" through drugs or alcohol, but instead seek to experience increased sensitization and capacity to respond to each other.

The extended-family arrangement does not exhaust possibilities for more rewarding relationships between adults and between children and adults. Surely there will be more instances of unmarried men and women deliberately choosing to have children whom they will raise themselves, of one man living with two women (perhaps a partial solution to widowhood), and more marriages between persons of the same sex (as in Rotterdam in July, 1967, when two homosexuals were married by a Roman Catholic priest), in addition to all of the existing varieties of monogamy.

Due in part to improved birth-control methods and chemical techniques of postponing the male and female climacteric, active sexual life will begin earlier and end later than is now the case, thus eliminating at least some of the physical and psychological distance between childhood and adolescence, on the one hand, and maturity and old age, on the other. One result of such a development will be a necessary adjustment of present concepts of the life cycle and ultimately a need to abandon entirely the assumption of an inevitable "gap" between generations. Attitudes toward sex as a form of play and relaxation for children as well as for adults will be enhanced.

These innovations in traditional sex and marital relationships will mark a partial return to themes that Freud regarded as characteristic of what he termed "the love life of antiquity." The "most pronounced difference" between the sexual behavior of the ancient world and our own, he commented in an early work, "lies in the fact that the ancients placed the emphasis on the instinct itself, while we put it on its subject. The ancients extolled the instinct and were ready to ennoble through it even an inferior object, while we disparage the activity as such and only countenance it on account of the merits of the object."[11] Freud is saying, in effect, that for the ancients the objects of love were regarded as less important than the instinct of love itself, whereas in the modern world the instinct is tolerated only insofar as it attaches itself to an approved object. Thus sexual relations are conventionally acceptable in a setting of marriage but not outside it, a restriction reflected in the numerous social prohibitions on marriage; ineligibles have included persons wishing to marry across racial lines, paupers, and close relatives. Indeed, the effect, if not the intent, of the shift from instinct to object has been to limit severely the choice of objects, thereby impoverishing the instinct itself. As Durkheim noted with respect to marriage, "It completely regulates the life of passion, and monogamic marriage more strictly than any other. For by forcing man to attach himself forever to the same woman it assigns a strictly definite object to the need for love, and closes the horizon."[12]

If, however, object choice can be both broadened and deepened in the directions indicated, the result may be a diminution of sexual violence and aggression, an amalgam of which has become increasingly evident in American sexual behavior. Since Freud observed that with some men the sexual instinct is inextricably linked with aggressive impulses, to the extent that the absence of the latter in a sexual relationship can render the male impotent, a commonplace observation is that sexual pleasure is frequently enhanced in a setting of violence and that violence of certain kinds is not without sexual overtones. The crude as well as subtle combinations of sex and violence are a staple of the Mike Hammer and James Bond type of literature, in which a woman is occasionally stabbed or shot to death by her lover while they are in the throes of sexual embrace. Even more familiar is the long-standing language phenomenon whereby slang terms for sexual intercourse are extensively used to express violent or hostile attitudes, as in "fuck you," "screw you," "go fuck yourself," etc. Since 1967 the term "motherfucker" has become so much a replacement for "bastard" and "son of a bitch" that in abbreviated form it is extensively used in newspapers and magazines.[13]

While such usage, common to most Indo-European languages, reminds us that there is an aspect of force in sexual intercourse, an important question is whether the varieties of sexual violence are increasing. Forms of sexual violence and the frequency of such language as "fuck you" apparently increase in proportion to the extent that violence as such is indulged and sexual expression as such deprived. Thus the incidence of violent action and language not only is highest in the armed forces but high as well in prisons, mental hospitals, and other environments in which, as previously noted, the sexual revolution has not penetrated; in wartime there is probably an element of rape in all sexual relations in occupied areas.

Although love and war can coexist, there is probably a fundamental antagonism between the demands of love and those of war. The tendency of war to depersonalize sex and to anesthetize affective relationships is well known. World War II and Korean War experience demonstrated that temporary or prolonged impotence and other sexual malfunctions are characteristic of many men involved in front-line combat operations, and similar disturbances occur in a society at war or severely troubled by internal dissension. The Vietnam War and domestic strife may have accounted in part for complaints in recent years, especially in the big cities, of sexual disorders of all sorts.

Orwell, Huxley, and other novelists to the contrary notwith-

standing, the relationship between the sexual condition of a society and its politics has not been demonstrated conclusively, but
this does not rule out possible connections. Perhaps the crucial
sexual event for politics is whether in the maturing individual the
cultural blocking of sexuality is experienced as guilt or as frustration. If, that is to say, the child or adolescent is made to feel guilty
about his developing sexuality, he may as an adult overidentify
with the authority institutions and symbols (religion, law and order, the flag, the Constitution, the system as such) and thus take
up a position in politics somewhere between moderate and extreme conservatism. If, on the other hand, the child or adolescent
experiences the cultural intervention as frustration, he may overidentify with challenges to authority institutions and thus take up a
position on the left. This psychic mechanism or something very
similar to it may explain why political conservatives tend to be opposed to sexual permissiveness and liberals to favor it, quite apart
from other considerations such as their religious affiliation, education, income, and so forth.

What determines whether the cultural blocking will be experienced as guilt or as frustration? A society whose attitudes toward sex derive from Pauline Christianity will inevitably generate
both guilt and frustration, but until recently in the United States
the stigmatization of the sexual drive as such as has been far more
significant in child-raising than the questioning of laws and customs restricting sexual expression. Moreover, as previously noted,
the rise of phallic culture and the seemingly greater sexual freedom enjoyed by many Americans does not prove that Sullivan's
"lurid twilight" has ceased to exist. On the contrary, there is good
reason to believe that a very large proportion of Americans suffer
from anxiety and conscious or unconscious guilt about their sexual fantasies and performance, and perhaps this abundance of anxiety and guilt is partly the cause of the political conservatism that
dominates so much of American history. If the strength of this
conservatism is increasing, it may be in part because the stimula-
tions and excitements of phallic culture produce a good deal of
anxiety and guilt that seek a release in politics. Perhaps, too, the
restlessness and rebelliousness of the young and many not so
young, the hedonism of certain countercultures, and the endless
search for "kicks" and "mind-blowing" experiences owe something to the quest for that absolute sexual gratification the phallic

culture holds to be tantalizingly within the reach of everyone. Freud, however, may have been right to caution that "something in the nature of the sexual instinct itself is unfavorable to the achievement of absolute gratification."[14]

Whatever the case, the conclusion can only be that phallic culture is simply the other side of the coin of Victorianism and that the so-called sexual revolution can be viewed as an expression in some degree of reactionary tendencies. A true sexual revolution would go beyond what is merely physical to a recognition that the most satisfying sexual relationship is based on the Martin Buber "I-Thou" principle, namely, that the other is the subject as well as the object of love and sex. The realignment of culture, morals, and practices in a genuine sexual revolution would end the "lurid twilight" of guilt, frustration, and masturbatory fantasy that is so characteristic of the American sexual scene at the present time.*

This is not to say that a true sexual revolution will solve all problems, any more than other revolutions have done. In the end, happiness, which includes sexual satisfaction, remains a personal problem and perhaps one that will be forever elusive. Still we can expect that the consummation of the sexual revolution will promote the sum of human happiness by removing some of the more important remaining restrictions on equality of sexual opportunity and one's freedom to give and receive love. Surely that would be no small accomplishment.

---

*Perhaps another characteristic of those who are "into" group sex, bisexuality, foursomes, swapping, and other phenomena is depression. A good many sexual activists apparently use sex as a means of warding off feelings of sadness. One is reminded of the observation of Edmond and Jules de Goncourt that "debauchery is perhaps an act of despair in the face of infinity."

5

City Blues

On the first day of December, 1972, a leading brand of Scotch whisky inaugurated the Christmas season in New York with the following advertisement in the New York *Times:*

> New York, New York
> It's a wonderful town.
> Where the scrapers go up
> (And the Cutty goes down).

Did the ad writer intend to convey the subliminal message that the height of buildings in New York was somehow connected to the quantity of whiskey drunk, or was the linkage neither more nor less significant than the lines that followed urging New Yorkers to "drink down even *more* Cutty Sark. . . "? Surely the writer was not hinting that city life is tolerable only if one consumes large amounts of alcohol, or was that indeed the suggestion?

Whatever his intention, the copywriter was not far off in rhyming "Cutty goes down" with "wonderful town." For some years now the word "down" has been so descriptive of most trends and developments in New York that such references to the metropolis as "wonderful town" or "Fun City," if used by New Yorkers at all, are used with the utmost sarcasm. *Down,* for example, is that total of corporations making their headquarters in New York, the number of jobs each year, the hotel-occupancy rate, the number of new housing units being constructed, the total applications from interns seeking jobs in hospitals, the number of leading retail stores, and much else. The only upward movement, many

New Yorkers despairingly believe, is registered by the growing numbers of junkies, muggers, persons on relief, and a veritable population explosion among the prostitutes, pimps, massage parlors, and pornographic film houses that constitute the city's erogenous zone west of Sixth Avenue and north of Forty-Second Street.

While there is much wrong with New York, as with other cities, New Yorkers are prone to exaggerate the ailments of their city as they exaggerate everything else and to prophesy gloom and doom at the drop of practically anything, whether it be the stock market or the neckline of women's dresses. Clearly there must be some reason why, despite all the problems, more than 8,000,000 people continue to live in the city[1] and why, further, New York retains its position as the world's first or second city for art, music, and the theater, not to mention its importance as a commercial and banking center. "Any musician or orchestra still has to conquer New York before an international reputation is made," writes music critic Harold C. Schonberg.[2] "If you're tired of New York," says a titled English lady, paraphrasing Samuel Johnson, "you're tired of life."[3] New Yorkers "sometimes forget," writes novelist Anthony Burgess, "that New York is a beautiful city. Ezra Pound once addressed it as 'beloved' and likened it to a slim girl without breasts. It is also, though full of potential death, a life-enhancing city."* Humorist S. J. Perelman, escaping to London from the perils of New York, returns after a year because he misses the city, and in London "there is such a thing as too much couth." Clearly New York can't be all bad.

We also do well to remember that if the urban crisis is more serious in America than elsewhere, city traumas nevertheless are no new thing in the world. The Dark Ages, during which many European cities virtually disappeared, the great plagues and pesti-

---

*"I often feel suicidal in Rome, Paris and London," he continues, "and there is no antidote there except drink or literature. In New York, when the desperate mood comes on, all I have to do is to descend to the subway after midnight and observe the omnipresent evidence of violence there, and then the urge to go on living rushes in with the speed of a suburban express. New York is a place where every taste is catered to, the most recondite gustatory urge, the most rarified form of art. It is also a jungle where one has to keep alert. . . ." (*New York Times Magazine*, October 29, 1972.) New York seems to appeal more to the British than to other foreigners, perhaps because it has some of the excitement that London possessed when it was the capital of the British Empire.

lences, the uncontrollable fires and other disasters, the sackings and invasions and bombings, all of these precipitated urban crises far surpassing any experienced thus far by an American city, and yet all were surmounted, although not in a short span of time or without great losses. Since, despite calamities of all sorts, the cities of the world have largely survived, we can only conclude that there is no alternative to cities and no adequate substitute for the virtues and values of city life. We can imagine living without states and nations as such and indeed have lived without them in times past, but we cannot imagine living without cities.*

But we may have to live, at least for some time, with cities very different from those of even the recent past. For the argument can be made that the American city itself is entering a Dark Age, not because of any invasion by barbarians—although the barbarian spirit is at large in cities everywhere—but because the city is becoming a fragmented pseudocity of decay, fear, violence, and breakdown. Unlike the medieval city, which was surrounded by walls to protect it from hostile outsiders, the modern American city is crisscrossed by invisible but nonetheless thick walls within— walls between rich and poor, white and black, young and old. There is, in effect, not one city within a given metropolitan boundary, but several cities that have less and less to do with each other even on ceremonial and ritualistic occasions, and not one citizenry the members of which belong to a common polity but several citizenries who regard each other with suspicion if not outright hostility. To be sure, not all cities have entered equally upon a Dark Age; there are, after all, degrees of darkness as there are degrees of light. But almost all American cities in recent years have had experience with increasing crime, violence, and physical deterioration and decreasing amenities and civilities. Add to this the paralysis of nerve and will that characterizes the centers of city government and the atrophy of civic consciousness that is wide-

---

*During the 1,000 years between the fourth and fifteenth centuries some formerly great cities reverted to the status of towns and villages. The barbarians, it is instructive to recall, did not like cities, and Rome was particularly affected. At the height of its power Rome was the largest city of the ancient world, with an estimated population of 800,000; at the end of the Dark Ages in 1400 the population had dwindled to fewer than 20,000. As late as 1600 London's population was probably no more than 40,000.

spread in the populace, and the scene is set for an urban Dark Age that is likely to be rather longer than shorter in duration.

While it is not easy to assess what has gone wrong—Americans as they confront the complexities of their society are like the blind men who were trying to identify and describe the elephant by touching its various parts, one the trunk, one the ears, one the tail, and so forth—much less determine how to put it right, an attempt to understand the urban crisis, touching as it does on so many facets of American life, can throw light on a variety of problems. For the travail of the city is inseparable from the travail of color and caste, poverty and profits, welfare and war (while American wars are customarily fought elsewhere than on American soil, the city is often the first to suffer and the last to recover from the costs of a major war). It was also one of the earliest victims of technology, in the form of the automobile, and the city-as-victim tradition continues in the shape of the jet plane spewing noise and pollution over city streets.

But the city, above all, has been victimized by the national unwillingness to accept the social consequences of the melting-pot tradition insofar as it implies a multiracial society. If unwillingness were not the case, the millions of white citizens who have fled the cities would have remained to carry on the necessary, if often frustrating and exhausting, task of integrating the blacks and Puerto Ricans into the mainstream of American culture and civilization. Instead, the cities have largely been deserted by the white educated middle class with the result that they have become not only black, brown, and poor but to a large and increasing degree unfit for any human habitation.

Thus almost every large city with a substantial nonwhite population contains blocks or whole sections that give every appearance of having been firebombed, blitzed, or abandoned to the ravages of rodents and weather. "Madison Street [on Chicago's West Side]," reports a De Paul University professor, "looks like it was hit by a holocaust. Maybe only one-third of the stores operating there 10 years ago are still functioning. A three-block area lined by storefronts before 1968 lies completely vacant."[4] Detroit's Twelfth Street, the scene of major rioting in 1967, has been only partially rebuilt; the black residents who live nearby must travel long distances to buy groceries and medicines. Miles of downtown

Trenton, Newark, and Camden are boarded up; Trenton, the state capital of New Jersey, has long since given up its hotels and most of its department stores and movie houses. Brownsville, a section of Brooklyn, "looks worse than the East End of London did after the Blitz," writes critic Alfred Kazin. "Apparently the roofs are regularly set on fire, for the tops of the old tenements, built of New York's usual cheap apartment house brown brick, are charred, blackened, fire-streaked. . . . I was stupefied by the look of rusted blood down so many windows, the heaps of garbage ostentatiously heaped in a continuing line down the middle of the avenue, the long line of empty boarded-up storefronts, and the dead angry silence in front of the stoops on the street. . . ."[5]

There is no need to labor the point that the most devastated cities are those with large nonwhite populations. The 1970 census showed that Chicago was almost 38 percent black, with a black population of 1,102,620. Detroit in 1970 was almost 44 percent black, St. Louis more than 40 percent black, Newark more than 54 percent black, and Trenton and Camden 38 percent and 39 percent black, respectively. More than 42 percent of Brooklyn's population was nonwhite in 1970, as compared with 35 percent for all five New York boroughs.*

Although blacks and Puerto Ricans constitute only 16 percent of the nation's population, they form a majority in six cities: Washington, D.C., Atlanta, Newark, Gary (Indiana), Compton (California), and East St. Louis (Illinois). In the fifty cities with the largest number of blacks, blacks average almost 45 percent of the population.†

*According to the Census Bureau, between 90 and 95 percent of Puerto Ricans classify themselves as white for census and other purposes. Taking the more conservative figure of 90 percent, New York City's population in 1970 was:

Whites (excluding Puerto Ricans)	5,102,761
Puerto Rican whites	946,080
Blacks	1,688,115
Puerto Rican blacks	105,120
Others (mainly Chinese and other Orientals)	177,906
	8,019,982

†Of these fifty cities, the ten with the largest black populations were:

City	Number of Blacks
New York	1,688,115
Chicago	1,102,620

Even more significant is the distribution of the nonwhite population. The black in particular, like the American Indian before him, is segregated and more or less restricted to certain areas of the city; in effect, he is confined to urban reservations which, in the course of time, expand in size but remain poor and over-populated. In New York as in most urban centers the white population moves to other areas of the city or leaves it altogether as the reservations spill over into what were formerly white neighborhoods. Thus in 1970, 85 percent of white New Yorkers lived in predominantly white sections, that is, parts of the city where at least three of every four persons were white, whereas only 64.1 percent of blacks live in areas more than 50 percent black. In Brooklyn, for example, almost 13 percent of the 780 census tracts had no black residents, and while only 21 percent of blacks lived in sections that were 90 percent or more black, 82 percent of whites (including Puerto Ricans) lived in sections that were 90 percent or more white.

These figures might suggest that the black population was more dispersed than the white population, and in a sense this is true. But the racially mixed areas are mainly poverty areas that include, in addition to Puerto Ricans, Orientals, Cubans, Mexicans, and other nonwhites, the poorest of the white population such as students, the elderly, and those on welfare. They remain in the spill-over areas rapidly becoming black not because they believe in integration but because they are too poor to move. The whites who leave, on the other hand, migrate to other city areas or suburbs that are predominantly white. In the case of New York this migration in the decade between 1960 and 1970 resulted in a net outward movement of 955,000 whites; if Nassau County in Long Island and four nearby New Jersey counties are included, the net loss of whites in the New York area was 1,160,000. Areas predominantly white, such as Suffolk County on eastern Long Island,

Detroit	660,428
Philadelphia	653,791
Washington, D.C.	537,712
Los Angeles	503,606
Baltimore	420,210
Houston	316,551
Cleveland	287,841
New Orleans	267,308

the counties to the north of New York City, and outlying sections of Connecticut and New Jersey, showed net white gains of as much as 314,000 (Suffolk County).

As the cities of America have become less white, they have become less rich, reflecting not only the revolt against racial equality but a revolt against economic and social equality as well. Of course, the revolt against equality is not new. As Tocqueville noted in 1835, the American seeks not to be equal to his neighbor but to demonstrate by a variety of symbols that he is his neighbor's superior. But in a general, if almost intolerably slow, way the economic advance of any particular ethnic group has been followed by at least some measure of social equality. Thus the successive immigrations of Irish, Germans, Italians, and Jews have progressed over two or three generations from sweatshop or blue collar to white collar, from tenements to apartments or ranch houses in the suburbs, from night schools to Ivy League colleges, and, finally, from marriage within the group to intermarriage. As it is exactly three generations from "Honey Fitz" to Jack Kennedy, so it is roughly three generations from the saga of Leo Rosten's Yiddish-speaking H*Y*M*A*N K*A*P*L*A*N to the social self-assurance of Norman Podhoretz's *Making It*.

Because blacks and Puerto Ricans have made little real progress toward integration, any black or Puerto Rican writing the equivalent of *Making It* would have difficulty finding a publisher for the book, and once it was published, he would have even more difficulty explaining to his friends back on the reservation how and why he managed to write such a book.* Although all groups in the

---

*Books by or about black superstars, such as *Rockin' Steady* by Walt Frazier and Ira Berkow (Englewood Cliffs, N.J.: Prentice-Hall, 1974), might appear to be an exception, but they are testaments to an ultra-affluent life-style instead of social acceptability. In *Rockin' Steady* we hear much about Frazier's Rolls-Royce, mirrored bedroom and mink-covered bed, 49 suits and 50 pairs of shoes, and 7 coats (one of them a full-length black mink), in other words, about how he spends the $300,000 he is paid each year by the New York Knickerbockers. An ad for *Wilt*, by Wilt Chamberlain and David Shaw (New York: Macmillan, 1973), quotes a reviewer: "Wilt has more than 10,000 phone numbers on file at home . . . he comes across as the Paul Bunyan of the bedroom." Perhaps, after all, there are no great differences between the tangible evidences of success; there are only differences between success and failure. In any case, it is only a matter of time until Frazier, Wilt Chamberlain, and other black celebrities are invited to intellectual soirees on Central Park West and Sutton Place.

population have benefited from the unprecedented economic growth since 1945, blacks and Puerto Ricans continue to lag far behind the white majority, and there is little likelihood that their relative position will change very much in the coming years. In 1973, for example, the median family income of blacks was $7,269 as compared with the median white family income of $12,595, a difference of more than $5,300. In the nation's metropolitan areas in 1970, 24.4 percent of black families earned less than $4,000 per year, whereas only 9.5 percent of white families were below that figure. Black and Puerto Rican unemployment is usually two to three times as high as white unemployment, and most of those on relief are blacks or Puerto Ricans; in New York in 1972, 48 percent of Puerto Ricans and 32 percent of blacks were welfare recipients, compared with 4 percent of whites.*

In some parts of the country, moreover, the relative income difference is increasing rather than decreasing. For example, in New York the dollar gap between white and nonwhite incomes in recent years has grown larger, as is shown in the following table:

Median Family Incomes in New York

Year	White Families	Black Families	Puerto Rican Families
1959	$6,091	$4,437	$3,811
1970	9,682	7,150	5,575

Thus, black family income as a percentage of white family income showed no improvement between 1959 and 1970, and the dollar gap rose from $1,654 in 1959 to $2,532 in 1970. Puerto Ricans in New York fared worse: their family income as a percentage of white family income decreased 5 percent between 1959 and

---

*Nationwide about 1 of every 14 persons aged between twelve and seventy is on welfare, but the welfare percentages are much higher in the cities. In New York and St. Louis 1 of every 6 persons and in Boston 1 of every 5 persons is a welfare recipient. The "working poor" in New York, that is, workers whose incomes are so low they are supplemented by welfare payments, total 133,000, or 11 percent of the welfare recipients. A government study of the years 1968–1974 has shown that "50 million persons were below the poverty line in at least one of the six years, and that perhaps as many as 85 million were eligible at some time during that period for welfare checks, food stamps, or public housing." (New York *Times*, July 2, 1974.)

1970, and the dollar gap in their case rose from $2,280 in 1959 to
$4,107 in 1970. If inflation is taken into account, the real increase
for all families was much less and for Puerto Rican families the
least of all. While all family incomes increased in real terms
$2,400, or 28 percent, between 1959 and 1970, and the black fam-
ily increase was $1,510, or 26 percent, the increase for Puerto Ri-
cans was a paltry $701, or 14 percent.

What these figures suggest is that the most recent immigrants to
New York, like those who came before them, arrived poor, but
that unlike their German, Irish, Italian, and Jewish predecessors,
they have remained poor. At the same time, those earlier arrivals
who succeeded in New York, first economically and then socially,
those who, so to speak, went not so much from rags to riches as
from rags to Richmond Brothers, have left the city for the suburbs and exurbs, although in most instances they, too, remain
economically dependent upon the city, albeit in a different way.
The result has been that the city, caught in a squeeze between the
resident poor and the commuting rich, is drained of its resources
by both populations, the former impoverishing it by demanding
welfare payments and services, the latter through earning swollen
incomes in the city that, relatively speaking, are city-tax-free.*

As a result, the city is increasingly forced to tax its poor or deny
them needed services; in effect, what one agency gives them
another takes back. Sales taxes, which fall harder on the poor, increase. Fares for buses and subways, more used by the poor than
by the rich, go up and up and up; because in many cities the number of riders, mainly black as well as poor, decreases, deficits grow
larger, and the rolling stock is allowed to deteriorate to the point
where the passengers' safety itself is endangered.† Garbage, trash,

---

*Thus a New York commuter with a wife and two children earning, say, a
gross salary of $25,000 annually, will pay a city income tax averaging $110. Although his salary is earned in the city and he avails himself of various city services and amenities, most of it is spent elsewhere.

†"Public transit increasingly is being used almost solely by the very old and
very young, the poor and near-poor. . . . In a few congested large cities such as
New York, Chicago and Washington, there are still significant numbers of
middle-income passengers. But poverty level residents account for more than
half of the transit ridership in scores of other cities—Houston, Cleveland, and
Atlanta, for example. . . . In Akron, Ohio, where city buses now carry only 5
percent as many riders as they did in 1945, transit officials estimate that at least

and junked or stripped cars accumulate in the slum areas as collections become less frequent. Death rates in municipal hospitals rise sharply because of shortages of medical personnel and equipment, and in many such institutions drugs including narcotics are openly bought and sold. The public schools, as they take measures against vandalism and hire so-called security officers to protect teachers and students, begin to resemble rundown penal institutions; not surprisingly, the quality of education as measured by tests of reading ability and aptitude scores drops rapidly. As the recent high school graduates begin to fill the available jobs, one notices a decrease in the efficiency and good manners of telephone operators, store clerks, waitresses, and other service employees, and this, too, contributes to the economic decline of the city.

Perhaps the most serious threat of all to the city's future, and one closely linked with other changes, is the closing or departure of major firms and business enterprises and with them the jobs and tax payments the city so desperately needs. While most large cities have lost factories, offices, and stores to the suburbs and small towns, several of the nation's most important cities have experienced a veritable exodus of industry in a relatively short time and a consequent severe net loss of jobs. Between 1963 and 1971 St. Louis lost 191 of its 3,217 manufacturing plants, and when the old-established firm of Emerson Electric decided to expand, it chose Arkansas, not St. Louis, as the site of its new facilities. Although New York is still the headquarters for more than 100 of the nation's largest corporations, in recent years it has witnessed the departure from the city of more than two dozen major firms, an average of two each year, including General Dynamics, General Telephone and Electronics (including Sylvania), International Business Machines, Panasonic, Nabisco, Shell Oil, American Can, and American Cyanamid. As against this list, fewer than a dozen large firms have moved all or part of their operations to the city, and while it is understandable that city officials should boast that the city is now home to Norton Simon, UMC Industries, and Atlantic Richfield, they can hardly claim that Crompton &

---

65 percent of today's passengers are low income blacks. . . . In Winston-Salem, about 80 percent of the bus riders are black. . . ." (New York *Times*, February 21, 1971.)

Knowles compensates for the withdrawal of Pepsico, the Borden Company, or Uniroyal.

What New York goes through on a large scale other cities experience to a lesser degree, but the smaller cities suffer more because they are less able to absorb losses. Thus when Prudential Insurance moves out of Newark or Sears, Roebuck ceases operations in Camden, the consequences for the city can be almost catastrophic. In the fifteen years between 1957 and 1972 employment loss occasioned by departing corporations and stores cost Camden approximately 60,000 jobs, and this at a time the black population was increasing to 40 percent of the population. Nor was there the equivalent of Norton Simon to take the place of the New York Shipbuilding Company. If and when Camden's two remaining major industries, Campbell Soup and Radio Corporation of America, leave the city and no new sources of employment develop, there is a very good chance that Camden itself will cease to exist.

Camden in 1972 had no department store other than a discount house and no centrally located supermarket, whereas New York, needless to say, is well supplied with shopping facilities of all sorts. Yet the future of New York as the leading retail center is also in doubt. Many of the stores on Fifth Avenue and Madison Avenue that have made the city attractive to shoppers from all over have left the city or are making plans to leave. Some, like Best & Company, The Tailored Woman, DePinna, Weber & Heilbroner, Arnold Constable, have gone out of business or consolidated operations elsewhere, while others, such as Georg Jensen, have moved to less space in an effort to reduce costs. As a result, less than half the frontage on Fifth Avenue between Thirty-fourth and Fifty-seventh streets is now given over to retail enterprises. The new Fifth Avenue is at least half office buildings, airline-ticket agencies, and banks, and perhaps the avenue's future is signaled by the discount houses and stores which seem to appear and disappear almost overnight, selling cut-rate rugs, clothing, jewelry, radios, and cameras.

New Yorkers who absent themselves from the city for even a short time have a very personal way of knowing that drastic changes are taking place. The small restaurant that was a favorite for lunch has been replaced by a pharmacy; where a grocery, dry-cleaning establishment, florist, and cigar store stood in June, there is in August an empty lot strewn with building rubble. Rendered useless by an occupancy rate that declined from 76 percent in 1969 to 62 percent in 1971, a well-known hotel is torn down to make way for an office building or becomes a flophouse for addicts, prostitutes, welfare families. Within one twelve-month period a shop on Lexington Avenue is given over, successively, to the sale of stereo equipment, lighting fixtures, and baked goods; none of the stores survives more than a few months. The galleries, antique shops, and specialty stores that made strolling on Madison Avenue such a pleasure, along with the groceries, butchers, and delicatessens, are gradually replaced by expensive boutiques and hairdressing establishments. With business rents doubling and in some instances tripling every five years or less—there are innumerable cases of store rents going from $250 to $1,000 per month at the expiration of a lease—only those enterprises that do not have to make a profit in their location, such as airline-ticket offices, or that can pass on the high rents or divide them among several tenants are able to survive. Nor can the small retail business that, in the past, contributed so much vitality and warmth to everyday life in New York escape, like the Olin Corporation, to other areas or, like Stern's, consolidate with its suburban branch stores.

But if the small retail establishment is one of the first casualties of inflated real estate prices coupled with declining profits, it is by no means the last. In almost all cities a departing corporation or vacant store means fewer jobs, and in the case of most large American cities the job attrition has been serious. Between 1969 and 1973 jobs declined 19.4 percent in Detroit, 11.8 percent in Baltimore, 11.3 percent in Dallas, 9.7 percent in St. Louis, and 8.9 percent in Milwaukee. In manufacturing employment the job loss was even greater: jobs were down 21.7 percent in St. Louis, 18.8 percent in Philadelphia, and 15.7 percent in Baltimore.

The employment decline in New York over the same period of time was 6.4 percent, but because New York is larger than other cities and frequently has a higher rate of unemployment—in mid-1974 the rate was 8 percent—the number of lost jobs was a substantial 316,500 between 1969 and late 1974. Moreover, the rate of employment loss was increasing rapidly in 1974: during the first four months of that year the job decline averaged 24,000 a month. In the manufacturing industry the number of people employed dropped from 1,000,000 in 1950, of whom 558,000 were working in the apparel, printing, and food industries, to 650,000 in 1974, 325,000 of whom were apparel, printing, or food workers. The only significant employment gain in that time was in federal, state, and local government, where jobs increased from 374,000 in 1950 to 580,000 in 1974.

The job decline was, as always, particularly hard on blacks and Puerto Ricans. In 1971 the "Negro and other" unemployment rate in the twenty largest metropolitan areas was 9.9 percent and in the urban poverty neighborhoods 12.4 percent.* For blacks aged sixteen to nineteen, however, the rate was 30.2 percent in urban areas and 38 percent in poverty neighborhoods. In St. Louis in 1973 an estimated 34 percent of black males aged sixteen to twenty were unemployed; the corresponding figure for New York in 1973 was between 30 and 40 percent (39.8 percent of male Puerto Rican teenagers were unemployed). Of blacks in the twenty to twenty-four age category, 16 percent had no jobs. Inasmuch as the median age of black males in New York is 23.1—in Brooklyn half of the black male population of 297,000 is under twenty-one years of age—the total black unemployed in New York, male and female, is not much below 150,000, even without including the 40,000 teenagers living in low-income areas who were neither employed nor in school.

Black unemployment figures are remarkably close to certain other statistics, for example, drug addiction. The estimated number of heroin users in the New York metropolitan area is over 200,000, which is not far from the estimated total of black unemployment. In Washington, D.C., writes columnist Tom Wicker, "nearly half the city's addicts live in a 7.7-square-mile area that is the most densely populated part of the city—the 'inner city,' or black ghetto. Within that large area lies the three-square-mile 'Model Cities' sector, just a few blocks north of the White House. In the Model Cities sector, 36 percent of all young men between 20 and 24 years of age and 24 percent of all youths between 15 and 19 are heroin addicts." Wicker goes on to note that the Model Cities sector not only has the densest population in Washington

---

*At the end of 1974 black unemployment was estimated at 12 percent, or about double the white rate. Almost 40 percent of black teenagers were unemployed, according to the Bureau of Labor Statistics.

"but also the highest number of welfare cases and of poor families."*

The Model Cities area, like other poverty sections of major cities, is also high in venereal disease, infant mortality, and crime, but the last, unlike disease and infant death, while highest of all in black neighborhoods, does not stay confined in the black ghetto. Police estimate that at least half of all robberies (including muggings), burglaries, and larcenies are related to drug addiction and that in New York alone heroin addicts steal an average of $3,000,000 each day.

Racism, poverty, crime, and heroin are the four horsemen of the urban apocalypse, and as they charge back and forth over our seemingly prostrate cities, they destroy much that is not within their path. Perhaps the first and most important casualty is civic loyalty, the sense of being a responsible citizen of the city and for that very reason feeling superior to those who live and work somewhere else. Perhaps no New Yorker ever experienced the fierce civic pride and loyalty Londoners feel for London and Parisians feel for Paris; probably no Chicago Samuel Johnson ever said to a Chicago James Boswell that the smartest thing a southern Illinois farmboy ever does is to take the highroad for Chicago.†

---

*New York *Times*, March 7, 1971. A black youth who became an addict at the age of thirteen succinctly sums up the relationship between heroin, race, and poverty: "[Heroin helped] my nose not to smell the urine-soaked hallways. I didn't feel the garbage underfoot. I didn't hear the sound of police sirens tearing through the black jungle." (Michael Tabor in testifying at New York's Black Panther trial, quoted in New York *Times*, February 5, 1970.)

†Not all Scotsmen, of course, then or now, would have agreed with Johnson that the "smartest thing a Scots lad ever does is take the highroad for London." A song beloved in Glasgow, of which there is no American counterpart, was made famous by the music-hall song-and-dance man Will Fyffe; the chorus runs:

> I belong to Glasgow
> Dear old Glasgow town,
> But there's something the matter
> With Glasgow
> For it's going 'round and 'round,
> I'm only a common old working lad
> As anyone can see,
> But when I get a couple 'a drinks
> On a Saturday
> GLASGOW BELONGS TO ME.

But there was a time, and it was not too long ago, when the praises of New York, Chicago, Boston, and many other American cities were eagerly sung by poets, composers, and playwrights, a time when the nostalgic eulogies of a George M. Cohan or a Damon Runyon were taken as realistic evocations of the city. Then the cities belonged to and were cherished by the people who lived in them or who were fortunate enough to visit them; in those days one did not wonder "how the [United States] Travel Service has the nerve to ask me to ask anyone, let alone a friend, to visit" New York and other American cities.[6] Now the average New Yorker, the typical Bostonian, or the Chicago man in the street dislikes his city, perhaps even loathes it, and if he has any conviction that his city belongs to someone, the conviction he defends with passion is the conviction that it belongs *not* to him but to "them." Our "unloved cities," in the phrase of Albert Eide Parr, are full of unloved and unloving people.

Because many urban residents believe that the city has been taken over by "them," and because in reality the city has become increasingly unlovable as well as unloved, it is the helpless target of a thousand grievances and the victim of a hundred punishments. Like a naughty child who is beaten for bad behavior, only to behave worse, for which he is beaten even more, the city is to some extent made to fail and then blamed for its failure. Since the parks are strewn with litter and debris, some do not hesitate to steal trees, shrubs, and flowers, and as the parks are stripped of their natural beauty, everyone finds it easier to treat them as garbage dumps. In the end a desperate but essentially losing effort to preserve what remains is made by chaining trees and shrubs to stakes in the ground; even so, the cost of vandalism in New York City parks is almost $1,000,000 each year.

Aggression against the city takes many forms. One of the more important is the deposit of dirt in practically every variety and shape known to humankind.* Just as the condition of a house

*Dog lovers will not like the suggestion that there may be a relationship between canine excrement on the sidewalks and citizen attitudes toward the city. The possibility exists that dogs are permitted to perform their natural functions where people walk because their owners feel they have been "shit upon" by the city, in reality or fantasy, and it is time the city was paid back. Of course, this may not be the reason so much of the 150,000 pounds of feces shat daily by New York City dogs is deposited on the sidewalks.

reflects the pride or indifference of its owners, so the quantity and distribution of city litter tell us much about the attitudes of its citizens. With rare exceptions some part of the filth and debris that accumulates in front of apartment buildings, unless there are conscientious doormen, and brownstones is likely to stay there, eventually to overflow into the street. The garbage pickup and street-cleaning services in many cities, utilizing the most advanced equipment, seem unable to keep sidewalks and streets even relatively clean; perhaps one reason is that the sanitation men, like those in New York, truck "the same garbage out of city dumps that they truck into them . . . so that they will not have to work as hard on the next swing through the streets of their collection routes."* City dwellers who would not tolerate in their flats the least gobbet of dust will accept almost any amount of street litter— garbage, dog turds, broken glass, junked mattresses and furniture, old newspapers—as long as it does not obstruct routes to and from their building. In American cities, unlike those in some parts of Europe, there is no concept that the street is one's front yard in the city and is to be cared for in much the same way one would care for a plot of grass in front of one's house in a suburb or small town.

The hostility of the alienated and anonymous poor is often highly visible, as in the graffiti that cover almost every subway car, subway station, and bus, but visibility is not its only motivation. While "Eddie 181" is most assuredly drawing attention to the insignificance of his life in a tenement on 181st Street, in defacing city property he also is expressing his hatred for the city and its white middle-class sensibilities. (Are American cities, one wonders, the only ones where the streets carry numbers instead of names?) The epidemic of set fires in slum areas and the sharp rise in false fire alarms, the latter making it more difficult to deal with actual fires, are more direct expressions of destructive hostility.† In effect, the poor, who are made to feel poor in a dozen different ways, take it out on the city almost any way they can. As sociologist

*New York *Times*, September 19, 1969.
†Approximately half of the fire alarms in New York City are false. The rate of false alarms is highest in the extreme poverty neighborhoods of Brooklyn and the Bronx and in areas of Queens north of Kennedy International Airport. No doubt the fantasy or wish accompanying many such alarms is that the hated city is burning.

Lee Rainwater has pointed out, their "physical world is telling them they are inferior and bad. . . . Their inability to control the depredation of rats, hot steam pipes, balky stoves, and poorly fused electrical circuits tells them they are failures as autonomous individuals. The physical and social disorder of their world presents a constant temptation to give up or retaliate in kind."[7]

The alienation of middle-class city dwellers has been remarked by many observers, and it, too, is visible, but in a different way. "I did not see a happy face," former New York *Times* theater critic Brooks Atkinson reported following a visit to New York. "Everyone looked tired and surly. Preoccupied with their own miseries they hardly knew other people existed. . . . People on the street and in the elevators seemed to be irritated with one another."[8] Perhaps such irritation gives way to an overt expression of dislike and an exchange of insults, but it is more likely to result in a sullen silence because the most typical form of middle-class hostility toward the city is a passive-aggressive stance that leaves all of its problems unsolved. Thus if the subways are unsafe, the middle-class city dweller avoids them, thereby making them more unsafe, and if his neighborhood begins to decline, he moves away, thereby ensuring further deterioration.* If the streets are clogged with traffic, he continues to drive a car; if trucks are double-parked everywhere, he continues to insist that packages be delivered regardless of size, and *promptly* delivered. Whatever goes wrong, he vehemently insists, is not his responsibility, and even less does he set about putting it right. Instead, he angrily curses the city, accuses the mayor, blames "them."

To be sure, the cities are hard to govern, and there are times when effective city government in certain cases would appear to be impossible no matter what the competence of the mayor or city

---

*This deterioration process can be observed in almost every city, but New York is one of the foremost examples. In recent years, for example, families have been leaving the residential West Side at a rate four times that of single persons. Between 1960 and 1970, during which its population dropped 18 percent, the number of families declined almost 24 percent. (New York *Times*, March 26, 1974.) In the same decade the departure of families from New York City as a whole averaged 2,100 families per year; from 1970 to 1973 the number of families leaving the city each year rose to 10,500. Since 1960 the number of unrelated individuals living in the city increased almost 24 percent. (New York *Times*, December 22, 1974.)

manager. Even "boss" mayors like Chicago's Daley, who would be at home in the local government of the Soviet Union or any other authoritarian system, cannot prevent physical deterioration and the frequent breakdown of city services; the increasingly rapid turnover in city halls throughout the country reflects the fact that the rewards of office are gradually being overtaken by the frustrations and sense of failure. Americans are ingenious violaters of rules and prohibitions they find personally inconvenient, and as citizens of cities they develop highly skilled techniques of getting around regulations and having their way at the expense of the common good. Even the best-governed city, if it is as large as New York, cannot ensure that every sanitation truck is full on its way to the dump and empty upon its return, or that every policeman is awake and on the job instead of asleep in the squad car, or that every taxicab stops when hailed and takes the passenger to his destination. So long as car owners evade parking regulations or truckers threaten to strike if given tickets for parking violations, no city can do much about traffic congestion except curse.

The governments of America, however, city, state, and federal, are hardly innocent of fault for the plight of cities; as will be demonstrated later, cities everywhere in the world face difficult problems, but many of them are coping better than American cities. One has difficulty understanding, for example, why the clean-air laws of many cities fall short of establishing standards health agencies deem minimally desirable, and equal difficulty making sense of decisions raising the permissible noise levels in the face of evidence that diseases and chronic illnesses in urban areas caused or made worse by pollution and noise are increasing.* On at least

---

*In a number of studies respiratory ailments such as asthma, chronic bronchitis, croup, and influenza have been linked to air pollution, and noise levels, which have more than doubled in the last forty years, to the increasing incidence of deafness, heart disease, hypertension, and mental illness. It is known that loud noises have adverse effects on the nervous system that are similar to those produced by a sudden awareness of danger. The heart action and adrenal discharge are speeded, blood vessels constrict, and muscles grow tense. Despite what is known about noise pollution, cities impose few restrictions on noise, and in 1974 New York raised the permissible decibel (sound unit) level of automobile horns on the grounds that at existing levels they could not be heard above competing city noises! Nor has any city done much to reduce subway noise, found in an official report to be unpleasant and too loud as long ago as 1931.

one occasion New York during a period of more than four years withheld information to the effect that tunnel employees were exposed to carbon-monoxide levels twice as great as the level regarded as dangerous.[9]

Los Angeles and San Diego, which have seen both smog and the number of private automobiles increase dramatically since 1947, have yet to restrict the use of cars and institute a comprehensive system of public transportation.* Nor is it clear why New York in 1971 was forced to collect garbage for $49 per ton as compared with Chicago's $22 per ton or why its streets, compared with those of other cities, are so full of potholes, broken surfaces, depressions, cracks, protruding or sunken manhole covers, and other paving faults, making a vehicle ride as comfortable as a drive on a rock-strewn beach after the tide is out. The "Manhattanization" of San Francisco, regularly condemned by the city fathers and most civic organizations, proceeds apace with more than forty buildings of at least twenty-five stories already constructed or scheduled to be built. Almost everywhere local governments seem unable to prevent the rape of their cities by the automobile—in many cities 60 percent of the ground space is covered by automobiles—and the despoliation of the urban environment by smog, sprawl, and the office tower constructed, in Ada Louise Huxtable's apt phrase, according to the "Unistyle commercial model by Skidmore, Owings and Merrill, considered suitable for use by any major corporation in any American city, with soap sculpture on the inevitable plaza. . . ."[10] New York, it appears, is even unable to ensure itself adequate voltage during the summer months, when one or more Con Edison generators fail, or successfully resist pressure to relax zoning regulations in favor of "fast food" outlets, stand-up snack bars, and motels, although these have an adverse effect on the survival of restaurants and other retail establishments that attract

---

*Of the 300,000 automobiles that travel into downtown Los Angeles each day, an estimated 79 percent carry one person. It is typical of law enforcement in the "Clean Air" area, as in other sectors, that the officials in charge are the first to concede that regulations cannot be enforced and that, therefore, they will distinguish between what is "legal" and what is "practicable." Thus the California "Clean Air" plan adopted in 1972 called for a 20 percent reduction in auto traffic in Los Angeles, San Francisco, and San Diego, but the state's Air Resources Board officials "conceded that no more than 10 percent reduction was really expected." (New York Times, January 14, 1973.)

families to mid-city areas. Such a nominal and desirable measure as the segregation of smokers in public places is beyond the reach of many municipalities, the most daring of which have rarely gone beyond a ban on smoking in elevators and supermarkets, and no one pretends that even these limited restrictions are enforced.

Whatever the recent caliber of those elected to political office in the city, the impression is widespread that the quality of civil-service employees has been declining. While bureaucracy and red tape are usually blamed for the length of time it takes to obtain a decision from a city government, the fault frequently is not with the procedures but with the employees who administer them. In the majority of municipal hospitals, schools, social-service agencies, staff offices, and other facilities a good many employees customarily arrive late and leave early, take long lunch hours and coffee breaks, and deal with their work much the same way a hypochondriac deals with a contagious disease. Because there is the risk of a strike and shutdown if a tenured worker is fired, the tendency is to transfer the poor performer to another office; in one city hospital nurses and paraprofessionals who fail on the job are regularly shipped off to the methadone clinic, regarded as the least desirable place to work. Perhaps the municipal civil service in many cities is far from being the last refuge of incompetents, but the truth is that a large number of city workers would not be employed for long by private employers.*

Even the best of city governments cannot provide, in an inflationary era, the kind of housing that would keep the white middle class in the city and raise the living standards and morale of the urban poor. In almost all the nation's cities there is a large gap between the rents paid by tenants in low-rent and rent-controlled buildings and the operating costs of landlords, a gap estimated in 1970 of at least $255,000,000. Without subsidies many landlords cannot afford to maintain buildings, which leads to their deterioration and eventual abandonment, but if rents are increased or

---

*Graft, corruption, and theft involving employees also are ways in which cities are exploited by those who are supposed to serve them. Almost every year in New York, Chicago, and other cities the newspapers feature fresh scandals of bribery, influence-peddling, and other corrupt acts in police departments, among building inspectors and purchasing agents, in licensing agencies, etc. "Ripping off" the city in one form or another, many of them petty, is even regarded as a legitimate activity.

rent control is abandoned, few city dwellers can afford to live in apartments; construction costs in many cities now average well over $100 per room in rent, or approximately $500 monthly rent for a two-bedroom apartment. Hence, New York City, relying mainly on private builders, must manage with less than a third of the minimum 70,000 new apartments needed each year, most of which are sold or rented to the rich and well-to-do. As the blocks of flats in low-income areas decay, they are neither repaired nor replaced with better housing, and many of them are taken over by addicts, prostitutes, pimps, and criminal elements of all sorts, hardly the best of neighbors for the families that remain or the most suitable companions for their growing children.

In principle, government subsidies could make it possible for builders to construct attractive apartments renting for as little as $45 per room or even less. Unfortunately, even in the days when there was much more of a commitment to public housing, the housing projects developed for low- and middle-income families were rarely attractive at the start and after a few years of use totally unattractive. In accordance with the private-enterprise ethic, which in general associates esthetic values with wealth, housing because it was cheap had to be, if not ugly, at least simple, unpretentious, and starkly functional.* As Robert Hastings, former president of the American Institute of Architects, once observed, "If you even tried to make [public housing] look good, the Federal Government thought you were wasting money."[11] Neither the poor nor those who serve the poor are permitted, of course, to try to make anything "look good."

But the ultimate cost of what is initially cheap or cut-rate, as every consumer learns eventually, can be greater than the ultimate cost of what is initially more expensive. Most of the nation's low-income public housing is monotonous and bleak in appearance and depressing within and without. Perhaps there is no better example of the fatal interaction of race, poverty, bad planning, and cost economics than the now-destroyed Pruitt-Igoe public housing complex in St. Louis. Constructed in 1955–1956 at a cost of $36,000,000, Pruitt-Igoe consisted of thirty-three eleven-story

*There is a tendency for Marxists as well to think that if something is beautiful, it must be costly and, because beyond the reach of the poor, immoral. It follows that public buildings in socialist countries should be as cheap and ugly as those in capitalist countries, and they usually are.

apartment buildings and ten related structures built on a site formerly occupied by slums. *The Architectural Forum* and city planners in all parts of the country hailed the design of Pruitt-Igoe as far superior to that of other public housing projects; they particularly liked the extensive use of brick and glass in the apartments, the emphasis on access and circulation, the open space between buildings. Pruitt-Igoe, in short, was to be a model for low-income housing developments everywhere.

Fifteen years later Pruitt-Igoe was a disaster area, reminiscent of the worst sections of Brownsville. Windows and doors were gone, floors torn up, plumbing removed, and the walls inside and out covered with graffiti. Many of the elevators worked sporadically or not at all. In 1970 some of the original tenants—no one knows for certain how many—were still living in the complex, but a large number had long since left, to be replaced by derelicts, street gangs, drug pushers, and hoodlums.

Almost from the beginning everything went wrong that could have gone wrong. Because of misguided efforts to save money on construction, elevators stopped only on the fourth, seventh, and tenth floors. Since there were no corridors connecting apartments at opposite ends of the same floor, people in a front apartment on, say, the tenth floor would have to go down to the ground floor and come back up in a different elevator to visit a neighbor in a rear apartment on the tenth floor. Children were burned because steam pipes were not adequately covered, and an unknown number of persons fell or jumped to their deaths in elevator shafts because elevator doors did not always close properly. There were no locks or other restrictions at the entrances to buildings, with the result that dubious characters and those bent on mischief could roam the corridors at will.

But the biggest mistake of the Pruitt-Igoe planners was to make the project all black and all poor. They apparently assumed that concentrating 12,000 poverty-level blacks in high-rise apartment buildings would spontaneously produce a city within a city or at any rate establish the basis of a community. If they were aware that 60 percent of the blacks were on welfare, or that two-thirds of the families had no male heads, or that more than 60 percent of the project residents were children, their plan did not show it, and there was even less awareness that the basic high-rise design of Pruitt-Igoe was incompatible with the needs of a poor, fragmented, and fundamentally demoralized population. Pruitt-Igoe, even when it was new, looked, felt, and smelled like low-income public housing. Perhaps the most imaginative planners could not have overcome the fatal stigma attached to it as to many such projects, namely, the stigma resulting from the popular belief that to live in a low-rent public housing development is to declare oneself poor, inferior, and undesirable. In any event, the Pruitt-Igoe planners and builders, like the larger society of which they are a part, seemed not to know that if people are treated, deliberately or otherwise, as if they were of little worth, they will behave, consciously or unconsciously, as if they were of little worth.

Not that the blacks of Pruitt-Igoe were treated worse than other blacks in St. Louis or elsewhere in the nation. Indeed, the ghetto areas of many cities are such that they could only be improved by the building of a Pruitt-Igoe housing complex; it is also important to remember that while this St. Louis effort to improve the housing available to the poor turned into a massive failure, the effort was made, and made in a city that has never been in the forefront of civil-rights actions. Nor have efforts elsewhere always been successful, whether to improve housing, education, or employment opportunities. Thus the Lindsay Administration in New York, after trying for several years to persuade the construction industry and building-trades unions to employ blacks, confessed failure and terminated the attempt, but again, as Mayor Lindsay declared at a press conference, the failure had not been through any lack of effort. In America in the seventies, where success in any area of civic improvement is difficult, if not impossible, to achieve, it is the effort that counts, for or against, and less and less the results, and it is in terms of their efforts rather than their accomplishments that political figures are judged and remembered.

Why, in America, political success should be crowned with efforts, whereas elsewhere in the world it is more frequently the other way around, is difficult to determine. Despite the ravages of twentieth-century technology and the centrifugal forces of urbanization, European cities by and large continue to be livable on a scale far beyond that of their American counterparts. Not only is there less crime and therefore less fear of dark streets and parks but there also are many more amenities and humanizing conveniences; everyday life in most European cities is, in short, easier and far more pleasant. London, once famous for its deadly fogs and odorous river, has taken great strides toward abolishing air and water pollution; prizes have been offered for the first salmon caught in the Thames, which is again home to numerous varieties of fish. The Paris Métro, in addition to being safer and less oppressive than the New York subway, is more visually appealing: the Franklin D. Roosevelt station features stained-glass reproductions of famous paintings; the Louvre stop offers the rider copies of the "Venus de Milo" and the "Winged Victory"; Défense contains a pet shop, banks, clothing stores, and a restaurant. The Moscow subway, also decorated with art, daily carries more than a million more passengers than the New York subway, yet it is clean, less noisy, and rush-hour trains are eighty seconds apart. One can avoid traffic congestion by taking a train from airport to city center in Paris, Brussels, and Frankfurt, and it will not be long before Zurich and London offer a similar shuttle. Most travelers agree that European and Japanese trains are the best in the world, in the sense that they are clean, fast, and comfortable. Unlike American rail passenger services, European railways simplify matters for travelers by indicating on the outside of cars their destination points and at the entrance of compartments whether they are for smokers or nonsmokers; in the newer trains a corridor sign lights up when the toilet at the end of the car is occupied.*

Americans, so eager to be copied or imitated by others, apparently are unwilling to learn from anyone else, even when they admit that there is something important to learn. Thus when the chairman of New York's Taxi Commission "discovered" during a European trip in 1972 that European taxi services were far superior to those of New York, a "discovery" long known to the millions of Americans who have been abroad, he was unable to make a single recommendation for the improvement of the city's taxi service. Although Chairman Michael J. Lazar returned from Europe an admirer of separate traffic lanes for taxis, more complete safety inspections, longer and more thorough training for drivers, emphasis on courtesy, and, in London, the type of taxi vehicle

---

*These touches, unknown in America even in the days when railroads were flourishing, are in addition to food vendors and dining cars on the long-distance trains. Indeed, one can dine better on such crack European trains as the Orient Express or the Scotsman or the Mistral than in most restaurants in the United States.

used (referring to the Leyland Austin taxi as "the classic taxi in use anywhere in the world"), he could not suggest any change in the admittedly inferior taxi system over which he himself presided. In a similar way, American state and municipal officials have long been aware and envious of the British Amenities Act, under which buildings, streets, squares, parks, and other natural or man-made constructions cannot be destroyed if they bring to an area a special charm or beauty or are otherwise deemed to be an irreplaceable asset. Such legislation is practically unknown in the United States, where, if buildings are protected at all, they are protected only if they have clear historical value and/or are of little interest to property developers. Because bus and subway route maps and stops are more clearly indicated in European cities than in New York—even New Yorkers cannot always decipher the subway route maps, sometimes covered by graffiti, whether or not they can read the fine print or at night and in bad weather make out the street signs from buses—it is easier for an American to get lost in New York than in London or Paris. But, again, little was done about it until very recently when New York began to copy the oval route map that is an easy-to-read feature of the London underground.

European cities, of course, are not without problems. There, too, there are slums, inadequate housing, and mean streets, and there, too, the city centers decay. While the total number of hard-drug addicts in the United Kingdom is officially judged to be no more than 2,000, as compared with the estimated 200,000 heroin addicts in New York alone, meth drinkers may be seen almost any evening in the Stepney district of London's East End, and, in general, the drug problem in Europe, like the crime rate, is increasing rather than decreasing. In Paris Les Halles is gone, and office towers have made their appearance in Montparnasse and elsewhere. The elegant nineteenth-century mansions of the Rond Point gained a reprieve following a public protest aimed at "reconstruction" plans, but the President of France, in defending the new high-rise construction, ominously declared that Paris "is not a museum." German cities have lost population and tax monies to the suburbs and as a result are in a precarious financial state, and Italy allows its ancient monuments to decay or be turned into gas stations. Because of pollution no beach from Genoa to Naples on the west coast of Italy is guaranteed safe for bathing. In Israel, although cabinet ministers are as apt to be archaeologists or historians as businessmen or lawyers, the models for urban development appear to be Tel Aviv and Miami Beach; and in Israel, too, the streets are full of litter. Prior to the Yom Kippur War of 1973 a Crusader castle more than 800 years old in the Golan Heights was scheduled to be transformed into a discotheque.

But Les Halles did not disappear without a struggle, and in Jerusalem the battle to preserve what remains of the ancient hills and streets, despite losses to the Wolfson and Hilton interests, is a hard-fought one. Americans, by contrast, often seem to gravitate between despairing resignation and false optimism. Those who believe the large city is doomed are eager to leave it as soon as they have the opportunity and meanwhile take little interest in its problems. Those who remain, whether through choice or necessity, appear to believe in the magic power of words, acting often as if the city can be preserved through repeated incantations and slogans. Thus in 1971 the businessmen of Detroit spent $135,000 on radio and television advertisements proclaiming: "It's getting better, it's getting better all the time." A 1972 Columbia University study, "New York Is Very Much Alive: A Manpower View," juggles statistics to prove that the city's crime rate is lower than that of such other cities as San Francisco and that there has been a net gain in jobs; in fact, New York ranks first among cities in violent-crime rates (murder, rape, robbery, aggravated assault), and the job gain is demonstrated only if the preceding ten years are used as the basis of calculation rather than the period since 1969.*

Still another approach to city problems is to attribute them, as does President William J. McGill of Columbia University, to "a verbal pollution filled with gross distortions, false charges and ri

---

*Even so, the gain of 89,000 jobs in a full decade was hardly impressive. The crime rate, which takes into account all types of crime including car theft, is even more deceptive since it understates the frequency of crimes against the person, the most feared crime of all. The Columbia figures, moreover, were for 1970. Had the study based itself on 1972 figures, it would have had to admit that three of the four serious crimes against the person showed a substantial increase, with murder up 15.3 percent, rape up 35.4 percent, and felonious assault up 9.6 percent. In 1973 New York City ranked first in the violent-crime rate (number of violent crimes per 100,000 population), that is, such felonies as murder and non-negligent manslaughter, forcible rape, robbery, and aggravated assault. (Source: Federal Bureau of Investigation, *Uniform Crime Reports for 1973*.)

diculous claims" made possible by the communications media. "Much of what concerns us about the deterioration of New York," McGill argues, "is manufactured out of essentially psychological forces, and it can be modified by powerful and equally dedicated psychological efforts."[12] But perhaps the highest award of the Optimists Club should have gone not to Columbia University but to former President Nixon for his declaration in 1973 that "the hour of crisis has passed" in America's cities.[13]

Most studies of cities conclude hopeful analyses of urban problems with statements "that there is nothing wrong with New York and other American cities that," in McGill's words, "$50-billion and a change of priorities wouldn't cure." Since there is no likelihood that the nation's major cities combined, let alone New York, will receive even half that amount from any present or future Congress—in recent years the federal government has favored the less populated states and the suburbs more than the heavily urbanized states and the cities—such a statement is tantamount to a declaration that there is *no* cure for the city's ailments. But even if the money were available, there could be no certainty that it would "buy" a solution to some of the most important problems; $100 billion and more, after all, did not "buy" victory in the Vietnam War. Quite apart from the waste, mismanagement, and corruption that almost certainly would occur on an unprecedented scale, would the political and economic elite of the city know how, when, and where to use the billions available? Considering what has been done with the much smaller amounts the city has been able to spend, there are no grounds for believing that a significantly larger sum of money necessarily would be better spent.

For example, would the city fathers devote some of the money to the control of population growth in New York? Many students of cities believe that New York, with a population density of more than 26,000 persons for each square mile (Manhattan's density is almost 68,000), is too crowded to afford its citizens an optimal living environment. No city in Europe is as densely populated, and some of the consequences of overpopulation are apparent to anyone who compares everyday life in San Francisco or Paris or London or Geneva with daily life in New York. There is no easy way to reduce the population size of New York and other crowded cities, but perhaps people would be encouraged to move elsewhere by giving them the equivalent of relocation allowances and finding them jobs and homes in the new localities. The idea is not a new one; corporations usually pay for the relocation of their management-level employees. As is often the case, the only new thought involved is that governments should take as much interest in the quality of the life led by citizens as corporations take in the quality of the work done by their executives.

A proposal related to city size originally put forward by David Rockefeller and the National Commission on Urban Growth Policy is the creation of new cities that perhaps would be modeled after Columbia, Maryland. The Rockefeller suggestion that there be developed 100 new cities of 100,000 people and ten cities of 1,000,000 would accommodate 20,000,000 persons.* Certainly such cities could help to relieve population pressure in the older urban areas, as well as ensure that the anticipated population increase by the year 2000 does not settle in parts of the country that are already congested.

There are fewer obstacles in the way of paying people to integrate, that is, paying them to move to or remain in racially mixed neighborhoods. In a similar way teachers could be paid more to transfer to or remain in troubled schools, and there could also be a large bonus for merchants and others who continue to maintain businesses in mixed neighborhoods. In effect, what is being proposed is the civilian counterpart of the combat pay given soldiers and government workers in war zones or, perhaps even more literally, the counterpart of cost-of-living allowances.†

Much could be done to make city housing more attractive at little or no extra cost. By now it is clear that the high-rise apartment tower is more conducive to crime and vandalism than the low-rise apartment building, and its physical plan—the empty and per-

---

*The estimated $10 billion cost (as of 1971) is less than 10 percent of the cost of the Vietnam War 1965–1972 and not quite 2 percent of total military expenditures 1965–1972. But the difficulty is not costs but attitudes and an unwillingness to deal with major city problems. According to the National Urban League in 1974, state and local governments have used only 1 percent of revenue-sharing funds for social services, 2 percent for housing, and 5 percent for health programs. Most of the money, scheduled to total $30 billion by the end of 1976, so far has been spent on capital improvements and "salaries for policemen and firemen." (New York *Times,* December 5, 1974.)

†This idea and related proposals bearing on the future of the city are further discussed in the last chapter.

haps dangerous lobby with its elevator banks, the long double-loaded corridors (apartments on both sides), and so on—contributes to the sense of alienation and depersonalization that afflicts many city dwellers. The high-rise building is also unsafe for raising children, as witness the number of children who die or who are injured each year as a result of falling down elevator shafts or out of windows.[14] The areas between buildings may be little used and at night attract prowlers, derelicts, and other undesirables. In the high-rise projects "defensible space," in the words of Oscar Newman, is practically nonexistent.

Contrary to popular belief, cities could provide "defensible space" and accommodate as many people in low-rise housing without increasing rents. As William H. Whyte, Jr., has shown, the population density of some New York City brownstone sections and "vest-pocket" projects is greater than that of some public housing projects. Space for additional housing, he suggests, could be found by reducing the number of parking lots, consolidating utility rights-of-way, and utilizing air space over railroad tracks, expressways, piers, and other facilities.[15] Even in those cities where the population density could not be reduced to fifty units per acre, or approximately the density of garden-apartment housing, a mix of three-story walk-ups for families with children and a few high-rise buildings for the elderly "could achieve a combined density of 70 units to the acre—a density that begins to be reasonable even for New York."[16]

Perhaps office towers in America must grow higher and higher until, in many cities, they are taller than the World Trade Center buildings in lower Manhattan. Still, as Whyte suggests, they could be designed with plazas for sitting, eating, talking, or simply gawking; many city people make more leisure-time use of the space in front of or to the sides of high-rise office buildings than they do of city parks and other areas deliberately intended for rest or recreation.[17] In sections where office towers are side by side with hotels and apartment buildings, the office towers could be required to devote some floors to apartments and even schools, with portions of the ground floor reserved for shopping areas.* In that

*The Olympic Airline building in New York, built by Onassis, could serve as model were it not that the cost of the apartments ensures their being sold only to

way the tendency of office construction to extend into residential areas and ultimately take the place of apartment buildings and hotels could be reduced.

In almost all cities only a beginning has been made in transforming streets into pedestrian malls and vacant lots into "pocket" parks. Why should not every large building project earmark space for a pocket park or at least a small area of greenery, benches, and, if possible, flowing water? There seems to be no good reason why automobiles should not be banned or severely restricted in certain sections of cities irrespective of air-pollution problems. Trucks could be prohibited from moving during rush hours, as is the case in some European cities, or made to confine their deliveries to the nighttime hours.

Traveling about in the city would be easier and far more pleasant if street signs were illuminated and low enough to be seen, say, by a bus standee; an alternative would be to substitute clear glass for metal in that part of the bus that is eye level with the standing passenger, thereby permitting him to see street signs and the streets themselves instead of advertisement cards. Stops could be called out or shown on lighted screens. If it is not feasible to bring back the double-decker bus, perhaps tandem buses would be practical.

Possibly nothing can be done about the subways, but one wonders what might be accomplished if neighborhoods served by a particular station were encouraged to decorate that station and given the necessary materials without charge. Would anything be lost if dirty and grimy subway walls and tiles lining tracks were turned into free space for ads or covered with low-cost reproductions of paintings? Surely there must be a better way of lighting subways than the naked lightbulb and fluorescent tubing. The French have demonstrated that the substitution of rubber for steel car wheels vastly increases the comfort of passengers by reducing noise and vibration; it also reduces the amount of metallic dust and thereby the incidence of lung ailments among subway motormen and conductors. Of course, none of these improve-

---

millionaires and to multinational corporations for use by their top executives as occasional *pieds-à-terre*. Olympic Tower is unlikely to do much for the preservation of Fifth Avenue as a residential shopping center.

ments would necessarily make the subways safer, but at least they would make it possible for subway riders to be mugged in more pleasant surroundings.

The substitution of pleasant surroundings for ugliness and grime might have a slight but beneficial effect on the crime rate, for in truth more crimes are committed in subways than in airports or bus stations. No doubt there are many reasons for the higher subway crime rate, but among them is the fact that there is a primitive, violence-tinged atmosphere in the subway that is lacking elsewhere and that induces in some individuals aggressive behavior and in others anxiety and fright. Even those riders who are free from fear and foreboding do not find subway travel an enjoyable experience.

But the larger issue remains: can our cities be rescued from further decline and, if so, by what means? Whatever the definitive answer to these questions, there can be no doubt that the American city is worth saving, if only because there is no social entity or organism that can substitute for New York or Chicago or Los Angeles just as there is no social entity or organism that can take the place of London or Paris or Rome. Surely a world without these major centers of culture, history, and vitality would be a much poorer world indeed, one in which many people would not care to live at all. Would it were true that the cities were, somehow, self-renewing and immortal, but unfortunately William Jennings Bryan was very wrong to conclude: "Burn down your cities and leave our farms, and your cities will spring up again as if by magic; but destroy our farms and the grass will grow in the streets of every city in the country." If "your cities" are destroyed—the use of the possessive, while revealing of agrarian attitudes toward cities, is hardly out of date—there will be little else worth saving. The future of the city, in short, is inextricably bound up with the future of man, and if man himself survives, no doubt the city in some form will survive as well. As was noted earlier, the cities have always been with us and presumably always will be, although there may be sharp fluctuations of size and population as a consequence of wars or natural disasters. Still, as a warning, let us call the roster of cities that have disappeared or have never regained the status of former times. Carthage, Troy, Jaffa, Sparta, Thebes, Antioch, Daphne. . . .

6

The Uses of Crime and Violence

In his *Souvenirs d'égotisme* Stendhal with characteristic prescience foresaw a time when it would be conventional to hold the ruling classes responsible for crimes of thieves and murderers. The insight was worthy of Tocqueville, with whom the great French novelist was almost contemporary, but neither Stendhal nor Tocqueville anticipated a future when the American ruling classes would themselves develop a taste for crime and when, partly as a result, there would be no accepted definition of crime itself. We have not quite arrived at that point, but the currency of such terms as "Establishment violence," "white-collar crime," and "politicized crime," not to mention Watergate, suggests that the concept of a criminal act cannot be understood except in the context of a social and political as well as a moral and legal setting. Thus, to take an extreme example, few would care to argue that a crime has been committed if the act in question has been committed or approved by everyone, whatever the moral or legal code. As a group of leading European criminologists a few years ago remarked, "What makes a person a 'criminal' is not the fact that he has committed a crime—because noncriminals also have done that—but the fact that he has been caught, tried, convicted and punished."[1]

So defined, the criminal is almost always in the minority because most of those who commit criminal acts are never punished, and indeed a very large number are not even caught. Much white-collar crime is undetected as well as unpunished, and whether or not the Vietnam War can be counted as an example of Establishment

171

violence, except for Calley no one was punished for any crimes committed in Vietnam other than violations of civil law or military discipline. Most shootings of blacks, especially black militants, by police are not popularly regarded as crimes, and probably a good many Americans have heard other Americans sometimes say, with reference to looters, communists, student radicals, pushers, hippies, and other troublemakers: "If it was me, I'd take 'em out and shoot 'em!"

According to the late FBI Director J. Edgar Hoover in 1970, only 20 percent of serious crimes are solved by the police. If that percentage holds for crimes committed by political figures, police officers, and others, and unfortunately there is no way of being certain that it does, then the reported crimes and corrupt acts of authority figures are only a fraction of the total. Even so, the theft by New York police of millions of dollars' worth of confiscated heroin and other drugs in 1972, not to mention the accounts of extortion and bribery collected by the Knapp Commission, is impressive.

But even more impressive and by far more significant is evidence that indictments of political officeholders for criminal and corrupt acts have been increasing at least as fast as other kinds of crime. Between 1969 and 1974, according to Department of Justice sources, at least 400 elected and appointed officeholders excluding police officers and sheriffs were indicted by the Justice Department for violations of federal laws. In the state of New Jersey alone, between September, 1969, and January, 1973, 59 past or present public officials were indicted or convicted of federal-law violations, not counting seven who were found not guilty after being indicted.

Those indicted, although not necessarily convicted, included the Vice President of the United States, four present or former Cabinet secretaries, among whom was the Attorney General, several high-ranking presidential assistants, two United States judges (of a total of five who had ever been indicted by a grand jury), two United States Senators or former Senators, five Congressmen or former Congressmen, one former governor, and two State Supreme Court justices. Indictments were also handed down against present or past attorney generals of three states, seventeen mayors, ten state legislators, and nineteen state officials. Charges against these officeholders ranged from extortion, bribery, and perjury to mail fraud and the submission of false income-tax returns.*

Given the example set by a large number of public dignitaries, one of them as highly placed as the Vice President, and leaving aside the significance of the Nixon resignation, it is hardly remarkable that the crime wave in political office has been attended by an increased crime rate in general. In the same period of time as that covered by the more than 400 indictments of political officeholders, namely, from 1969 to 1974, the number of reported serious crimes rose from a little over 5,000,000 to approximately 8,600,000 and the crime rate from 2,483 offenses per 100,000 population to almost 4,100 offenses per 100,000 population.[2] But not all serious crimes are reported; law-enforcement agencies such as the FBI estimate that half to two-thirds of burglaries and robberies are never brought to the attention of the police.[3] This would suggest, since burglaries and robberies constitute the bulk of all serious crimes, that the actual crime total is at least 1,000,000 to 2,000,000 more than the number reported in an average year, 80 percent of which will not lead to any arrests and convictions. In 1971, for example, total arrests as a percentage of the number of serious crimes committed was 19 percent. Not all of those arrested were formally charged, and in the end only 4.8 percent were found guilty as charged. Of the remainder who were formally charged, 1 percent were found guilty of lesser offenses, 2.3 percent were acquitted or had their cases dismissed, 5 percent were juveniles referred to juvenile courts, and the rest were cases pending.

In other words, for every 100 serious crimes that were committed in 1971, only 5 persons excluding juveniles were convicted on the original charges. The range was from 23 persons for each 100 acts of murder or nonnegligent manslaughter to 2 persons for every 100 car thefts. Clearly, crime not only "pays" but in a number

---

*Based on information supplied by the Public Information Office of the Department of Justice. The indictment list furnished by the Public Information Office did not include the names of all officials charged with violating federal criminal statutes, and as noted above, indictments do not always lead to convictions. Because it may be years before a case is finally disposed of, no estimate can be made about the number of indicted officeholders who will finally be judged innocent or guilty. Apparently no private or public agency systematically collects information regarding the crimes and corrupt acts of public officials.

of instances pays well. Considering the billions of dollars' worth of property that is stolen and never recovered each year, there can be no doubt that the profession of criminal in the United States entails relatively high rewards at relatively low risk for those who enter it.*

Were this not the case, the crime rate, currently increasing at an annual rate of between 5 and 10 percent, would be less inflationary, but as it is, and taking into account the scarcity of jobs available to ghetto youth, there is every prospect of a continuing crime escalation. Most criminal acts involve property of some sort, and because blacks make up the bulk of the American poor, they account for more than 60 percent of robbery arrests and more than 50 percent of all arrests for crimes of violence.[4] Allowing for the fact that the ratio of blacks to whites is almost one to fifteen, the black arrest rate is almost four times the white arrest rate for all crimes, but for violent crimes it is more than eight times the white rate. Of all black arrests for crime, 30 percent are for violent crimes and 70 percent for crimes against property, whereas for white arrests the comparable figures are 14 percent and 86 percent.[†] The majority of those arrested for most crimes are white, and it is possible that a "true" crime rate, that is, a rate based on all criminal acts and not just those reported to police, would diminish

*Federal Bureau of Investigation, *Uniform Crime Reports for 1971.* In New York in 1970 the Vera Institute of Justice estimated that 177,000 defendants in nontraffic cases had not been brought to court during the preceding ten years because the police department's warrant squads had failed to execute court-ordered arrest warrants. (New York *Times,* June 19, 1970.) A Rand Institute study of the city's criminal-court system revealed that of 330,000 felony and misdemeanor charges in a single year, defendants in 15,000 could not be located, and that 80 percent of 55,000 felony charges were either dismissed or reduced to misdemeanor or violation status. (New York *Times,* March 28, 1970.) In 1972 only nine of 647 persons charged with rape, sodomy, or attempted rape in New York were convicted on the original charge. The charges against 342 were dismissed outright, and of the remainder, 147 were convicted on a lesser charge such as assault or disorderly conduct, 51 were released on probation, and 13 were released after being fined. (New York *Times,* November 13, 1973.)

†The total number of black arrests per 100,000 black population is about 2,087.1, compared with a white total per 100,000 white population of 525.3. The overall black-white arrest ratio of almost four to one reflects the balance between the property-crime black-white arrest ratio of slightly more than three to one and the much higher violent-crime arrest ratio that ranges from almost six to one for aggravated assault to more than fourteen to one for robbery.

the significance of black participation in crime.* Since black crime is frequently street crime, it is more "visible" than white crime, and blacks are more often arrested and dealt with severely by the criminal-court system. This no doubt partly accounts for the finding of a Philadelphia study that one of every two black youths born in 1945 had been arrested at least once before he was nineteen years old, whereas the corresponding figure for white boys was 28.6 percent.[5]

But while much crime is poverty related, a significant and increasing proportion of crime in the United States involves violence resulting in personal injury and some type of vandalism. Homicide, rape, assault upon teachers and destruction or defacement of school property, participation of teenagers and young adults in youth gangs, and outbreaks of mayhem without any apparent aim or motive—these and other crimes and delinquencies have been increasing faster than most types of crime against property. The most serious of all crimes, homicide, has increased to the point that it is now the seventh leading cause of death among all nonwhite males, and it ranks second, or just behind accidents, as a cause of death among black and white males between fifteen and twenty-four years of age.†

A growing proportion of these activities, moreover, have involved children—in at least one instance, children of four and two years of age, respectively, the former as murderer and the latter

---

*This may be what District Court Judge James B. Parsons had in mind when, in the course of sentencing five blacks for mail fraud, he warned blacks to avoid committing "slick white man's crimes" because they lacked the expertise necessary to commit such crimes and not be caught. Judge Parsons, who is black, listed the "white man's crimes" as counterfeiting, mail-fraud schemes, business and technological manipulations, large-scale embezzlement, jewel theft, and safecracking. These crimes, the judge added, "call for vast know-how in legitimate business, banking and technology. Because society has prevented Negroes from getting into that world, from developing sophisticated techniques and skills, Negroes go about such crimes in a crude way. . . . I don't feel that the police arrest Negroes faster for these types of crime than they would white men. It's that Negroes commit more faux pas out of inexperience in the legitimate field in which they are trying to perpetrate their fraud." (New York *Times*, May 4, 1969.)

†Dr. Stefan A. Pasternack in *Medical Tribune*, January 23, 1974. According to Pasternack, on "a typical day someone is wounded or killed by gunshot every 90 seconds." He estimates that more than 800,000 Americans have been "gunned down" since 1900.

as victim—and women.* If one effect of this burgeoning crime rate is that the average American has been or expects to be assaulted or robbed in any given twelve-month period, another consequence is that Americans in recent years have become the most armed people in the Western world.† In the six years 1964–1969 (published figures do not go beyond 1969), 24,-700,000 handguns, shotguns, and rifles were produced, imported, and sold in the United States.[6] Inasmuch as there is no reason to believe that the level of gun purchases has declined much, if at all, since 1969, and allowing for a certain amount of attrition, it seems reasonable to estimate that about one of every five men, women, and children in the country owns a gun of some type.

The increasing violence no doubt owes much to the decline of

*According to the FBI's *Uniform Crime Reports,* the increase in the rate of women arrested for serious crimes rose 246.2 percent from 1960 to 1972, as compared with the 81.7 percent increase in male arrests. For all crime the arrest-rate increase was 85.6 percent for women and 28.2 percent for men. In other words, the rate for such crimes as homicide, aggravated assault, robbery, and burglary, regarded as serious crime, committed by women increased more than three times as much as the rate for men. In 1974 the sharpest increase in crime was among juveniles and teenagers and in the suburbs and rural areas. Most crime, of course, continues to be city crime, but the popular impression that it is the largest cities that have the highest crime rate needs correction. The *Uniform Crime Reports* listing of city crime rates puts New York in eighth place for total crime. Of the top thirty metropolitan areas ranked in terms of crime, nine are in California and six are in Florida. In another study of city crime rates, however, New York was in thirteenth place for crimes of violence, with 36 such crimes per 1,000 residents aged twelve and over. The twelve other cities, in descending order, were Detroit; Denver; Philadelphia; Portland, Oregon; Baltimore; Chicago; Cleveland; Los Angeles; Atlanta; Dallas; Newark; and St. Louis. (From a survey conducted by the Census Bureau for the Law Enforcement Assistance Administration, reported in New York *Times,* April 15, 1974.)

†A Gallup Poll in 1973 reported that one of every three city residents and one of every five suburbanites were victims of crime in 1972. The difference between these figures and corresponding FBI statistics of 5.4 percent and 3.9 percent may be due to the fact that the Gallup report included all forms of vandalism; vandalism accounted for approximately a third of the crime-victim total. It also appeared, in keeping with earlier studies by criminologists, that perhaps as much as half of all crime is never reported by those who are its victims. Since the Gallup Poll did not show any difference between whites and blacks, both reporting percentages of 21—and it is well known that black ghettos are high crime areas—it must be assumed that much more than half of all crime in these areas is not notified to police.

the superego that was noted in an earlier chapter and related changes in the structure and role of the family. Perhaps, too, more complete and systematic reporting of certain crimes, such as rape, accounts in part for the increase.* Other factors, ranging from the Vietnam War to the "female reinforcement of male impulses toward violence . . . emasculation too often accomplished, intentionally or not, through the offices of women . . ." have been cited as causes, and in addition the alleged propensity of Americans to resort to violence whether the provocation be great or small.[7] There is evidence that children who lack affection and who are neglected or mistreated in early life are more prone to violence in later years than children who have been loved and cared for, and that certain kinds of brain damage, the effect of which is to disrupt normal patterns of electrical discharge in the temporal lobe and other parts of the brain, precipitate or promote violent behavior.[8] Population density and high-rise apartment construction have been linked to many types of sociopathological activity; there is evidence, for example, that men who commit violent crimes are more sensitive to the physical closeness of others than those who commit property crimes.[9] And millions of people, of course, believe that violence in human affairs and even war itself ebb and flow with the movement of the stars and the circulation of the planets.

Of all these hypotheses about the roots of violence, the most

*Nevertheless, there is no reason to believe that the increase in rape and other violent crimes is entirely due to more complete reporting. Between 1960 and 1970 the rate of forcible rape increased 90 percent as compared with an increase in murder of 60 percent. Aggravated assault in the same period rose 92 percent and robbery 186 percent. Between 1970 and 1972 the increase in reported rape was 21 percent, whereas murder and assault increased 14 percent and robbery only 5 percent. The rate of rape in the United States is twelve times as much as the rape rate in England and Wales and three times the Canadian rate. In the last several years the rise annually for reported rape in American cities, such as New York, has been substantial; the New York rate for the first four months of 1974 increased 16 percent over the same period in 1973. Attitudes toward women and other general explanations for rape hardly account for differences between countries or even differences between areas within a country. For reasons not clear, a woman's chances of being raped are three times as great in Chicago, Detroit, and Denver as in New York, Philadelphia, and Baltimore. (According to a study by the Law Enforcement Assistance Administration, reported in New York *Times,* April 15, 1974.)

persuasive in terms of evidence and applicability are those suggesting that the conditions of early life and the population density that is typical of urban poverty are crucial for the determination of future violence. Poverty alone does not produce violence, but a child who grows up not only poor but deprived as well of parental love is headed toward an antisocial adolescence and adulthood that may well include crime. If, further, the child is abused by his parents or siblings—and in recent years child abuse has been increasing—it is even more likely in later life that he will commit violent crimes.* When this ill treatment and extreme deprivation are experienced in a more or less segregated slum from which escape in the normal course is almost impossible, the likelihood becomes a practical certainty.

These and other conclusions have been established not only with reference to particular cases but on the basis of numerous experiments with animal colonies where conditions in some respects resembled those of America's urban ghettos. Rats, rabbits, monkeys, and cats that outgrow their living space become seriously disturbed and begin to behave in pathological fashion. Mothers neglect their young to the extent that most of their offspring do not survive; in rat colonies many of the helpless young and smaller rats are eaten by the larger males, some of which behave as tyrants, while others are treated as pariahs confined to the outskirts of the group. There is more disease, both physical and emotional, and a significantly higher mortality rate. Especially striking and relevant are certain changes in normal sexual behavior in the direction of hypersexuality. In the majority of stressful animal colonies studied, males compulsively seek to mate with unreceptive females, essentially the equivalent of rape, and with each other.†

---

*Almost twenty years ago an influential study of aggression in children found that "the way for parents to produce a nonaggressive child is to make abundantly clear that aggression is frowned upon and to stop aggression when it occurs, but to avoid punishing the child for his aggression." (Robert Sears, Eleanor E. Maccoby, and Harry Levin, "The Socialization of Aggression," in *Patterns of Child Raising* [New York: Row, Peterson, 1957], p. 266.) Perhaps the more urgent need now confronting the United States and other countries is to find ways of producing nonaggressive parents and adults from whom children can learn to be affectionate and nonaggressive toward others.

†On animal hypersexuality as a function of overcrowding, see John B. Calhoun, *Scientific American*, February, 1962. Galle *et al., op. cit.,* found that human population density, defined as the number of persons per room, may be the most important factor in the development of certain social pathologies such as juve-

Hypotheses generated by studies of child-raising patterns and population density may account not only for violence in the ghetto, where family life is brutalized or nonexistent, or for the higher rates of crime in America's high-rise cities with their overcrowding and anomie, but for the rising incidence of crime and violence everywhere. To be sure, American rates are higher than rates elsewhere, especially for violent crimes, and surely that reflects the economics as well as the psychology of racism. In addition, the decline of the family and the deterioration of the cities have been under way longer and have proceeded at a faster rate in the United States. But almost everywhere in the world, whether London, Paris, Cairo, Tel Aviv, or Moscow, crime and violence also have been increasing, and there, too, family life is becoming more fragile and the cities more inhospitable. By all the measures that correlate with pathological social behavior, that is, poverty and slum housing, the failure of superego development, the incidence of families without fathers, child abuse (some of which results in brain damage) and extreme deprivations of affection and nurturing, and a sense of futility and hopelessness about the future, most urban societies elsewhere are moving in the same direction as the United States with respect to crime and violence, and they may expect similar results.*

------

nile delinquency. In other experiments, such as those reported in the February, 1964, *Bulletin of Atomic Scientists,* stress-induced overactivity of the pituitary-adrenal system was associated with heart and liver disease, sexual deviation, and starvation in the presence of an abundant food supply. Calhoun's work with wild Norway rats suggested a relationship between population density and the neglect of the young. Rat mothers in overcrowded dens "forgot" how to build nests and care for their infants, most of which died before weaning. According to a report in *Medical Tribune* of January 30, 1974, in India, where rhesus monkeys are allowed to roam freely in both cities and rural areas, the city monkeys are ten to fifteen times more aggressive than the country monkeys.

*Thus in the Paris region between 1964 and 1970, according to *Le Monde,* murder and attempted murder rose from 176 to 255, holdups from 26 to 133, "robberies with violence in public places," from 1,231 to 2,751, and break-ins from 3,975 to 36,121. (*Le Monde Weekly,* March 25–31, 1971.) Violent crime in London increased 10 percent from 1970 to 1971, the largest percentile increases being recorded for robbery and rape. (New York *Times,* July 16 and August 27, 1972.) Of course, the total number of crimes committed annually in other countries remains small by American standards. In 1971 there were 177 murders in England and Wales, and in Tokyo in 1970, 213. Perhaps Tokyo is the safest of modern cities: in 1970 robberies totaled 474 as compared with 74,102 in New York!

Even the culture of make-believe violence that once was thought to be peculiarly American—the panoply of toys, sports, comic books, movies and television, cowboys and Indians, cops and robbers—has taken root abroad. In Bangkok a little boy, dressed in a cowboy suit, happily shoots any and all passersby with his toy revolver, while in London in 1971 the most popular television offerings included those American programs rated the "most violent," namely, *Mannix, The Untouchables, The Baron, I Spy,* and *Hawaii Five-0.*[10] The most popular American-made movies, such as *The Godfather, Dirty Harry, Straw Dogs,* and *A Clockwork Orange,* with their explicit renderings of rape, maiming, gouging, and murder, do as well in the export market as in our crime-ridden cities and suburbs, thereby suggesting that almost everywhere there is the same willingness to love, in the words of movie critic Pauline Kael writing about *A Clockwork Orange,* "the punk sadist . . . who gets kicks out of violence . . . [and who] makes you root for his foxiness, for his crookedness. . . ."* Even the American penchant for body-contact athletic events has spread overseas, where the Japanese have taken up with enthusiasm football, our foremost spectator sport.† No doubt it is only a matter of time until such American neologisms for violence as trashing, wasting,

---

*"For most of the movie," Ms. Kael continues, "we see [Alex] tortured and beaten and humiliated. So when his bold aggressive punk's nature is restored to him it seems not a joke on all of us but, rather, a victory in which we share . . . . The look in Alex's eyes at the end tells us that he isn't just a mechanized choiceless sadist but prefers sadism and knows he can get by with it. Far from being a little parable about the dangers of soullessness and the horrors of force whether employed by individuals against each other or by society in 'conditioning,' the movie becomes a vindication of Alex, saying that the punk was a free human being and only the good Alex was a robot." (*New Yorker,* January 1, 1972.)

†Would football, our most favored sport, be as popular if it were less violent? In an average year most men who begin the season as starting quarterbacks are disabled by broken arms, legs, and collarbones, concussions, torn ligaments or cartilages, and other injuries. Many of the players who inflict these injuries, mainly the linemen, believe that pay raises depend on their ability to "rack up" key men on the opposing team, which requires them to survive bruising encounters with the defending "bodyguards," whose average weight is as much as 250 pounds. As a result, experienced players tend to look "like somebody who was in the front seat of a bad automobile wreck and was then treated by an old country doctor." (Bill Surface, "Pro Football's Broken Men," *New York Times Magazine,* October 26, 1969.)

and fragging, which are still another legacy of Vietnam, are wide-ly used expressions in German, French, and Italian, among other languages.

The American willingness to accept and even condone violence in behalf of certain ends can also be increasingly found in other Western countries, but, again, nowhere as much as in the United States. Most people everywhere probably would resort to violence and even killing in defense of themselves and their families; in one University of Michigan study of American men 89 percent felt that killing another person was permissible in self-defense, and 93 percent accepted killing in defense of one's family. But 58 percent endorsed killing in defense of one's house, and almost a third expressed the view that the police in confronting ghetto ri-ots should "sometimes" shoot to kill, while 61 percent agreed that the police should shoot at rioters, although not to kill. Significant-ly, 85 percent regarded looting and 65 percent burglary as vio-lence, but only 35 percent viewed the police shooting looters as vi-olence. More than a third, on the other hand, or 38 percent, were on the opinion that student protest is a form of violence, and more than half, or 58 percent, regarded draft-card burning as violence.[11]

These responses suggest that a majority of Americans support violence to the point of killing when it is in self-defense or in or-der to protect property and that large numbers favor violence by the police and other agencies when, in their view, there is a threat to established institutions. In effect, there is a disposition to accept violence by and in behalf of the Establishment and a tendency to condemn protest and demonstrations when they are perceived to be anti-Establishment. Such inclinations make it possible to un-derstand why the public in the late sixties was in general tolerant of the rough treatment accorded protesting blacks and students by the police in many instances and opposed and hostile to the protestors themselves. As the Michigan study pointed out, men "who rate students or blacks as untrustworthy or troublemakers as a whole, tend to condone police violence. . . ." Given the sizable number of Americans who view blacks and students with suspi-cion, the police in some sections of the country could conclude at the time of the anti-Vietnam War demonstrations that they en-joyed a free hand in dealing with alleged rioters and lawbreakers, and indeed there were few efforts anywhere to punish those re-

sponsible for the worst excesses in the police treatment of protestors.

In a society that more or less approves of Establishment violence, those who are determinedly against the existing order, for
whatever reasons, will increasingly exercise violence to bring
about social change. The situation of America is particularly unstable in this respect because while all Western societies must deal
with growing discontent and unrest as a result of their failure to
solve crucial problems, the prospect that dissent in the United
States will take a violent turn is more pronounced. To begin with,
there is no viable radical political party and no important economic or social movement advocating major change. Both of the leading political parties—Gore Vidal has termed them the Property
Party—are consensus parties of the moderate middle rather than
ideological parties of the Right and Left. In fact, from the perspective of European political history with its tradition of monarchical, clerical, Tory, Whig, socialist, and communist politics,
the Democratic and Republican parties can fairly be classified as
conservative parties dedicated to the preservation in its essentials
of the status quo. Both parties have looked backward in American
history for their inspiration, both have rejected ideology and the
dogma of class politics, and both have repeatedly tamed, disarmed, and swallowed up the occasional radicalizing impulse
from within and challenge from without. The Republican Party,
to be sure, has always been the more Tory of the two, but the
Democratic Party even at its most liberal moments has never gone
much beyond the pragmatic reformist philosophy of the great
British conservative Edmund Burke.[12]

As a consequence, the increasing tendency of those who insist
on the need for radical change, but who despair of such change
taking place within the existing political framework, will be to
work underground and engage in acts of political violence. Thus
far the underground organization of revolutionaries has been ru-
dimentary, and their acts of violence, such as assassinations,
bombings, and kidnappings, sporadic. In fact, the behavior of
revolutionaries in the United States, unlike that of revolutionaries
elsewhere, has always been characterized much more by restraint
than by daring. Few political figures have been assassinated for
political reasons, and it is not yet certain that any kidnapping has
been carried through by revolutionaries. While there was much

civil unrest between 1963 and 1968, the violence of those years accounted for only 220 lives, of whom twenty were civil-rights workers and most of the rest blacks; the death rate, therefore, was 1.1 per million population as compared with a European civil-strife rate of 2.4 per million.[13] Clearly the incidence and fear of violent civil unrest were exaggerated in recent years, and reports of imminent revolution, like the famous account of Mark Twain's death, were at the very least premature.

Little is now heard of the Black Panther Party or the more recent Symbionese Liberation Army, but even when they were more active, the Panthers, despite the rhetoric of Eldridge Cleaver and Huey P. Newton, were never fully committed to revolution. The SLA apparently never enrolled more than a handful of members, many of whom were white women. Neither movement was led well, and neither was able to mobilize even a fraction of the black community. The organizations of students that existed in the sixties, such as the Students for a Democratic Society, were even less effective, and in any case, one tends to doubt that students, who inevitably leave behind their status as students as they graduate out and into society, could ever form a genuine revolutionary vanguard. Unfortunately for those older Americans with fantasies about the "greening of America" and regeneration at the fountain of the nation's youth, students do not remain students in the same way that workers remain workers or blacks remain black. Student "revolutions" for the most part are "soft" revolutions motivated more by psychological factors than objective needs and almost always relatively short-lived. Ultimately students accept and even welcome the fact that they are a privileged class.

Short of a serious and prolonged depression much worse than the Depression of the thirties, or defeat in a major war, or successful efforts to resegregate society, Americans in any significant numbers will not turn to revolutionary solutions. The probability is also low that the communist and socialist parties can have even peripheral influence on politics, and if leaders as brilliant as Lenin were to appear, they, like Lenin himself for more than a score of years, would have to await their opportunity. Of course, as the concluding chapter tries to make clear, the possibility of a massive economic and social collapse is not so remote as to be ruled out, but in that event the consequent political shift is likely to be not to the Left but to the Right.

The immediate prospect, however, is for an increasing number of severe and violent disruptions of urban life patterns, mostly undertaken by isolated or small groups of individuals, justified in terms of revolutionary symbols. In a society prone to inaction rather than radical social change, the politics of disruption carries a powerful appeal not only to frustrated political activists, alienated youngsters, and those serving life sentences in the ghetto but to all those of whatever class and status whose essential condition is rootlessness. For the rootless in America, that is, people who have no fixed place in society and no sense of belonging, are not now entirely disposed to exercise their traditional options of crime and suicide. Some of them are gradually discovering that revolution and disruption are not only available options here as elsewhere in the world but that as options they are preferable to crime, suicide, and other forms of self-destruction toward which the American rootless have always been drawn.*

Thus far, and considering the large and increasing number of rootless persons, the disruptions inflicted upon urban society have been minimal, although there is a sense in which crime, inasmuch as it generates widespread fear among citizens and tends to restrict their movements and general freedom of action, can be regarded as disruption. In 1968 a Gallup Poll reported for the first time since scientific polling began in the mid-thirties that "crime and lawlessness" were viewed by the public as the foremost domestic problem facing the nation and second only to Vietnam among problems in general. Since then the crime issue has seldom been seen as other than the top problem and one that steadily worsens. A Gallup Poll in 1972 found that six of every ten women and 41 percent of both men and women were afraid to go out alone at night.

The disruptive possibilities of urban guerrilla warfare extend far beyond the occasional snipings and shootings of police officers or such a *cause célèbre* as the ransoming and recruitment into the SLA, whether voluntary or forced, of Patricia Hearst in 1974. Nor does it require much imagination to list the disturbances which, if carried through successfully, would enable revolutionaries to

---

*Suicide as used here includes addiction to alcohol and drugs as well as self-inflicted death. But the suicide rate as such has been rising steadily among blacks and youth.

bring urban life to a gradual halt. The demonstrated vulnerability of cities to power failures may invite efforts to blow up generators and power transmission lines. Since it takes only a few stalled cars or trucks to block completely a major street or throughway at peak travel time, liberationists may choose to disable vehicles and to sabotage commuter trains and buses. Hit-and-run marksmen, stationed at the road approaches to major cities and shooting from rooftops and windows, could cause terrified motorists to abandon their cars and thereby bring traffic to a halt. Attempts to contaminate reservoirs and food supplies, firebomb airports and commercial centers, and make meeting places of all types unsafe would have far-reaching disruptive effects on the nation's economy as well as on city life. In other words, the basic routines of urban society could be effectively terminated or at least severely curtailed by a small band of dedicated revolutionary guerrillas even if they stopped far short of adapting to American conditions most of the terrorist techniques developed by the Irish Republican Army or the Palestinian liberation movement.

Just as we can confidently assume, given the worsening anomie and rootlessness of American society, that crime and suicide rates will continue to rise, so we can assume that the disruptions will initially take place wherever economic and social conditions, characterized by such problems as high unemployment, deteriorating housing, and hostile police, are perceived to be intolerable and where not everyone affected by them has been so demoralized as to make action impossible.* Because the ranks of those who will become the future Oswalds, Rays, and Bremers have also been growing, assassinations of prominent citizens will become more numerous. This is not to imply that in the past they have been infrequent; since 1865 one of every five Presidents, or four altogether, has been killed by an assassin, and one of every three has experienced an attempt on his life. If the average time between assassinations remains unchanged, that is, twenty-seven years, by 1990 one more President will be dead at the hands of an assassin,

*Surveys of twenty cities in which civil disorders took place in 1967 showed that the chief grievance in fourteen of these cities was police practices, in seventeen cities unemployment or underemployment, and in fourteen inadequate housing. Fewer than half the cities reported grievances connected with education, recreation, or the functioning of the political system. (Source: *American Almanac for 1974*, p. 151.)

and by 1980 an attempt, successful or otherwise, will have been made on the life of a President.* It is probable that the ratio of ideological to nonideological motivations in the acts of assassins will rise.

The continuing high level of kidnappings and bank robberies, whether for personal profit or as fund-raising ventures in behalf of revolutionary causes, will increase. In the four years 1969 through 1972 approximately forty-five persons were convicted each year on kidnapping charges, but in 1973 the number grew to seventy-one. The FBI in the first two months following the disappearance of Patricia Hearst reported ten "major" kidnappings, "major" being defined as a case the FBI pursues to the end rather than turns over to state or local authorities.[14] The number of bank robberies rose 409 percent between 1960 and 1970, more than any other type of robbery; one wonders whether a growing proportion of these robberies are undertaken for political reasons.

Since there is ample evidence that many Americans are willing to pay, and pay well, for protection from crime, as witness the millions spent annually on alarm systems, guard dogs, private security agents, and other safety measures, an increasing number of citizens will resort to payoffs and bribery to safeguard themselves and their families. Indeed, all professions, trades, and businesses, legal or illegal, concerned with "protection" should flourish.†

Still more certain is the prospect of increasing political corruption if for no other reason than the politician's eagerness and the voter's resigned willingness to accept the fact that officeholding is or can be made to be one of the most rewarding of enterprises. For who can doubt, after the *enrichissez-vous* scandals of the

---

*The assassinated Presidents since 1865 were, in addition to Lincoln, Garfield in 1881, McKinley in 1901, and Kennedy in 1963. Attempts were made against Theodore Roosevelt, in 1912, President-elect Franklin D. Roosevelt in 1933, and Harry Truman in 1950. Strictly speaking, Theodore Roosevelt as well as Franklin D. Roosevelt should not be included since in 1912 Theodore Roosevelt was a former President campaigning for reelection.

†In 1974 youth gangs in northern Brooklyn were extorting as much as $1,500 weekly "protection" money from some 200 merchants. "We can't prove a thing," said a police lieutenant, because storekeepers "are afraid to death of these kids. They don't make an official complaint." In return for their money, businessmen were "protected" from fires, broken windows, and destructive fights on their premises. (New York *Times,* February 25, 1974.)

Nixon-Agnew Administration, that a good many Americans who go into politics still do so, as they did in Lord Bryce's time, as a means of personal gain? Now, as almost a century ago, much of the public believes that the politician who dies broke is almost as rare as the whore who departs this life *virgo intacta*. As Illinois Secretary of State Paul Powell once put it—Powell himself was worth more than $3,000,000 when he died, although his salary had never exceeded $30,000 a year—"There's only one thing worse than a defeated politician, and that's a broke politician."[15] Perhaps the average American, like the average policeman, according to the Knapp Commission testimony of police officer David Durk, is "convinced that he lives and works in the middle of a corrupt society, that everybody is getting theirs and why shouldn't he, and that if somebody cared about corruption, something would have been done about it a long time ago."[16]

The honest politician may have as difficult a time of it as the honest cop. In 1972 corruption was uncovered in the police departments and sheriffs' offices in at least twenty-three states and the District of Columbia, and a distinguished Yale sociologist specializing in police studies expressed his "conviction that there is extensive corruption in almost every major and many medium-sized police departments in the United States."[17] The more than 400 federal indictments mentioned earlier embraced public officials, not including police officers and sheriffs, in fifteen states and the District of Columbia. If for every such indictment there are four corrupt acts not detected and brought to trial, as is the case with serious crimes—and no one can doubt that political corruption is much more difficult to detect and investigate—then the total of indictable corrupt acts and violations of federal law committed in the five-year period 1969–1974 was at least 1,600 and involved many more than fifteen states. Moreover, neither indictment figure includes officeholders prosecuted by states for violations of state laws.

But even if the known total of indictments was not 400 or even 4,000 but 40,000, it is highly unlikely that outraged citizens would begin to march on their state capitols. By the midsummer of 1974, Gallup Polls reported, almost half the electorate was bored by Watergate and had begun to lose interest in the proceedings. Their reaction to Watergate and to the corruption issue as such is reminiscent of the response of the titled British lady at the turn of the century who, when told that the British servant class was behaving in an immoral manner, responded that she didn't care what they did as long as they didn't do it in the streets and frighten the horses. Like the noble lady, what Americans care about is what happens in the streets, especially if it is crime, and understandably they feel much more threatened by crime and civil disruptions than by corruption. Indeed, they probably would accept much more corruption if, somehow, more corruption meant less crime. When you are being followed on a dark street at night, they would argue, any cop will do, even a corrupt one. In America in the seventies the wish to be safe in one's home or on the street is considerably stronger than the desire to have an honest man in the White House or, for that matter, anywhere else in the government.

Politicians and the police, it appears, can be forgiven almost every shortcoming but indifference or laxity toward crime. Because this is understood at City Hall and police headquarters, although not in circles that would reform both, the increasing professionalization of the police is being accompanied by an intensification of methods used to combat violent crime. The professionalization, in any case, has been largely confined to raising educational requirements and standards for recruitment; in a number of cities police applicants are examined by psychiatrists or receive some sort of psychological screening. Many communities with large minority populations require their police to attend lectures and courses dealing with what is euphemistically termed "community relations," that is, the causes and manifestations of minority-group discontent and ways to avoid provoking it needlessly when the police are operating in ghetto areas. As a consequence, many observers feel, the relations between police departments and blacks, in such major cities as New York, Los Angeles, and Detroit, have improved in recent years.

On the other hand, low minority representation, incompetence, and poor work performance remain urgent police problems. A survey published in 1974 showed that, despite efforts to increase minority representation on police forces, only 6 percent of police officers belonging to the surveyed 493 departments were blacks or other minorities, and if Washington, D.C., and Hawaii, both with large minority representations, were eliminated, the percentage dropped to 4.* All but 6 percent of departments require no more than a high school diploma for employment, and almost half are willing to hire persons who have been convicted of adult misdemeanors.†

The police, like other Americans, have been demanding more and better protection against the possibility of violence, in particular, weapons and other equipment that will reduce the toll of police fatalities, which rose from 48 in 1960 to 187 in 1971. Police unions and fraternal organizations have been insisting that officers on patrol be equipped with shotguns as well as automatic weapons, bulletproof cars, armed helicopters, and more sophisticated electronic detection devices. In some instances police squads have resorted to equipping themselves with weapons specifically banned, such as machine guns, automatic rifles, and handguns more powerful than the regulation .38-caliber revolver that is supplied by most jurisdictions, while in others, and despite protests from minority groups, orders have been relaxed to permit police to switch to the more deadly .357 magnum handgun and to use hollow-point bullets.**

---

*In the fifty largest cities, however, 9 percent are blacks; in Atlanta in 1974, 20 percent of the police force was made up of blacks. In contrast, only 1.5 percent of state police are black, and another 1.5 percent are Hispanics, Indians, and other minorities. Alabama has the largest percentage of black state policemen, with Maryland second. (New York *Times*, December 10, 1974.)

†The survey by the Police Foundation, a Ford Foundation-supported police research organization, was reported in the Washington *Post*, April 21, 1974. While some cities, such as Los Angeles, will not accept men who score lower than 110 in IQ tests, other cities including New York have experienced a downward trend in average IQ scores of police recruits. Average scores of 107.7 in 1962 had declined to only 105.7 by 1967, but two years later, in 1969, the average was down to 98.2. There is no agreement among police experts, however, that high IQ is necessary for effective performance of police duties. (New York *Times*, July 23, 1970.)

**In 1974 the .357 magnum was being used by an undetermined number of police departments and, in addition, the New York, New Jersey, and Connecticut state police, the FBI, and the Treasury Department. Unlike regular bullets, hollow-point bullets hitting a human target expand to almost twice their size in the first two inches of flesh, thus inflicting much more damage. According to the American Civil Liberties Union, hollow-point or "dumdum" bullets are used by police in Massachusetts, Virginia, Texas, Tennessee, Wisconsin, California, Mississippi, Washington, Connecticut, Pennsylvania, and Hawaii. (New York *Times*, October 27, 1974, and January 16, 1975.)

The police also appear to be taking fewer risks in dealing with activists and revolutionaries, especially black ones, and in some cities to be operating on the principle that bullet-induced cardiac arrest is superior to all other forms of arrest. The 1969 deaths from police gunfire of Illinois Black Panther leaders Fred Hampton and Mark Clark, both of whom were in bed at the time and possibly asleep, may have been the result of an ambush, according to a subsequent investigation, and the deaths of other Panthers among the more than thirty who have been killed since 1967 smack more of police executions than the outcomes of gun battles. The shootout in May, 1974, between six SLA members and the Los Angeles police, during which the six died, involved 410 police officers, twenty-nine of whom were firing weapons, an official police report later revealed. Clearly the police were taking no chances.[18]

No doubt it is inevitable, although regrettable, that increasing crime and violence should be accompanied by increasingly violent means to combat them, but new and more powerful police weapons or the Nixon-Agnew call for "an end to permissiveness" (a call issued before permissiveness ended for them) are not likely to have much adverse effect on the crime rate. Nor will vigilantism of the type advocated by the National Rifle Association and Attorney General John Mitchell in 1970 or the murder of drug pushers and other criminals by underground law-and-order organizations make homes secure and the streets safe.[19] Despite claims to the contrary, no test of children as young as six to eight years of age can predict that they will become delinquents and criminals even if there are tendencies toward misbehavior, and even if there were such tests, no one can say how they could and should be used to prevent crime.*

*In 1969 Dr. Arnold A. Hutschnecker, who was and perhaps still is Nixon's occasional physician, recommended to Nixon that all six- to eight-year-old children, and possibly all children, be tested for "delinquent tendencies." At that time, apparently, Dr. Hutschnecker suggested that children showing such tendencies should become involved in "After School Programs" and be given group therapy. More time was needed, he told Nixon, "in order to determine the most effective and least costly method . . . to detect . . . violent and homicidal tendencies." In a New York *Times* article of October 2, 1970, on which this account is based, Dr. Hutschnecker, an internist, described himself as a fellow of the American Society of Psychoanalytic Physicians, and in press reports he is often referred to as a psychiatrist. So far as is known, his medical training has never included either psychiatry or psychoanalysis.

While most Americans, according to many polls, favor stiffer punishments including the death sentence for those who are guilty of crimes, especially violent crimes, there are many reasons to believe that these measures, too, fail to provide a solution. Prison terms, partly because of the primitive and brutal conditions obtaining in most prisons, tend to confirm those sentenced in their criminal and antisocial tendencies, and the longer the sentence, the more hardened such behavior becomes. Rehabilitation efforts, according to criminologists, are a farce even in the best of penitentiaries and a total travesty in those, the majority, that range from bad to worse. Capital punishment has not been shown to discourage the commission of violent crimes or to have much effect on the homicide toll one way or the other. Although permissiveness is widely regarded as a major cause of the soaring violent-crime rate, it is cruel and abusive treatment of children, as was earlier suggested, not permissiveness, that significantly correlates with violence.

Indeed, the evidence suggests that prison sentences should be reduced, not increased, or abolished altogether. For the condition of almost all of America's 400 prisons and 40,000 jails and the treatment accorded their inmates are such as to make one hope that Dostoevsky was wrong in declaring in *The House of the Dead* that "the degree of civilization in a society can be judged by entering its prisons." The point is not only that the average prison cell is small, dingy, and bare of any furnishings except the essential cot, sink, and toilet, or that a typical meal consists of rice, peas, chocolate pudding, and Kool-Aid (this was lunch one day recently in the Bronx jail), or even that in many prisons punishment for rule infractions, however minor, is cruel and sadistic. All this is bad enough, but the worst feature of prison life is that it succeeds in destroying forever in most of its victims whatever is left of their humanity and decency and eventually returns to the streets not persons who have improved or who are capable of improvement but total human wreckage.

The dehumanizing process is such, in fact, as to almost justify substituting "is designed to destroy" for "succeeds in destroying." In California's Soledad Correctional Training Facility—the name is both ironic and suggestive of Orwell's "Newspeak" in *1984*—a section known as "O" wing houses in isolation men who have violated rules or who have difficulties with other prisoners. There the cells measure ten feet by six feet, and the inmates are fed through a slot in the door. They are allowed out of their cells for one hour of exercise a day and are not permitted to read anything other than religious and legal material. In principle "O" wing inmates are there only a relatively short time; in practice a prisoner may spend six months or more in an "O" wing cell. Some of these cells, known as holes, are reserved for those regarded as "troublemakers" by the guards. The holes are smaller than other cells, contain no cot or other furnitue, and do not release their prisoners, who see no visitors and receive no mail, even for an hour's exercise.

Each year in America's prisons many hundreds of inmates and guards are killed or injured in riots, fights, brawls, and assaults. At Soledad an average of between five and ten prisoners and their keepers, but always many more of the former than the latter, die of violence each year. The deaths at Attica of twenty-nine inmates and ten guards held as hostages in September, 1971, were exceptional, but the deaths of more than 100 California prisoners and guards, along with fifteen inmates and their custodians in West Virginia, in a recent three-year period were not. Prison authorities account for some of the inmate deaths by saying that the guards sometimes must shoot to kill in order to prevent an escape, as allegedly happened in the case of black militant George Jackson at Soledad.

A prisoner who is not beaten or shot to death by guards is not necessarily safe from harm and abuse. The guards and convict trustees may extort money from him if he has any, in return for extra cigarettes or favors, or he may be cheated, as happened recently at Mattawan State Hospital for the Criminally Insane, by being deliberately overcharged or made to pay for fictitious purchases at the commissary. In many penal institutions the prisoners themselves administer "discipline" and determine who is to be punished and who is to receive special privileges as a reward for good behavior. Even well-administered prisons cannot do much about voluntary and involuntary homosexuality, given the universal practice in America, unlike that of Mexico and some other countries, of denying male and female prisoners any opportunity for heterosexual satisfactions. In many institutions younger prisoners, especially if they are physically attractive, may be raped or threatened with rape unless they submit to older inmates, and even without the threat they may involve themselves with someone more influential and knowledgeable about prison ways simply to make their years in the "pen" as livable as possible. The homosexual problem, of course, would be almost nonexistent if all American prisons instead of just a few followed the Swedish example of permitting men to visit their families every other month and to spend private hours each week with their wives or girlfriends. Certainly homosexuality would be less important if prisoners, like those in Denmark, were given access to pornography as an encouragement to masturbation.*

If, somehow, a prison inmate survives the years of inhuman treatment to emerge, at the conclusion of his sentence, relatively intact in mind and body, society makes it all but impossible for him to lead a decent law-abiding life. In most states he cannot work at any civil-service job or any employment that requires licensing, bonding, evidence of good character, or a security check. Usually he is not allowed to handle money or other valuables, and he needs special permission to practice a profession. To tide him over until he finds a job, which may take weeks or often months, he is supplied, as a rule, with one suit, a sum of money rarely exceeding $50, and, if he is a parolee, the name of his parole officer, to whom he must report weekly and from whom he requires permission to drive a car, travel, drink alcoholic beverages, and marry. But however long it takes him to find employment, and it need

---

*Since 1970 Danish prisoners aged fifteen and older have been supplied with all types of pornography including sadistic literature. Although initially there were fears that inmates would be "overstimulated to excessive sexual behavior," the result of providing "adequate psychosexual stimulants . . . [was] salutary. . . . Prisoners no longer complain of sexual problems. We have demonstrated that pornography leads to phantasy, not . . . objectionable action." (Dr. Berl Hutchinsky of the Institute of Criminal Justice, University of Copenhagen, in *Medical Tribune*, February 20, 1974.) The American "solution" is, in some cases, to administer electroshock therapy to jailed homosexuals in an effort to "cure" them and in almost all cases to ban books containing any reference to sex. Some prisoners in Massachusetts, California, and a few other states are permitted to take occasional furloughs home or have private visits from their wives, but the only American state prison which gives men and women prisoners any opportunity to be together, the minimum-security Massachusetts Correctional Institution at Framingham, prohibits sexual relations, defined to include kissing in public, even between those married to each other. The only body contact permitted is hand holding. By contrast, even maximum-security prisons in Sweden, such as Kumla, permit prisoners to have sexual intercourse with visitors, including prostitutes.

hardly be emphasized that ex-convicts are not the first hiring choices of most employers, in many states he is ineligible for unemployment benefits. No wonder that about half of all those released on parole return to prison within five years.[20]

A longer term in prison, in other words, is hardly a solution. The question of stiffer sentences, moreover, reduces to the question of: stiffer sentences for whom? Increasing the length of sentences would simply add to the gross unfairness of the existing law-enforcement system, in accordance with which most of those who commit criminal acts are not caught and those who are caught receive vastly different sentences for the same or similar offenses. A New York study of criminal justice, for example, found that Mafia racketeers brought to trial had their cases dismissed or were acquitted five times as often as other defendants, and of those who were convicted, 46 percent received suspended sentences or were fined.* The day following the sentencing of former Vice President Spiro T. Agnew to three years' unsupervised probation and a $10,000 fine for failure to pay taxes on income received in the form of bribes, a man in California was sentenced to seventy days in jail for fishing without a license and having in his possession seven striped bass under the legal size limit.[21]

In fact, distortions in trial judgments and the severity of sentences appear to be increasing. By such methods as plea bargaining, so extensively used in the Watergate trials, many of those charged with criminal acts can ensure nominal sentences for themselves or verdicts that amount to no more than reprimands. Still another device, which with exaggeration could be regarded as a sophisticated form of jury tampering, is the selection of jury members in accordance with psychological principles and other factors so as to produce in the end a jury decision favorable to the defendant. The acquittal of black militant Angela Davis in 1972 and Nixon Cabinet secretaries Mitchell and Stans in 1974 owed something, perhaps even a good deal, to the jury-selection advice

*The study by the State Joint Legislative Committee on Crime covered the period 1960–1970, during which there were 1,762 cases in state courts involving organized crime. On the same day, before the same judge, in the same court, in 1967 a Mafia chieftain with a criminal record dating back to 1925 was fined $250 for bribery of a police officer (to which he had pleaded guilty), while a young Puerto Rican was sentenced to a maximum of five years in the Elmira Reformatory for robbing a drugstore. (New York *Times*, September 25, 1972.)

received by defense lawyers from five black psychologists in the first case and to the ability of the defense in the second case deliberately to choose jurors who, with one exception, were from that section of the population that heavily supported the President.* Such tactics, of course, are not guaranteed, and certainly it is not enough, as the guilty verdict in the trial of Nixon aide John Ehrlichmann demonstrated, for defense attorneys, some of whom are black, to confront a jury that is all or predominantly black. The point, however, is not that juries can be, in effect, brainwashed by a variety of subtle techniques of manipulation but that verdicts of guilt or innocence, as well as the length of sentences, often depend less on the facts of the case than on techniques of manipulation.

But even if justice were foolproof, which it can never be in any epoch because of human fallibility, punishment, however severe, cannot be expected to do more than satisfy society's ancient demand, sanctified first by religion and later by law, that an eye pay for an eye and a tooth for a tooth. Even that statement, however, is too simple, because no society has ever insisted that all eyes, much less all teeth, are equal. Many a thief has been celebrated in fable and song, and more than a few, as recent events remind us, have been rewarded with high honors and office; many a murderer or assassin has gone on to become a national hero. Our shock, therefore, should be reduced when we read that a convicted burglar has become an idol in parts of the youth community or that a suspect in twenty-five slayings has become a civil-rights symbol to

---

*In the Davis trial the psychologists, who were present in the courtroom, advised not only on prospective jurors but on how Ms. Davis should present herself to the jury. (New York *Times,* September 2, 1972.) The Mitchell-Stans defense, drawing on a "jury profile" prepared by the head of a "communications think-tank," sought to select a jury made up of blue-collar workers who were primarily Catholic, earned an average of $8,000 to $10,000 annually, and read the New York *Daily News.* There were no Jews or what the "think-tank" president called "limousine liberals" on the jury, but instead persons "who would associate the dour Mr. Mitchell with John Wayne." (New York *Times,* May 5, 1974.) The "first effort to make systematic use of the social sciences in jury selection," according to *Science,* occurred in Harrisburg, Pennsylvania, in 1971 in connection with the trial of Father Philip Berrigan for allegedly conspiring to kidnap Henry Kissinger. Since 1971 techniques similar to those used in Harrisburg have been employed in the Wounded Knee, Attica, and Ellsberg-Russo trials, among others. (*Science,* September 20, 1974.)

young Chicanos.[22] In a country where being black, Puerto Rican, Indian, or Mexican is in itself grounds for suspicion when a crime has been committed and where many other citizens have at one time or another broken the law but escaped punishment with regard to their income-tax returns, shoplifting, or pilferage, who is to say that this person is a criminal and that person a victim?

For in many court proceedings it is not a man or a woman who is on trial but poverty and discrimination that are being tried, and it is these that should be found guilty and sentenced. In the absence of such a verdict, violence for some, like sex for others, can be viewed as affirmative acts in a society that no longer has sufficient confidence or will to affirm itself. Or perhaps "gentleness." Frantz Fanon, Sartre wrote in an introduction to Fanon's *The Wretched of the Earth,* "shows clearly that this irrepressible violence is neither sound and fury, nor the resurrection of savage instincts, nor even the effect of resentment: it is man recreating himself. . . . No gentleness can efface the marks of violence; only violence itself can destroy them."[23]

Those concerned about crime would do well to ponder, not so much whether Fanon and Sartre are correct about some uses of violence but whether Sartre is right about the word "only."

7

Toward Another "Final Solution"?

T he theme of a popular joke in America concerns a man who fakes being hit by a Cadillac, as a result of which he pretends to be crippled for life. He successfully sues the wealthy owner of the Cadillac and collects a huge sum of money as compensation. The attorney for the Cadillac owner, however, is suspicious, and the attorney tells the "cripple" that when he leaves the hospital, he will be followed by an agent for the attorney, and the moment the agent sees him walking again the attorney will reopen the case. "Ah," says the "cripple" from his hospital bed, "when I leave here I will be carried to an ambulance on a stretcher, and in the ambulance I will be transported to JFK, and from there I will be flown still on the stretcher to Orly in Paris and transported from there in another ambulance to Le Bourget, where I will be carried onto another airplane and flown to Lourdes. When I get to Lourdes, your agent is going to witness one of the greatest miracles of all time!"

The joke, of course, is a variety of ethnic humor, and the "cripple" in most versions is Jewish or Irish or Italian or Scots. He is never black, presumably because a black body, whatever its state, is worth much less than a white body, and hence, if the "cripple" in the joke were black, the humor of the story would be sharply reduced. But just how little a black life is worth most Americans have no reason to know unless they work for insurance companies or are policemen or prison guards. They know, especially the insurance companies, and thus, when a six-year-old boy whose mother was on welfare was killed by an automobile while running across the street, the insurance company offered to settle the case for $800. The boy's mother and her lawyer rejected the offer but accepted the second and final offer of $2,000. When writer Elliott Liebow protested the award, he was told by the lawyer, "You've got to face the facts. Insurance companies and juries just don't pay as much for a Negro child." He might have added, says Liebow, especially a Negro child on welfare.[1]

The accident that killed six-year-old Anthony Davis was not the fault of the driver, but then there are the other "accidents" and the remarks that accompany them. When two black students were killed and eleven others wounded on the campus of Jackson State (Mississippi) College in 1970, one of the policemen called into his radio: "You better send some ambulances, we killed some niggers."[2] In Chicago on December 4, 1969, the police apparently shot their way into the headquarters of Black Panther leader Fred Hampton, who was killed while still in bed. Deborah Johnson, who was in the apartment at the time, remembers a policeman saying: "'He's barely alive, he'll barely make it.' . . . So then . . . they started shootin' again . . . the Pig said, 'He's good and dead now.' The Pigs run around laughing—they was really happy, ya know. . . ."[3] No doubt their happiness was shared by a great many white Chicagoans and, for that matter, Americans everywhere. Studies show that the death of Martin Luther King, let alone the deaths of Malcolm X and George Jackson, occasioned relatively little regret in the population at large.*

None of this, of course, makes the case for genocide, as some extreme critics of America's race mores have charged. But American society as a whole may be guilty of what E. James Lieberman, MD, has called genasthenia, a neologism he defines as "a systematic weakening of a race." Genasthenia, according to Lieberman, was characteristic of Selective Service policy during the Vietnam War, in that it selected blacks who were high achievers, played down their medical problems and placed them in military positions where there were greater risks of death or injury. As evidence Lieberman cites the fact that almost twice as many whites as blacks were rejected for military service on medical grounds, al-

---

*An independent investigation of the Hampton shooting, launched by Ramsey Clark and former Associate Supreme Court Justice Arthur J. Goldberg, strongly suggested that Hampton, in Clark's words, was "murdered in the legal sense of the word." Nevertheless, the Cook County state's attorney and thirteen others who were involved in the incident and who were tried for conspiracy to obstruct justice were acquitted.

though blacks of all age levels have much higher death and disability rates. He accounts for this by pointing out that "privileged whites have a better chance of being excused than less privileged whites and blacks because good private medical care gives the affluent a medical record which an even worse-afflicted poor person may not have."*

Genasthenia directed at blacks and others is not confined to draft calls, nor is it any new thing for a society to fill out the ranks of its army and navy with those who have no future in civilian life, as witness the British practice for centuries. Isolation, obliteration of the indigenous culture, avoidance, and confinement to reservations destroyed the American Indian, and all of these practices have been successfully used against the American black, although their reservations are mainly in urban centers and bear names such as Harlem, Hough, and Watts. Still another form of genasthenia is the creation of conditions that foster drug addiction, drunkenness, malnutrition, and chronic illness, conditions that undermine the mind and spirit no less than they undermine the body. Self-abuse of all sorts, sexual mistreatment, aggressive behavior, and crime are daily features of life on these urban reservations, and these, too, insofar as they are sanctioned or encouraged by the larger society, constitute a kind of genasthenia.† Finally, genasthenia requires that the militant leaders and suspected trou-

---

*Letter to *Medical Tribune*, March 9, 1970. In a letter to New York *Times* of May 26, 1971, George Margolis, MD, quoting Lieberman, adds that while only 19 percent of "Anglos" were drafted, 45 percent of eligible Mexican-Americans were drafted, and they made up 20 percent of the American population. Still another contrast reported by Margolis is that only 3.6 percent of Congressmen had sons or grandsons who fought in Vietnam, and of the total of twenty-six who saw service in Vietnam, only one was wounded. More than 1,000,000 American families, says Margolis, by 1970 had a close family member either killed or seriously wounded. Half of the 234 draft-eligible sons of Congressmen were deferred. (Figures based on *Congressional Quarterly* survey, February 13, 1970.)

†As Clayton Riley and others have observed, the law-enforcement agencies are far more vigilant about drugs and crime in white neighborhoods than in black ghettos. Some critics, wondering why so little is done to end the heroin traffic in Harlem and elsewhere, have suggested that the police *like* the Harlemites sedated, spaced out, stoned. If there was any doubt that the thousands of blacks who can be seen every day dozing in doorways, sleepwalking, or shuffling along owe something to the police, that doubt was ended with the discovery in 1972 that the millions of dollars' worth of confiscated heroin and other hard drugs that had been stolen from police headquarters in New York had been resold to addicts and pushers.

blemakers be removed from the scene through either death or imprisonment; as there was no place for the Chief Josephs and Sitting Bulls of a century ago, so today there is no place on or off the reservation for their black counterparts.

White attitudes toward the Indian, as political scientist Michael Rogin has shown, were not dissimilar to those many Americans display toward blacks, and certainly there are many similarities of treatment.[4] Yet it is easier to understand, although not to justify, the destruction of the Indian than to understand the destruction of the black American. The Indian, after all, had something white men wanted very much, namely, land, forests, minerals, fur-bearing animals. Regarded as savage and aboriginal, he probably would have suffered the same fate had he not been in the way of westward expansion, but attitudes alone do not account for the genasthenia of the Indian.

Apart from his labor power, which has always been cheaper than white labor power, the black has never possessed anything that white America wanted, and in large areas of the country even his labor power is no longer needed as a result of technological change. But while he owns nothing of any value and is so far a stranger to white society as to be almost, in Ralph Ellison's phrase, an "invisible man," he continues to be the principal victim of genasthenia. Indeed, the variety of feelings and emotions aroused by blacks, most of them negative, is such as to suggest that the white-black situation in the United States can be understood only in terms of psychopathology. The black, in effect, is seen by many as a threat, menace, and evil and by some as a hero and rejuvenator, but he is not quite all things to all men. In the mythologies of race, in which he appears as either feared savage or envied superman, he is not quite a human being.

Psychiatrists and others who have examined white-black relations have noted that the black arouses a number of anal fantasies and aversions that have their root in bodily processes.[5] Indeed much that mankind dislikes or fears is in reality dark-colored or is pictured as dark-colored, with excrement being the best-known example. But it is not only feces and dirt that is black or brown. The night is black, and so is the devil and the angel of death. Ham, the youngest son of Noah, who was banished from the Ark, was black. The child's fear of the dark has been observed in almost every culture, and creatures that are used to frighten children into behaving better are usually black or have dark complexions. An angry temperament is often referred to as a black or dark mood, and we may say of an evildoer that he has a black heart or a dark soul. "Don't blacken my name," we admonish a malicious gossip; an old term for a scoundrel is blackguard. The son in the family who does not do well in life or who is less liked than the other offspring is the black sheep. And almost everywhere a light skin, unless it has been fashionably tanned by the sun, is preferred to a naturally dark skin; even in Israel blond and fair-skinned girls are preferred to their darker sisters, not least because a dark skin is associated with the largely lower-class North African and Levantine Jewish immigrants.

Sexuality as well is frequently connected with racism, usually in the form of a belief that the despised or allegedly inferior race has unusual sexual proclivities and/or parts. A conviction of many anti-Semites is that Jews lust toward gentile maidens and tend, in general, to be sex-ridden people; such belief is frequently stated in Hitler's *Mein Kampf*. Rape fantasies often attach themselves to members of minority groups and, in addition, invaders and occupiers of one's country, persons in authority, strangers, and deformed individuals, among others.

But the connection between sex and race does not always exist. The American Indian was widely regarded as both uncivilized and uncivilizable, but atrocities attributed to Indians, such as the murder of white women and their infants, were not of a sexual nature. Indians could be brutal in their treatment of their own and captured women, but the brutality did not involve sex. As Winthrop Jordan has commented: "Negroes seemed more highly sexed to the colonists than did the American Indians. . . . Far from finding Indians lusty and lascivious, they discovered them to be notably deficient in ardor and virility. [Eventually and almost inevitably a European commentator announced that the Indian's penis was smaller than the European's.] And the colonists developed no image of the Indian as a potential rapist. . . . In fact the entire interracial complex did not pertain to the Indians."[6]

The conviction that blacks are highly sexed is no less firm today than it was in colonial times, and it intrudes at every point in the discussion of black integration. Whatever the reference, whether to housing or schools and busing or jobs, the thought, if not the utterance, in the minds of many Americans is that the effort to extend equal rights will end in a bedroom containing a black man and a white woman. While the old cliche: "Would you want your daughter to marry one?" is heard less often than it was a generation ago, and there is even evidence, to which we shall return shortly, that public acceptance of racial intermarriage has been slowly but steadily growing, much anxiety and hostility of a sexual nature continues to mark white-black relations. Thus in 1970, when buses carried twenty black children, in response to a court order, to the doors of Lamar (South Carolina) High School, one of the 200 angry white men present exclaimed: "Things keep going like they is and in five years all our women will be nigger prostitutes." [7]

The statement, of course, is revealing, not only of the extent to which the black man has been eroticized beyond all fact and reason but also of the extent to which some white men have been victimized by their own generalized castration anxiety. For the statement implies that white women, given the opportunity, will sell or freely offer themselves to black lovers in preference to their own husbands, that, in effect, there is an overpowering sexual attraction on both sides. Since this fantasy has no basis in reality—which is not to deny the existence of normal male-female sexual interest across racial boundaries—it is clear that in "forecasting" the future of school desegregation, Lamar's white resident is giving expression to a variety of deeply held anxieties and insecurities about himself.

No doubt some of this anxiety is rooted in Southern history, in particular the history of sexual relations between the races. Both before and after the Civil War there was miscegenation in the South, almost all of it involving white men and black women; indeed, well into our own day in many small Southern towns any black girl on the streets after sunset was deemed to be fair game for any white male and his friends who happened to be passing. Guilt about the sexual exploitation of black women or, more precisely, the expectation that the black will take his revenge on history by, so to speak, getting his own back, unquestionably plays a role in the opposition to integration.

The black, however, is a victim of the white unconscious in still another sense, and it may be the most important of all. As was noted in an earlier chapter, for almost 2,000 years, or roughly since the beginnings of Christianity, sexual impulses have been regarded as base, unclean, and, above all, sinful unless related to procreation within the framework of marriage. Even in the era of the so-called sexual revolution we still refer to a sexual joke as a dirty joke and accuse the person who told the joke of having a dirty mind. Sex and dirt, in short, have never been entirely separate in the psyche of Western civilization, nor have they ever been entirely acceptable.

But while the instinctual apparatus to which Freud referred as the id has repeatedly been driven underground, through such mechanisms as repression, sublimation, denial, and projection, it has just as often reemerged, but usually in a form that enables us to avoid any sense of our own sin. The pagan world, for example, freely indulged the sexual demands of the id, but when Rome converted to Christianity, the id was exiled, as it were, to those parts of the world that were outside the Holy Roman Empire, and its sexual component assigned to non-Christian people, such as the Jews, Orientals, and Saracens. When, after some centuries, the id was once more in the ascendancy and Pauline doctrine in decline, the Protestant Reformation, in a sense representing another conversion to Christianity, again drove it underground. Viewed from this perspective, Calvin and Luther did not so much extend the work of Saint Paul as revive it, with the result that it again became necessary to repress, deny, sublimate, or otherwise refuse to acknowledge man's natural sexual appetites.

But now to the list of those figuring prominently in the projected erotic fantasies of Europeans was added a new group. By the beginning of the sixteenth century black Africa had long since been discovered, and the year 1562 marks the beginning of the slave trade between Africa and the Americas. The sexuality that had undergone a new repression at the hands of Calvin and Luther reemerged as the imagined attribute of the black slave; less than a century after Luther posted his 95 theses on the door of Wittenberg Palace Church, the black-slave-as-phallus reached the shores of North America.

The argument that there is a connection between white sexual repression and the belief that the black's id, so to speak, is very large and exceedingly active is supported by the fact that the African did not impress all early travelers as a particularly sexual creature, although he impressed some, and those whose observations underplayed the sexual element were fully supported by the later work of anthropologists. African kinship and family structures were not only relatively stable but governed by a variety of sexual taboos that were, in total, far stricter than those that have prevailed in the West during large periods of history. Nor is there evidence that the black slave was more sexually active than his forebears; what is certain is that slaves were sometimes forced into sexual activity by their owners, either for their owners' pleasure or in connection with a slave-breeding program designed to augment the owners' capital. But even these aspects of slavery had been exaggerated. The most recent research suggests that slave women typically were not forced to have sexual relations with whites or blacks, were not promiscuous and generally abstained from sexual relations until out of their teens, and on the average did not give birth to a first baby until the age of twenty-two.[8] In short, whether the context be Africa or the New World, the hypersexual black was a white invention and, from another point of view, the "return of the repressed." *

Having eroticized the black because we could not accept, much less enjoy, our own eroticism, there was no need to eroticize the American Indian and less need to fantasize the sexuality of ethnic groups that arrived later, such as the Jews, Irish, Italians, and Slavs. Moreover, these later arrivals were not objects of guilt projections related to sex or outlets for anal-sadistic fantasies to the same degree as the blacks; what is noteworthy, in fact, is the extent to which these later immigrants came to share the stereotyped images of the black that prevailed when they arrived. Although the black was not part of *their* history, he easily and quickly became part of their psyche, since among them, too, the instinctual apparatus of the id pressed heavily against religious belief and the dominant Protestant mores of the society to which they had

---

*In a similar way and for somewhat similar reasons the popular belief for a long time was that the higher primates devoted much of their time to sexual play, with the dominant male reserving most of the females for himself. Careful observation of primate behavior by ethologists and others has established that sexual activity is largely confined to female estrus periods and that during such periods females will have intercourse with all or most of the mature males and not only the dominant male. In general, the sexuality of the animal world has been grossly exaggerated, whether with reference to the jungle or the barnyard, so that in the end—an awful prospect!—it may turn out that the only truly sexual animal is man himself.

immigrated. Prejudice against blacks and others, but especially against blacks, has always been strongest in those who were most religious.

Of course, white-black relations cannot be understood entirely in psychological terms. There is an important economic side to discrimination, without which and despite psychic obstacles, blacks would have achieved much greater equality. For if there is psychic profit to whites in the conviction of black inferiority, there is hardly less economic profit to the white majority in the lower status of blacks. The employer who pays his black labor at lower rates than he would have to pay white workers, the landlord who can turn his tenement into an overcrowded rooming house and neglect repairs, the shop owner who can charge more for inferior products because there is nowhere else to shop, the housewife who has a maid or cleaning woman because there is little demand for unskilled black female labor—all these and many more people derive economic benefit from the enforced lower status of blacks.

If, for example, blacks holding the same jobs as whites were paid the same wages, black income would rise 27 percent, and if they received equal pay and also held the same proportion of various jobs that whites hold, black income would increase 45 percent.[9] While black income would increase if unemployment among blacks was not always higher and in some years twice that of whites, the amount of increase would be negligible if unemployment simply was transformed into underemployment at subsistence wages, and it would not be very great if the new jobs were found in the lowest-paid sectors of the economy. Much has been made of the narrowing gap between white and nonwhite family income, but the gap widens appreciably when black income is figured on a per capita rather than a per-family basis. On a per capita basis, which reflects the fact that black families are on the average larger than white families, black income continues to be not much more than half that of white income. Where black family incomes begin to resemble those of white families, the explanation usually is that the black income is based on two or more jobs in the family.*

*In December, 1971, for example, the Census Bureau reported that among black families in which only the husband worked there had been no income gain relative to whites between 1959 and 1970. Income averages of young Northern

In those areas where there has been an increase in black employment, the greater part of the increase is almost always in the jobs paying the least. Thus the number of blacks holding professional and technical positions, according to Federal Reserve Board member Andrew F. Brimmer, showed a dramatic increase of 109 percent during the 1960's, but one-fifth of the blacks, or approximately the same proportion as in 1960, remained in the lowest-paying jobs. Brimmer in 1974 also demonstrated that more than 25 percent of all business firms employing fifteen or more workers had no black employees in any job.[10] In the construction industry, despite a variety of governmental and private programs designed to promote minority-group employment, the minorities' share of the total 2,900,000 "skilled trades" jobs (excluding ordinary labor) in 1971 was 218,000, or about 8 percent of the "skilled trades" work force. Most of the 8 percent were carpenters, bricklayers, or workers in other "trowel trades"; few blacks and other minority-group members were employed as skilled metalworkers, electricians, plumbers, or pipe fitters. Especially rare is a black or Puerto Rican working as a crane operator or foreman.*

The reason is not simply the scarcity of jobs or the reactionary hiring policies of employers and unions, although these factors exert influence. Behind the exclusion of blacks and other minorities is a realization, more often unvoiced than articulated, that so long as these minorities remain poor, they cannot follow the more affluent whites to the further suburbs and exurbs, let alone

---

black families were closer to those of white families because 63 percent of black wives worked, compared with 54 percent of white wives, and 52 percent of the black wives worked year round while only 36 percent of the white wives did so. For further discussion of income and other economic differences between blacks and whites, see chapters 3 and 5.

*Nor has the so-called Black Capitalism program been more successful. Of the nation's 7,489,000 business firms in 1969, the total minority ownership was 322,000, or 4.3 percent. The black share, however, 163,000, or 2.2 percent of all firms, was a share roughly equal, despite the population-size difference, to that held by Chinese, Japanese, Mexicans, Latin Americans, Puerto Ricans, American Indians, Filipinos, etc., combined. In 1970, following two years of efforts by the Nixon Administration to increase gas-station and auto-dealer franchises held by minorities, only a few thousand gas-station owners and forty car dealers were members of minority groups. (In 1967 there were 216,000 service stations and 62,000 new- and used-car dealers.)

patronize the better watering places, country clubs, ski resorts, and golf courses. For whites perceive that few blacks with families would choose to remain on the reservation if they were provided with the means to leave, that is, decent jobs and incomes. White Americans understand that the geography of their America, and above all its social life, will remain white only if black America remains poor. Perhaps if economic equality *alone* were involved, job and other kinds of discrimination would be less, but since social acceptance cannot really be separated from economic equality, there is widespread opposition to and little solid progress toward equal economic rights for blacks and other minorities.

Since, in America, there is an intimate connection between economic achievement and self-esteem, it would be absurd to expect that extreme poverty generates among blacks, in particular, proud and confident images of themselves. The poverty of other minority groups may be no less, but their self-images are bolstered by an established and often respected cultural or national tradition that frequently is supported by a separate language and some vestiges of the life-style practiced in "the old country." The desperate and, one may fairly say, pathetic search in recent years for a black identity—the short-lived Africanist vogue of learning to speak Swahili or Yoruba and to wear dashikis or djellabas, and the establishment of black-studies programs in many colleges and universities—could only result, at best, in an ersatz identity, for the black's roots in Africa were irretrievably severed long ago. Many blacks and most whites to the contrary notwithstanding, the black in the United States is an American or he is nothing.*

The status of "nothing," to which the black has been consigned for most of our history, inevitably has produced much anger and hostility toward whites; taking into account the cruelties and in-

---

*This is not to slight the importance of courses dealing with the history and achievements of blacks in America, given in 1974 at more than 1,200 colleges and universities. The Africanist orientation, however, is another matter. The long-term effect of the "discovery" of Africa may be limited to a slight influence in the world of fashion. African-style clothes and dresses made from African cloth are seen less on 125th Street than on Madison Avenue, where they adorn such "smart" women as Jacqueline Kennedy Onassis, Barbara Walters, and Mrs. Jacob Javits, among others. Built-up heels and soles on men's shoes are a similar phenomenon but with the difference that the style has not been abandoned by blacks among whom it originated. Here, again, the relationship to black identity—the effort to "stand taller," as it were—can be recognized.

justices the black has experienced in the United States, the miracle is that there is not more anger and hostility. But given the dangers of openly expressing such feelings, inevitably a good part of the anger and hostility will be directed inward and there be transformed into rejection and self-hatred. The demoralization of blacks, however, is more than a matter of attitudes and moods. It finds expression in crime and drug addiction, in mental illness, in violence of all sorts, in sexual abuse, and above all in the precipitous decline of the black ghetto family as a nurturing and socializing agency. Perhaps no statistics are so revealing of the essential black condition in America, so indicative of how little real improvement has been achieved, as statistics showing that between 1950 and 1972 the percentage of black families *headed only by women* increased from 17 percent to 32 percent. Such families, of course, are not necessarily unstable ones, but they are almost certainly poorer than other black families, and they have higher rates of crime, delinquency, and premarital pregnancy.*

There is even evidence, according to a Michigan study, that the demoralization of blacks is responsible, at least in part, for the rising death rate of black men. For the nation as a whole in the decade 1961–1971 the life expectancy of black females rose from 66.5 years to 69.3 years, whereas that of black men showed a slight decline from 61.5 years to 61.2 years. From 1960 to 1970 the average life expectancy of black men in Michigan declined 2.6 years, whereas the life expectancies of white men and women and black women increased, the life expectancy of black women by as much as two years. One result of this decline, which "experts attribute to soaring drug and alcohol use, poverty and hard jobs," is that black women in Michigan, with an average life expectancy of 70.1 years, can expect to outlive their men, whose life expectancy in 1970 was

---

*The increase in the two years from 1970 to 1972 was 4 percent, or only 1 percent less than the total increase 1950–1960. The percentage of white fatherless families, by contrast, has remained fairly constant at 9.4 percent, and although the percentage of other nonwhite fatherless families (Puerto Rican, Chinese, etc.) has increased during the last two decades, it remains below that of black families. In 1972, 64 percent of poor black families, that is, nonfarm families earning less than $4,275 a year, were headed by a female, compared with 33 percent of poor white families. The median family income of black families headed by women was 62 percent of the median income of poor white families headed by women.

61.4 years, by almost 9 years.* If black women in Michigan increase their life expectancy within the next decade to 75.4 years—the life expectancy of white women—and there is no change in the life expectancy of black men, the average black woman will live fourteen years longer than the average black man.

The unemployed or poorly paid black man who is psychologically as well as economically unable to support his family may take to the streets and, quite literally, become a nonperson so far as society's awareness of him is concerned. In the 1960 census an estimated 15 percent of black males aged between fifteen and thirty-four were not counted, and perhaps as many as 10 percent were missed in the census of 1970. Most of these, presumably, are homeless "street corner" men without any fixed address or regular job, and certainly they have little reason to cooperate with the Census Bureau or any other government body. If the missing 10 percent were counted, the figures for black unemployment and poverty-level incomes would almost certainly increase, but the ratio of black men to women, estimated in 1970 at 83 men for every 100 women aged thirty-five to forty-four, would be more equal.

The missing men, however, are unlikely to be fathers living at home or, for that matter, men who are involved in long-term relationships with women. For there is some evidence that the never-ending war between the sexes rages more fiercely in the black community than elsewhere. Hostile aggressive feelings that cannot be discharged in the larger world may find outlets in domestic battlefields where men, who have internalized mean and debased images of themselves, confront women whose self-images are no better and who, in addition, must cope with children, home, job, bills, social workers, and, not infrequently, the police. Ironically, in view of the way he is regarded by white Americans, the black male is also threatened by castration anxiety and sexual malfunctions, and he may choose desperate measures to assuage his insecurities. There is not much he can do about being made to feel

*New York *Times,* February 11, 1973. Dr. Kurt Gorwitz, director of the Center for Health Statistics of the Michigan Department of Public Health, included among the responsible factors a rise in the violent-death rate among black men. Of the 693 homicides in Detroit in 1972, 78 percent of the victims were black and 70 percent black men.

half a man in the white world, but he can and sometimes does take action when he is made to feel half a man by his wife or children or neighbors. If black fiction and nonfiction is any guide, many a black woman and child have suffered the wrath that was inspired by, and in a reasonable world would have been directed back toward, the whites responsible not only for the occasional insults, slurs, and innuendos but for the conditions that make humiliation an everyday certainty.*

As a consequence, relations between black men and women, to judge by novels, plays, and films, are characterized by massive displacements of hostility and ambivalence. In Maya Angelou's film *Georgia, Georgia,* for instance, the heroine is a black singer who, while on tour in Sweden, has an affair with a white photographer. The principal black men in the film are presented unattractively: one in the singer's entourage is homosexual and the other, rather seedy in appearance, leads a group of Vietnam defectors. Nevertheless, the singer, because she has chosen a white man as her lover, is strangled to death by the black woman who is her combination mother figure, chaperone, and wardrobe mistress and who detests whites. Although the film was generally understood to express the view that sexual relations between a white man and a black woman were a betrayal of black identity—certainly this was the point conveyed to black audiences, who usually cheered or otherwise expressed approval during the strangulation episode— this was not Miss Angelou's intention. Instead, the purpose of the film, she explained to a reporter, was to demonstrate that racism

---

*The mortality rate from such diseases as hypertension, the incidence of which is three or four times higher among blacks, also plays a role in the death rate. Among black males whose ages range from twenty-four to forty-four hypertension accounts for a death rate 15.5 times that of white males of the same age and a death rate for black women 17 times that of white women. (*Medical Tribune,* May 15, 1974.) The enforced inferior position of blacks in America probably is in whole or in part responsible for the higher incidence of other diseases as well. Also relevant is the finding that when protein-deficient diets comparable to those of poor blacks and other poverty groups are fed to animals they leave "the animal's nervous system with a life-long hypersensitivity—a tendency to overreact to environmental disturbances." (New York *Times,* October 10, 1974.) Blacks in ghetto areas are less able to escape city air pollution even for short periods of time and therefore undoubtedly suffer more from ailments associated with pollution than whites who commute or who escape from the city weekends.

is particularly hard on black women "not only because they must bear up under conflicting internal impulses but also because they must shoulder such troubles without their men." Miss Angelou, in accounting for the murder of the singer, added: "The sadness among blacks today is that we don't allow our heroes the luxury of being in love," but she went on to make it clear that her greatest reservations were with reference to black men, not black women who became involved with white men. "For instance, I haven't had a substantial relationship with a black American man in 21 years. I'm more attracted to African men. . . . They call me sister in a way that means more than just going to bed." Her next film, she declared, would be designed "to help clear the air in black America, because, as I see it, that's what needs to be done. I'm going to write in 'Caged Bird' about all those black men with their fists balled up who talk about nation buildin' time, then go home to rape their nieces and step-daughters and all the little teen-age girls who don't know beans about life. I'm going to tell it because rape and incest are rife in the black community."[11]

For such statements, were Ms. Angelou white, she would stand accused of blatant racism; she is giving voice, after all, to sentiments not very different from those expressed by the white farmer in Lamar. But what is more important is that she is directing her anger and resentment not to white society which has made the black man what he is or, rather, what she says he is (there are no reliable statistics about the incidence of rape and incest among blacks), but to the black man himself. In saying that he is incapable of treating women as other than sexual objects, that he is capable only of sexual excesses, she is, in effect, also making him pay for her own unhappy autobiography, and she is doing so by talking not about any typical or average black man, but about a caricature of such a person.*

Even if Ms. Angelou is right about the frequency of rape and incest in the ghetto, to write about them is not necessarily "to help clear the air in black America. . . ." She does not know, nor does anyone else know, whether all or most or only some black men regularly abuse "their nieces and step-daughters," any more than

*Ms. Angelou's personal history, as told to the *Times,* includes a sexual assault at the age of seven, an illegitimate son at sixteen, and two failed marriages, one to an "African revolutionary" and the other "to a Greek."

she or anyone else knows whether all or most or only some black parents drink to excess or beat their children or engage in shop-lifting and other forms of theft. The pathology of the ghetto is such, however, as to justify the statement that it is fertile ground for delinquent acts of all types. Of the estimated 2,500,000 children who are physically abused every year, more than half may be black and other nonwhite children; in a sample of 1,380 reported child beatings in 1967 more than half involved blacks and other minorities.[12] There is evidence that many ghetto children who in school seem to be retarded are, in reality, not retarded but behave that way because they have lived all their lives in the midst of aggressive and sadistic behavior and, as a consequence, their learning ability has been inhibited by a conscious and unconscious preoccupation with violence.[13] Other ghetto children who appear retarded and children and adults who give the impression of being sullen, hostile, or withdrawn are suffering from malnutrition and/or severe depression; for millions of blacks and other minorities in the United States hunger and chronic depression, at times becoming acute, are among the everyday facts of life.

No doubt there is much sexual abuse in the ghetto as well, but this, too, is a function of pathological conditions. Numerous experiments with monkeys, rats, and other animals suggest that there is a loose relationship between rage or aggression and hypersexuality. As was noted earlier, tests with animals show that population congestion, anger and violence, or even simple excitement will produce in some animals a sexual frenzy characterized by compulsive mountings of both a homosexual and heterosexual nature. The sexual behavior of animals in captivity is, in general, very different from their behavior in the wild, and while some caged animals show little or no interest in sex and cannot be induced to breed, the males of various species can be restrained from sexual activity only by separating them from the females. The ghetto or reservation is not an exact cage, of course, but those who live there because they have no other place to live often sense they are confined, and there, too, sexual behavior often takes a pathological form.

Given the poverty and pathology of so much black life in America, it is fatuous in the extreme to suggest, as Daniel P. Moynihan did in 1970, that "in quantitative terms, which are reliable, the American Negro is making extraordinary progress. . . . The nineteen-sixties saw the great breakthrough for blacks." Although Moynihan admitted in his memo to President Nixon that the "breakthrough" had largely been confined to economic improvement and education—citing figures that later were found to be incomplete or inaccurate—and placed heavy stress on the increase in female-headed families, rising illegitimacy among blacks, and "the extraordinarily high" incidence of "anti-social behavior among young black males," he nevertheless urged that the Nixon Administration devote less attention rather than more to the problems of blacks. "The time may have come," he suggested, "when the issue of race could benefit from a period of 'benign neglect.' The subject has been too much talked about. The forum has been too much given over to hysterics, paranoids and boodlers on all sides. . . ."[14]

Presumably the Moynihan memorandum found favor with Nixon because it was not long after it that the recommended policy of "benign neglect" became, with reference to housing, school integration and busing, poverty and welfare benefits, and other areas of government intervention, an operating program of malignant indifference. Despite rejection of its premises by every major civil-rights leader and its tacit repudiation by the United States Commission on Civil Rights, the memorandum substantially weakened the commitment of the federal government to the promotion and enforcement of equality for backs and other non-whites.*

Less than three years later there was no doubt that civil rights were low on the agenda of the Nixon Administration, so low that former Chief Justice Earl Warren found it necessary to admonish Nixon "obliquely but plainly . . . not to be another Rutherford

---

*Others who did not share Moynihan's bland assumptions were former Chief Justice Earl Warren and former President Lyndon B. Johnson. In November, 1970, accepting an award from the American Jewish Congress, the former Chief Justice warned that the eradication of race prejudice was the foremost problem facing the country and one which would "determine whether we will be able to live in peace and harmony at home and abroad." (New York *Times*, November 23, 1970.) More than two years later former President Johnson in one of his last public appearances admitted, "I'm kind of ashamed that I had six years and couldn't do more . . . [of the 31,000,000 papers in the Lyndon Baines Johnson Library in Austin, that part dealing with civil-rights work] holds most of myself within it and holds for me the most intimate meanings." (New York *Times*, December 17, 1972.)

Hayes and allow the country to slip back into a period of oppression and neglect where blacks are concerned."[15]

But even had Moynihan recommended otherwise, Nixon never would have appeared before Congress, as Lyndon B. Johnson did, to declare, "We shall overcome." Nothing in Nixon's background indicated a commitment at any time to civil rights or civil liberties, and whereas Roosevelt's patricianism was broad enough ultimately to embrace the blacks, Nixon's Middle Americanism was exclusive rather than inclusive. It essentially was directed to the business class and those who earn good salaries or wages in regular jobs, to the self-employed and the farmers, to the suburbs and small cities and towns, to the white ethnics, to all those, in short, who are lost in Jeffersonian reveries and memories of an America that never was.

Most of these Americans voted for Nixon in 1972, and whether or not race was *the* issue that gave Nixon his second term, there can be no doubt that it was uppermost in the minds of many voters. Asked whether "minority groups are receiving too much, too little or just about the right amount of attention," 40 percent of voters on the eve of the 1972 election replied "too much," and of this group of four out of ten voters, 80 percent said they would vote for Nixon.[16] Perhaps the obsessive quality of the race issue was nowhere better illustrated than by an incident in Michigan. There the Democratic candidate for Senator, Frank Kelley, saw a line of people waiting for unemployment compensation. Kelley went up to one man and asked him what was on his mind in the election. "Busing," the man answered.[17] Presumably he belonged to the 66 percent of Americans who were strongly opposed to busing, notwithstanding the fact that busing impinged little or not at all on the lives of most citizens. A Gallup Poll in March, 1972, found only 3 percent of public-school parents saying that their children were affected by busing designed to achieve racial balance in schools.[18]

A possible interpretation of "benign neglect" is that it was intended not only to help win the election of 1972 but to win support for the Nixon foreign policy that began to emerge toward the end of his first term in office. Many of the Nixon votes came from those who previously had been strongly identified with anticommunism policies at home and abroad and hence were strongly opposed to any détente with the Soviet Union, and most of them were even more strongly against extending any form of recognition to Communist China. To keep these voters from bolting the Republican Party in 1972—it would have been fatal if they had merely stayed at home on Election Day—Nixon had to locate an issue that aroused emotions and feelings stronger than those generated by his flirtations with Moscow and Peking. That issue undoubtedly was race. Of course, Nixon was greatly helped by the poor image and ineptitude of the McGovern campaign. Had the Democratic candidate been more conservative and had he attacked Nixon from the right, he might very well have won the election. Nevertheless, there is a sense in which Nixon, consciously or otherwise, sacrificed the blacks in behalf of his foreign-policy goals. Had the Michigan unemployed worker replied, "Communists in government" or "Red China," or had the charge been made and sustained that Nixon was "soft on communism," the election probably would have had a very different outcome.

But while blacks became increasingly aware that the Nixon Administration was "anti-Negro," as the chairman of the board of directors of the National Association for the Advancement of Colored People put it in 1970, and as a consequence increasingly hopeless and despondent about the future, they did not flock in great numbers to join the Panthers or any other revolutionary party or significantly multiply the resorts to violence either singly or in groups. In fact, in large numbers they did not even bother to vote; black turnout in the 1972 presidential election was less than in 1968, and in 1974 black voter registration in major Northern cities ranged from a third to a half of those eligible to register. Random shootings of policemen and others by self-claimed revolutionaries, not all of whom are black, do not constitute a race war, and an increase in slum fires that may or may not have been set by blacks does not satisfy Moynihan's prediction in his 1970 memorandum that "Unless I mistake the trends, we are heading for a genuinely serious fire problem in American cities."* Although we

---

*Two lengthy paragraphs were devoted to this "problem," in one of which Moynihan made the curious statement: "Fires are in fact a 'leading indicator' of the social pathology for a neighborhood. They come first. Crime, and the rest, follows. The psychiatric interpretation of fire-setting is complex, but it relates to the types of personalities which slums produce." The factual basis for this statement, as for other statements in the memorandum, is, to say the least, questionable.

lack studies on the subject, for every black reader of Eldridge Cleaver's *Soul on Ice* or Bobby Seale's *Seize the Time* or Huey P. Newton's *Revolutionary Suicide* there are a hundred or more white readers, chiefly college students, intellectuals, and so-called white liberals. Indeed, by the mid-seventies what remains of the Black Panther Revolutionary Party has largely been transformed into a literary movement much given to black-and-white cocktail parties on Nob Hill and weekends at Quogue or Stinson Beach.*

It would require a succession of Nixons and many years of "benign neglect" to change black discontent into violent activism, and even then the activists would be far outnumbered by the optimists and the fatalists. While violence and disruptions of community life are likely to increase in the future, for the majority of blacks alienation is much more likely to express itself in apathy and sociopathic acts than in radical political action, let alone revolution.

What immediately is to be feared, in fact, is not black guerrillas but white vigilantism, which, in the name of "law and order" and in preventing "crime in the streets," brings about the establishment in America of something very similar to South Africa's apartheid. For the "crime in the streets" issue—the widespread impression that everyone who lives in a large city has been mugged or knows someone who has been mugged—generates passions not unlike those that were inspired in the past by the spread of plague and other infectious epidemic diseases. An even more serious threat to civil rights and integration is evidence alleging that genetic inheritance is more significant than environment in accounting for intelligence differences between blacks and whites. According to engineer William Shockley and psychologist Arthur R. Jensen, the principal reason blacks score an average of fifteen points lower than whites on IQ tests and, in consequence, earn less money relates to, in Shockley's words, "racial genetic differ-

---

* Such gatherings are not to be confused with what Tom Wolfe called "Radical Chic" with reference to the famous fund-raising cocktail party given for the Panthers in January, 1970, by Mr. and Mrs. Leonard Bernstein. For some whites "Radical Chic" was fun and excitement: "I've never met a Panther," said Mrs. Peter Duchin, wife of the orchestra leader. "This is a first for me." Others, mainly white liberals who were also Jews, in supporting the Panthers could simultaneously indulge their feelings of guilt and self-hatred, since the Panthers never made any secret of their equating Judaism with Zionism, colonialism, imperialism, and capitalism.

ences in neurological organization. . . ." Shockley, Jensen, and others therefore have recommended that persons with low IQ scores should be paid bonuses for allowing themselves to be sterilized. Other studies suggest that heredity, to quote one researcher, "plays some role in both psychopathy and criminality," the latter terms defined to include personality disorders, observation for psychopathy or probable psychopathy, character deviation, and such conditions as criminality, alcoholism, or drug abuse.[19]

From a scientific point of view, most of these studies prove little or nothing about the role of heredity in determining intelligence or delinquency, much less establish that there are important differences between ethnic and racial groups. Biologist S. E. Luria, Nobel laureate in 1969, has referred to the evidence on which such studies are based as "shaky and probably meaningless" and has drawn attention to an "elegant analysis" by Bowles and Gintis showing that whether or not IQ is predictive of school success, it "turns out to be almost irrelevant to economic success in life. The son of an industrialist with an IQ of 90 has an enormously better chance of success than a black boy with 120."[20]

Moreover, Luria adds, if IQ is inheritable and racial differences significant, nothing sensible can be done about it short of strict segregation or concentration camps. Of course, there are those who would go that far, but those persuaded there is such a thing as racial inferiority should be reminded not only that the evidence is weak but that geneticists, too, are influenced by social factors and movements of opinion that have little to do with science as such. Science historian William B. Provine has pointed out that between 1930 and 1950 geneticists in England and the United States moved first from a position condemning race mixing to one of neutrality or "don't know." This was followed by a shift to the belief that race crosses were "at worst" biologically harmless, a shift that took place during and shortly after World War II. Both movements of opinion were based not on new evidence about race and heredity, but on "revulsion" to Nazi race doctrines and their use in the destruction of European Jewry.[21]

The probability, however, is that many Americans will continue to insist that "scientific evidence" argues the desirability of racial segregation. When this "evidence" is joined to statistics demonstrating that while the black reproduction rate is falling, it is falling at a slower rate than the white net reproduction rate, thus suggesting that the proportion of blacks in the population is likely to increase for some time ahead, the fantasy that begins to form in the minds of white Americans is the fantasy of taking some action to ensure that the black population becomes once again small, docile, and cheerfully available for the menial work of the society, a population, in short, that once again "knows its place."*

The fantasy, to be sure, is not that of a "final solution"; short of civil war or a prolonged severe economic crisis, we are unlikely to move toward concentration camps and gas chambers. But if and when the black is perceived not just as undesirable and unwanted, but as The Enemy, is there any reason to suppose, given our history, that he will not be treated as we have treated other "enemies" in our history? Lord Jeffrey Amherst (1717–1797), commander of British forces during the French and Indian War, solicited the views of Colonel Henry Bouquet on the question whether a small-pox epidemic could be started among the "perfidious" Indians so as to "extirpate that Vermine. . . ." The noble lord would have had no trouble understanding our dropping the A-bomb on Hiroshima and Nagasaki or our systematic defoliation of millions of acres of Vietnam. Surely he would have thought the My Lai massacre of March, 1968, an action on too small a scale against another species of "Vermine."†

*According to the Census Bureau, the black population increased 5 percent between 1970 and 1973, while the white increase was 2 percent. The median age of blacks in 1973, at 22.9 years, was also much lower than the 29.2 median age of whites. But growth rates of both blacks and whites have been decreasing, in the case of blacks from 1.73 percent in 1970 to 1.41 percent in 1973, as compared with a white decrease from .91 percent to .6 percent during the same period of time. As Ernest B. Attah has shown, extremist fears on both sides are unmerited. Based on certain assumptions about female life expectancies and net reproduction rates, the percentage of nonwhites in the population could exceed 50 percent in 100 years, but is not likely to given a continuing birth decline; conversely, assuming the nonwhite population attained a decrease of .28 percent annually by the year 2100—a rate that would entail genocide, according to some black critics of population control—"it would take approximately 6015 years for the nonwhite population to become extinct." ("Racial Aspects of Zero Population Growth," *Science,* June 15, 1973, pp. 1143–51.)

†He also would have had no trouble accepting the sentencing of three New Mexico white teenagers to an average of two years each in reform school for the murder of three Navajo Indians in 1974. According to the presiding judge, the sentences were those prescribed by law. (New York *Times,* August 31, 1974.)

Of course, no one can doubt that much progress has been made toward racial equality since the *Brown* v. *Topeka Board of Education* school integration case of 1954, especially during the past decade. The 1974 Supreme Court decision banning busing across school district lines to achieve integration was, to be sure, a significant setback, but considering the closeness of the 5-to-4 decision, the Court's verdict may not stand for long. In any case, important gains in recent years in education, housing, employment, the integration of public facilities in the South and elsewhere, and even a small increase in the number of interracial marriages suggest that substantial gains have been achieved. More than half the population now disapproves of laws "making it a crime for a white person and a Negro to marry," according to recent Gallup polls.* The young are less prejudiced than the old, a hopeful indication in itself. Surveys report there is much less bias in textbooks, particularly those used in history courses, and blacks and other minorities are more frequently seen in the theater, television commercials, concert orchestras, and even comic strips such as *Tarzan* and *Peanuts*. Although black elected officeholders represent one-half of 1 percent of all elected officials, the increase of 121 percent between 1969 and 1973 was substantial; in May, 1973, there were 2,621 black elected officeholders.[22] In 1973 blacks were elected mayors of four major cities, one of them in the South, and more than 600 blacks held public office in the eleven Southern states. Following the 1974 election, ninety-four blacks were serving as senators and representatives in state legislatures throughout the South, and three were members of the House of Representatives.†

Even recent criticism of "affirmative action" (the admission to

---

*According to the Census Bureau, the number of black men with white wives rose from 25,496 in 1960 to 41,223 in 1970 (the number of white men with black wives decreased from 25,913 in 1960 to 23,566 in 1970). While this increase was less than that registered by marriages between American Indian men and white women, the 40,039 total of which was almost equal to the total for black men–white women marriages, the percentage increase was an impressive 63 percent. Of the 44,597,574 marriages on record in 1970 interracial marriages of all types amounted to .70 percent of the total, as compared with .44 in 1960.

†Nevertheless, as late as 1970 the Louisiana State House of Representatives passed a bill declaring a person to be white "having one-thirty-second or less of Negro blood." Thus a person one of whose eight great grandparents was black would not qualify as white under the Louisiana measure.

schools and hiring of minorities on the basis of quotas rather than qualifications) by educational bodies and other organizations, criticism interpreted by some as "antiminority," can be regarded as a step forward. To begin with, the fact that such a position can be taken implies that there is less sensitivity, both black and white, to stating views that can be misunderstood as favoring race exclusion and denial of opportunity. But what is more important is the growing recognition that no one gains if the effect of hiring blacks and members of other disadvantaged groups, such as women, is to lower academic standards in colleges and universities, place persons in jobs at which they cannot do well, and deny these same jobs to people who can perform them. Both the DeFunis case, involving a white student denied admission to the University of Washington Law School as a result of "affirmative action," and the 1974 report of the Carnegie Commission on Higher Education emphasize that the most affirmative action would be to increase the number of qualified blacks and other minority members who can compete with whites on their own merits, not move ahead on the basis of "reverse discrimination." For "affirmative action" discrimination is not only, like other forms of discrimination, undemocratic; by forcing a lowering of standards and a consequent decline in the quality of education, it cheats blacks and whites of their effective opportunity to acquire the skills necessary for advancement in our highly complex technological society.

Despite these problems and many others, one can discern in America, if not the faint tracings of an interracial society, at least the outlines of a society in which there is more tolerance and mutual respect. But if the lyrics of Billie Holiday's "Strange Fruit" now seem dated and Amos and Andy almost as remote as the shadow box of the nineteenth century, if in advertisements and the names of restaurants Little Black Sambo has become a white lad and in the movies the stereotype of Stepin Fetchit has long since been replaced by Shaft, we still do well to remind ourselves that the idea of progress in race relations may yet prove as ephemeral as the idea of progress in general. So long as the black remains a stranger in our midst—and despite the gains, he continues to be the unknown American upon whom all sorts of anxieties and fears can be projected—there remains a danger that one day he will become The Enemy. "It can't happen here," we assure ourselves, but what we really mean is that it *hasn't* happened here, which implies very little about the future. The fate in our own time of the Jews in Germany and the melancholy history of Armenians, Greeks, Bulgars, Turks, the Indians of Brazil, Saracens, Huguenots, Hutu, the American Indians, and others, the prevalence of torture and mutilation, the popularity in many parts of the world of public executions, and everywhere the widespread indifference to cruelty underscore the point that in every society, no matter how advanced its culture and laws, there is a potential victim.

8

The Pursuit of Suburbia

Americans in 1776 were the first people to make the pursuit of happiness an avowed national goal. While Thomas Jefferson did not define what he meant by the pursuit of happiness in the Declaration of Independence, we know something about his life-style and can make certain inferences. A substantial income, earned or unearned, was essential, and also important was a comfortable home in a decent neighborhood. Family and friends, ample leisure time, good food and drink, creative employment and freedom from drudgery, books, music, travel—all these apparently were indispensable to Jefferson's happiness, and many of them have been indispensable to some Americans ever since. But among the important differences between Jefferson's time and ours is the shrinkage of physical space. In the eighteenth and nineteenth centuries an American could go west in pursuit of happiness or leave the city for the farm or start a business, and perhaps a very large number of Americans—we will never know for sure—came within striking distance of their goal. In the twentieth century, however, the pursuit of happiness has become more and more illusory. Americans may still migrate to Oregon or to California, may leave the city for suburbia, may change jobs, but the ending is usually *plus ça change.* . . . Forever a restless people, one out of every five of whom changes his residence each year, Americans move and move and move, only to find that . . . *plus c'est la même chose.*

The tendency of things to stay the same, if not to become worse, finds perfect expression in the vast exodus to the suburbs that began after World War II. While Americans have always distrusted the city, in accordance with sound Jeffersonian principles and nostalgias, one can hardly believe that the flight from the city would have become a mass migration had it not been for the discovery by blacks that urban life to some extent could offset rural poverty and discrimination. With the black awareness that urban reservations such as Harlem, however economically depressed and slum-ridden they may be, are preferable to the helplessness and isolation of the rural South, the mass departure of whites was assured, first, from the core or central city to the outskirts, then to the suburbs, and, finally, to the so-called exurbs, whose relationship to the city is increasingly tenuous. By 1970 almost one of every four persons in the country's sixty-seven largest metropolitan areas was black, and in twenty years or less most large cities and their nearby suburbs will have predominantly black populations.

The population movement alone would have doomed the city as a continuing melting pot, thus further depriving the blacks of that essential acculturation and socialization experience that had earlier transformed Italian peasants, Irish stevedores, and Jewish peddlers into middle-class Americans. But in recent years a development even more momentous has occurred that ultimately may prove fatal for the city as such. Formerly the exiting whites worked in the city, that is, they commuted back and forth, five days each week, from suburban or exurban homes to city jobs. Inevitably some of the money they earned stayed in the city, and no doubt some measure of caring for and about the city remained a part of the commuting experience. All this has been changed by the movement to the suburbs of the office buildings, factories, and stores that provide jobs, shopping opportunities, and recreation. Formerly the typical suburban family was a married couple with children; the flight to suburbia of the unmarried young and the increase in single-occupancy apartments are particularly notable.* As a result, a growing number of Americans rarely or never spend even as much as a full day in the city, and if they seek entertainment at night, such excursions are likely to be on a one-evening-per-month basis or confined to special events.

*Between 1960 and 1970 the number of suburban apartments increased 96 percent as against a 17 percent increase in single-unit houses. There are now two suburban apartments for every four city apartments. As one housing authority commented, "It's the ultimate urban irony—apartments and town houses 25 miles from town." (New York *Times*, December 9, 1971.)

But whatever the fate of the city, the transformation of suburbia into shopping centers connected by major auto routes and surrounded by homes and apartment buildings has neither recreated urban advantages nor preserved rural amenities. Greenbelt is gradually disappearing under miles of concrete slab, and the flickering neon along the dreary stretches of U.S. 1 or El Camino or the misnamed "Miracle Miles" in all parts of the country is a reminder of the ubiquity in American life of the automobile, tubular glass, and plastics. Moreover, the blacks and the poor are also escaping the city, with the expected result that the suburbs themselves are fast becoming low-profile city slums. In 1970 almost 5 percent of suburbanites were black, and for every three poor people in the city there were two in the suburbs, but these are figures for the entire nation and, therefore, understate the migration of blacks and the poor to the suburbs of major cities. Between 1960 and 1970, for example, blacks in the suburbs of Cleveland increased by 453 percent, while in Los Angeles a total of 124,000 blacks moved from the central city to the suburbs.*

Predictably, the suburbs, too, are experiencing deteriorating schools, rising crime rates, and drug problems. The suburbs are still safer than the cities, especially in terms of criminal acts directed against persons, but in recent years the violent-crime rate in the suburbs has been increasing faster than the city rate of increase. No doubt for some time to come criminal activity in the suburbs will involve mainly property, but there is every reason to expect that crime in general, like everything else, will follow the migration pattern from the city to the suburb to the exurb. In fact, assuming a continued lower efficiency for suburban police departments and the reluctance of property owners to invest in costly electronic surveillance devices, suburbia is likely to afford the professional criminal a safety and security relatively greater than that available to him in the city. In a great many instances he

---

*Because the suburbs have been almost entirely white until recently, the percentage increase relative to numbers tends to be inflated. Thus the migration of 2,000 blacks to Minneapolis suburbs represented an increase of 223 percent. Nevertheless, the proportion of blacks in the suburbs of many cities is greater than the overall national average of almost 5 percent. In Miami the proportion is 12 percent, in Houston 9 percent, in Washington 8 percent, and in St. Louis 7 percent.

will become a commuter in reverse, living in the city and working in the suburbs.*

For wives and children living in suburbia, the center of life outside the home is the shopping center, in effect the equivalent of the city's downtown area before the blight. Consider one such center of forty-plus acres surrounded by developments and low-rise office buildings—let us call it Fairbrook Mall—with one corner forming the intersection of two four-lane highways. Fairbrook Mall is in the Eastern United States, but it could be almost any one of the more than 13,000 shopping centers in the United States. The large board directory at the main automobile entrances lists almost 100 enterprises including department stores, specialty shops of all sorts, boutiques, restaurants and snack bars, a bowling alley, banks, a cinema, and even a religious chapel for "meditation." The stores cater to a variety of incomes and tastes, but most are in the middle- and lower-class range; in an upper-income suburb, say, Palo Alto, California, or Grosse Point, Michigan, Gimbels and Bambergers give way to Saks and I. Magnin. Approximately 200,000 people live within ten miles of Fairbrook Mall, and twice each day, usually around ten in the morning and three in the afternoon, the huge parking lot will have very few empty stalls.

The mall absorbs more than 70 percent of the shopping dollars of the local population, a spending pattern that has practically destroyed the downtown business of nearby towns and cities.†

---

*The inability of police departments to cope with rising crime rates is reflected in the growing popularity of civilian patrols. Equipped with two-way radio cars and baseball bats or other types of wooden weapons, the patrols began in the cities and have spread into the suburbs and exurbs. A romanticized view might see them as the successors to the posse and deputy sheriffs of Western days; a more realistic approach might emphasize the vigilante aspect of the nightly neighborhood prowl in the patrol car. Certainly these patrols enjoy their work; in several metropolitan areas they have campaigned *against* expansion of the regular police force. Wives and older children have been enlisted as well, usually in the guise of auxiliaries or "junior" club members. In 1974 the popularity of the movie *Death Wish*, in which the central character takes it upon himself to "execute" muggers and rapists, suggests that vigilantism is finding increasing favor as a response to violent crime.

†The International Council of Shopping Centers estimates that the Fairbrook Malls of this country account for more than 50 percent of the retail trade in

Where once the shopper could choose between stores and prices downtown and in the mall, the choice is now between mall stores and enterprises to the extent there is any choice at all. The butcher, baker, and candlestick-maker are long since gone from Main Street, as is the movie house, the only local seafood restaurant, and what was, from 1921 to 1972, the town's only hotel. Fairbrook Mall, on the other hand, has few "For Rent" signs in store windows, and shoppers can see and hear, off to one side, bulldozers leveling the ground for a mall extension. A current rumor is that the 100-year-old Church of the Sacred Heart is negotiating for space in the projected new area.

But the social life of the mall has little appeal to adults. The bars cater mainly to grim, solitary drinkers whose eyes stare fixedly at television screens that are never turned off. There are no indoor or outdoor cafés where adults may linger over a social cocktail or cup of coffee; if one orders only coffee in one of the restaurants or snack bars, the waitresses make their displeasure very apparent or silently point to a small sign on the wall inscribed: "Minimum Charge: $1.00." Since the food is mediocre, "eating out" at one of Fairbrook Mall's several restaurants or dining at one of the numerous drive-ins that line the nearby highways is invariably a disappointing experience out of all proportion to the cost. Unfortunately, as the local residents incessantly complain, there is no place else to go within an hour's driving distance. The lack of amenities, however, does not bother the manager of the mall, or the various service clubs and civic organizations, or the assorted councils and commissions that govern the township in which Fairbrook Mall is located. They apparently agree with the head of the Chamber of Commerce, who says: "Fairbrook Mall welcomes shoppers, not loafers." Accordingly, the forty-plus acres provide exactly three wooden benches upon which tired shoppers may rest.

Toward late afternoon these benches are full of teenagers, and Fairbrook Mall begins to undergo a strange and even mysterious transformation. As the shoppers depart, they are replaced by hundreds of junior high school boys and girls riding grocery carts around the increasingly deserted parking lot or, disregarding the

twenty-one of the largest metropolitan areas. In some New Jersey communities, such as Paterson and Passaic, the figure is 79 percent; in Hartford, Connecticut, 68 percent; in St. Louis, Missouri, 67 percent.

"Keep Off" signs, lying on the grass listening to transistors. Business in the mod-clothing boutiques and record stores, slow earlier in the day, begins to pick up; the snack bars, movie house, and pizza parlor are jammed to capacity. Activity slackens as the stores begin to close toward dinner time, but accelerates again with the onset of early evening, especially if the weather stays fair. By dark many of the teenagers have returned, but now there are young adults as well, and the atmosphere of Fairbrook Mall has undergone a subtle change. Small groups of people stand quietly but watchfully in front of the closed, brightly lighted stores, while others sit in automobiles listening to car radios, talking little. Here and there joints are passed around, and money is furtively exchanged for capsules, pills, and glassine envelopes. Squad cars drive in and out of the parking lot; every so often one will remain for some minutes, its engine and lights turned off. Uniformed security guards, swinging nightsticks, patrol the mall itself. The talk and smoking cease as they pass the clusters of young people. Glancing briefly at the boys and girls, men and women, who are leaning against the storefronts or sitting on the benches, the guards walk by in silence. They know without turning around that the watching eyes are unfriendly and full of mockery.

Once the atmosphere was different at Fairbrook Mall or South Hills Village near Pittsburgh or Southcenter Shopping Center on the outskirts of Seattle. Only a few years ago there were no private security guards employed by the mall, but then burglaries and vandalism began to increase. The mall has since doubled the number of guards and is now making every effort to discourage those its manager refers to as "loungers." There was a time, another mall manager recalls, "when we thought [shopping centers] should be like the old Roman forums, where people could not only buy but be entertained and meet their friends. But when they also come to loaf and use us as a place to hang out, we've had trouble. They've been pushing dope, loitering in the walkways, and using obscene langauge. I had no choice but to close that coffee house, I'm sad to say." The advertising manager of Seattle's Southcenter Shopping Center remembers "a day when shopping centers would do anything to draw people. We don't take that approach anymore. We don't try to duplicate the downtown community. Now we don't do anything unrelated to our main purpose, which is merchandising."[1]

As the shopping center is not and in the nature of things cannot become downtown, so it is difficult to view the suburb as anyone's hometown, although the phrase is clung to because it is useful in the context of the perennial question Americans meeting for the first time ask each other: Where are you from? Significantly, the answer to such a question is not where one lives now, which can be an address to which one has recently moved or a trailer park or a furnished apartment, but where one was born and grew up even if it has not been visited for many a long year. The newer suburbs and exurbs, especially, lack not merely neighborhood stores and other meeting places that contribute to a sense of community but any facility that promotes contact between their adult citizens. Thus there may be a usable sidewalk on only one side of the street, forcing those on the other side to do their strolling in the street or give it up altogether. The lawn or fenced-in front of a suburban house, lacking a porch or stoop, provides no place for a casual neighborly meeting or chat; family activity outdoors takes place in a closed-off area back of the residence that is accessible only from the house itself.* There may be few if any streetlights, and since they are spaced far apart, the house numbers and street signs are not easily read. It is usual in the evening for the streets to be deserted except for persons walking dogs, and these excursions are apt to be short and businesslike. Late at night an unrecognized person on the street will attract attention, and if he is black or poorly dressed or is not moving along purposefully, he is apt to attract something more than attention. Suburbs do not welcome strangers.

Suburbia no less than the city reflects not the closeness of the American family—"togetherness" was never more than an advertising slogan—but its retreat into a private affluence that is intended to compensate for the absence of civil amenities. It is not only that our traditional openness has been replaced by suspicion as a consequence of generalized anxiety about race and crime but that many Americans have ceased to expect from the community that it provide them with anything more than the basic police, fire, school, and sanitation services. Hence the increasing unwilling-

---

*One is reminded of the notice that was attached to the driveway gate of Frank Sinatra's home in Beverly Hills some years ago. It read: "If you haven't been invited, you better have a damn good reason to ring this bell."

ness of the suburbs to tax themselves in behalf of civic improvements, much less to rescue the nearby city from impending total collapse.* If the schools begin to deteriorate, the solution is not to spend more on construction and the hiring of able teachers but to send the kids to private school. If garbage disposal becomes a problem, the answer is not compulsory recycling but the purchase of a landfill from any seller, public or private, within trucking distance. If the park areas become dangerous and subject to vandalism, the outcome is that the parks will be closed at sunset or even earlier. While the wealthier suburbs usually maintain public libraries and playing fields, rarely does one find in any suburb an art museum or concert hall or civic center, and in many suburbs the future of the library, indeed of any cultural facility dependent upon public funds, is in doubt.

Even rarer, however, is any awareness of cultural deprivation, presumably because culture, like politics, is largely viewed as marginal or irrelevant to everyday life. Of course, the mass of citizens in every country is little interested in its great writers and artists, but why Americans, who have had more years of higher education than any other people, should be so indifferent to cultural affairs still is far from clear. In 1972, for example, the government's support of the arts was significantly less than that of any government in Europe. Whereas the West German contribution in dollar terms amounted to $2.42 per person, and the contributions of Sweden and Austria totaled $2 per person, the support accorded by the federal government was the striking figure of $.15.† One consequence is that most Americans outside of cities never have the opportunity to see great art or attend a play or hear live classical music performed by a distinguished orchestra, although this is not to say that they would avail themselves of any

*In most states the suburb has taken the place of the rural county as the leading opponent of legislation benefiting the city. The battle for reapportionment, designed to give the cities greater representation in state legislatures at the expense of the farming areas and small towns, has in many instances merely substituted the "crabgrass brigade" of suburban representatives for the "cornstalkers."

†The fiscal 1972 appropriation for the National Endowment for the Arts was $30,000,000. The American contribution of $.07 compares with $1.40 for Canada, $1.34 for Israel, and $1.23 for Great Britain. The budget figure was significantly increased in fiscal 1974, but mainly in connection with the approaching bicentennial in 1976. Even so, per capita spending was only $.33.

such opportunity if offered. People do not usually stand shoulder to shoulder in the great museums of America, nor do long lines form outside of concert halls featuring the foremost symphony orchestras.*

In fact, were it not for the British Broadcasting Corporation and heavy subsidization by the Ford Foundation and a handful of corporations, Americans who watch television would have few alternatives in dramatic fare to *Marcus Welby, M.D.* or *All in the Family*. Apparently, the combined resources of the three major networks cannot do for Hawthorne and Melville what the BBC was able to accomplish for Galsworthy and Henry James, Stendhal and Balzac. To be sure, the audience response to serious drama and public-affairs programs as measured by Nielsen ratings is not reassuring to advertisers. Midweek movie night on television reaches between 17,000,000 and 21,000,000 households on the average, whereas an evening of public affairs may be viewed by only a few million families. Neither *The Forsyte Saga* nor *Père Goriot* can compete with Flip Wilson or Archie Bunker, and programs devoted to the plight of migrant workers and other so-called problem areas are no match for *Gunsmoke* or even reruns of old favorites.

But do these several million families, many of them suburbanites, care much about the quality of television programming? Evidently not, since there are no reports of organized efforts to improve television format other than in the direction of curbing depictions of sex and violence, and even these efforts have achieved little. Clearly most Americans are satisfied with the way things are, and the minority that is not satisfied appears to be resigned to the situation. Few have any desire to repeal the Gresham's law of television to the effect that bad programs tend to drive out the good.†

* Perhaps the future of classical music, like the future of classical literature and art, is in doubt, given the tendency of much modern culture to be produced by and for those with no talent and little taste. "Just match the numbers on the paints," says a Macy's ad, "to the numbers on the canvas and [in larger type] you can paint a beautiful oil picture. $2.49. It's a cinch. Anyone can paint with a Craftmaster set. Doesn't matter if you're young or old, artistic or not. Here's your chance to make like Rembrandt."

† Similar tendencies are at work in other areas of culture and where there is much less reason to copy the obsessive commercialism of television. Thus *Harper's* editor John Fischer noted some years ago that few of the 4,000 to 5,000 short stories submitted to *Harper's* were "of much interest to the consumer. Apparent-

Indeed, were such programs to be removed or sharply curtailed, the official and unofficial guardians of the public interest no doubt would allege that First Amendment freedoms had been violated and call for a full-scale congressional investigation.

While bad books do not necessarily drive out good ones, they do make it more difficult for good books to be advertised and sold and perhaps also to be reviewed, for in publishing, as in war and love, nothing succeeds like success. Thus a book that begins to sell widely, for whatever the reason, will usually have its advertising budget substantially increased even if the publisher has a low opinion of the work, whereas a book that is poorly received by the public will be advertised very little or not at all, no matter what the publisher may think of it. As publishers are fond of telling each other and their complaining authors, "You can't advertise a book into a best seller," and presumably you shouldn't try. But there was a time when a publisher or senior editor would go to great lengths to promote a book he thought important even if there was little chance that the book would pay for itself. Had it not been for such publishers, the protest and "muckraking" literature of a generation and more ago, books that have been influential in shaping the American present, might still have been published, but it is doubtful that they would have come to the public's attention.

Protest and "muckraking" books continue to be published, but because there is little public interest in these volumes, they are advertised, sold, and read less and less. Indeed, the best-seller lists of recent years reflect not only the escape to private affluence, of which suburbia is the most perfect expression, but an almost total avoidance of confrontations with the major problems of our time.

---

ly the reason for this is a theory, assiduously propagated by our universities, our critics, and by a good many writers themselves, that a writer shouldn't pay any attention to the customer, anyway; that he should write to express himself, to massage his own soul and not be influenced by the markets or the editors or the readers. If you consider fiction as a form of self-administered psychotherapy, I suppose this is a fine thing, but I shouldn't expect anyone to anticipate that he should get paid for it. If a person wants to make a living by writing fiction, or in producing hotdogs or automobiles or anything else, probably it is necessary to give the customer what he wants." (Quoted in Bennett Cerf's "Trade Winds" column, *Saturday Review*, December 15, 1956.) The substitution of "consumer" and "customer" for the term "reader" is suggestive of the extent to which a merchandising approach is as characteristic of middle- and high-brow cultural circles as it is of those pandering to mass tastes.

Looked at another way, the best sellers, like television and the movies, suggest that the defense mechanisms of denial and repression have become, in effect, an essential part of our national behavior.

Thus few books popular with the public deal with the power structure of American society or foreign policy or race or poverty. During the entire period of the Vietnam War only one book about the war became a best seller, and no book about the decay of the cities has ever appeared on the best-seller list. The staples of the list, year after year, are do-it-yourself therapy books of the *I'm OK, You're OK* type, sex and marriage manuals, biographies, popularized accounts of history, and works of nostalgia and mood, such as *Paris Was Yesterday*. Little of this literature, no matter how well done, helps Americans locate themselves in the stream of events or make connections between developments that only superficially are unrelated. Few books of any sort penetrate the tough surfaces of our institutions and practices, with the result that most Americans know nothing about the workings of the great corporations or the organization of universities or the infrastructure of the government.* But because such books do exist, we can only conclude that Americans do not seek to become informed, indeed will go to great lengths to avoid being informed. And again, the paradox is that Americans in the formal sense are the most educated people in the world.†

---

*How many Americans, for example, are aware that blacks are much more the victims than the perpetrators of violent crime, or that the poor pay more in taxes than they receive back in the form of government social services, or that the nation spends more on diet pills and reducing exercises than some African countries spend on food?

† In 1973, for example, fifty paperback books had print orders of 900,000 copies or more. The ten paperbacks with the largest print orders were:

Richard Bach, *Jonathan Livingston Seagull* (6,650,000 copies)
Dr. Thomas A. Harris, *I'm OK, You're OK* (3,800,000)
Norris and Ross McWhirter, *Guinness Book of World Records*, 11th ed. (3,600,000)
Xaviera Hollander, *Xaviera* (3,572,000)
Erich von Däniken, *Chariots of the Gods?* (3,080,000)
Arthur Hailey, *Wheels* (2,600,000)
Robert Atkins, MD, *Dr. Atkins' Diet Revolution* (2,400,000)
Herman Wouk, *The Winds of War* (2,200,000)
Xaviera Hollander, *The Happy Hooker* (2,100,000)
Larry Collins and Dominique LaPierre, *O Jerusalem!* (2,100,000)

What, then, is the nature of the affluent private life to which Americans retreat behind their suburban fences or the police locks and burglar alarms of their city apartments? Put another way, what constitutes the pursuit of happiness two centuries after Jefferson ranked it third in importance behind life and liberty? The evidence is that Americans know what happiness is *not* but are by no means certain what happiness is.

Thus they are fully aware that happiness is *not* being poor or old or sick or alone in the world, and many will go to enormous lengths to avoid these conditions. Male Americans are likely to believe that happiness is *not* being female; rarely does a man wish that he had been born a woman, although the contrary wish, that of a woman who wishes she had been born a man, is far from uncommon. White Americans with few exceptions do not wish to be black, but probably most blacks at times have wished they were white. For some, happiness is being in love or simply drunk, while for others happiness is and always will be dependent on an avoidance of the responsibilities of life.*

The American pursuit of happiness is first of all a pursuit of affluence. The good life as depicted on television and in the family magazines is devoid of worries about paying bills; even the television Archie Bunkers, who presumably are not affluent enough to join the other working-class Archie Bunkers in moving from increasingly "mixed" neighborhoods in Brooklyn or Queens to Rockland County, were not shown to be having difficulties making ends meet until the rampant inflation of 1974. The good-life essentials, apparently, begin with an income large enough to afford a comfortable house or apartment in a decent neighborhood, a once-a-week cleaning woman, ample food and drink, a modern kitchen, one or more television sets, a meal out at least one night a week, and an annual vacation. In the suburbs the good life re-

---

The only paperback selling over a million copies that dealt with politics and current affairs was David Halberstam's *The Best and the Brightest*, the print order for which was 1,200,000.

*Hence the myth of the happy drunkard, the carefree vagabond, and the resilience of the expression "happy-go-lucky." The popularity some years ago of "happiness is. . ." definitions is also revealing, albeit in a less serious way. One was: "Happiness is three martinis on an empty stomach." Another (more ambiguous definition) ran: "Happiness is when your pregnant secretary marries her boyfriend."

quires at least one new automobile every two or three years, a stereo-equipped family room or den, a minimum of two full bathrooms, and an outdoor barbecue. More and more *de rigueur* is the provision for each adolescent family member of his or her own bedroom, television, and record player and for the children their own telephone number if not also their own private telephone.*

But all this is only the beginning. A goal of those who strive for affluence and an achievement of the better off may well be a swimming pool, weekend country place, and a full-time maid. Financial status in the suburbs often is measured by moves from one house in one section to a more expensive dwelling in a more fashionable part of town; to remain in the same house for long is to reveal that one is no longer advancing in terms of job and income. Status-consciousness and the good life also stand revealed in the driveway—a foreign import such as a Mercedes or Jaguar confers more prestige than an American vehicle—or in the choice of wines offered guests or in the collection of pre-Columbian sculpture that is conspicuously displayed.

So described, the American affluent way of life is the envy of the world, sought after and copied everywhere. In many countries it is probably more influential than religion in shaping values, more decisive than ideology in determining what the mass of the people want. Yet, by a gross irony of history, Americans themselves, as measured by certain vital statistics, may be among the Western world's least happy people. The most affluent society in history has the eleventh highest suicide rate and leads the world in divorce, alcoholism, drug addiction, and the number of people who see psychiatrists. At a time when longevity is increasing in most countries, the death rate in the United States, after half a century of improvement, appears to be worsening. Between 1964 and 1968 the mortality rate rose for all ages between 15 and 74. Death rates for white males aged between 15 and 19 increased 21 percent, not including battle deaths; for nonwhite males the increase was 35 percent.[2] American males are outlived by males in Israel,

---

*In 1970 almost 30 percent of families owned two or more cars and two or more television sets. More than 90 percent of families possessed washing machines, vacuum cleaners, and refrigerators, and almost a quarter were equipped with dishwashers. By 1972 Americans owned more than 9,000,000 boats of all types, 1,250,000 snowmobiles, and 75,000,000 bicycles. About $100 billion was spent on so-called leisure-time activities.

Sweden, Japan, the Soviet Union, the United Kingdom, and fifteen other countries, and perhaps what is more important, they are outlived by their women an average of seven and one-half years. At ages 45–64 the mortality rate of white males is double that of white women, which means that a white male must reach the age of 57½ years before he has the prospect of living until he is 75, a prospect enjoyed by females at birth.[3]

Nor is this the only evidence of a fundamental disturbance in the American affluent way of life, assuming it cannot be demonstrated that happiness kills and that happy people suffer more than unhappy people. The ulcer, once regarded as a disease typical of the hard-driving ambitious business and professional man, is becoming increasingly common among children, particularly teenage boys whose parents belong to the upper-income group. Basing itself on Erie County hospital records from 1946 through 1961, one study found that the average annual incidence of childhood ulcers rose from .5 per 100,000 youngsters in the period 1947–1949 to 3.5 per 100,000 in the years from 1959 through 1961. The sharpest increase was among fifteen-year-old boys from the highest socioeconomic class.[4]

While the suicide rate among young people appears to be rising in a number of countries, the rate has been increasing more rapidly in the United States than elsewhere. In the ten years 1957–1967, the latest period for which detailed statistics were available in 1974, the suicide rate for white males in the 15–24 age group increased more than 60 percent, while for white females the rise was over 70 percent. In the 25–44 age bracket the increases were 25 percent for white males and 63 percent for white females. Also noteworthy in the 1960–1970 decade was the rapid increase in the suicidal-death rate of young women as opposed to the rate of attempted suicide, which has always been higher for women that for men.* At the present time outpatient mental clinics serve more persons in the 10–19 age group than in any other

---

*Medical Tribune, April 12, 1972; January 3, 1973; New York Times, April 2, 1972. The suicide rate of older white men, however, has been falling, a development that some attribute to Medicare and improved economic conditions for the elderly. The 200-odd suicide-prevention centers in the United States estimate that a significant proportion of deaths caused by drug overdose and auto accidents are, in reality, suicides and that the overall suicide rate is at least twice the official count of 25,000 deaths each year.

decade of life, and the National Institute of Mental Health predicts that the hospitalization rate of young people will more than double during the next decade.

But even those affluent Americans who manage to avoid both an early grave and the mental hospital give little evidence of contentment with their lives. Judging by the incidence of depressive illness and the character and increasing frequency of encounter groups, awareness meetings, and consciousness-expanding rap sessions in the suburbs, those who suffer most from the frustrations and boredom of everyday existence are the wives of commuting husbands, and certainly they have reason. For the men can escape from the nation's Westports and Athertons to careers that, whatever their drawbacks, do usually allow for long lunches in the better restaurants and business trips that are not wholly given over to business. Their wives for the most part are tied to house and children until they have reached the threshold of middle age, and here it little matters whether a particular wife has graduated *magna cum laude* from Radcliffe or abandoned a promising career for marriage and family; all women are equal in the car pool and the PTA.* No wonder that for many wives in the suburbs the most important distinctions are less those of status and money than of degrees of freedom from domesticity. As sociologist Philip Slater trenchantly observes: the busy routines of the American housewife are designed to "mask the fact that the housewife is a nobody" living a life of "emotional and intellectual poverty."[5]

Suburbia and its discontents, however, rarely induce a searching inquiry into the causes and consequences of a commuting economy, much less raise questions about its indispensability. Thus husbands who spend three or more hours each day on trains or buses, often returning home only after the youngest children are ready for bed, complain not about a corporate system that makes commuting necessary but about the woefully decrepit

---

*Every professor can number among his best students over the years a good many women who, in a given class, were far superior to the men present, but rarely is anything heard of them after graduation. Whatever happened to Kathy M. or Sally C., one wonders, remembering the eager curiosity and bright sparkle of their student days. Perhaps it is better not to know, since the women who do keep in touch often have little to talk about other than their husbands' careers and their children.

and even dangerous condition of commuter trains and buses. And wives who are bitter about the fact that the main burden of maintaining the house and raising the children falls on them, or who resent the twice-daily drive to the station to wait for trains that are often late, focus not on the policies that have made the city an unsuitable place for children but on the institution of marriage itself and inequalities in the relationship between men and women. "I don't know if it's really possible to be free and married," says a Fairfield County housewife. "I think of marriage as an oppressive institution." For another unhappy suburbanite a step toward happiness was taken when she and her husband "switched roles. My husband does the marketing and I do the mowing and yard work. I love to dig in with a pickax and make holes for trees, and he hates it." The husband of another "loves to do the laundry. He finds it soothing to his brain, and I've become aware that I've always liked to do male-type chores, like putting up cabinets." For a Chappaqua wife "awareness" began when she stopped feeling sorry for her husband because he had to commute. "All winter the trains would be an hour or an hour and a half late, and I'd wait for him and tell him how terrible it was that he had to sit in the train all that time." But then her husband blew his cover by telling her "he hadn't even noticed." And she continues, "it's not the men who suffer over commuting. It's the women. For a man, the train is a welcome cushion of time when he can be alone, when the phone won't ring and no one will bother him."[6]

Presumably rare among these women is the thought that rap sessions and the like may serve to divert them from some real issues and that in any case, the sterility and boredom of their lives will not be resolved by discussing their problems with other women whose lives are equally sterile and dull. Nor does it occur to their husbands that there may be viable alternatives to the so-called rat race, provided they are willing to question the goals and values which have led them willingly to take part in it. Here psychiatry, encounter groups, and women's liberation can offer little assistance because, no matter how successful they are in dealing with interpersonal problems, they cannot and do not wish to change the fact that, so long as the money is in the city and the home is in the suburbs or exurbs, husbands and wives must spend almost half their lives apart and in very different worlds. In other words, until the city again becomes a fit place to live and raise a family, and ways are found by which husbands and wives can share everyday lives and not merely function as appendages to offices and businesses, husbands will continue to commute and lead separate lives, while wives continue to languish in the suburbs.

Of course, there is a major difficulty here. Many husbands would be unhappy if their wives were closely involved in their careers, and despite the earlier examples, few husbands like to do the laundry or wash the floors or make beds. Their jobs may be drudgery or, except for financial returns, unrewarding, but drudgery and unrewarding only by comparison with more interesting or challenging jobs elsewhere, never by comparison with housework, which most men are glad to be free of. As the leaders of women's liberation have correctly intuited, men in general do not wish their women to be equal in *all* respects, and they especially do not want them to be equal around the house. In fact, many a father who is uncomfortable or impatient with small children will delay as long as possible his return home from the office in the hope that by then his children are in bed, and with luck his wife will have a drink waiting, dinner almost ready, the table set, etc. Perhaps the popularity of such weekend entertainments as golf, boating, fishing, and above all watching televised sports events reflects to some extent the desire of many men to reduce family time to a minimum. No doubt the increased popularity of weekend escapes to motels, during which the entire family is indulged to a degree not possible at home, tells us something about certain regressive aspects of homelife or at least some unspoken feelings about those Saturdays and Sundays when the husband ceases to commute and the children are out of school.*

Granted that someone, the husband or wife or maid or all three, must attend to the house and the kids, can anything be done to reduce the distance between city and suburb, husband and wife? One answer is that we do not know for certain because Americans, the most innovative and experimental people in

---

*Motel owners report that the weekenders usually are families with young children for whom the motel with its cocktail lounge, restaurant, and pool functions as a relatively inexpensive resort. While no one knows how many of the 2,000,000-odd motel and tourist-court rooms are occupied by such families at a given time, motel managers testify that many families spend an entire vacation in a motel that may be only a few miles from home.

science and technology are among the least creative in areas of social invention. Paradoxically, many countries that can least afford social experimentation because of low living standards or unbalanced economies have been among the most innovative—one thinks of the British "New Towns" program after World War II, the Israeli *kibbutz,* the Chinese commune—whereas the world's richest nation, the United States, has been the least willing to take risks.* The consequence is that we lack alternatives to the city-suburb-exurb life into which we have drifted, as we have drifted into much else. There has been no lack of ideas, as witness the library of books about community planning and urban reconstruction; there has been simply a lack of desire to rank human needs ahead of profit margins and land values and to take chances.

But even assuming no large-scale social reform, the possibility remains of shifts of emphasis that would make possible incremental changes in life-style. In some parts of the world, for example, lunch periods are long enough to allow employees to return home for several hours; in effect these periods constitute midday vacations.† The thirty-five-hour week, already a reality, is gradually being transformed into a four-day week, but perhaps employees could be given a choice of arrangements, some electing to work alternate weeks of five days and three days with others preferring six-day followed by two-day weeks. There seems no good reason why only professors should enjoy sabbaticals and three-month vacations with pay; it is doubtful that the economy would collapse if

*The reason may be our national obsession with increasing productivity and gross national product and our neglect of the human costs involved. But would it really matter if the entire auto industry, say, lost new-car production devoting a year to experimental ways of dealing with factory and office organization, work routine, the relation of work to home and family life, commuting, and so forth? Employees, suppliers, and new-car dealers would have to be paid, of course (here the cooperation of the federal government would be essential), but if there were little or no auto production during that experimental year, who would care? With more than 100,000,000 cars on the road, would the nation really miss the cars that might not be manufactured? If experience with the moratorium on new-car production during World War II is any guide, the answer must be no.

†In Spain and Israel offices and stores are usually closed between twelve and three or one and four and then open again until seven. While no one could be expected to go back and forth to Greenwich in a few hours, those Americans who live on the outskirts of small or medium-sized cities and who drive to work could certainly manage to lunch at home at least some of the time.

everyone were entitled to take six months off every seven years. The suggestion that wives be paid for housework and mothers for tending children has yet to be discussed outside of women's liberation circles, much less put into effect.

The loneliness and boredom of domestic chores could be reduced by the return of the eat-in kitchen with fireplace as central gathering room for the entire family and the elimination or at least recycling of the misnamed family room or den, usually given over to dad and the television set, located in that part of the house that is farthest from the wife and kitchen. Perhaps, too, we could learn to manage with a smaller number of rooms that must be cleaned—for instance, by returning to the practice of having brothers and sisters share rooms—fewer conveniences and less spick-and-span. Whether or not cleanliness is next to godliness, no one has ever shown that a happy home is one that is spotlessly clean and equipped with every modern convenience. "One of the most enjoyable houses I know," historian Regis A. Courtemanche recalls for his and our benefit, "has electricity only in one part, is drafty, possesses one ancient toilet, and leaks. Yet I would gladly spend all my days there, because its natural materials show the hand of man everywhere. The dining room floor is stone, worn by many feet. The wood-paneled living room reflects the soft glow of a table lamp. Stained glass windows at the top of the stair invite the late afternoon light, while in other rooms wainscoting reaches halfway up the wall and is marked by the hand prints and toy scuffs of small children."[7] Given the opportunity to acquire such a house, how many American women, one wonders, would send out immediately for painters, plumbers, decorators, electricians, cabinetmakers, roofers, and appliance dealers?*

---

*The sterility in design and furnishing of many modern homes clearly owes something to the understandable desire of women to avoid housework drudgery, one alternative to which is a house or apartment constructed with materials that do not show dirt and can be easily cleaned. But a woman who is soon finished with her household chores or has them performed by someone else may find herself pondering if not the question, "What does a woman want?," posed by Freud, at least the question of what to do with the time not spent on housework. Whether or not Freud's view of women reflects Victorian prejudices and sexism, as many feminists believe, one is somewhat puzzled that women find this view more offensive than a full-page *Cosmopolitan* magazine advertisement depicting the "Cosmopolitan Girl" as saying: "When do you suppose I'll begin to feel guilty about the money I spend on clothes (straw hats with streamers are this

Modernity, in other words, which many people think of as synonymous with progress, destroys not merely the relics and artifacts of the past but a way of life that permitted a close fit between man and his domestic environment. Yesterday's families may not have been happier than the families of today, but in an atmosphere of physical proximity, shared tasks, and mutual dependence, closeness, at least, was possible. Many of the older houses gave off and continue to give off a feeling of warmth because they were built and furnished with warm materials: wood, local stone or brick, wool, cotton. It is no accident that the modern functional look is often cold in feeling; chemical products such as plastic, vinyl, nylon, and synthetics in general, so often used in furnishings, are cold materials as compared with products found in nature and animal and vegetable fibers, which are warm. Nor has anything been invented that will center a room and gather its inhabitants together as effectively as an open fire.

Indeed, much of what is heralded as the utmost in modern home decorating is not only cold in feeling but somewhat schizoid. Thus the book *Underground Interiors* features living rooms without windows or furniture, frames without pictures (the "anti-picture room"), neon-light sculpture, the "womb room," and a "one-way mirror to sit in: a huge reflecting sphere that you can get inside of and sit invisibly while you survey the room around you." For those "into" the sexual revolution there is the "underground four-poster" with an overhanging canopy mirror and the "counter-culture bathroom painted in shiny black enamel with toilet and bidet encased in industrial sheet metal frames"; an alternative bathroom study is the "bathroom parlor with all the customary fixtures plus living-room amenities."[8]

"Underground interiors" no doubt are preferable to dark cheerless flats with conventional furnishing, nor can it be disputed that most big-city apartments are dreary in appearance and claus-

---

week's weakness), on *beaux* (men deserve presents, *too!*), on trips to Port-au-Prince and Hyannis Port [sic] (a girl has to *travel*), on the hairdresser and my Shih Tzu's veterinarian, not to mention my record collection and a party every week or so. Frankly, I may not *ever* feel guilty. My favorite magazine says earning big and spending big on things you love are important 'perks' for a smart girl. . . . I can go into tax-free municipals (or worry about the children's orthodontia!) *later*. . . ." (New York *Times*, July 24, 1974). Whatever Freud wrote about women, he never attributed to them an imbecilelike vacuity.

trophobic in mood. But the answer may not be to eliminate windows because they look out on walls or garbage-littered lots, and
paint ceilings "the blue of an unpolluted sky with fluffy cumulus
clouds." For man is not an underground creature who can live in
a sealed-off environment without becoming sealed off himself. He
cannot, that is to say, spend his nights in a "diaphanous bed-pock-
et that gives you the feeling you're sleeping in the hive of some
mysterious insect" without developing an insectlike blindness to
the world outside the hive. The whole purpose of the "underground interior" is to induce a fantasy that one is not living in a
decaying city or in a slum area or in an overpriced apartment that
is too small, and to that end almost everything that constitutes the
"underground interior" is either make-believe or pseudo-erotic.
Not only do the senses shrivel and die, as happens in environments that totally lack stimuli, but they are deceived into taking as
real what is only apparent or downright fake. Inevitably the sensory experience itself becomes more and more detached from reality and more and more self-absorbed with the analogues of masturbatory images. As the "bathroom parlor" suggests a relationship between modernity and decadence, so the bed with the canopy mirror reflects the extent to which, in America, sensuality is
identified with exhibitionistic gratification and autoeroticism.
Since every exhibitionist's preferred object is himself, it is altogether fitting that the last person one sees at night before turning
off the light and the first person one sees after awakening in the
morning should be oneself.

Of course, the "underground interior" and the life-style it con-
jures up is not for everyone. Nor, for that matter, are all wives in
the suburbs lonely and bored and all commuting husbands running hard in the rat race. Encounter groups, women's liberation
and psychoanalysis have yet to make an appearance in most of the
small towns of America, and there the pursuit of happiness has
not yet become incompatible with the Protestant ethic. Indeed, if
we exclude certain geographical areas, such as the conurbations
of Boston–Washington, San Francisco–Los Angeles, and perhaps
Chicago and the North Shore, we would be on safe ground in stating that the American way of life largely consists of the *Reader's
Digest,* church suppers, color television, high school sports events,
Miss America contests, the Rotary Club, and the bowling alley.
Thus Muncie, Indiana, the "Middletown" of Robert S. and Helen

M. Lynd in 1925 and 1935, has changed relatively little since the Lynds first visited the city fifty years ago.[9] Still 90 percent white and 95 percent Protestant, Muncie continues to believe in the free-enterprise system and minimum government, thrift, early to bed and early to rise, and that you get ahead in life through hard work and self-improvement. With few exceptions the townspeople dress conservatively, "nor do men wear their hair long or grow sideburns or beards (even double-vented jackets are uncommon)."[10] Although the 10,000-odd blacks, like blacks everywhere, are mainly poor and badly housed, militancy is rare. Even population growth in Muncie sets the town apart from many other municipalities. From 1935 to 1960 the population grew from 50,000 to 69,000 or about 38 percent, which is close to the national population increase of 40 percent, but from 1960 to 1970, when the national increase was more than 13 percent and growth in Indiana almost 11 percent, Muncie added a total of 479 people to its population.[11] A stable population, clearly, is an important reason for the relative absence of change. In the Muncies of America, one is tempted to say, Poor Richard and Horatio Alger are alive and well.

Nor are they deceased elsewhere. Because we are inclined to think that every city resembles New York and every suburb Scarsdale and that every college student is a pot-smoking member of the youth counterculture, we overlook the fact of what might be called attitudinal lag or the tendency of the mores and manners of the country to respond only slowly to changes in the culture of big cities as reported in the media and embrace more slowly still the most *avant-garde* opinion. Hence the shock of some sophisticated circles when a state referendum defeats a proposal to legalize marijuana, especially if that state is California, and the dismay when it is reported that a majority of Americans wishes to restore capital punishment. Americans, it can hardly be stressed too much, have always been a conservative people who, in almost every age, have viewed with suspicion if not hostility nonconformists, eccentrics, deviants, radicals, atheists, and intellectuals in general. So-called Middle America not only has always been with us; with the exception of certain short-lived periods, Middle America has dominated the nation's morals no less than its politics.

Hence, for every marriage ceremony that breaks with tradition,* there are scores that do not, and for every couple experimenting with group sex, experiments which are said to be increasing, there are hundreds for whom a departure from conventional arrangements would be even more unthinkable than voting Communist. Consider, as one example, Dominick and Margaret Denio of Melrose, New York, married twenty-three years and with eighteen children, for whom, says Mrs. Denio—no "Ms." there!—"it's been beautiful." Dominick Denio is a high school teacher, football and basketball referee, and in the summers a park recreation director, whose total income is $18,000 a year. The two older children, both boys, are employed, and most of the others attend school or college. Mrs. Denio, until the number of children passed the eleven mark, managed to attend a local college at night and is only thirty hours away from a degree. The Denios are regular Roman Catholic churchgoers and are involved in many activities: sports, 4-H, a women's club, sewing, needlepoint, cookouts, cheerleading, chorus, dramatics. None of the children has ever been in trouble. "I've got Mr. Wonderful," says Mrs. Denio of her husband. "He works so hard. He's kind, conscientious—he's everything. And I know this sounds Pollyanna, but our sex life is the same as it was 23 years ago. That's just the way it is. . . . We don't have the right to be as happy as we are."[12]

Those who are worldly, sophisticated, or merely cynical would find it easy to make fun of the Denios, who are, in a word, squares. But to do so is to miss the point. The Denios believe in the older virtues and values and somehow have managed to act on them. "I'd probably make more on relief if I didn't want to work," says Dominick Denio, "but I would never do it, of course. We're too able-bodied and too proud around here. But nobody could have it any worse, moneywise, than me." Yet the Denios feel rich, not just

*Such as the marriage of Adelia Moore and Tom Gerety, one of the more appealing examples, on October 7, 1972. For the ceremony at the Adirondack camp owned by the bride's family, the prospective couple and some of the guests arrived by canoe, the groom dressed in an open Walt Whitman shirt and blue corduroys. Although the bride's father is the Episcopal bishop of New York, neither he nor any other minister conducted the ceremony; instead the bride and groom wrote and performed their own vows. The bride intends, the *Times* story further reported, to retain her maiden name, and to be addressed as "Ms." (New York *Times*, October 8, 1972.) It is difficult to imagine this taking place in Muncie.

because they are a happy family, which is how they would account for their feeling, but because they have never lost their innocence. Apparently they do not worry about war, poverty, and drugs any more than they worry about the population explosion, to which they have made their own rather impressive contribution. For the Denios, one may presume, the urgent problems are those that impinge most directly on their lives, such problems as crime and inflation, and not the fate of America's migrant workers, much less the traumas of starvation in Bangladesh. In other words, it is not that the Denios know something that other less satisfied Americans don't know. It is that they do *not* know something that other less happy Americans know or have experienced. In a vital sense they are new at being Americans, indeed, almost as new at becoming American as their parents and grandparents who emigrated here from Italy, and hence for them America continues to be the land of opportunity and promise.

For Dominick and Margaret Denio, in short, America is a success, and perhaps it will be a success as well for their children and grandchildren. But one can already detect that their innocence has begun to falter, that they have begun to suspect that in America, as elsewhere, virtue is not its own reward. In declaring, "I'd probably make more on relief if I didn't want to work," Dominick Denio inferentially is not only maligning those who are on relief, most of whom want to work but are unable to find employment. In calling attention to the fact that despite his many jobs, "nobody could have it any worse, moneywise, than me," Denio is revealing just the slightest discontent about his place and condition in society and illustrating, once again, the precariousness in America of both innocence and happiness.

9

Expecting the Barbarians

Man, it seems, is the only murderous animal. Whereas other vertebrates kill for food—but rarely their own kind—and are capable of aggression when competing for food, females, or territory, men kill each other for reasons that have nothing to do with survival. Furthermore, they are characteristically—one is tempted to say chronically and compulsively—aggressive.* An authoritative study of war undertaken at the University of Michigan has established that in the 150 years between 1816, the end of the Napoleonic era, and 1965, there were a total of ninety-three international wars, fifty of them involving two or more sovereign states. The world's nations averaged more than six wars in each decade; wars were fought in all but twenty-four years during that century and a half. The Michigan study estimates that deaths in battle alone amounted to 29,000,000 but this may be too small a figure even excluding civilian deaths.[1] According to behavioral scientist Lewis Richardson, between 1820 and 1945, "59,000,000 human beings were killed in wars, murderous attacks, and other deadly quarrels." If we include the slaughters of the last thirty

*Archaeologist Louis S. B. Leakey has advanced the view that aggressive acts did not become a feature of human society until about 40,000 years ago. Until then, Leakey suggested in 1971, men lived in small family groups that lacked incentives for violence. But with the growth of population and increasing territorial pressure and competition for food, men turned on each other. If Dr. Leakey is correct, aggression is relatively recent in the long span of human history, which goes back more than 2,000,000 years, but if that is the "good news," the "bad news" is that men have been killing each other for 2,000 generations, and that is a very long time indeed.

years in the Korean and Vietnam wars, the civil wars in China, Indonesia, Nigeria, and elsewhere, the tribal conflicts in Africa, the Pakistan-India-Bangladesh war, and the outbreaks of internal strife everywhere, the total for the 155 years between 1820 and 1975 is probably not far short of 65,000,000 persons.[2]

This horrendous toll of death is likely to seem remote to Americans, who, in general, have had little direct experience of war. Viewing themselves as idealists and peace lovers, from which perspective they occasionally are forced into war by the aggression, malevolence, or expansionist ambitions of nations led by dictators and despots, Americans thus far have never needed to take war as seriously as, say, the British or the Russians. No foreign enemy has invaded the country since 1812, and no war has been fought on the continental soil of the United States since 1865. Put another way, few of the 65,000,000 lives lost in the last 155 years have been American lives.

But however the wars have come about in which the United States has participated, they have occurred with an impressive frequency during the past 200 years. Since 1776 Americans have fought at least nine major wars, which average out to about one war every twenty-two years.* Approximately thirty-three of the 200 years of our history have been occupied by these nine major wars, or, roughly, one year in every six since the founding of the Republic.

These figures may suggest that Americans, compared with certain other peoples, have waged peace much more than they have waged war, and indeed there is some truth in this; between 1816

---

*The following list excludes military engagements against the Indians (such as the so-called Black Hawk War of 1832) and the numerous "expeditions" of American forces in Latin America and elsewhere:

Wars of the United States	Dates
War of Independence	1776–1783
War of 1812	1812–1815
Mexican War	1846–1848
Civil War	1861–1865
Spanish-American War	1898
World War I	1917–1918
World War II	1941–1945
Korean War	1950–1953
Vietnam War	1965–1973

and 1965 the British and French each engaged in eighteen major wars, the Russians in fifteen, and the Italians in eleven. (The total for the Germans, somewhat unexpectedly, is six!) But before congratulating ourselves as the world's foremost peace-loving nation, we should note that the United States did not become a world power until this century and that four of the nine major wars were fought after 1900. All of these wars, moreover, unlike those of the nineteenth century, took place far away from mainland United States. If we take account of the frequency and duration of these latest wars, we can observe that Americans of this century are more often at war than in the past and that these modern wars tend to last longer. Roughly fifteen of the last seventy-five years have been given over to war, or, on the average, one year of every five.

Assuming that we have never been forced into war by economic necessity, such as the need to find sources of food, raw materials and cheap labor, or outlets for population, what is the reason for our increasingly frequent recourse to military action? The answers to such a question are extremely complex, but one simple fact about the relationship between war and the United States is significant: however the costs are measured, Americans have suffered very little from war since 1865. In terms of casualties, for example, *battle deaths from all wars combined* total only 650,000, many fewer than the British *or* French *or* Russians *or* Germans suffered in World War I alone, leaving out of account population differences.* The wars of this century, especially the two world wars, have generated much economic growth, and they have been important in producing high levels of employment, rising living standards, and greater opportunity. Directly and indirectly they have made a positive contribution to standards of medical care and the health of citizens, educational levels, scientific and technological innovation, and much else. Truly, for almost all Americans

*The British lost 419,654 in the Battle of the Somme alone. Total battle deaths in World War I have been estimated at slightly more than 8,600,000, of which the British share amounted to 908,000 and that of the French 1,350,000. Had American casualties been in the same proportion to the population as British casualties, losses would have been more than 1,980,000 instead of the actual total of 53,500 battle deaths or 116,000 deaths from all causes combined. Had the proportions been similar to the French, American losses would have reached 3,400,000.

except those who have been killed or wounded in military actions and their families and close friends, war has been, as Randolph Bourne observed almost sixty years ago, "the health of the state."

Bourne was not thinking primarily of the impact of war on the economy; but with the possible exception of the Vietnam War, to be discussed later in this chapter, recent wars of the United States have contributed much to the viability of the economy. The Great Depression of the 1930's, for example, did not end until World War II, despite the "pump priming" of the New Deal. Unemployment during that period never fell below 7,000,000 and in 1938–39 totaled approximately 10,000,000, or roughly one out of every five of the work force. According to figures presented by economist Isador Lubin to the Temporary National Economic Committee (TNEC), between 1929 and 1938, assuming that the amount of wages and salaries paid in 1929 remained the same, American wage earners lost $119 billion, farmers $38.4 billion, and investors $20.1 billion. The loss in national income averaged $1,000 for each man, woman, and child in the country. It was as if every worker had taken an unpaid vacation of one year and two months.

World War II, of course, began September 1, 1939, when Germany invaded Poland. By the end of 1939 manufacturing employment had increased ten percent and payrolls in general sixteen percent. The index of industrial production, which in August, 1939, had stood at 106 percent of the 1935–1939 average, had increased to 125 percent in December. Much of this increase was owed to the $12 billion Congress had appropriated for military needs by July, 1940; By April, 1941, the total appropriations had reached $35 billion, a figure greater than that for the entire period of World War I. By mid-1942 the industrial index had climbed to 174, and already there were labor shortages in the major industrial cities. Between August, 1939, and March, 1942, the prices paid to farmers rose 66 percent. Employment went from approximately 45,000,000 in April, 1940, to almost 50,000,000 in December, 1941, with average weekly wages increasing from $29.88 to $38.62 over the same period of time.

Following the war the economy continued to operate for some time at high production levels to supply the goods that had not been produced or purchased during the war; overall the 1945–49 years were years of replenishment and reequipment. In 1949–

1950 there was a slight recession, or, as it was sometimes called, a "readjustment," in agriculture especially but also in manufacturing. Production and spending were reduced, and there were especially sharp effects abroad as a result of a fall in United States imports from Western Europe (one consequence, at least in part, was the devaluation of the British pound in 1949).

Perhaps the economy would have turned upward without the stimulus of the Korean War, but there can be no question about its impact. When the war began in June, 1950, annual defense spending averaged $13 billion. Three years later, in 1952–1953, the annual defense expenditure was more than four times that amount; by June, 1953, over $160 billion had been appropriated (although not all of it spent) for the Korean War, and once again there were labor shortages in major cities. In 1952 defense needs absorbed 15 percent of steel production, 50 percent of machine tools, 60 percent of electronics, and 15 percent of farm machinery. Of a total work force of 66,000,000 persons in public and private employment (including 3,600,000 in the armed forces) at the end of 1952, 10,600,000 were directly or indirectly in defense production or the military sector; in other words, about one of every six employed Americans owed his job to the defense effort.

Moreover, every war fought by the United States since 1898 has been followed by a vast expansion of American economic and political influence abroad. The Spanish-American War gave us Puerto Rico, Guam, and the Philippines, thereby extending American power to the far reaches of the Pacific. The aftermath of World War I saw a substantial increase in American investments in Europe and for the first time participation in international conferences of many types. Following World War II there was a further impressive spread of American influence in almost all parts of the world except those areas dominated by communist governments; thirty years after the end of the war American troops continue to be stationed at 367 major bases in twenty-six foreign countries and United States territories, and American naval units can be found on every ocean and sea.* Under a variety of

*As late as April, 1974, American troops in Asia totaled 168,000, most of them in Japan, Okinawa, Thailand, and South Korea. In addition to major bases the United States maintains 1,800 other installations overseas. Total land-based forces stationed in foreign countries were estimated in mid-1974 at 438,000, with another 426,000 military personnel attached to the four Atlantic and Pacific

treaties the United States is pledged to come to the defense of more than four dozen countries in Europe, Asia, Latin America, and the eastern Mediterranean and to supply an additional score of countries with military equipment. The United States, it need hardly be said, does not intervene in every war, everywhere, but wherever there is war, whether between Indians and Pakistanis, Israelis and Arabs, or communist Chinese and nationalist Chinese, American involvement of some sort is never absent, and only rarely is it even concealed.*

During the past thirty years our interventions and involvements have been justified in terms of a communist-fomented Cold War designed to promote communist interests almost everywhere in the world by a variety of means including military force, subversion, terrorism, infiltration, and territorial expansion. The

---

fleets. In January, 1975, the total number of military personnel outside the United States was reported to be 512,000. (*Defense Monitor,* Vol. 4, No. 1 [January, 1975].) In 1973–1974 the United States was the world's leading supplier of military hardware, selling some $8.5 billion worth of arms to a number of countries, most of them in the Middle East. The Soviet Union and its allies are estimated to have sold military goods worth a quarter of that amount in the same period of time, with most of it also going to Middle Eastern countries, although not to Israel. (New York *Times,* July 10, 1974.)

*Thus the Nixon Administration made no secret of either its support for Pakistan during its war with India that began in late 1971 or its opposition to the Allende regime in Chile. Measures taken in favor of Pakistan included suspension of the aid program to India, the dispatch to the Bay of Bengal of the nuclear aircraft carrier *Enterprise* carrying 2,000 Marines, and insistence that the Indian ambassador to the United States "not . . . be treated at too high a level." For reasons that have never been made clear, the pro-Pakistan policy, the wisdom of which was questioned by American Ambassador to India Kenneth B. Keating and other State Department officials, originated with President Nixon himself, who, according to Henry Kissinger, then Nixon's adviser on national security matters, gave him "hell every half-hour . . . that we are not being tough enough on India." The long-term results of this attitude, the effects of which were to strengthen anti-American feeling and increase Soviet influence in India, remain to be determined.

In Chile between 1970 and 1973 more than $8,000,000 was spent on covert activities by the CIA in an effort to undermine Allende. According to CIA Director William E. Colby, the agency had intervened in Chile as early as 1964 by subsidizing the presidential campaign of Eduardo Frei Montalva against Allende, who subsequently lost. (New York *Times,* September 8, 1974.) See also Victor Marchetti and John D. Marks, *The CIA and the Cult of Intelligence* (New York: Knopf, 1974).

assumptions behind our Cold War policies and tactics have been remarkably consistent through the administrations of five Presidents of—at times—sharply opposing points of view on most other issues of policy. The consensus is all the more striking considering that some of these assumptions were never shared by an impressive number of informed students of communism and scholars in the field of international politics or, for that matter, by experts in the government itself if their memoirs of office can be trusted. In effect, the Presidents and their key advisers came and went during these years, but the assumptions remained whether the Presidents inclined toward liberalism or conservatism at home and caution or brinksmanship abroad.

The principal assumptions were four in number. The first was that the doctrines of communism were unalterably opposed to and in essence at war with the values of free societies everywhere, and that these doctrines were incapable of change from within or without in the direction of the values espoused by free societies. In other words, the foreign-policy makers assumed that communism, whatever its claims, was inevitably and permanently a totalitarian system of political and social organization. The second assumption was that all communist leaderships, whether of established governments or guerrilla movements, hold the same beliefs and subscribe to the same policies, especially in the area of foreign relations and military strategy. It followed from this assumption that there was no such creature as an "independent," "native," or indigenous communist movement that was not under the control of either Moscow or Peking.* The third assumption was that communism was driven by its own inner necessities and logic toward expansionism by whatever means were appropriate at a given time, not least among which were treachery and deceit. Therefore, the assumption dictated, there could be no meaningful collaboration with communists in any coalition or common effort, let alone any so-called popular front government. Finally, the policy planners assumed that wherever and for whatever reasons communism came to power anywhere, neighboring areas and states

*Thus the expression "international communism" was and still is widely used, although it would have struck almost anyone as absurd to speak of "international democracy" or "international capitalism" in view of the differences between nations which, overall, are democratic and/or capitalistic.

would sooner or later come under communist domination—this was the famous "domino theory." Consequently, the United States was obligated to use its resources and, on occasion, its manpower to prevent a communist takeover anywhere in the so-called Free World.*

By now the second assumption of communist bloc solidarity has been shattered by the enmity between the Soviet Union and China and the increasing tendency of several bloc countries, especially Rumania, to steer their own course in domestic affairs and, to a lesser extent, foreign policy. The assumption that there could be no collaboration with communist regimes has been weakened by the success of joint peacekeeping efforts and other shared undertakings, although these efforts have been cautious, limited, and above all characterized by abundant mistrust on both sides. The other assumptions of our Cold War policy, however, remain in force, and they are the most dangerous of all. For, on the one hand, they express the view that communism, however benign and reasonable it may appear at times, is and will remain the Antichrist, a pagan force in the world that is, forever, the enemy of the West;† and, on the other hand, they assume, almost as a truism, that if the remaining dominos are not to fall, they must be bolstered at the least by American military assistance that since 1950 has amounted to more than $40 billion and a war-preparedness program that since World War II has totaled approximately $1.5 *trillion.*

The expression "since World War II" is, of course, misleading, for it was the military phase of the Cold War, not the Cold War itself, that began after World War II. The conventional dating

---

*Large parts of the Free World, of course, were not and are not free in the sense of liberty and democracy; the term "free" meant essentially: free of communist and/or Soviet domination. Not infrequently "free" also meant: open to American capital and economic influence. Hence the Free World came to embrace dictatorships in Spain and Portugal, military juntas in Greece and Turkey, one-man imperial rulerships in Iran and Ethiopia, and the feudal sheikhdoms of the Middle East, in addition to the democracies.

†This was the view, for example, of John Foster Dulles shortly before he became Secretary of State. In his book *War or Peace,* published in 1950, Dulles wrote: "Soviet Communism starts with an atheistic, Godless premise. Everything else flows from that premise." (Quoted in Townsend Hoopes, *The Devil and John Foster Dulles* [Boston: Atlantic Monthly Press, 1973], p. 83.)

point is March 5, 1946, when Winston Churchill, in the presence of Harry S Truman, announced that a Soviet-manufactured "iron curtain" had descended across Europe. Behind that curtain, Churchill declared, "lie all the capitals of the ancient states of Central and Eastern Europe. Warsaw, Berlin, Prague, Vienna, Budapest, Belgrade, Bucharest, and Sofia. . . . Athens alone—Greece with its immortal glories—is free to decide its future at an election under British, American and French observation."*

It was appropriate that Churchill should have announced the opening of the post-World War II period of the Cold War in Fulton, Missouri, the heartland of what later came to be called Middle America. The abhorrence of communism was as natural to most of his audience as it was to Churchill himself, who had been a Cold Warrior since 1917, when the Bolsheviks first raised the Red Flag over Moscow and Leningrad. Nor did Truman require convincing that communism was the enemy. However much he felt that Stalin personally was "all right" and was "as near like [Missouri political boss] Tom Pendergast as any man I know,"

---

*Churchill did not mention that between the two world wars Greece had been a battleground fought over by monarchists, liberals, and extremists, with one monarch being assassinated and all four of his sons exiled or deposed at various times. Twenty years after his speech another iron curtain, this one of local military manufacture, would descend on "Greece with its immortal glories" without calling forth any comparable statement from any Free World leader. Quite the opposite: the extinction of Greek democracy by the Colonels' Coup of 1967 received warm support from Vice President Agnew and Secretary of Commerce and chief Nixon election fund-raiser Maurice Stans. As Ambassador Henry J. Tasca put it to touring Congressmen, "This is the most anti-Communist group you'll find anywhere. There is just no place like Greece to offer these facilities [for investment and trade] with the back-up of the kind of government you have got here." (Quoted by Charles Foley, correspondent for London *Observer*, July 1, 1973, from a diary kept by one of the Congressmen.) The diary also recorded the remark of "an American two-star general that "it's the best damn government since Pericles." Apparently it was also one of the most heavily subsidized governments in terms of covert funding by the CIA. According to a story by David Binder in New York *Times* of August 2, 1974, Colonel George Papadopoulos, who led the 1967 coup, had been on the CIA payroll since 1952, along with a large number of other military and civilian political figures. To what extent the United States was involved in the removal of Papadopoulos and his associates in November, 1973, is not clear. On July 23, 1974, the military junta that had overthrown Papadopoulos resigned, and Greece was restored to civilian government.

Truman never shared the view of Admiral William D. Leahy and others that the Russians were being reasonable in their demands for security in Eastern Europe. Even before the war was over, Truman declared his opposition to Soviet hegemony in Poland, and in a memorandum of January 5, 1946, to Secretary of State James F. Byrnes, which anticipated Churchill's Fulton address by two months, he established the principles that later became the basis of the Truman Doctrine and American foreign policy in general. In his characteristically blunt style Truman enunciated his suspicion of Soviet intentions in the Mediterranean and went on to declare:

> There isn't a doubt in my mind that Russia intends an invasion of Turkey. . . . I do not think we should play compromise any longer. We should refuse to recognize Rumania and Bulgaria until they comply with our requirements; we should let our position on Iran be known in no uncertain terms and we should continue to insist on the internationalization of the Kiel Canal, the Rhine-Danube waterway and the Black Sea Straits and we should maintain complete control of Japan and the Pacific. We should rehabilitate China and create a strong central government there. We should do the same for Korea.
>
> Then we should insist on a return of our ships from Russia and force a settlement of the Lend-Lease debt of Russia.[3]

Perhaps a different stance on the part of the Truman Administration could not have averted the later wars in Korea and Vietnam; the final determination, by historians, political scientists, and others, of responsibility for the Cold War itself, if ever there is a final judgment, will not be made in this chapter or, probably, in any chapter written by anyone during the present century.[4] But the fact remains that in 1946 "the United States made no concessions of significance to the Soviet Union."[5] Although a convincing argument could be made that Soviet efforts to extend control and exert influence in adjoining areas were not inconsistent with her legitimate interests and traditional balance-of-power considerations, the United States with rare exceptions regarded every Soviet claim or demand as expansionist. Nor did the fact of Russia's exhaustion following World War II, an exhaustion that owed much to a combined military and civilian death toll estimated at more than 20,000,000 persons, preclude expectations in the West that the Soviets were capable of still another military effort and were, therefore, a direct threat to Iran, Greece, Turkey, and even Western Europe itself.* Hence, Russian assertions of a sphere of influence in Europe and the Middle East were met by the dispatch of an American fleet to the eastern Mediterranean, a move toward the "tacit dismemberment" of Germany rather than unification with its risk of eventual Soviet domination, the decision that "a nuclear arms race was preferable to the adoption of a less-than-foolproof scheme for the international control of atomic energy," and, in March, 1947, the Truman Doctrine.[6]

At the same time the United States was actively pursuing a so-called containment policy primarily directed toward the Soviet Union, it was rejecting or displaying total indifference toward a variety of conciliatory initiatives and friendly overtures emanating from communist leaders in Asia. Indeed, one of the saddest developments of the entire postwar era was the rejection by the United States of requests for support and cooperation that came from revolutionary movements, not all of them Soviet- or Chinese-dominated at that time, the cadres of which imagined that America, given its own history of colonial revolution, would become an ally in their struggle for independence. Again, there can be no certainty that the Korean and Vietnam wars could have been avoided and no confidence that a policy of coexistence with communist China could have begun a score of years earlier, but one is tempted to speculate what might have been the result had the Truman Administration responded positively to Ho Chi Minh's appeals for support against the French in 1945–1946. In fact, so far as is known, there was not even a reply to a number of letters sent by Ho to President Truman.† Nor was the United

---

*Soviet battle deaths alone amounted to 7,500,000. Had the United States suffered equivalent casualties, the American battle death toll in World War II would have been approximately 5,500,000.

†According to the Pentagon Papers, in late 1945 and early 1946 Ho Chi Minh "wrote at least eight letters to President Truman and the State Department requesting American help in winning Vietnam's independence from France." (Document #1 of *The Pentagon Papers*, as published by New York *Times* [New York: Quadrangle, 1971], pp. 5, 27–28.) The cablegram dispatched to the State Department on February 27, 1946, by an American diplomat identified only as "Landon" suggests that Ho's model for a future independent Vietnam was the "Philippines example." Following independence in 1946, the Philippines enjoyed a special relationship with the United States, and perhaps Ho wanted to es-

States more responsive some months earlier in January, 1945, when Mao Tse-tung and Chou En-lai secretly informed President Franklin D. Roosevelt that they wished to travel to Washington to discuss with him the improvement of relations and the possibility of economic and military assistance to China. Once again there was "no response to the overture,"* although it is probable that the major Chinese motivation was "to avoid total dependence on the Soviet Union."† Four years later, with the war against the nationalists almost over, the Chinese communists again took the initiative toward improving Sino-American relations, and again there was no immediate response. Their invitation of May 13, 1949, to United States Ambassador J. Leighton Stuart to visit Peking in order to discuss future relations between the two countries was not answered for almost two months, and when it was answered by the State Department on July 2, the answer was no.**

Given this history and the assumptions discussed earlier, few

---

tablish a similar relationship between America and Vietnam. Certainly Ho was capable of imaginative proposals. In 1946 he offered Jews, through David Ben-Gurion, a home in exile in Vietnam!

*Barbara W. Tuchman, *Notes from China* (New York: Collier Books, 1972), p. 77. For a fuller account of this extraordinary story, see her chapter "If Mao Had Come to Washington in 1945," pp. 77–112, and the comprehensive account of American policy toward China in Joseph W. Esherick, *Lost Chance in China: The World War II Despatches of John S. Service* (New York: Random House, 1974).

†Quoted from testimony presented on June 28, 1971, to the Senate Foreign Relations Committee by Allen S. Whiting, former American deputy consul general in Hong Kong (New York *Times*, June 29, 1971). According to Whiting, who based himself on official State Department records, the visit of the Chinese communist leaders was opposed by Secretary of State Dean Acheson, who "suppressed all information about [Chinese communist overtures] in the 1949 White Paper" on China. It was also Acheson in the Truman years who, insisting that France was the mainstay of the anticommunist coalition in Europe, argued for American support of the French position in Indochina on the grounds that a French defeat in Southeast Asia would weaken her elsewhere. For an account of Acheson's role, see Senator J. William Fulbright, "Reflections: In Thrall to Fear," *New Yorker*, January 8, 1972.

**New York *Times*, July 23, 1972. The *Times* story was taken from Seymour Topping, *Journey Between Two Chinas* (New York: Harper & Row, 1972). The invitation to Stuart is not mentioned in State Department documents covering the period of Stuart's memoirs, *Fifty Years in China*. The *Times* further reported that Topping was denied permission by the State Department to examine documents relating to 1949.

will find it difficult to understand the American refusal to respond positively to several peace overtures from Hanoi and the Vietcong between 1967 and 1973.* A leading principle of our foreign policy, although one infrequently articulated, is that there be no recognition of any communist regime until every possible effort short of all-out war has been made to get rid of it and/or there is no longer any chance that it will be overthrown from within. In accordance with this principle, the Soviet Union was not accorded recognition for sixteen years, by which time it was clear that there was no alternative to recognition. In the case of the Chinese communists a somewhat longer period was required, mainly because of lingering hopes for a quarter of a century that Chiang Kai-shek somehow would manage to topple the regime from his Formosan retreat; even now, when such hopes are no longer entertained in responsible circles, relations with the Chinese communists continue to be both limited and strained. In the last few years there has been some acceptance of the reality of Castro in Cuba, and after fifteen years a thaw in relations is possible, if by no means certain.

In Vietnam, however, the American awareness that the choices and alternatives were few is of recent origin. Not until the closing months of the Johnson Administration in 1968—some would put the date much later—was it realized in the highest policy-making circles that if the war could not be totally lost, neither could it be totally won. Initially, in keeping with the decision to support the

---

*According to British Labor Party leader Harold Wilson, in February, 1967, he—Wilson was Prime Minister at that time—and Soviet Premier Aleksei N. Kosygin attempted to arrange peace talks, but their efforts, initially welcomed by President Johnson, were subsequently thwarted by "the Washington hawks." (London *Times*, May 16, 1971; and the New York *Times*, same date). During the election campaign of 1972, Democratic Vice Presidential nominee Sargent Shriver, supported by W. Averell Harriman and Cyrus R. Vance, charged that the Nixon Administration in 1969 "blew" a chance to end the Vietnam War by refusing to accept a Hanoi offer to withdraw 90 percent of its troops from the two northernmost provinces of South Vietnam. (New York *Times*, August 16, 1972.) In 1971 British Labor MP John Mendelson reported the confirmation by State Department officials that an "offer of secret talks had been made by the N.L.F. [Vietcong] and had been turned down." Mendelson was astonished to discover that "most people" he had talked with in Washington, including Congressmen, were "completely unaware" of "the refusal of the United States Government to engage in real negotiations about a political solution. . . ." (New York *Times*, October 5, 1971.)

French against the Vietminh, the United States steadily escalated its financial contribution by increasing its payments from 40 percent of the war's cost in 1951 to 80 percent in 1954.[7] Between 1955, by which time we had abrogated the Geneva agreements, and 1961, American military aid to South Vietnam averaged about $200,000,000 per year.[8]

American manpower, meanwhile, had also begun to make an appearance. In May, 1950, the first American economic mission arrived in Saigon, and it was followed in July, a few weeks after the beginning of the Korean War on June 25, by a military mission. Four years later, following the French defeat at Dien Bien Phu, the CIA dispatched a team of agents to Saigon with orders to engage in "paramilitary operations" and "political-psychological warfare" against North Vietnam; the missions of the CIA group, directed by Colonel Edward G. Lansdale, included sabotage of the Hanoi city buses and rail lines, the printing of false leaflets that were attributed to the Vietminh, the training of Vietnamese counterinsurgency agents, the bribing of astrologers to predict dire events for the Vietminh and good prospects for the South Vietnamese government, and, perhaps not least, holding English-language classes for the mistresses of key government and military officials.[9]

In the end, inevitably, the exploits of Colonel Lansdale were more dramatic than effective, but they were important in communicating to those interested a continuing if partial American commitment to President Ngo Dinh Diem and his government. By 1956 there were 350 military advisers in South Vietnam, and in May, 1960, the total reached 685. December of 1960 saw an increase to 900, and by December, 1961, only eleven months after John F. Kennedy's inauguration, the number of military advisers was 3,200. One year later the total had increased to 11,300, and in October, 1963, on the eve of Kennedy's assassination, there were 16,732 military advisers in South Vietnam, or almost the equivalent of a full infantry division.

Compared with this horde of military advisers, the first American ground combat unit of 3,500 Marines that arrived in Vietnam on March 8, 1965, "to protect U.S. bases," was something of an anticlimax. A seasoned observer of that event, and there were some, might have doubted, in the light of the decade just ended, that 3,500 or 35,000 or even 350,000 armed Americans could win the war for South Vietnam. But such observers were few in 1965 and their misgivings muted. Most Americans that year found it impossible to believe that overwhelming technological power and military force could not win a war against an enemy who, however skilled a foot soldier he might be, possessed little or no air force or navy and very few tanks and other advanced weapons of war. The only dire possibility, in this context, was that the Chinese would intervene, as they had done in Korea with disastrous consequences for American forces, or that the Russians would take some advantage and cause trouble elsewhere in the world.

There was also a tendency on the part of many Americans, for the most part unspoken, to think of the typical Vietnamese, North or South, as a primitive "Wog," "Gook," "Slope," "Slant," or "Dink," as the counterpart of the alien and heathen Indian of our frontier wars a century ago, as, therefore, people who are less human than we are and beyond the reach of our empathy. Perhaps for this reason we did not hesitate to use the most modern weapons of extermination against the North Vietnamese and Vietcong, as we earlier did not hesitate to destroy the Indians with our superior weapons and numbers; and as we do not mourn the vanished Indians, so we do not mourn the millions of dead Vietnamese.*

*University undergraduates aside, among whom books such as Dee Brown's *Bury My Heart at Wounded Knee* (New York: Holt, 1971) became a best seller in the 1970's, Americans have never been stirred by the fate of the Indians and thus memorial expressions like "Wounded Knee" arouse much less emotion than "the Alamo" or "Bastogne." Hence only Stanford University in recent years has ceased to use the Indian symbol to represent its football team. The nation's capital remains the hometown of the Washington Redskins football team, and when the Redskins were matched with the Miami Dolphins in the 1973 Super Bowl game in the Los Angeles Coliseum, the Miami *Herald* featured a full-page ad in the Washington *Star-News* with the caption over a photograph of the stadium: "Site of the last great Indian massacre." The ad continues: "For the Redskins, Los Angeles Coliseum will be Wounded Knee, '73." (Washington *Star-News,* January 12, 1973; New York *Times,* January 13, 1973.) Equally instructive are the names of American aircraft and operations in Vietnam. As Tom Hayden has pointed out, helicopters and gunships were named *Cheyenne, Mohawk, Chinook, Iroquois,* and *Thunderchief.* The bombing of the North was called "Operation Rolling Thunder." Johnson advisers frequently made use of Indian terminology in referring to the war. (Hayden, *The Love of Possession Is a Disease with Them* [New York: Holt, 1972], pp. 109–11.) Still another aspect of the American attitude toward the Vietnamese was expressed in the "branding" by the First Infantry Division of more than a square mile of jungle northwest of Saigon with the

The point may seem outrageous until we remember that American excesses in the conduct of war largely have been confined to Asian wars against peoples who are neither white nor Western nor, in significant numbers, Christian. Indeed, of the three Asian wars the United States so far has fought in this century, two have occasioned the American use of weapons never before employed in war and one of them on a scale that is unique in world history. In August, 1945, we became, in the final days of the war against Japan, the first nation to use the atomic bomb, and in the Vietnam War we were the first nation to make widespread use of chemicals, herbicides, and related defoliants. Between 1964 and 1972 more than 5,000,000 acres, or 12 percent of South Vietnam, was sprayed with defoliating chemicals.[10] Altogether some 7,100,000 tons of bombs were dropped on Indochina by the end of 1972, more than three times the total for World War II, and 400,000 tons of napalm used, as compared with the 14,000 tons used during World War II.

Nor was this all. While American casualties were not inconsiderable, the 50,000 battle deaths fade into insignificance when compared with the estimated 900,000 North Vietnamese and Vietcong and the 600,000 South Vietnamese soldiers and civilians who died.* "Operation Phoenix," part of the so-called Pacification Program aimed at the elimination of suspected Vietcong agents, alone accounted for more than 40,000 dead, most of them executed without trial. Wounded South Vietnamese—the number of Northern wounded is not known—totaled another 1,400,000, and more than 8,500,000 were refugees by the end of 1972.[11]

American atrocities in war were not unknown before Vietnam; General William Tecumseh Sherman during the Civil War laid waste to a broad belt across five Southern states in accordance with a scorched-earth policy that left no building standing except

---

division emblem. A huge "1" within a five-sided enclosure was cut into the jungle by bulldozing an area one and one-half miles long and one mile wide. To photograph the "Big Red One" emblem, an Army cameraman in a plane was forced to fly to an altitude of 6,000 feet. (New York *Times,* April 5, 1970.)

*Again, casualty projections based on population are revealing. Had the United States suffered equivalent deaths to those experienced by the North Vietnamese, the American toll would have been almost 9,000,000, and, on the same basis as South Vietnam, more than 6,000,000.

churches and slave cabins. But not since the Indian wars had American soldiers systematically hunted down women, children, invalids, and old people, as they did in My Lai and My Khe on the morning of March 16, 1968.[12]

Only in the Indian wars did American soldiers cut off and keep as souvenirs parts of the bodies of dead enemy soldiers—these earlier souvenir hunters sought the ears of the enemy dead—and perhaps not even in the Indian wars were there "mad moments" when soliders "who were bored were allowed to fire weapons with abandon at anything they wanted."[13] According to sworn testimony, American soldiers in Vietnam, on one or more occasions, also:

> —used the wiring of field telephones to inflict electric shocks on the genitals or breasts of suspected Vietcong, practices they referred to as the "Bell Telephone Hour";[14]
>
> —refrained from taking live prisoners;[15]
>
> —gang-raped Vietnamese nurses, afterwards shoving hand flares into their vaginas and exploding their stomachs;[16]
>
> —went through the villages and searched people [and] the women would have all their clothes taken off and the men would use their penises to probe them to make sure they didn't have anything hidden anywhere and this was raping but it was done as searching;[17]
>
> —flung suspected Vietcong from helicopters;[18]
>
> —tortured suspected Vietcong by shoving bamboo splints under their fingernails, or amputating fingers;[19]
>
> —blew up brothels to avoid paying.[20]

In no previous war, so far as is known, have we deliberately sought out and destroyed hospital and other medical facilities, leper colonies, schools, and churches or assigned military commanders "kill quotas" and made leaves of absence dependent upon "body counts." And there were other Vietnam "firsts": generals shooting unarmed civilians from helicopters, falsifying reports, and ordering unauthorized air strikes. Most important of all: Vietnam was the first war fought by the United States in which more than one high-ranking officer stood formally accused by other officers and men of war crimes not unlike those committed by the Germans and Japanese during World War II.*

The accused Americans, however, unlike the Germans and Japanese, with a lone exception, have either not been tried for these crimes or if tried have not been convicted. Although the Army itself in an official report of inquiry charged the two senior generals of the Americal division involved in My Lai with a total of forty-three specific acts of misconduct or omission, the only punishment meted out was the censure of Major General Samuel W. Koster and Brigadier General George H. Young, Jr., the demotion of Koster to brigadier rank, and the revocation of both generals' Distinguished Service Medals. Of the twenty-three other officers and enlisted men of the Americal division implicated in the atrocity, charges against all but six were eventually dismissed, and of these six only First Lieutenant William L. Calley, Jr., was tried and convicted of the premeditated murder of "not fewer" than twenty-two Vietnamese civilians.† Thus far no one charged with any other atrocity in Vietnam, including actions similar to those of My Lai, has been brought to trial and convicted; charges were dismissed against the two officers accused of murdering six and two civilians respectively by taking "pot shots" at them from helicopters. General John D. Lavelle, who was responsible for the unauthorized air strikes against North Vietnam and for falsifying reports, was reprimanded, demoted two ranks, and retired—but retired with the $27,000 annual salary of a four-star general. The courageous few responsible for exposing My Lai and bringing

---

*It is of interest that the only previous case in this century involved a brigade commander in another Asian country. Brigadier General Jacob H. Smith, serving in the Philippines in 1901, was court-martialed for giving orders that "no prisoner should be taken" in an operation on the island of Samar, that "there should be extensive killing and burning . . . and that all persons above the age of ten years should be killed because they were capable of bearing arms." Smith was convicted and sentenced to be admonished. President Theodore Roosevelt ordered him retired. (New York *Times,* June 3, 1971.)

†Estimates of the My Lai dead, almost all of whom were unarmed old men, women, and children, ranged from the official but secret Army figure of 347 to more than 500. (Seymour Hersh, *Cover-Up: The Army's Secret Investigation of the Massacre at My Lai 4* [New York: Random House, 1972].) Calley's own preferred word for what he and his platoon had done to the villagers was "wasting"—the villagers had not been murdered or killed, just "wasted."

charges against Lavelle—Sergeant Lonnie Franks, Lieutenant Delbert R. Terrill, Jr., Ronald Lee Ridenhour—presumably could confront our record in Vietnam because they could confront their own guilt in the ravishment of that unfortunate country. Most Americans, to judge by their acceptance of the acquittals and the haste and ease with which the war has been forgotten, presumably could not.* And with the knowledge that the commanding generals who issued orders and those who carried them out are not guilty of war crimes, there is the reassurance that no one is guilty.

History, nevertheless, is almost certain to view the Vietnam War itself as an atrocity and American participation in it as not only costly to Vietnam but to the United States as well. Indeed, the historians of the future may well want to raise the question whether both countries would not have gained had the elections scheduled in 1956 under the Geneva agreements been held and Ho Chi Minh come to power in a unified Vietnam. For all students of Vietnam agree that Ho Chi Minh was much more a Vietnamese patriot than he was a communist and much more a communist of independent mind than a puppet of the Chinese or the Russians. Had he and his Vietminh won the election in 1956, and it is probable that a victory for Ho and his forces would have been the result, Vietnam undoubtedly would have become an instructive blend of Marxism, the Chinese heritage, indigenous Vietnamese culture, and French influence. Instead, there is much death, mutilation, and destruction everywhere, and while the North remains culturally intact, according to accounts, South Vietnam until it fell to the North was another matter.

The most attractive features of the American way of life, apparently, like some of the best wines, do not travel. The so-called Americanization of South Vietnam, therefore, created in the cities especially a bastard society that combined what was ugly, sordid, and commercialized in the American style of life with what was cheap, imitative, and corrupt in Vietnamese culture. The resulting mix, almost all travelers to the country agreed, was some-

*Thus there was general relief when Calley's life sentence was reduced to twenty years and support for President Nixon's order that Calley be released from the Fort Benning stockade and confined to house arrest. On April 16, 1974, his sentence was further reduced to ten years. These actions and the response to them made it highly unlikely that Calley would serve out his sentence, and on September 25, 1974, he was ordered released by a federal court judge.

where between the PX and Times Square, on the one side, Pigalle and Shantytown on the other. Looked at another way, Saigon "is like a stewing Los Angeles, shading into Hollywood, Venice Beach, and Watts," wrote Mary McCarthy in 1967. "Street vendors and children are offering trays of American cigarettes and racks on racks of Johnnie Walker, Haig & Haig, Black & White (which are either black market, stolen from the PX, or spurious, depending on the price); billboards outside car agencies advertise Triumphs, Thunderbirds, MGs, Corvettes. . . . There are photocopying services, film-developing services, Western tailoring and dry-cleaning services, radio and TV repair shops, air conditioners, Olivetti typewriters, comic books . . . you name it, they have it."[21]

At night the PX gave way to Pigalle and Times Square, as Saigon began to look "like a World's Fair or Exposition in some hick American city. There are Chinese restaurants, innumerable French restaurants (not surprising), but also *La Dolce Vita, Le Guillaume Tell,* the *Paprika* (a Spanish restaurant on a rooftop, serving paella and sangria). The national cuisine no American wants to sample is the Vietnamese. . . . Saigon has a smog problem, like New York and Los Angeles, a municipal garbage problem, a traffic problem, power failures, inflation, juvenile delinquency. In short it meets most of the criteria of a modern Western city. The young soldiers do not like Saigon and its clip joints and high prices. Everybody is trying to sell them something or buy something from them. Six-year-old boys, cute as pins, are plucking at them: 'You come see my sister. She Number One fuck.'"[22]

With the rate of inflation estimated at 65 percent a year in 1974, almost every Vietnamese was forced to supplement his earnings in one way or another, and since even an Army officer could not support his family on his pay, American goods of every variety found their way into a flourishing black market. In 1973 South Vietnam exported products worth $62,000,000, whereas imports totaled $740,000,000, or almost twelve times the amount exported; while no one knows the exact figures, perhaps a quarter of the imports, most of which were paid for by the United States, never reached their legitimate destination.[23]

Whether or not a PX by day and Pigalle by night, and whatever the extent of the corruption and black market, Saigon and those sections of South Vietnam not under the control of the Vietcong existed within the framework of a police state. Although the government pretended otherwise and made occasional gestures in the direction of fundamental liberties, there were no free elections, no free press, and no right of *habeas corpus* or fair trial. Those suspected of sympathizing with the enemy, a "subversive" category that included anyone protesting the war or lack of rights, could be imprisoned without trial for an indefinite period of time. In 1972 the South Vietnamese Committee on Prison Reform estimated that there were more than 100,000 prisoners in Vietnam jails, most of whom have never stood trial.[24] Torture was commonplace and often went on under the eyes of American advisers, at least one of whom was attached to every prison and interrogation center. In short, American lives and money were no more successful in ensuring democracy in South Vietnam than they were successful in purchasing victory over the communists.*

The war's effects on the American home front were different, but casualties and war damage aside, they had a good bit in common with the consequences in Vietnam. In America, too, there were, and there continue to be, widespread doubts about the necessity for the war and our motivations and goals in becoming involved. While no President suffered the fate of Premier Ngo Dinh Diem during the period when America was most active in Vietnam, the retirement from office of Lyndon B. Johnson was largely caused by a general lack of confidence in his handling of the war, and the continuing "credibility crisis" of the Nixon years with reference to policies in Cambodia and Laos no doubt helped estab-

---

*As the bereaved father of one of the American war dead put it, following a visit to Vietnam early in 1974: "It was my hope that in going to Vietnam I might find some consolation for his loss if there was evidence that his sacrifice had somehow served the Vietnamese people. . . . I would not have believed it had I not seen for myself what can only be called a total police state. . . . We were overwhelmed with the personal impact of talking with people who had actually suffered torture and the brutality of prison life . . . we saw little evidence that American money was being used for anything but support of the Thieu military regime. . . . The fact is that the American presence now, as before, remains a disaster, not only as a result of the wartime devastation, defoliation and displacement of people, but as a continuing financial presence that maintains a government of military officers that clings to power, no matter what the cost to peace, freedom and democratic principles." (Robert C. Ransom in New York *Times*, February 19, 1974.)

lish the later conviction during Watergate that the President was a chronic liar. The rate of inflation and the reductions in spending on vital domestic needs and services also owed much to the financial costs of the Vietnam War.

Unlike in World War II and the Korean War, however, our role in Vietnam did not develop at a time when the economy was moving in a downward direction. In 1964, the last year before the war was escalated, the nation was close to full employment, and the preceding five years had seen a substantial rise in corporate profits and the value of corporate stocks. The average worker with a family in 1965 was earning approximately 11 percent more in spendable income (adjusted for inflation) than he had earned five years earlier. In short, the Vietnam War, unlike the two other wars, did not constitute a massive "pump-priming" operation for a faltering economy, and it cannot be argued, therefore, that Vietnam was an economic necessity.

But because real wages, profits, and the stock-market index substantially declined between 1965 and 1970, it does not follow that defense expenditures as such are of little or no benefit to the economy. Although annual military expenditures for Vietnam rarely amounted to more than a third of defense expenditures 1963–1973, the total spent on defense did not fall below $50 billion annually, with the exception of fiscal 1965, and in all but three years exceeded $75 billion. In 1969, when defense spending approximated $78 billion, of which the Vietnam share was $21.5 billion, the *Wall Street Journal* estimated that one of every nine jobs was "in the defense field." If, added the *Journal*, wives, children, and other dependents were included, "Americans who rely on defense work for their financial support constitute a very significant fraction of the U.S. population—perhaps nearly one-fifth." According to the *Journal* article, within the civilian work force one of every five electrical and mechanical engineers, two of every five airplane mechanics, two of every five nonteaching physicists, and three of every five aeronautical engineers were working on defense-related projects at that time.[25]

Since defense-related employment is unevenly distributed, some sections of the country are much more dependent than others on military contracts for production and procurement. In 1972, for example, twelve states received over $1 billion each in prime military contracts,* and twenty-two states were awarded contracts of between $100,000,000 and $1 billion. The population in 1970 of the twelve high-award states was 104,800,000, and while the per capita value of defense contracts may be small in the case of such heavily populated states as California and New York, the contracts are nevertheless important in providing direct and indirect employment. The economies of the New England states, California, Texas, and Florida undoubtedly would become severely depressed if defense spending were heavily curtailed.†

There is, however, little prospect of that happening in the foreseeable future, given a continuing American commitment to the assumptions stated earlier. The crucial question, then, concerns

---

*The twelve states were: New York, New Jersey, Pennsylvania, Ohio, Virginia, Massachusetts, Rhode Island, Connecticut, Florida, Missouri, Texas, and California. (New York *Times,* January 26, 1973.)

†The economic stability of some sections of the country probably would be increased if the government itself wholly owned and operated firms, such as aircraft manufacturers, that depend almost entirely on military-procurement contracts for their business. Perhaps the ultimate cost to taxpayers would also be less. Certainly the recent history of the Grumman Corporation is instructive and not without a certain bemusement. To begin with, a Grumman bid to build the Navy's F-14 fighter was accepted, although the bid was $100,000,000 more than the next lowest bid. Grumman difficulties with design and production of the plane forced it to borrow from the Navy $52 billion beyond the amount originally advanced, and in 1974 it applied for an additional $100,000,000. In the course of hearings on the request, held by a Senate subcommittee, Grumman disclosed that it had invested $24,000,000 of the original loan in short-term securities such as Treasury bills and bank certificates of deposit, thereby earning $3,000,000 in interest. While the Navy itself had no objection to this practice, which in effect enabled a private manufacturer to make a profit on money borrowed from the government, a number of Senators questioned the wisdom of lending the company still more money in view of its dismal production record. On June 6, 1969, shortly after Grumman successfully bid on the F-14, the *Wall Street Journal* in a front-page story reported that the Navy had an option to purchase 463 F-14s at a cost of $7,300,000 each, or a total of almost $3.4 billion. By August, 1974, the cost per plane had increased to $17,800,000, or $6.4 billion for 336 planes. (New York *Times,* August 1, 1974.) By November, 1974, the announced cost per plane had risen to $19,800,000, and according to Senator Thomas F. Eagleton, the Navy had requested an additional $100,000,000 "to correct deficiencies in its F-14 fighter plane, particularly in the radar system." In a Senate speech on November 21 Eagleton asserted that the radar systems were failing every 2.2 hours; Vice Admiral Robert B. Baldwin, representing the Navy, "reportedly assured the Senator that this figure had been raised to 16 hours." (New York *Times,* November 22, 1974.)

the long-term effects of what President Eisenhower termed the military-industrial complex on the American way of life, and in answering this question the real or imagined dependence of the economy on arms expenditure may be the least important consideration. The interest of industry in lucrative military contracts, the fraternal relations between corporate executives and high-ranking military officers and the ease with which such officers retire to important positions in business firms, the ferocity with which state governments and congressional delegations compete for procurement awards and defense installations, all this may be accepted and, at least up to a point, lived with in the framework of American democracy.[26]

Evidence exists, however, that the military-industrial complex is gradually becoming politicized into a garrison state in which the interests and influence of the military are increasingly dominant in traditionally civilian areas. No doubt any Thirty Years War—and the United States has been at war with communism to one degree or another for at least thirty years—inevitably would witness a shift toward the militarization of any society no matter what the strength of its civil institutions. The Cold War, however, is a special case in that it is a war that can never be wholly won or wholly lost and in which there are few if any spectacular victories or spectacular defeats. Indeed, on the two occasions thus far when the Cold War turned hot, namely, Korea and Vietnam, there was no clear-cut result, much less a triumph for the United States. Instead, there was a good deal of humiliation in military circles and resentment of civilian "meddling" and interference, much evidence of demoralization and the breakdown of discipline within the armed forces, and increasing skepticism everywhere about the character and capabilities of the men and women in uniform, whether officers or enlisted personnel. The Cold War, by diverting the nation's resources and energies elsewhere, also ensured the neglect of vital domestic problems, many of them related to racial injustice and the deteriorating quality of life, almost to the point of no return.

In view of these suspicions, doubts, and misgivings, one finds it understandable, if regrettable, that the military establishment, feeling itself to be somewhat off-balance, should regard the anti-war movement not merely as misguided but as directly or indirectly communist-inspired and include among its enemies hippies, liberals, the mass media, and certain "girl students from Vassar College and the State University of New York at New Paltz [who] will offer sex to [West Point] cadets who sign an antiwar petition."[27] But there is discontent in some military circles that goes far beyond the issue of whether the Army may properly conduct "an extensive domestic surveillance program" aimed at the peace movement and its sympathizers, including those in Congress.[28] In Vietnam the discontent found expression in the authorization of air strikes at North Vietnam between November, 1971, and April, 1972, in defiance of instructions from higher authorities, and in the systematic falsifying of reports concerning the heavy bombing raids. Discontent is also reflected in the charge that the "attack on the military establishment" emanates from "radical journalists" bent on creating confusion, from which it follows that "Communist strategy aimed at defeating the United States not on the battlefield but on the home front has succeeded."[29] Hostility toward traditional freedoms, such as freedom of the press, is manifest in criticisms of the mass media on grounds that the "vast amount of information over television and other instant news media [is] one way or another, in my judgment . . . a disservice to the security of the country" and in the accompanying proposal that there be created a "national information program, such as maybe every week a half-hour program . . . starting out with defense issues."[30]

Much of this restlessness and discontent suggests not only a fundamental impatience with the constitutional principle of civilian control of military affairs but an insistence that the military have a significant role in the determination of policy, especially in the foreign field. This insistence presumably underlay the efforts in 1970–1971 and thereafter of a high-ranking military spy ring in the White House and National Security Council to obtain and deliver to the chairman of the Joint Chiefs of Staff secret policy documents stolen from the files of Henry A. Kissinger and others; and it also plays a role in the increasing tendency to replace civilians in key government positions with generals and admirals.*

---

*In 1947, when the Department of Defense was created, there were no flag-rank officers serving as Deputy Assistant Secretaries of Defense. By 1964 there were three such officers and, ten years later, a total of eleven. In combining the two positions formerly held by H.R. Haldeman and John Ehrlichman and by

Such developments encourage a suspicion that significant elements in the military hierarchy are prepared to accept continued civilian control of policy only if they are permitted to participate in the decision-making process and, in certain cases, exert a decisive influence.

To be sure, in the modern world the United States could not, as a major power, make foreign policy without reference to the military interests and capabilities of those involved in treaty commitments and security arrangements. Aid programs, trade negotiations, access to key waterways, the balance of forces, even the question whether or not to recognize a new regime, all these and many more policy areas can hardly be separated from a military component of greater or lesser importance. A foreign policy that was made with no reference to any military equation would be as unrealistic as a military strategy that was executed in total isolation from foreign-policy considerations. Hence no Secretary of State, however strong his desire to be awarded the Nobel Peace Prize, can afford not to consult with other members of the National Security Council and the Joint Chiefs of Staff.

But the present system of consultation may not be compatible with a long-term continuing dependency on high levels of preparedness and military expenditures. Given such dependence, the military establishment almost certainly will seek to gain influence not only in foreign policy but in areas of domestic national life that, in the eyes of the military, relate to morale, our cohesiveness as a nation, and discipline. There is bound to be increasing awareness in military circles of the deficiencies of the schools, the mass media, and the political system itself and, accompanying this awareness, a growing number of officers embarking on political careers.* In proportion, as the usual military-recruitment processes serve to attract alienated and addicted white and black

---

appointing General Alexander M. Haig, Jr., to fill the post, President Nixon in 1973 became the first President to have a senior military officer as his closest adviser.

*The Korean and Vietnam wars, perhaps because they were not total victories, have produced few heroes and no Grants or Eisenhowers. The only major political effort so far of a military nature is that of former commander in Vietnam and Army Chief of Staff, General William C. Westmoreland of South Carolina, who in 1974 announced his candidacy for the South Carolina governorship but was defeated in the primary.

dropouts, much given in the Army to drugs, "fragging," racial brawls, and crime, pay scales and other emoluments will be raised sufficiently to enlist larger numbers of young men and women from the white and black educated lower-middle and working classes; in short, the armed forces will gradually become an elite corps of well-paid professionals presiding over an increasingly complicated and expensive technology of warfare.* Finally, the resulting garrison state would undoubtedly witness a strengthening of the authoritarian institutions of society and a partial return to the older values and traditions, although not necessarily the older mores.†

But whatever its internal form or condition, the garrison state can exist only in the framework of a prolonged international crisis that constantly threatens and occasionally reverts to war. Failing an occasional successful military venture, the garrison state either ceases to exist or, enlarging upon and accelerating certain inherent tendenceis, gradually evolves into an authoritarian system. The mere threat of war, probably, is not enough in the long run to sustain the level of effort and expenditures, just as at the community level the threat of crime is not enough to sustain the police force at an impressive strength. What is needed is actual war, actual crime, if the garrison state or police force is not to wither away.

Taking the past as a guide, there will never be a need to lament

---

*These trends were well under way 1974–1975. Aided by rising unemployment, recruitment in January, 1975, went beyond the goals set by the services, and the quality of recruits received, especially black recruits, was steadily improving. At that time recruits received, in addition to food, clothing, shelter, and free medical and dental care, pay of $344.10 a month. Those recruits who were high school graduates were given bonuses of $2,500 if they volunteered for the combat units. At the same time, the Army was also training special elite combat forces, such as the First Ranger Battalion, for "rapid deployment by air wherever a United States military presence is required." (New York *Times*, October 25, 1974.) In January, 1975, the Pentagon announced that blacks constituted 20 percent of the Army, of whom 4.5 percent were officers, and 13 percent of the Navy. (New York *Times*, January 26, 1975.)

†It is conceivable, for example, that the garrison state would continue to permit a good deal of sexual freedom and experimentation in life-styles, provided that such "permissiveness" did not threaten the politico-military order. The possibility that "permissiveness" would work not against but for authoritarianism is discussed in the final chapter.

the absence of war for very long, and this not only because there are political, economic, and ideological causes of war. Nor is it enough to suggest that wars occasionally are due to accident, miscalculation, power and aggrandizement, and even simply incompetent advice (the "explanation," in some accounts, of American intervention in Vietnam). Unfortunately all such accounts neglect the psychology of aggression and war and by so doing fail to explain the ubiquity of war in the human experience. The best of them involve a myth of some sort—any alleged cause of war that invokes altruism is a myth—while the worst serve to confuse issues or belabor the other side. Equally naïve is the belief that war as such someday will be ended by the adoption everywhere of this or that economic or political system. Such beliefs are simply not in accord with more than 4,000 years of recorded history.

Instead, if this history be read without cultural blinders, it teaches us that Freud was essentially correct to posit in man a basic aggressive instinct that is hardly less important than any other instinctual need, an instinct, moreover, that is encouraged to express itself in a variety of group settings, especially those based on race or nationality.* The psychology of war, like the pyschology of prejudice, makes use of manipulations and projections of all sorts. Almost all the qualities that we dislike about ourselves—all that we consciously or unconsciously regard as base, mean, greedy, lustful, and aggressive—can be attributed to the enemy, and by that means we shore up that always-fragile sense of our own goodness that is forever beset by guilt and anxiety. War, in other words, is not only the health of the state, as Bourne suggested. In a somewhat different psychological sense, it is the health of the individual.

---

*The instinct of aggression, or aggressive drive, should not be confused with what Freud called the "destructive instinct" or "death instinct." In his last statement about the "destructive instinct" Freud maintained that its "final aim" is to reduce "living things to an inorganic state. For this reason we also call it the *death instinct*. If we suppose that living things appeared later than inanimate ones and arose out of them, then the death instinct agrees with the formula we have stated, to the effect that instincts tend toward a return to an earlier state. . . . So long as that instinct operates internally, as a death instinct, it remains silent; we only come across it after it has become diverted outward as an instinct of destruction." (*An Outline of Psychoanalysis* [New York: Norton, 1949], pp. 20–22.) The dilemma for the individual, as Freud saw it, was that the expression of aggres-

But the Cold War, in particular, may perform another function. The American response to Nazism and fascism, it has long been observed, was remarkably more temperate than the response to communism. Attempts to explain this difference range from the quasi-Marxist argument that there is an affinity between fascism and big business to the somewhat more acceptable view that the true nature of the Nazi threat to Western civilization was not understood for a good many years. No doubt there is some truth in these and other efforts to account for appeasement and the related belief in the 1930's that is was possible to "do business" with Hitler.

Additionally, however, it is worth noting that a psychological appeal of fascism is to the father or leader principle, which, as psychoanalyst Alexander Mitscherlich and others have noted, is rooted in the wish to be dependent on and protected by the all-powerful father, a wish that originates in childhood but is by no means ever entirely given up later in life.[32] Fascism, from the standpoint of psychoanalysis, is the return of the father, or, to put it more precisely, the substitution for the missing, weak, and fallible father of a "new one of still undiminished strength."[33] Because fascism, quite apart from other considerations, fulfills a need for security and reassurance that goes back to childhood, it is experienced as less threatening even by those who are not themselves fascists and who do not, in their own societies, support fascist movements.

Communism, on the other hand, in threatening to do away with the father principle, arouses the most profound anxiety and the deepest enmity among those whose childhood dependency needs are very great. In its appeal to brotherhood and fraternity rather

---

sion exposes him to all sorts of dangers, but "holding back" on aggression "is in general unhealthy and leads to illness." In a similar way, a society that resorts to war may invite its own destruction from the superior force of its enemy, but if it "holds back," the aggressive drive may turn inward and threaten the stability of the society. Freud, in effect, despaired of finding any solution to the problem of aggression; there were perils and penalties either way, whether aggression was discharged or contained.

Not all psychoanalysts accept Freud's postulation of a death instinct, but almost all agree that, clinically speaking, aggressiveness and aggression are facts of life.[31]

than fatherhood, communism, in effect, revives the uncertainties and anxious rivalries of the sibling relationship while at the same time removing the security provided by paternal authority. As Mitscherlich puts it, the collapse of the father ensures that the "relationship of the sons between themselves is intensified and reinforced by the libidinal and aggressive ties previously attached to the father."[34] Whereas communism underestimates the significance of sexuality—hence its tendency toward sexual puritanism—fascism utilizes primitive homo- and heterosexual components and sexualizes aggression. The hypothesis, then, is that fascism is experienced as less threatening than communism because it is, in part, an attempt to rescue the father principle from oblivion and to utilize all varieties of sexual feeling.

That fascism gains and communism loses *in appeal* from the universal hunger for a powerful father is not difficult to understand in the larger context of history. Just as in religion the principle of God the Father has always elicited more devout support than the principle of men as brothers, so in politics all political systems, whether communist or democratic, industrial or agrarian, have moved inexorably from ideologies of brotherhood to the actualities of strong and powerful leadership. Thus the emergence of the Lenins and Stalins, the Maos and the Castros, in the communist countries and the clamor in the democracies for leaders in the mold of a Churchill, a Roosevelt, or a de Gaulle.[35]

In one respect, however, the psychological strength of communism is far superior to that of either fascism or democracy, the economies of which are based essentially on capitalistic principles. Wherever there is extreme poverty and suffering—and the "wherever" takes in most of the world—communism or some variety of it appears to offer the most promise of improvement in the general condition. In that crucial respect communism, however authoritarian, rather than Western democratic capitalism has become not so much, in William James' phrase, "the moral equivalent of war" as an acceptable alternative to desperate want and early death from disease, in short, almost all the miseries that afflict the great mass of humanity.[36] Thus far the West has developed no social alternative to the motivations of self-interest and private greed and hence no solution to most of the problems for which communism presents itself as the remedy. Until "moral equivalents" are found, there will be an endless succession of immoral equivalents exemplified by but by no means confined to wars of the Vietnam type.

Meanwhile, in the name of military preparedness, scarce resources are further depleted, urgent economic and social crises are not resolved, and the quality of life in every Western nation deteriorates at an ever increasing rate. Perhaps it is time to conclude that the real enemies of democracy are within our own societies and within ourselves and that the battle to preserve what is best in the Judaic-Christian tradition will be won or lost on these battlefields. Perhaps, in other words, it is time to raise the question posed by the Greek poet C. P. Cavafy in his poem "Expecting the Barbarians."[37] The poem tells of a people whose rulers can do nothing, not even pass laws, because they are awaiting the "barbarians." All day the Emperor and the Senators, the consuls and praetors, sit and wait, but the "barbarians" do not come. Finally it is night, and when some travelers arrive from the frontier and say that "there are no longer any barbarians," the people return to their homes deep in thought. "And now," asks the poet,

> what shall become of us without any barbarians?
> Those people were a kind of solution.

10

The Abdication of One-Eyed Kings

Presidential candidate George McGovern has much to recommend him, playwright Arthur Miller commented on the eve of the 1972 election, but "he lacks that touch of larceny which we enjoy in our leaders." Novelist Norman Mailer, no less astute, had noted earlier that a caucus of McGovern supporters at the Democratic Convention in Miami, while appealing in terms of the "open" faces of the delegates, was boring because "there was insufficient evil in the room."[1] Neither Miller nor Mailer could have known at the time how much prophecy as well as insight was contained in their remarks, and indeed few if any Americans in 1972 could have guessed to what extent the nation's politics in the coming years would be dominated by more than a "touch" of larceny and evil.

Feeling themselves to have been, in a sense, gang-raped by the Nixon Administration and only slowly emerging from the trauma of that event, many Americans understandably think of Watergate and the associated high crimes and misdemeanors as sometime things and believe, with James Reston, "there is little danger that we will have another White House gang like this one. . . ."[2] One hopes, of course, that such optimism is justified, but a careful study of recent presidential history does not suggest that Nixon was in every respect *sui generis* or that the violations of law committed by his staff were unique. While Nixon's personal biography is essential to an understanding of his behavior, we should not forget that he and his close associates are fairly representative of a system of values that enjoyed and continues to enjoy widespread support in the United States. Because of this, Nixon himself, even after the adverse judgments of both the Supreme Court and the House of Representatives, was far from completely out of favor with an impressive number of citizens, especially those who were among his enthusiastic backers before 1968, not to mention 1972. Even in late June of 1974, 58 percent of businessmen, with whom Nixon has always been extremely popular, were opposed to his impeachment by the House, and 72 percent were against either his conviction by the Senate or his resignation. A Gallup Poll of June revealed that only 48 percent, or fewer than half of Americans, regarded Watergate as a "serious matter," with 43 percent dismissing it as "just politics." As late as April, 1974, both Gallup and Harris polls showed that Nixon still enjoyed the approval of a quarter of the total electorate and close to a third of those who were white Protestants, small-town and rural voters, business people, Southerners, and citizens over fifty years of age.* Given these attitudes and the willingness of many Americans to accept, if not condone, much political immorality if it does not threaten their immediate economic interests, one would be naïve to believe there will not be other Nixons, not to mention other Haldemans and Ehrlichmans, in the White House from time to time, just as there will be other Oswalds and Bremers awaiting their opportunity in the anonymous ranks of the rootless.

But whatever the future may hold, to suggest that the nation's acute crisis of leadership did not begin with Nixon, and will not end with his successor is not exaggerating or stretching the bounds of reason too much. For a variety of complex reasons, *all* recent Presidents, not only Nixon, have left the office of the President somewhat diminished in honor and respect and the American people with shrunken confidence in their political institutions. If one consequence of these presidential failures is a political culture characterized by leaders who cannot or will not lead, another

*For details see the New York *Times* of April 14, 1974, and July 11, 1974. The report on businessmen is based on a *Times* questionnaire sent in late June to the top executives of the largest 500 corporations, 167 or a respectable 34 percent of whom responded. No one can tell how many of these executives voted for Nixon in 1972, but a *Times* survey on the eve of that election found 91.4 percent of 430 executives saying they would vote for him. In contrast to the 28 percent of businessmen who favored conviction or resignation, the June Gallup Poll reported that 44 percent of Americans believed that Nixon should be removed from office.

more serious result is national anomie or panic of the type described by Freud not long after the collapse of the Austro-Hungarian Empire. "The loss of the leader in some sense or other," Freud wrote in 1922, "the birth of misgivings about him, brings on the outbreak of panic . . . the mutual ties between the members of the group disappear, as a rule, at the same time as the tie with their leader. The group vanishes in dust. . . ."[3]

Certainly one is tempted to view much of the turmoil and unrest, the anomie and alienation, the mayhem and violence of recent American history as a kind of panic marked by the dissolution of bonds that have traditionally made for unity and to account for it in terms of the loss of leaders and "the birth of misgivings" about them. Prior to 1964, apparently, the public's confidence in the nation's political leadership was fairly high. A University of Michigan survey in 1964, for example, found 62 percent of adults expressing "a high degree of trust in the Government," with relatively little difference between those who favored immediate withdrawal from Vietnam and those who supported an escalation of the war.[4] By June, 1968, or more than six months before Nixon took office, a Harris study reported that only 13 percent of Americans felt that the political leadership of the country was "better" than in the past, whereas 38 percent believed it was "worse" and 42 percent thought it was "about the same." But particularly significant was the finding that no other leadership field scored as low on the "better" side; in medicine, science, and business comparable figures were 88, 79, and 64 percentiles.[5] In a 1973 Harris survey conducted for the Senate Subcommittee on Intergovernmental Relations, those Americans expressing "a great deal of confidence" in the executive branch had declined to 19 percent; in 1965 and 1972, Harris further reported, the comparable percents were 41 and 27.[6] While no one can know precisely when the seemingly endless credibility gap first became manifest, it existed in mature form at least as early as February, 1967, when 65 percent of Gallup Poll respondents expressed doubts about the reliability of information being supplied them by the Johnson Administration. Four years later, with Nixon as President, the proportion had increased to 69 percent.[7]

The political alienation of blacks is even more striking. According to a 1974 study by the Joint Center for Political Studies, toward the end of the Eisenhower years the federal government enjoyed the confidence of as many blacks as whites, and in 1964 black trust in government was greater than that of whites. In the mid-sixties whites became increasingly distrustful of government, and their confidence remained low until the election of Nixon in 1968. Black confidence in government, on the other hand, dropped sharply between 1968 and 1972, especially among youth, professionals, and persons over age fifty.

No doubt the credibility gap reached its most exacerbated state during the presidential years of Johnson and Nixon, when many Americans believed that one President was a habitual liar, bungler, and vulgarian, while the other, also a liar, was in addition somewhat paranoid and a crook. But Nixon, whose record was much worse than Johnson's, perhaps even the worst in the entire history of the Presidency, did not evoke the same emotional response, especially among young people. Nixon was distrusted, certainly, and toward the end intensely disliked, but he aroused more contempt than anger.

Some part of the murderous hostility toward Johnson that existed among youth, a hostility that was at least partly responsible for his decision not to seek another term, may have derived from the unconscious suspicion that he was not entirely innocent of some connection with the death of John F. Kennedy. In the unconscious of some young people the death of Kennedy at the hands of persons unknown other than Oswald but including LBJ may have been experienced as the murder of a younger, more virile son (and brother) by an older, impotent father, a father jealous of the son's very youth, good looks, vigor, and greater success— for Johnson, too, had sought the nomination in 1960. If this was the unconscious fantasy, certainly one could imagine or want to believe that LBJ was somehow implicated in the assassination and, believing this, hate him, mock him, want to destroy him. The popularity of the venomous satire *Macbird!*, the anti-Johnson jingles and buttons, the posters belittling his masculinity, and the obscene slogans and chants support such interpretations. As a popular anti-Vietnam War jingle put it, "Hey, hey, LBJ, how many kids did you kill today?" The reference to killing children is in almost perfect accord with the hypothesized fantasy.

The fantasy itself, of course, is well known in mythology, in which there are numerous instances, as science-fiction writer Isaac Asimov has pointed out, of "hostility between royal father and heir-apparent son" leading to the death of the latter. For example, Cronos, having castrated his father and replaced him, swallowed his sons to ensure that he would not suffer a similar fate at their hands. Neither Zeus nor his brother Poseidon would marry Thetis, with whom they were in love, because it had been decreed that she would bear a son mightier than his father. Daedalus killed his nephew and pupil Perdix out of "overwhelming jealousy, when that young man showed signs of becoming superior to his teacher."[8] These myths, in addition to revealing that there never has been much love lost between generations, tell us that no son can vanquish a father without guilt and feelings of rivalry and that no father can give way to a son without resentment and some sense of defeat.

There are few, if any, Greek elements in the Nixon tragedy. Those Americans who have not already forgotten it may regard the Watergate era as a singular nightmare in our history, from which, like Stephen Dedalus in Joyce's *Ulysses*, they are trying to awaken.* Once awake, they are not likely to look back on Watergate with the same sadness with which they look back on the Johnson years, remembering what never was but what might have been. Had it not been for Vietnam, Johnson, for all his limitations, might have touched greatness. With Nixon there was never any question of what might have been and no possibility of greatness.

But in fairness to Johnson, who lied to protect the war, and to Nixon, who lied to protect himself, one may observe that Americans rarely are told the whole truth by their political leaders, and when they are, it usually is in regard to matters of small moment. Kennedy admittedly was evasive about the American involvement in the abortive Bay of Pigs invasion of Cuba and about his own role in the overthrow of Ngo Dinh Diem in 1963. Nor can it be denied that Truman withheld from Congress and the public a good deal of information pertaining to his conduct of the Korean War. What the White House tapes were for Nixon on a scale that no one could have imagined, the Pentagon Papers were on a lesser

---

*The nightmare image made an early appearance in President Ford's first address to the nation when he said: "My fellow Americans, our long national nightmare is over." He could not say, for obvious reasons, that there is such a thing as a recurrent nightmare.

scale for Kennedy and Johnson, and in recent years a number of published diaries and memoirs dealing with Roosevelt, Truman, and Eisenhower enabled Americans who read them "at last to match the lies they told us with their secret truths."[9]

Despite these accounts, much remains to be known about the American role in overthrowing the legal governments of Guatemala, Iran, Chile, and Greece and the agreements that were responsible for ending the so-called Yom Kippur War of 1973 between Israel and the Arab states. All of the Presidents since 1945 have either been silent or less than honest about the influence of the CIA in foreign elections and other political events abroad and have evaded questions about the extent to which the agency is under their effective control.[10]

Presumably many political leaders assume that the public is infinitely gullible and will believe almost any statement if it is delivered in an earnest and authoritative manner. Thus Nelson Rockefeller in 1969, not long before his reelection as New York's governor, expected to be believed, and perhaps was believed by his audience, when he declared that in a matter of months the Long Island Railroad would be the best commuter line in the country. Months and, for that matter, years later, as the governor must have anticipated when he made his statement, the Long Island rail service was still among the worst, if not the worst, rail passenger service in the nation. Rockefeller's declaration may have been less momentous than President Kennedy's assurance that the United States was not implicated in the murder of Ngo Dinh Diem or President Johnson's insistence on September 28, 1964, that there were no plans at that time to bomb Vietnam when, in fact, plans had been made three weeks earlier, but it was hardly less a deception.*[11]

Politicians, of course, are deceptive everywhere; lying is hardly unknown in the higher echelons of both democratic and au-

---

*Given the increasing tendency of politics, like the theater, to make of deception a fine art, one is not surprised that it should appeal to former actors or that certain politicians *manqué,* such as former New York Mayor John V. Lindsay, should be drawn to appearing in films and on television. Perhaps the actors-turned-politicans and the politicians-turned-actors are performing fantasies of themselves. Certainly the histrionics, poses, and elaborate gestures of certain political figures remind one much more of stage Lears and Hamlets than of law-office backgrounds in Boston or rural Illinois.

thoritarian governments abroad. But American political leadership is not just deceptive. If felony indictments of officeholders, described elsewhere, are any guide the governing elite is, in large measure, corrupt as well on a scale that is almost beyond comprehension in any other democratic country. It is also inclined toward a good deal of questionable ethical behavior, for example, the practice of being paid legal or consulting retainers while holding office. Nor is it unknown for the relatives of political persons to hold highly paid but essentially absentee jobs in government and for the persons themselves to be reimbursed for expenses, such as those incurred in trips abroad, that are only remotely connected with the public business.

Legislators are fortunate that relatively few citizens attend sessions of Congress and the state assemblies or read the *Congressional Record.* Much time, on the floor and in committees, is devoted to such urgent matters as the history of the turkey, the forthcoming 100th anniversary of the founding of an obscure Iowa town, and the question whether the nation's newspaper-delivery boys should be honored with a postage stamp. Not infrequently visitors are left wondering when and how important public business is transacted by their elected representatives.

But the least edifying spectacle in American politics is the capitulation of officeholders to forces and pressures they know to be misguided or wrong. To be sure, those who resist often pay a heavy price in terms of careers abruptly terminated. The wreckage of recent years includes a number of able and in some cases distinguished men and women who refused to take a militant anticommunist position during the McCarthy era, especially with reference to the China policy then in force. The harsh treatment accorded officials who opposed the Vietnam War and other policies of the Johnson and Nixon administrations is evidence of the fact that criticism of those in power is apt to be as costly as it is courageous.

Even the Presidents have not been immune to displays of weakness at crucial moments. Although Truman made no secret of his distaste for Senator McCarthy, this did not prevent his cooperating with the anticommunist extremists by instituting the loyalty investigations in 1947–1948, the trials of the Communist Party officials under the Smith Act, and, shortly before he left office, the harassment of Charlie Chaplin. Eisenhower, who also personally detested McCarthy and who, as a Republican and a respected figure, was better placed than Truman to take unpopular positions, was also disabled morally by his failure to deal with McCarthy and McCarthyism, despite the Senator's cruel treatment of Eisenhower's wartime chief and friend General George C. Marshall; only after McCarthy's assault upon the Army itself did Eisenhower clearly separate himself from the Senator and his circle.

No President in almost fifty years was ever able to insist that J. Edgar Hoover and his FBI be subject to the normal regulations affecting government agencies, although some of them privately were extremely critical of Hoover's dictatorial methods and well-known habit of leaking confidential information to his political friends and cronies. Despite Hoover's involvement of the bureau in partisan political activities and in other violations of rules, Kennedy reappointed Hoover as FBI director almost immediately following his inauguration, and in 1964 Johnson waived the retirement law under which Hoover would have been forced to leave office at age seventy in 1965. Hoover was still head of the FBI when he died in 1972 at the age of seventy-seven.*

Hoover, like other archconservatives, was fond of attributing the nation's troubles to permissiveness and "moral degeneracy." The thought did not occur to him, as it does not occur to other members of the governing elite, that the Establishment itself may deserve blame for many of the problems. Although there is much evidence, some of it presented in earlier chapters, that the authoritative institutions and elites have lost the capacity to govern in a responsible manner, the nation's leaders rarely question, much less criticize, their own behavior. The villains, so to speak, are always outside the Establishment and the fault always elsewhere than in the power centers. As a consequence of this view, Establishment wisdom is fond of moralizing about the state of the union, but it rarely draws any moral that would apply to itself.

Thus the malaise of recent years has been traced to the nihilism

*Under Hoover the FBI's 15,000 employees were outside the civil service, and they were not permitted to form a union or join one. Although Hoover himself had a taste for high living and was, among other things, a frequenter of race tracks, women employed by the bureau were not allowed to smoke or even take a coffee break. In 1967 Hoover, a lifelong bachelor, fired a clerk for spending the night with a girlfriend.

of intellectuals, to both technology and astrology, to drugs and the absence of drugs. According to presidential adviser Daniel P. Moynihan, "What is at issue is an adversary culture firmly entrenched in higher education . . . for years, not months, it has been evident that an almost classic form of nihilism has been taking root in upper-class culture in the United States. . . . It would follow that increasingly higher education will come to stand for the humiliation of traditional America." Those who would curb technology in the name of survival are more influential than the astrologists, but astrology was clearly implicated when the president of the New York City Board of Education in 1971 suggested that the school-behavior problems of some youngsters may be due to "birth signs" that conflict with those of other children or their teachers. At about the same time the president of the American Psychological Association stressed that aggression and hostility between nations could be curbed by giving certain drugs to political leaders. According to Elliott Roosevelt, the country was ripe for a "true revolution" that would probably begin during Nixon's second term, but a multimillionaire friend of California Governor Ronald Reagan saw no need for a revolution even in the ghetto: "I see no objection to ghetto living," he told a reporter. "I see nothing wrong with it. There are a lot of advantages. You have your friends around you. . . ."

Chief Justice Warren E. Burger assailed "adrenalin-fueled lawyers [who] cry out that theirs is a political trial," and he castigated other "hot-heads" in calling for "civility if we are to keep the jungle from closing in on us and taking over all that the hand and brain of man has created in thousands of years. . . ." Associate Justice Lewis F. Powell, Jr., contrasted American family life with the portrayal of Tevye and his family in *Fiddler on the Roof* and found the Tevye version "sadly . . . not the portrait of contemporary American life." Justice Powell went on to wonder "if persistent and often destructive self-criticism is not a cause of the alienation of so many young people. . . . It is said that religion is irrelevant, our democracy is a sham, the free enterprise system has failed, and that somehow America has become a wholly selfish, materialistic, racist society—with unworthy goals and warped priorities . . . excessive self-flagellation can weaken—or even destroy—the ties that bind a people together."

For Leonard Bernstein, on the other hand, there was hope in

The Principle of Hope, a book by German philosopher Ernst Bloch. "He describes an aspect of consciousness that goes beyond Freud," Bernstein told his students at the Berkshire Music Center, "which he calls the 'Not-Yet-Conscious'—*Das Noch-Nicht-Bewusste*—which is the psychic representation of the Not-Yet-Become (the Not-Yet-Happened, *das Noch-Nicht-Gewordene*)—in other words, that which has not yet happened, but which is sensed in anticipation. . . . This built-in Anticipation is a *quality* of man (he calls it 'Dreaming Ahead,' 'Dreaming Forward. . .')." The trouble, Bernstein continued, is that dreaming ahead doesn't always produce immediate social change, and "Youth today cannot wait; their great problem is massive impatience . . . [but] thank God you're impatient, because impatience is a certain signal of hope."[12]

Whatever the status of the "Not-Yet-Conscious" and the "Not-Yet-Become," there can be no doubt about the reality of the "Not-Yet-Happened," among which nonevents can be included, in addition to revolution and adversary culture, the acceptance by the Establishment of at least some responsibility for the alienation that afflicts Americans of all ages, not merely young people. Such enlightened organizations as the Urban Coalition and Common Cause, both of them public-spirited lobbies opposed to "special interests" but working within the Establishment and financed, in part, by substantial contributions from the Ford Motor Company, Time Inc., and John D. Rockefeller III, do not offset the widespread loss of faith in the leadership of the country, nor do Establishment mavericks like John H. Knowles and Ramsey Clark compensate for Watergate. Perhaps not even the second coming of a Lincoln or a Franklin D. Roosevelt could resolve the massive crisis of confidence in America's political institutions, but certainly it will not be resolved by the men and women in public life of whom it could be said what John Maynard Keynes said of European leaders after World War I. "Many are strong and rich," Keynes wrote in a poem,

> and would be just,
> But live among their suffering fellow-men
> As if none felt: They know not what they do.*

*The poem appears in Keynes' *The Economic Consequences of the Peace* (New York: Harcourt, 1920), p. 297. Since the poem does not appear in quotation

Nor are other leaderships and social institutions more deserving of respect. The men and women of God, in particular, are supposed to be immune to the temptations of materialism, but the Billy Graham blend of religious fundamentalism and sharp business methods is not unknown in other church circles, and it hardly hurt the "God is dead" movement when the Watergate investigation indirectly raised questions about his tax returns.* Norman Vincent Peale, another pillar of religion, prepares his sermons, we are told by his wife, either in his twelve-room cooperative apartment on Fifth Avenue "overlooking the Metropolitan Museum of Art," or in his sixteen-room house on 225 acres in Pawling, New York, "complete with sauna, covered swimming pool and Norwegian antique furniture. . . ."[13] He also collects stamps, and while we do not know the value of the collection, perhaps a hint in that direction is supplied by the coin collection of the late Francis Cardinal Spellman, archbishop of New York. At the time of his death in 1967 Spellman's coin collection was worth more than a quarter of a million dollars.

One is tempted to dismiss this or that grotesquerie as an individual aberration rather than any reflection on the Establishment as such and to argue, as many now argue in relation to Watergate, that it may have happened once but it won't happen again. But what is to be said about the integrity of *noblesse oblige* (the obligation of those in high positions to behave responsibly) when Supreme Court Associate Justice Abe Fortas, a prospective Chief Justice of the United States, is not aware of any conflict between his Court responsibilities and his entering into a contractual relationship with a foundation, paying $20,000 annually, controlled by a financier with a questionable reputation who was also

---

marks, one assumes that it was written by Keynes himself, who was, in addition to being a distinguished economist, a devotee of the ballet, art collector, gifted writer, and occasional poet.

*On July 16, 1974, the House Judiciary Committee released a memorandum dated October 1, 1971, in which an aide to H. R. Haldeman asked Haldeman, "Can we do anything to help?" The memorandum, on which Haldeman wrote, "No—it's already covered," dealt with an Internal Revenue Service investigation of a Graham tax return. According to the New York *Times* background story, apparently based on previous testimony by John J. Caulfield, Graham at the time "was under investigation for allegedly receiving income he never reported in the form of construction and decorator work and tuition payments for his children, who were in school abroad." (New York *Times,* July 17, 1974.)

in legal trouble? Or when Jacqueline Kennedy, foremost in public esteem, marries not someone of comparable position but an aging Greek playboy millionaire whose previous close companions largely consisted of opera singers, actresses, and junta generals? Or when men bearing some of the nation's proudest names are frequently seen in the presence of women who are not their wives? Whether or not these developments, not to mention the Nixon scandals, demonstrate that the ruling elite no longer has a sense of the things that are not done, they do suggest that it is unaware of any significant moral distance between the higher reaches of politics and law and the lower depths of money-grubbing, jet-setting, and ass-chasing.

Even those who would insist that these are extreme statements, that those who hold power can be neither bought nor seduced, are confused about the definition, much less the requirements, of leadership. Thus a 1974 *Time* cover story on leadership, emphasizing that "there are in America a great many leaders, both actual and potential," nowhere discusses the meaning of the term. Perhaps as a consequence, *Time*'s collection of 200 "faces for the future" under forty-five years of age tends to blur distinctions between leaders and celebrities and not discriminate between those who are influential and those who are merely newsworthy. Perhaps certain television personalities, like Barbara Walters, are leaders, but is newscaster Dan Rather a leader, and if so, in what sense? Are such sports stars as Bill Bradley and Billie Jean King leaders, and if they are, on what grounds is pacesetter Joe Namath not included? Approximately half of those on *Time*'s list are active in politics, but there is no mention of black militant Angela Davis, and by not naming anyone closely associated with Nixon, did *Time* mean to imply that there is no political future for anyone connected with Nixon, however innocent he may be of wrongdoing?

The faces of Jacqueline Kennedy Onassis and film producer Peter Bogdanovich were not included among "faces for the future," although either is far more influential than Father Salvatore Polizzi, associate pastor of St. Ambrose Roman Catholic Church in St. Louis.* Even less understandable is the inclusion of

*Mrs. Onassis, to be sure, was only two weeks away from her forty-fifth birthday, but she still qualified as "under 45" when the *Time* feature was published.

five priests among the six religionists, with the combined total equal to the number of scientists. According to *Time,* a policeman has as much chance of becoming a leader as an Indian: the list features one of each, both of them chiefs.[14]

But perhaps the most remarkable aspect of "faces for the future" is its failure to discuss the ethics of leadership or raise the question of how it was possible for a nation characterized by "a great many leaders, both actual and potential" to choose Richard M. Nixon as President. Considering that many of the 200 "faces" must have voted for Nixon in 1968 and 1972 and that *Time* itself supported him, in the context of the impeachment proceedings surely some hindsight or *a posteriori* reflection would have been in order. Instead, Watergate as such was little mentioned and Nixon hardly at all. It was almost as if Nixon had never happened, as if he were one of Bloch-Bernstein's events that had "Not-Yet-Become."

As suggested earlier, however, there is a probability that there are other Nixons in the nation's future and a certainty of it unless the lessons and implications of Watergate are carefully studied. Nor is it enough to reform the election laws and change the rules governing campaign contributions. From 1789 to the present the government has been active in behalf of one economic interest or another, mostly businessmen and farmers, despite the lip service that everyone has paid to laissez-faire, and as long as it has favors to bestow and the power to make some men rich and others poorer than they were, the Nixons of American politics will always find the money somewhere. Nor will those with the money, in a nation where wealth counts for much more than birth, wisdom, or virtue, ever suffer from any lack of Nixons.*

---

*Even the best sleuthing of the Watergate investigators was not able to trace the sources of all the money contributed to the two Nixon campaigns or determine how it was spent. Their efforts did show, however, that antitrust and other actions against certain corporations were coincidentally suspended following secret contributions by the officers of these corporations. Following a $250,000 contribution from executives of the Amerada Hess Corporation, an oil company, the Interior Department ended an investigation of the company's operations in the Virgin Islands. (New York *Times,* March 20, 1974.) According to finance writer Philip M. Stern, there is a connection between the large campaign contributions of the oil industry and milk producers and Nixon's rejection in 1970 of his Cabinet's recommendation to abolish oil-import quotas and 1971 decision

The corrupt bargain, in fact, had been struck long before Watergate, even long before Nixon reached the White House. In 1952, when Nixon was the vice presidential candidate on the Republican Party ticket with Eisenhower, a group of Southern California businessmen, more or less on the extreme right wing of the party, established a secret $18,000 fund for Nixon's unspecified use. When the fund became known, there were reports that Eisenhower wanted Nixon to withdraw as a candidate; had the general insisted that he give up the nomination, Nixon's ambition for a higher office than Senator probably would have ended or at least been severely set back, much as the ambition of another vice presidential candidate, Senator Thomas Eagleton, was set back twenty years later. Whatever Eisenhower's intentions, Nixon, far from resigning from the ticket, delivered his famous "Checkers" speech proclaiming his innocence of wrongdoing. The themes emphasized in that address, its technique and style, even the manner in which it was delivered, mark it as an early version of the speeches and statements Nixon was later to deliver in connection with Watergate. Indeed the two Nixons, the Nixon of "Checkers" and the Nixon of Watergate, are mirror images of each other.[15]

Thus in his "Checkers" speech there was the theme, later to become so familiar, that the secret fund story had been concocted by political enemies: "When I received the nomination for the Vice-Presidency, I was warned that if I continued to attack the Communists in this government, they would continue to smear me. And, believe me, you can expect that they will continue to do so. They started it yesterday. They have tried to say that I had taken $18,000 for my personal use."[16] Nixon's effort to make light of the matter: "Now, was that wrong?" was not unlike his later attempt to present Watergate as "the broadest but thinnest scandal in American history, because what was it about?"[17] There was the insistence that he had done nothing wrong: "The purpose of the fund simply was to defray political expenses that I did not feel should be charged to the Government"; the purpose of the two secret campaign funds of the 1968 and 1972 campaigns, the first

to raise government support prices for milk. Stern estimates that the oil policy cost consumers $5 billion a year in higher prices and the decision benefiting dairymen $500,000,000 to $700,000,000 a year in higher milk prices. (New York Times, November 16, 1973.)

amounting to $1,098,000 in cash and $570,000 in checking accounts, the second totaling almost $1,500,000 in cash, was also to pay legitimate expenses, Nixon maintained, not to finance the purchase and expenses of his two estates.[18] Finally, there was the claim that he had done nothing others had not done and his display of magnanimity toward them: "Mr. [Adlai] Stevenson, apparently had a couple [of funds]—one of them in which a group of business people paid and helped to supplement the salaries of state employees. . . . I don't condemn Mr. Stevenson for what he did. . . . Mr. [John] Sparkman . . . had his wife on the payroll. I don't condemn him for that. . . ." In the course of the Watergate investigation Nixon frequently stressed that President Johnson and other distinguished Americans had made similar tax deductions, not that he blamed them for it, and that there had been a good deal of wiretapping, influence peddling, and campaign "dirty tricks" during the Kennedy and Johnson administrations.

In retrospect, the early-warning signals of the Nixon scandal were as numerous as they were unnoticed at the time. On Christmas Day, 1969, less than one year into Nixon's first term, a story in the New York *Times* noted that the Justice Department under Attorney General John N. Mitchell was becoming "the strong right arm of the White House," thereby causing "concern among traditionalists who believe the agency should pay homage first to the law and secondly to the President." Mitchell was staffing key positions in the department, the *Times* further reported, with men whose background was essentially political, such as Richard G. Kleindienst, former Arizona Republican chairman and field director in the campaigns of Nixon in 1968 and Goldwater in 1964.* Only one of Mitchell's assistants "had an established reputation as a lawyer," and he was Richard W. McLaren of the Antitrust Division, later to be a special target of Nixon's wrath because of his role in antitrust proceedings against ITT. (If McLaren continues with these proceedings, Nixon told Kleindienst on April 19, 1971, "McLaren's ass is to be out within one hour. . . . I do

---

*Kleindienst, who later pleaded guilty to perjury in connection with the ITT inquiry, told James N. Naughton of the *Times:* "The Department of Justice is probably more sensitive to political philosophy than any other department of Government . . . to turn this place into a bunch of technicians [sic] would not take account of the plebiscite of every four years."

not want McLaren to run around prosecuting people, raising hell about conglomerates. . . . Or either he resigns. I'd rather have him out anyway. I don't like the son-of-a-bitch.")[19]

Early in 1970 two former commissioners of Internal Revenue revealed that Nixon had authorized staff member Clark R. Mollenhoff to look at any tax returns he thought it desirable to see, a practice contrary to policies that had long been in effect in the Tax Service and, in addition, a violation of the Internal Revenue code.[20] Throughout 1970 doubts regarding Nixon's credibility were expressed by a number of observers, and in June reporters discovered that transcripts of presidential news conferences were regularly altered by the White House, a revelation that takes on added significance in view of the later Watergate tape erasures, deletions, and alterations. (The sole purpose of these changes, press secretary Ronald L. Ziegler said at the time, is "the purpose of clarity and to be factual. . . ."[21])

Not long after Ziegler's statement an assessment of the President's character was volunteered by the late newscaster Chet Huntley. "I've been with Nixon socially," Huntley declared in an interview. "I've traveled with him in his private plane; I've seen him under many conditions. The shallowness of the man overwhelms me; the fact that he is President frightens me."[22] Another disturbing characteristic of Nixon's was noted by Walter J. Hickel following his dismissal as Secretary of the Interior: "He repeatedly referred to me as an 'adversary.' Initially I considered that a compliment because to me an adversary within an organization is a valuable asset. It was only after the President had used the term many times and with a disapproving inflection that I realized he considered an adversary an enemy. I could not understand why he would consider me an enemy."[23] In November, 1970, special counsel to the President Charles W. Colson stated that advertisements attacking eight Democratic senatorial candidates were ordered by "someone in the White House"; the ads accused the candidates of supporting violence and extremism and of favoring, or at least not opposing, the use of drugs.[24]

Early in 1971 a House Banking Committee report revealed that Commerce Secretary Maurice H. Stans owned Penn Central Railroad subsidiary stock worth about $300,000 at the time the Commerce Department was involved in negotiations concerning a government loan to the railroad of $200,000,000 to save it from bankruptcy. According to Senator Vance Hartke, chairman of a Senate transportation subcommittee, Stans did not reveal his ownership of the stock during confirmation hearings on his appointment to the Commerce Department position.[25] Two years after the 1968 election and their departure for Washington the New York law firm in which Nixon and Attorney General John N. Mitchell had been partners still carried the listing in the telephone book: "Nixon Mudge Rose Guthrie Alexander and Mitchell." That the President *and* a prestigious law firm should leave such an important detail uncorrected for two years—a firm spokesman referred to it as "a goof"—struck some observers as almost incomprehensible; whatever the explanation, the "goof" was hardly one that hurt the firm's business.*

These and other incidents demonstrate that Nixon and many of his close associates were indifferent to ethical questions on those occasions when they did not consciously resolve them in favor of irresponsible or illegal behavior. Some part of this behavior was motivated by cupidity, for it was never true, despite his avowal to Rabbi Baruch M. Korff, that Nixon "never cared much about money," just as it was not true that he left office, as he told the nation in his "Farewell" speech, with no "more of this world's goods than when he came in. No man or no woman [in the Nixon Administration] ever profited at the public expense or the public till."[26] Instead the evidence, especially his handling of his income taxes and expense accounts, supports the hypothesis that Nixon as a boy was scarred by his family's lack of resources and bitter about the wasted opportunities and "bad luck" that doomed the Nixons to remain lower middle class. All of his life, apparently, Nixon has envied those who were wealthy and earnestly sought to become one of them. In this respect, no less than in others, Nixon departs from the example set by other Presidents from modest backgrounds, none of whom endeavored to become rich by exploiting his position as President.†

*By 1970 the Mudge firm had increased from sixty-five lawyers at the time Nixon joined it to 115 and from three floors at 20 Broad Street in New York's financial district to five floors. When Nixon and Mitchell left for Washington early in 1969, the firm employed 102 lawyers. (New York *Times*, September 26, 1970.)

†For someone who cared little about money, Nixon lived very well even before he became President. As a partner in the Mudge law firm his salary was close to

But if there was any single factor that led to Nixon's undoing, any single explanation, as it were, for the Watergate burglary and the Ellsberg break-in, for the obstructions of justice and the "dirty tricks" of the Committee to Re-elect the President, the likely one was the climate of paranoia that permeated the White House and clouded the thinking of Nixon and his closest associates. That climate, first of all, led the President to believe that the continuation in office of his administration was so crucial to the welfare of the country that any action that would continue it in office was justified. Those who moved in such a climate found it natural to value power above all other considerations and to regard the winning of votes and elections as the most important measure by which a policy was to be deemed effective. It was a climate that viewed effective government as essentially a matter of effective public relations and the public's judgment as vulnerable to infinite manipulation. It was also a climate that generated the worst suspicions of opponents and critics and produced opinions that were guarded even in their estimates of friends. Finally, it was an angry climate of vindictiveness and the relentless pursuit of those stigmatized as the enemy, a climate that treated politics as a war in which there are no atrocities, no victims, no regrets. There are only winners and losers.

Because paranoia involves, among other things, the projection onto others of feelings one cannot face in oneself, the paranoid person is someone who acts from basic weakness. To put it another way, the paranoid individual tries to conceal doubts and fears about himself behind a façade of toughness. He does not see himself as base or sinful; he sees the other side; it is not he who is hostile and aggressive, it is the other side again. The paranoid, in a reversal or counterfeit of the golden rule, proceeds on the principle: do unto others what they have done to you or would do to you if they had the opportunity. As someone once observed, the paranoid is not infrequently someone who was mistreated in the

---

$200,000 a year. He owned a spacious cooperative apartment on Fifth Avenue and was driven to and from his office in a chauffeured limousine. He joined the exclusive Metropolitan and Links clubs and was able to send one daughter to Finch College and the other to Smith. He also invested in the stock market and, according to his own account, owned shares worth $300,000 in addition to other property when he was elected President in 1968.

past, or, in other words, someone who in this special sense has a "reason" to be paranoid. And since, often, there is a personal history of abuse or cruel treatment, the paranoid person sees the world as a cold and unfriendly place where there are few if any people to be trusted.

Insofar as others in his circle share this view, one may refer to the circle as a paranoid community, by which is meant a group of persons whose outlook is permeated by ideas with traces of paranoid origin regarded by the group members as rational and objective truths. While neither Nixon nor anyone else on his staff could be diagnosed, clinically speaking, as a paranoid personality, there is a good deal of paranoid thinking in the taped conversations. To begin with, everyone involved, the President especially, makes an almost obsessive use of the tough he-man language more often associated with the barracks and the battlefield than with political circles, let alone the White House. When the Watergate cover-up is not going well, someone, usually Nixon himself, declares it may be necessary to "bite the bullet," "prick the boil," and "cut our losses"; "cool" is a favorite expression. Rarely using a polite expression if an expletive is available, the President frequently refers to those he dislikes as "sons-of-bitches," "bastards," and "assholes"; when he has no interest in something or does not care about the consequences of an action, he "doesn't give a fuck" or "doesn't give a shit." The contrived he-manship of these occasions, much like the "us-guys" atmosphere of a locker room, is also expressed in the occasional lapse into ungrammatical language and slang: "There ain't a vote in it. . . . There's no votes in it, Bob. . ." (June 23, 1972).

Insights into the relationship between Nixon and his aides is provided throughout the tapes. For the most part, it is Nixon, not Haldeman, Ehrlichman, or the others, who does the swearing; it is as if, by unspoken agreement, Nixon alone, in accordance with the principle of *droit du seigneur,* was permitted to use the strongest language, thereby reserving for himself the foremost tough-guy role. Repeatedly he asks one or the other of his assistants to reread his *Six Crises;* during the Watergate investigation Colson reportedly told the House Judiciary Committee that he had read the President's book fourteen times. On June 23, 1972, Nixon, inspired by something he had written in *Six Crises,* says to Haldeman: "Why don't you re-read it?" He also demands of them constant reassurance that he is on the right track, that he is doing the correct thing, and from time to time they behave as a Greek chorus, feeding him with the echo of his own voice. When Nixon, on September 15, 1972, declares that "things are going to change now," that he is going after "all those who tried to do us in," Dean exclaims: "What an exciting prospect." "Thanks," says the President. Haldeman, not to be outdone, chides Nixon for past restraints: "You and your damn regulations. Everybody worries about not picking up a hotel bill."*

Though the election is a foregone conclusion by mid-September of 1972, the President and his aides can hardly get off the topic of "those who tried to do us in"; it is as if he can neither forget nor forgive those who had the temerity to oppose him and to be disturbed by the Watergate break-in the previous June. "Just remember," he tells Dean and Haldeman on September 15, "all the trouble we're taking, we'll have a chance to get back one day." Later: "This is a war. We take a few shots and it will be over. Don't worry. I wouldn't want to be on the other side right now. Would you?" Then Dean informs him that he is compiling notes "on a lot of people who are emerging as less than our friends . . . and we shouldn't forget the way some of them have treated us." To this Nixon replies: "I want the most comprehensive notes. . . . They didn't have to do it. If we had had a very close election and they were playing the other side I would understand this. No—they were doing this quite deliberately and they are asking for it and they are going to get it. We have not used the power in this four years as you know. We have never used it. We have not used the Bureau [FBI] and we have not used the Justice Department . . . ." With this Haldeman as well as Dean is in perfect accord. Referring to a General Accounting Office audit of White House staff expenditures that is then in progress, ordered, according to Dean, by the Speaker of the House, Haldeman suggests: "Maybe we better put a little heat on him." The President and Dean agreeing, Haldeman continues: "You know, we really ought to . . . call the Speaker and say, 'I regret . . . your calling the GAO down here because of what it is going to cause us to do to you.'"

On February 28, 1973, Nixon is incensed that in connection

---

*Haldeman presumably was referring to regulations requiring White House staff members to pay their own hotel bills and other traveling expenses.

with Watergate "they talk about a 35-year sentence. . . . There were no weapons! Right? There were no injuries! Right? There was no success! Why does that sort of thing happen? It is just ridiculous!" Dean is convinced that Senator Sam Ervin "is merely a puppet for Kennedy in this whole thing. The fine hand of the Kennedys is behind this whole hearing. . . ." Again the President agrees: "Yes, I guess the Kennedy crowd is just laying in the bushes waiting to make their move. I had forgotten, by the way, the talk about Johnson using the F.B.I. Did your friends tell you what Bobby did?" Two weeks later it is no longer the Kennedys but "the establishment" that is behind the Watergate investigation. "They've just got to have something to squeal about it," the President remarks on March 13. "They are having a hard time now. They got the hell kicked out of them in the election. . . . The establishment is dying, and so they've got to show that . . . despite the successes we have had in foreign policy and in the election, they've got to show that [we are] wrong, just because of this. They're trying to use this as the whole thing."

By "establishment" Nixon meant, as he indicated frequently, the "liberal establishment," consisting of influential newspapers, universities, intellectuals, and other "leftist" circles, mainly in the Northeast; on one occasion he referred to the Northeast as "the playground of the limousine liberal set. . . ."[27] The "establishment," he seemed to believe, was dominant everywhere: in the media, in which it controlled such newspapers as the New York *Times* and Washington *Post & Times-Herald* and the CBS and NBC networks; in the government itself, in which its power was particularly felt in the agencies that dealt with the economy and antitrust policies; and in the Kennedy-Johnson wing of the Democratic Party. "The big question," he told C. L. Sulzberger of the New York *Times* on March 10, 1971, "is: Will our Establishment and our people meet their responsibilities? Frankly, I have far more confidence in our people than in the Establishment. The people seem to see the problem in simple terms: 'By golly, we have to do the right thing.'" But at other times Nixon made it clear that his respect for ordinary Americans was no greater than his confidence in "the Establishment." On November 5, 1972, he confided to an interviewer: "The average American is just like the child in the family. You give him some responsibility and he is going to amount to something. If, on the other hand, you make him completely dependent and pamper him and cater to him too much, you are going to make him soft, spoiled and eventually a very weak individual."[28]

Whatever this statement may tell us about Nixon's true feelings for ordinary people, it is consistent with his view that he has few allies anywhere: "Nobody is a friend of ours," he tells his staff on March 13, 1973. "Let's face it!" Toward those who were not friends and who were perceived as hostile or simply incompetent, the President habitually displayed a cold anger and not infrequently a vindictiveness that was almost hysterical in mood. Thus he was not satisfied to hope, one April day in 1972, that the weather would clear over Vietnam so that the bombing could resume; instead, "the bastards have never been bombed like they're going to be bombed this time, but you've got to have weather."[29] Shortly after the attempted burglary at the Watergate headquarters at the Democratic National Committee, Nixon asks Haldeman: "Well, who was the asshole that did it? Was it Liddy?"[30] Like a ferret closing in on a rabbit, Nixon on April 19, 1971, cannot abandon the pursuit of the unfortunate McLaren and an unidentified "bad guy" in the San Francisco office of the Small Business Administration. To Ehrlichman and George P. Shultz, then director of the Office of Management and Budget, the President says, in connection with the antitrust action against IT&T: "It's McLaren, isn't it?" Ehrlichman replies: "McLaren has a very strong sense of mission here." The following dialogue then takes place:

P. Good—Jesus, he's—Get him out. In one hour—
E. He's got a—
P. One hour.
E. Very strong.
P. And he's not going to be a judge either. He is out of the god-damn government. You know, just like that regional office man in, in, in, San Francisco. I put an order into Haldeman today that he be fired today.
E. Yeah.
P. Today. Anybody that didn't follow what we've done per the latest'd have his ass out . . . one of the reasons . . . that you got to act on that SBA guy—I don't care if he's a kid with eight—a guy with eighteen kids—is that we have no discipline in this bureaucracy. We never fire anybody. We always promote the sons-of-bitches that kick us in the ass.

. . . Now, I don't care what he is. Get him out of there. Get him out of San Francisco. . . . the head is got to roll. . . . You get that guy fired, George. . . . Get him out of there. And by—I want it all, I want it to ricochet all around. . . . And let people know that when they don't produce in this Administration, somebody's ass is kicked out. This will be the first person we've fired except Hickel. Now, goddamn it, those are the bad guys—the boys down in the woodwork. We better get one. This guy goes. He's out. Fast.

Also "out," or, rather, condemned to stay out were those who refused to serve in Vietnam, for a man who could be vindictive in such small matters as the fate of an obscure official in remote San Francisco could hardly be less punitive in dealing with such large questions as the amnesty issue. While he had sympathy for those who made mistakes, Nixon told a press conference of February 1, 1973, nevertheless, "it is rule of life, we all have to pay for our mistakes. . . . Now, amnesty means forgiveness. We cannot provide forgiveness for them. Those who served paid their price. Those who deserted must pay their price, and the price is not a junket in the Peace Corps, or something like that. . . . The price is a criminal penalty. . . ."

Throughout his public life Nixon frequently displayed anger or was short-tempered in his encounters with the press, as on the famous occasion in 1962 when, following his defeat in the California gubernatorial contest of that year, he told a gathering of astonished newspapermen: "Just think how much you're going to be missing. You won't have Nixon to kick around anymore because, gentlemen, this is my last press conference." There were occasions, to be sure, when anger was appropriate to the occasion, but Nixon was often angry when there was little or no visible provocation. The tapes, in fact, reveal that in private as well as at press conferences and other public gatherings, Nixon was almost characteristically angry, suspicious, hostile and vindictive. What could have led him to make these responses?

One clue to Nixon's inner self is supplied by references to his parents, Frank and Hannah Milhous Nixon, in his farewell remarks to the White House staff. In the course of listing his father's various jobs, Nixon referred to him as "a great man because he did his job," although they "would have called him sort of a—sort of a little man, common man. . . ." The facts, however, do not quite establish Nixon's father as "a great man" in any sense, and because the facts as well as the family myths and legends throw light on Nixon's more recent career, they deserve at least brief mention. Frank Nixon, most of his life, was a loner and a loser. He never finished grade school, never held a job long, and never made the money he was determined to make. According to Gary Wills, the elder Nixon worked at everything from painting pullman cars to drilling for oil; he was, by turns, a trolley-car motorman, farmer, orchard grower, carpenter, gas-station operator, and proprietor of a grocery store that gradually became a general store.[31]

In character Frank Nixon was pugnacious, proud, impatient, easily made angry, argumentative, and jealous of those who were more successful in life. Toward his five sons, two of whom died in childhood (one older and one younger than Richard), he displayed little affection; he is remembered by them and others as a fierce disciplinarian and taskmaster who, in the words of Donald Nixon, the President's brother, "worked us kids to death."[32] Those of his sons who misbehaved were physically punished, and apparently the future President learned early to avoid saying or doing anything that would displease his father. He kept anger and resentment to himself, or, in the words of Donald again, "he did not explode himself. He saved things up. . . ." As Nixon himself put it: "Dad was very strict and expected to be obeyed under all circumstances. If he wanted something he wanted it at once. He had a hot temper, and I learned early that the only way to deal with him was to abide by the rules he laid down. Otherwise, I would probably have felt the touch of a ruler or a strap as my brothers did."[33]

Nixon's mother, Hannah, he told his staff at the farewell meeting, "was a saint," and perhaps this was less exaggeration. A college graduate and a practicing Quaker, Hannah Milhous Nixon was a patient and generous woman in whom people found it easy to confide. She presided over her family as she presided at the store, dispensing much more kindness and understanding than she could have hoped to get back in return. She rarely was heard to complain, and those who knew her could remember few times when she had lost her self-control, including the occasions that were marked by the deaths of two sons, one as a result of meningitis and the other after a five-year struggle with tuberculosis.

For more than two of these five years Hannah nursed her tubercular older son in Arizona. Some interpreters of Nixon, notably psychohistorian Bruce Mazlish and political scientist Michael Rogin, have suggested that the young Nixon must have been deeply hurt by his mother's absence for such a long period. As Rogin and John Lottier express it: "The sense of desertion induced in Richard by this separaton, occurring during the onset of puberty, must have been traumatic. . . . The loss of a mother at this stage typically induces in a boy the anxiety that his oedipal feelings have driven his mother away. Worse yet, the death of a younger brother . . . and the oldest son . . . a few years later . . . must have reinforced Richard's emotional impoverishment. . . . Other evidence suggests that Nixon's personality was, in [Erik] Erikson's words, 'weakened by an initial loss of trust.' "*[34] Mazlish, making a similar point, argues "a strong possibility that he unconsciously viewed his being sent away to live with his aunt as some sort of punishment, or lack of real affection on the part of his mother . . . we may surmise that he unconsciously perceived his beloved mother's leaving him for two years as a betrayal . . . [and] the birth of his brother Donald, only a little over a year after his own birth, as 'taking' his mother away from him, thus laying the first seeds of his own feelings of the precariousness of life and love."[35]

From this experience Nixon may have derived his tendency toward seclusion and withdrawal from the world when faced with severe adversity and deeply conflicted emotions, as he was during the last few weeks of the Watergate crisis. His other mood of hostility and suspicion, the need to act tough and be "cool," is traceable to Nixon's identification with his father. Perhaps Frank Nixon in part is responsible for a certain rootlessness in his son's life

---

*Psychoanalytic studies of children's reactions to the deaths of siblings have found a wide range of responses, including "depressive withdrawal, accident prone behavior, punishment seeking, constant provocative testing, exhibitionist use of grief and guilt, massive projection of superego accusations and many forms of acting out." Quoted from A. Cain et al., 'Disturbed Reactions to the Death of a Sibling," American Journal of Orthopsychiatry, Vol. 34, p. 743, in Charlotte Sempell, "Bismarck's Childhood," History of Childhood Quarterly, Vol. 2, No. 1 (Summer, 1974), pp. 116–17.

and a persistent inclination, nowhere more clearly seen than in Nixon's behavior following his overwhelming defeat of McGovern, to snatch defeat from the jaws of victory. One can also detect the father in the son's attitudes toward "the Establishment" and the "Limousine Liberals" of the Northeast and in Nixon's emphasis on the values of individualism and self-help. His inveighing against "permissiveness" and his rejection of "welfarism" owe much to Frank Nixon's stubborn independence and refusal, according to his son, to hospitalize his two ill boys at public expense although the family was in dire financial straits at the time. Even Nixon's efforts, with Rabbi Korff, to demonstrate that Watergate was not another Teapot Dome because no one made any money from it may reflect something of his father's influence; the Teapot Dome scandal was almost an obsession with Frank Nixon.

If Nixon was only his father's son and the chief choreographer of Watergate, his speeches as President stressing the importance of moral principles and honesty in government, his invocations of God, motherhood, the American family, peace, truth, and justice could be regarded as little more than the vote-getting hypocrisies often associated with public office. The Nixon of the pieties and displays of rectitude, however, reminds us of the "saintly" parent Hannah and suggest that she, too, was a significant figure in his early years. But a case can be made that Nixon's identification with his mother is more symbolic, as in the speech images, and more confined to his private life, in which, so far as is known, he has been an exemplary husband and devoted father. Indeed, the feminine side of Nixon, apart from certain gestures and mannerisms that are somewhat effeminate and may have been copied from his mother, was largely hidden from the public view; like most other men, Nixon reserved his tender, feeling side for his family and close friends.

While there were reflections of Hannah in his public performances, they were likely to make their appearance when Nixon was under severe strain or depressed. Perhaps the most notable occasion was the farewell gathering when, almost immediately after Nixon spoke of his mother as a "saint," he related the moving account by Theodore Roosevelt of the death of his first wife "when she had just become a mother, when her life seemed to be just begun. . . . Then by a strange and terrible fate, death came to her. And when my heart's dearest died, the light went away from my life forever." Nixon on that occasion was not, as he said and as others thought, identifying himself only with Roosevelt but with Roosevelt's young wife as well, dead before her time, who was loved for "her saintly unselfishness," and through her with his dead mother, Hannah, also a "saint," who would "have no books written about her." Nixon is saying, in effect, that he, too, though "saintly" and "unselfish," has suffered "a strange and terrible fate" and has died before his time.

History is not likely to agree with this judgment, and historians in the future may be equally critical of the political and social processes that elevated Richard M. Nixon to the nation's highest office. Certainly until Nixon Americans could believe that criminal behavior and political corruption stopped short of the Presidency, however much they were characteristic of lower-echelon positions. That conviction, the origins of which go back to 1787, can no longer be held. Certainly few Americans now would endorse Alexander Hamilton's view, put forward in one of one of the *Federalist Papers,* that "the process of election affords a moral certainty that the office of president will never fall to the lot of any man who is not in an eminent degree endowed with the requisite qualifications. Talents for low intrigue and the little acts of popularity may alone suffice to elevate a man to the first honors in a single state; but it will require other talents, and a different kind of merit, to establish him in the esteem and confidence of the whole Union." Clearly in this forecast, as in much else, Hamilton was wrong.

The self-congratulatory mood of the nation and the tributes to the durability of its political institutions and the effectiveness of the impeachment process are understandable and in some measure deserved. But the conditions that produced Richard Nixon and Spiro Agnew and the corrupt bargains that made them President and Vice President still exist, and in any case, their resignations do not remove the leadership decay that befouls so many city halls and state capitals. Nor can anyone be certain that the Presidency itself has escaped long-term damage; the critical years for the White House began, after all, in 1963, if not earlier, not in 1968 or 1972. Much depends on what can be achieved by Nixon's successors, and both the nation and the world will demand more from them than honesty and a desire to uphold the Constitution.

Whether more will be forthcoming from President Ford and

Vice President Rockefeller or from those who follow them is a major question, perhaps *the* major question, for the future. Thus far President Ford, honest though he may be, has provided little evidence that he understands the important problems facing the country, much less the international community, and there is even less evidence that he has any solution for them. The honesty and integrity of Vice President Rockefeller were scrutinized when he was nominated and resolved in his favor; not yet decided is the question whether a member of the nation's wealthiest family should be placed in a position from which he can succeed to the nation's most powerful political office. But that may be, in the long run, a less important issue than the issue of capability. Unfortunately, Rockefeller's declaration late in 1974 that "we've got the greatest system in the world. We've just got to find a way to make it work" does not encourage confidence. The utterance somehow is reminiscent of one of President Coolidge's famous statements when he was asked to explain unemployment. "When large numbers of people are unable to find work," said the President, "unemployment results."[36]

In other words, the old adage that "in the country of the blind the one-eyed man is king" has long since lost its relevance. Americans can no longer afford to be blind and to be ruled by those with limited sight. If peace cannot be preserved, if the economy cannot be made healthy and poverty eliminated, if blacks and whites cannot learn to live together, if the cities cannot be saved, then the country itself will not survive.

If further "panic," to revert to Freud's term, is to be avoided, America must regain confidence in its leaders, and the leaders must regain confidence in themselves and especially in their capacity to perform miracles of inspiration and direction within a democratic framework. They must become, in other words, miracle workers, and since, at present, they are something less than that and are not likely to improve much in the foreseeable future, that becoming would be the greatest miracle of all.

11

The Twilight of the Gods

George Santayana wrote that those who do not remember history are doomed to relive it. Perhaps those who remember it too well also are doomed to relive it, for surely much about America today resembles a past we have hardly forgotten. There is the political leadership, so similar to the faltering and fumbling leadership of the 1920's, the corruption so reminiscent of the scandals of the Grant and Harding administrations, the manners, morals, and taste recalling the social atmosphere of the Jazz Age, and the reports of "shocking conditions" in mental hospitals, prisons, nursing homes, mines, factories, child-care centers, migrant-labor camps, and slum tenements so like those written by the muckrakers at the turn of the century.* Even the celebrations of the very rich have a *déjà vu* quality, for is it not impossible to guess whether it was in the 1890's or the 1970's that a party lasting three days cost the host more than $250,000, while at another banquet the guests consisted of dogs owned by friends of the (human male) host, all of which dined on choice meats and seafood? In the later period, too, as in the earlier one, there was no lack of "cynics and feeble good men," to borrow a phrase from John Jay Chapman, and those who had begun as radical critics of the social order and ended as fervent apologists for the status quo.

*An outstanding example of what might be called, borrowing from Freud, the "repetition compulsion" as applied to society is the tendency of corruption to occur in regular cycles. Arthur M. Schlesinger, Jr., has observed that scandals involving the White House have taken place "every half century—the Grant scandals of 1873, the Harding scandals of 1923, the Nixon scandals of 1973." (*The Imperial Presidency, op. cit.*, pp. 259–60.) According to New York's Knapp Com-

The similarities between past and present reflect the profound ambivalence of American attitudes toward the values associated with democracy, especially the value of equality. This ambivalence is manifest not only in the tendency of reform movements, as Hofstadter puts it with reference to the Populists, to reject the entire political culture of industrialism in "looking backward with longing to the lost agrarian Eden, to the Republican America of the nineteenth century," but the behavior of even those liberals who are rooted in the realities of twentieth-century urban life and class politics.[1] For it is a commonplace observation that once radicals are elected to office, they are inclined to compromise, modify, hedge, and frequently betray the principles to which they appeared to be committed. Nor is this tendency confined to American reformers. As British historian E. H. Carr observes, "History everywhere shows that, when Left parties or politicians are brought into contact with reality through the assumption of political office, they tend to abandon their 'doctrinaire' utopianism and move towards the Right, often retaining their Left labels and thereby adding to the confusion of political terminology."[2] Thus, when the New Deals, Fair Deals, Square Deals, Social Democratic and Labor parties come to power, their achievements invariably fall short of what was promised, and among their followers there are cries of "betrayal" and "sellout."

No doubt many leaders of Left parties and movements are consciously or unconsciously motivated in their politics by personal factors rather than ideological convictions. The biographies of these leaders show that many of them sought power as a means of compensating for real or imagined deprivations and disappointments they experienced as children, especially ill treatment and the loss of love. As Franz Borkenau observed of revolutionary leaders, "Whether they spoke of the necessity of political liberty,

---

mission investigation in 1971 of police corruption, the time intervals for police scandals are reflected "in 20-year cycles of scandal, reform, backsliding, and fresh scandal." The commission's investigation of police corruption in New York produced reports similar to those of the 1875 Select Committee of the New York State Assembly, and it was the "worst dream" of the commission members that "around 1990 a group very much like them" would declare, following another investigation of the police, that corruption is "widespread" and recommend "basic reforms" to eliminate it. (New York *Times,* August 7, 1972.)

of the plight of the peasant or of the socialist future of society, it was always their own plight which really moved them. And their plight was not primarily due to material need: it was spiritual."[3] In the case of some leaders of social democratic and reformist parties, conspicuous among whom is Ramsay MacDonald, who led the British Labour Party fifty years ago, not to mention numerous trade-union officials and spokesmen for underprivileged groups, one suspects the "plight" that moved them first to join a radical movement and later to abandon it was a combination of spiritual and material factors. In any case, once the personal motivation is satisfied, a movement toward a more conservative outlook usually can be discerned.

But even those who do not fit Borkenau's description and who are by no means MacDonalds may hold ambivalent attitudes toward those radical principles they enunciate with so much passion, an ambivalence that is apt to emerge when they are in a position to give effect to such principles. Ambivalence, of which they are usually unaware, may be rooted in unconscious resistance to the radical change or reform being advocated; in effect, a conscious commitment to the change or reform is undone by an unconscious wish to keep things as they are. For just as idealism and pacifism when carried to extremes may reflect an underlying urge toward or obsession with violence,[4] in which event the idealism and pacifism can be viewed as a defense (or, more technically, reaction formation) against unacceptable impulses, so an extreme emphasis on social justice and an end to inequality may mask intense aggressive, competitive strivings and an unconscious need to lord it over others. In radicals and reformers whose conscious attitudes clash with unconscious predispositions, the frequent result is ambivalence toward policies designed to promote social justice and equality.

While such ambivalence can take many forms, a characteristic expression of it in governing liberal circles is an insistence that genuine reforms are being effected when, in fact, few basic reforms are under way or, in truth, desired. Another phenomenon at the level of individual behavior is the authoritarian liberal whose commitment to radical principles is so ambiguous and compromised by internal conflicts that he tolerates little personal or ideological opposition. He is almost always inclined toward coercive rather than persuasive methods of exercising authority.* The surface confidence and apparent certainty of purpose often conceal an inner doubt that the party program makes sense. Accompanying it is a corrosive suspicion that key party personnel are inferior in talent and ability to those on the conservative side.

Students of Left movements have observed that some radicals and liberals are not free of guilt feelings about their role as reformers; the rhetoric of social change often has about it a slightly apologetic tone, almost as if the advocate of the change regretted that it was necessary. Perhaps any challenge to the institutional environment, as Arthur Koestler has suggested, carries with it a price, "and the price is neurotic guilt. There never was an intelligentsia without a guilt-complex; it is the income tax one has to pay for wanting to make others richer. An armaments manufacturer may have a perfectly clean conscience, but I have never met a pacifist without a guilty look in his eyes."5 The reformer's tendency to feel ill at ease in promoting change may be reflected in the characteristic liberal fantasy that their opponents on the Right, and history itself, are moving in their direction, that in reality "we are all liberals now." In America in recent years the fantasy has taken the form of imagining that Senator Barry Goldwater is, somehow, a liberal at heart in his position on certain issues, and of assuming that no social gathering of liberal intellectuals in New York is complete without William F. Buckley, regarded by many of them as "the Kennedy of the Right."6 Unlike conservatives who expect to be loved because their prejudices and beliefs are in accord with most of human history, liberals need to be loved because their beliefs and prejudices are somewhat contradictory of that history and even of some of their own deeper feelings.

Reform efforts may fall short of their goals, in other words, partly because they encounter what has been repressed and unconsciously resisted in the reformers themselves. Insofar as we project onto blacks and other minorities our own sexuality and

---

*One is reminded of psychoanalyst Edward Glover's "typical example" of "the reaction formations of social pity and humanitarianism, which express the barrier against cruelty and yet, by insisting on penalties for cruelty, give a certain scope for retention of the original impulse." ("The Neurotic Character," *International Journal of Psychoanalysis*, Vol. 7 [1926], p. 25.) The authoritarian liberal counterpart is the individual who loves everyone irrespective of race or color and would imprison or otherwise punish those who do not.

aggressiveness, the existence of which we deny in ourselves, we can hardly be wholeheartedly in favor of integration no matter how fervent our declarations supporting it. Our efforts to promote integration, therefore, must inevitably suffer some inhibition unless and until we can integrate in ourselves much of what the black and other minorities, in our unconscious, have come to represent. In a similar way, our attempts to identify with the poor, the aged, and the downtrodden in general stumble against our rivalrous, competitive strivings and the need to deny our own passivity and feelings of weakness. Indeed, most endeavors to improve the lot of mankind, including the perennial peace crusades and share-the-wealth programs, fail at least partly because the resistance to these efforts that is conscious and articulate in most conservatives has its unconscious and repressed counterpart in the minds of reformers. From this point of view, liberalism itself, psychologically speaking, is a defense or reaction formation against what is illiberal and primitive in the nature of man.

If, as suggested here, reforms come up against not only conscious hostility in conservatives but also unconscious ambivalence in reformers, the combination of which is usually fatal to any achievement of major change, the probability is not great that the United States can solve most of the problems discussed in preceding chapters. For the solution to these problems requires fundamental changes in attitudes and life-styles, together with institutional reforms, on a scale far beyond any that has been proposed by the nation's leadership. Americans, of course, are not unique in offering resistance to social change, nor are their leaders consistently less imaginative or courageous than those of other countries. But in the world's largest democracy, foremost industrial and military power, and leading consumer nation, the consequences of resisting change are more serious than the consequences elsewhere. The problem is not just that the quality of life within the United States is at stake, although that is serious enough. An American failure to succeed as a multiracial egalitarian society will carry America and much of the world toward inevitable war and barbarism.

But even an American success does not guarantee peace and civilization even as far as the year 2000, much less until the nation's tricentennial in 2076. Given the increasing availability of nuclear weapons of all types and a continuing lack of effective ma-

chinery for the settlement of international disputes, there is a
practical certainty that one nation or coalition of nations with a
grievance someday will use nuclear technology against another.
Indeed, if they possess such weapons, poorer nations will be particularly tempted to use them since, in theory at least, the effective
use of nuclear weapons obviates the need for costly conventional
armaments, including manpower, and a long-term military
effort.* Even if nuclear wars can be avoided, population growth,
assuming it remains unchecked, will be hardly less calamitous
since it ensures, according to some estimates, that before the end
of the century as many as a billion people will starve to death and
that many more than a billion will be suffering from chronic malnutrition and the diseases associated with permanent near starvation. Nor will life necessarily be rewarding for those who manage
somehow to avoid war, eat well, and have access to clean air and
water. For unless there is some final catastrophe, wherever they
go and whatever they do, there will be more and more people going and doing. If the world's population continues to grow at the
current rate of 2 percent each year, the present total of approximately 4 billion will increase to 7 billion by the end of the century
and to almost 40 billion when the United States celebrates its
300th birthday in 2076.

Granted the future is impossible to predict—the present was
not forecast in any futurology scenario that was developed in the
past—still one is hardly surprised that most gatherings of futuro-
logists do not generate cheerful toasts to what lies ahead. The outlook is optimistic only with regard to areas of scientific advance
and disease control, such as exploration of the far reaches of
space and the establishment of colonies in space and the eradication of cancer and infectious diseases. Biologist H. Bentley Glass,

---

*Until the advent of the atomic bomb, the rich industrial nations were at a con-
siderable advantage in military technology and, in general, had little to fear from
the so-called underdeveloped countries, the armed forces of which were ill
equipped for modern warfare. Nuclear weapons, however, can be developed
and manufactured by relatively poor nations, such as India, whose technology
and living standards are well below those of Western Europe and the United
States. Of course, an industrial nation with nuclear weapons still holds an advantage, but a poor country with a few atomic bombs is more than equal, militarily
speaking, to a rich country without them. World opinion has yet to register a full
appreciation of the momentous change in the historical balance of forces that
nuclear weapons have made possible.

for example, anticipates that in the next twenty-five years the life expectancy of most Americans will reach to the ages of ninety or 100 and that defective body parts will be replaceable, even prenatally.[7] Geneticist Herman J. Muller and other natural scientists are confident that parents will soon elect to conceive babies from frozen sperm cells and to choose the sex of the baby, as well as determine whether there is to be one baby or twins;[8] some reproduction scientists predict that in a matter of years it will be possible to conceive babies artificially, that is, without any reproductive services being performed by parents. Other forecasts include pollution-free and ultra-high-speed methods of transportation, total weather control, systematic mining and farming of the ocean, and more efficient communication systems as replacements for the letter and telephone.[9]

Most such predictions are preceded by an "if" or "provided that," generally a reference to world economic and social conditions, about which no confident predictions are made. The advances are possible, as Muller put it in 1957, "provided that the world does not fall prey to . . . war, dictatorship of any kind, overpopulation or fanaticism." The world as a whole has not so far "fallen prey" to these calamitous developments, but since each of these conditions exists in some part of the world and several of them are increasing in frequency and severity, Muller's "provided that" could be interpreted to rule out effectively at least certain types of scientific and technological progress in the future. Even apart from that, few scientists and scholars expect social advances to keep pace with those in science and technology; indeed, they anticipate a good deal of backward, regressive movement in society. The behavior of mankind, says the French anthropologist Claude Lévi-Strauss, reminds him of maggots in a sack of flour: "When the population of these worms increases, even before they meet, become conscious of one another, they secrete certain toxins that kill at a distance—that is, they poison the flour they are in, and they die . . . what's happening on a human scale is a little the same sort of thing. We are secreting psychological and moral toxins . . . the time may be coming when humanity will have such a feeling of getting in its own way that we will enter an era of massacre beside which these colonial wars would be absolutely nothing."[10] According to biologist Albert Szent-Gyorgi, who won the Nobel Prize for his discovery of vitamin C, man's chances of survival are dropping toward 50 percent and by the end of the century may be lower than that. American society, Szent-Gyorgi suggested in 1970, is "death-oriented," and both America and the rest of the world are governed "by a terrible strain of idiots."[11]

Most social scientists who have endeavored to look ahead are not more hopeful than the biologists and geneticists. Economist Robert L. Heilbroner sees mankind threatened by population increase, nuclear war, pollution and spoilation of the environment, and ruthless industrialization "whetted by the values of a high-consumption society"; he has little confidence that the democratic way of life can survive these threats. The judgment of political scientist Andrew Hacker, focusing on the United States, is that "America's history as a nation has reached its end. The American people will of course survive. . . . But the ties that make them a society will grow more tenuous with each passing year. There will be undercurrents of tension and turmoil, and the only remaining option will be to learn to live with these disorders. For they are not problems that can be solved with the resources we are willing to make available. They are, rather, a condition we must endure."[12]

By far the most recent influential as well as most pessimistic forecast of the future, and one that continues to arouse much controversy, was made in a 1972 study undertaken for the Club of Rome by MIT Professor Dennis H. Meadows and his associates. The Meadows Report, published as *The Limits to Growth*,* was based on computer analysis of data in the five areas of population, agricultural production, natural resources, industrial production,

---

*New York: Universe Books (Potomac Associates), 1972. The Club of Rome, a forum for research and discussion of world problems, was organized in 1968 by the Italian industrialist Dr. Aurelio Peccei. The membership of fewer than 100 persons from more than thirty countries includes scholars, businessmen, scientists, and government officials who meet periodically to discuss what the club refers to as the "Project on the Predicament of Mankind." In 1970 the club commissioned Meadows, a computer scientist, to form a project team that would develop a global model of growth. Such a model, it was hoped, by specifying the problems of unlimited growth, would facilitate discussion of the quesion whether there was a limit to growth beyond which the world could proceed only at the risk of mass starvation and death. The model developed by Meadows *et al.* was based on the more elaborate systems model of Jay W. Forrester, another MIT professor, whose conclusions are somewhat similar to'those of *The Limits to Growth.* See Forrester's *World Dynamics* (Cambridge, Mass.: Wright-Allen Press, 1971).

and pollution. The analysis led to the conclusion that growth limits would be reached in 100 years or less "if the present growth trends in world population, industrialization, food production, and resource depletion continue unchanged. . . . The most probable result will be a rather sudden and uncontrollable decline in both population and industrial capacity." Present economic growth rates, moveover, not only ensure relatively rapid depletion of resources but are "inexorably widening the absolute gap between the rich and the poor nations of the world." The only alternative to ultimate world collapse as a consequence of population increase and resource exhaustion, *The Limits to Growth* argued, was a state of global equilibrium characterized by the following "minimum requirements:" (1) "the capital plant and the population are constant in size," with birth and death rates and capital investment and depreciation rates equal to each other; (2) "all input and output rates—births, deaths, investment, and depreciation—are kept to a minimum"; (3) the levels and ratio of capital and population "are set in accordance with the values of the society. They may be deliberately revised or slowly adjusted as the advance of technology creates new options."[13]

Exponents of growth assailed what they termed the Malthusian conclusions of the Meadows Report with a vigor not unlike that inspired by Malthus himself in 1798 when he published his gloomy *An Essay on the Principle of Population*. The growth model was criticized for its rigidities and exclusion of such regulating factors as price effects and what one reviewer referred to as "the important adjustment mechanisms that have helped the world avoid similar catastrophes to date."[14] The data base in *The Limits to Growth* was said to be too restricted, with neither producers nor consumers able to shift from one resource to another. A pessimistic bias, it was alleged, had governed the choice of assumptions, a bias that denied the possibility of technological breakthroughs and the discovery of new resource reserves. Management authority John Diebold went so far as to reverse the report's conclusions in predicting that by the early 1980's the world would be suffering from a food glut, enough economics in the use of raw materials to turn the terms of trade against raw-material-producing countries, especially the oil producers, and an "excess of controls on pollution."[15]

In the debate on *The Limits to Growth* its egalitarian implications

were lost sight of. Certain critics had imagined that the Meadows
Report, in effect, recommended a freezing of the present unequal
distribution of wealth. To be sure, a zero-growth rate would intensify competition for resources; and to the extent that affluent
societies and individuals were unwilling to consume less so that
poor societies and individuals could consume more, the result
would be increased social conflict of the sort that some of the
Founding Fathers predicted in the Constitutional Convention.
But the main emphasis of the report is on the freedom each society and, by extension, the world community would have to raise or
lower living standards by altering the balance between population
and resources. If, for example, the decision was that the social
goal should be more equality rather than less, any decrease in
population and increase in capital stocks would tend to promote
greater equality, whereas the reverse process would have opposite
results. There is no chance, the Meadows Report insists, that living standards can remain the same as they are at present, much
less improve, if population continues to grow at its present rate
because the resources simply do not exist in sufficient quantity.*

Further, *The Limits to Growth* envisages the possibility that in
the equilibrium state new, imaginative solutions might be found
to problems other than resource allocation. It is conceivable,
argues the report, "that a society released from struggling with
the many problems caused by growth may have more energy and
ingenuity available for solving other problems. In fact, we believe . . . that the evolution of a society that favors innovation
and technological development, a society based on equality and
justice, is far more likely to evolve in a state of global equilibrium
than it is in a state of growth we are experiencing today."[16]

Whether or not Meadows and Heilbroner are correct about the
need to adjust the balance between population and resources, neither they nor their critics, with very few exceptions, assume that
the world can adequately support a population of 7 billion or
more by the first years of the twenty-first century. McGeorge
Bundy, for example, in a scenario for the future couched in terms

*One estimate is that income per head in most less-developed countries would
increase 3.0 percent a year if their population growth rate of 3.025 could be reduced by half. "Halfing fertility also results in a third more capital per worker af-
·ter thirty years." (Economist Stephen Enke, "Birth Control for Economic Development," *Science,* May 16, 1969, p. 801.)

of "looking back" from the perspective of the year 2024, anticipates "Great Famines" in 1979–1981 that, with their attendant disorders, will cost 65,000,000 lives.[17] Such population experts as Bernard Berelson, president of the authoritative Population Council, sociologist Kingsley Davis, retired General William F. Draper, economist Joseph Spengler, anthropologist Margaret Mead, and almost all those who contemplate the population future agree that, in Mead's summary of the agreement reached at a United Nations Population Conference, "continuing, unrestricted worldwide population growth can negate any socioeconomic gains and fatally imperil the environment."[18] Computer scientist Jay W. Forrester goes so far as to predict "that the future of the world would undoubtedly see the practice of triage [the selective sorting of population] on a relatively widespread and nonwar basis," by implication the selective determination of who is to live and who is to die.[19]

If the practice of triage comes to pass, no one can doubt that the millions who do not survive will include a disproportionately large number of those from the underdeveloped countries which cannot muster a military challenge to the affluent nations, in other words, a disproportionately large number of brown and black people on the Asian subcontinent and in Africa. But triage may not stop there, for in every country, including the United States, there are an increasing number of people who do not possess any skills that their society wants, whose raw labor power is not needed, and who, therefore, cannot earn enough to provide for themselves. And in America these people, too, are mainly brown and black. They constitute the discontinued classes of society, in the sense that the problem is not that they are unemployed at any given time but that they are unemploy*able*. When are added to them the aged and the chronically ill and those who were employed in occupations that have been phased out by technological change, the conclusion unavoidably reached is that there are in the world and in each society individually a very great many persons who have become, to use a cruel but unavoidable word, obsolete. Again, who can believe that triage will be sparing of them?

But even if the surplus population somehow is minimally fed, housed, and clothed, the problem of living standards and the distribution of wealth is far from solved. On the one hand, available world resources will not permit a significant improvement in living standards of the poor countries unless the richer Western nations decide to consume less and not then unless population is stabilized at or near present levels. On the other hand, the world poor will not agree to remain poor, while at the same time the middle class everywhere wishes to possess still more; for both the rich and the poor yesterday's luxuries inexorably tend to become today's necessities. The tension between population and wealth, therefore, is almost certain to increase and with it competition for resources within societies and between nations that perhaps cannot be resolved by nonviolent means.

Indeed, for hundreds of years the world has been moving toward such a crisis, but until this century at a relatively slow pace. So long as the masses of mankind believed that eternal life in the next world mattered more than a short miserable life in this one, they were willing to starve, suffer, and die in desperate poverty and to do so silently. When they began to abandon this belief, a development over time that marks the end of the age of faith and the beginning of the age of materialism, the institutions, habits, and expectations of 1,000 years were radically transformed. But this transformation was gradual; not until fairly recently could the masses articulate their misery, much less any demand for a share of the wealth that had been acquired by a privileged minority. To be sure, there were always spokesmen for the poor, but it was one thing to plead their cause in the name of charity and the common humanity and quite another to thrust them, as Marx did, to the center stage of history. For Marx put their case not only in terms of bourgeois decline and the dialectic of fate. As powerful as these arguments were, his most revolutionary idea, which in its simplest terms could be as easily understood by those who were illiterate as by those who had read the whole of *Das Kapital*, was that the common workers of society through their labor were the source of society's wealth, a large part of which was taken from them by their employers, who, in that fashion, became rich. Capitalism, Marx was saying, is based on theft, or, in other words, the right of the rich to steal from the poor, from which it followed that the workers and, by extension, all of the underprivileged, in dispossessing the capitalists and landowners, were only taking back what had been stolen from them.

Marx expected that the workers' revolution would put an end to poverty and exploitation and free mankind from the habit of greed and the urge to accumulate possessions. He did not envisage that the workers, too, would become acquisitive and would acquire a taste for property and that socialism, whatever it set out to accomplish, would ultimately promote in some societies what capitalism had already achieved in others, namely, industrialization, modernization, and the democratization of values and aspirations that once had been exclusively confined to the middle class. For in an age of material plenty, the leading nations of which were those most addicted to consumption, there never was any reason in heaven or on earth why the workers should settle for less than the middle class unless, of course, they had no alternative to settling for less. Socialism in a variety of guises was that alternative, and in those parts of the world that are poor and where there is little individual opportunity to improve one's income and living standard, it remains an alternative.

If this interpretation is correct, socialism is less to be understood as an ideology opposed to capitalism than as a form of protest within the broad framework of capitalist society. Its limitations as a form of protest have been manifest in the traditional alliance between socialism and nationalism, an alliance inclusive of patriotic wars, and the equally traditional refusal of Marx's "workers of the world" to unite for any purpose whatever. While socialism has fared less well in the United States than in Europe, the similarities between European socialism and such American protest movements as progressivism and reformism are also revealing. Among them, in addition to nationalism, are a shared commitment to gradualistic processes and procedures rather than to an effective implementation of basic change in the economic order, an explicit or implicit endorsement of some forms of social stratification, the treatment of power structures and bureaucracies as inevitable and even desirable, a rejection of the concept of class struggle in favor of an emphasis on the need for cooperation between opposing interests and groups, and an indulgence in prejudice and ethnocentrism. Indeed, the resemblance between European socialists and American liberals is so marked as to suggest that in Europe as well as America there is no such thing as socialism; there are only varieties of progressivism and reformism.*

*The willingness of the socialist movement almost everywhere, but particularly in Western Europe, to abandon its ideological radicalism and settle for re-

But whatever the labels attached to parties and movements, the political momentum everywhere in the world is generated by a demand for higher living standards, a demand that is obliterating differences of history and culture between nations no less than it is obliterating ideological differences. This desire for a substantial improvement in the material conditions of life constitutes the real revolution of our time, and it confronts affluent classes in the United States and Western Europe with a difficult choice between two options. The first entails a decision to divert wealth and resources to the poor within a given society and to the poorer nations by sharply reducing military expenditures and curtailing wasteful and extravagant consumption. Were this to be done on a large-scale basis over an extended time, the probable result would be the elimination of poverty in America and Europe and a substantial rise in living standards elsewhere, assuming population stability in the poorer countries.

Within the United States a reduction in spending on private affluence, changes in the tax laws, and a reduced military budget would free a large amount of money for social experimentation and the improvement of factories, schools, hospitals, institutions for old people, and prisons. Worker autonomy, rotation of work schedules with more time off, substitution of teamwork for traditional assembly-line methods, and other humanizing innovations, similar to those that have been successfully tried in Sweden and Norway, would reduce the monotony of much factory work and boost employee morale. School study-work-leisure programs could be developed for all ages on an eleven-month basis, thereby eliminating the boredom of long summer vacations. Changes in hospital architecture, size, room arrangements, and staffing would abolish the overcrowding, neglect, and impersonality that are so characteristic of medical-care facilities at the present time. The aged could be provided with cottages, each with its own garden or outdoor area, instead of dreary nursing homes operated for private profit. A transformation long overdue could replace

---

forms that are acceptable to conservatives, is responsible for such statements as Sir William Harcourt's in London almost ninety years ago that "we are all socialists now." In declaring "we are all socialists now," a statement hailed by persons of all political persuasions at the time, Sir William was really saying that "we are none of us socialists now."

our huge fortresslike state mental hospitals with bungalows resembling the ones now available to patients at some of the better private mental hospitals. Perhaps similar structures could be created for prisons, and inmates offered programs comparable to those organized in the schools.*

The other option involves a decision that those citizens already surfeited with food and possessions should continue to be overfed, overclothed, and overhoused while the poor are maintained at or near their present levels, a detemination that of necessity requires a continuing high level of military expenditures. For if the resources are to remain available and supply lines kept open for their shipment to the major consuming nations led by the United States, the armed forces and intelligence networks must be able to deal with any threat from local populations who wish to keep the resources for themselves or obtain more favorable terms for their sale. At the same time, because the poor within the affluent societies remain poor and become more hopeless about their condition, rates of crime and violence can be expected to increase and with them public spending for police protection and private security services. But these measures are not likely to halt the steady deterioration of city and suburban life; the inevitable consequence of prolonged "benign neglect" is certain to be a more rigid social divison between white and black, rich and poor, with increased segregation of the well-to-do in heavily guarded housing, work, and recreational enclaves.

All this is only a beginning. In response to constant pressures at home and permanent threats abroad, such a society would become, sooner or later, a full-scale garrison state, the dominant classes of which resorted to force and repression as a means of maintaining their power and privileges. Those who sought to change the existing order or who were alienated from it in ways deemed to be undesirable would be subject to "pacification" programs utilizing, in addition to coercive measures, psychotropic drugs and techniques of behavior modification in conjunction with mandatory work projects. Meanwhile, efforts by the raw-

---

*These proposals, which some will regard as outlandish, are neither original nor new. Schools, hospitals, old-age facilities, and prisons of the type suggested already exist in some countries of Europe, notably the Scandinavian countries, and in China.

material-producing countries to exploit their position through the manipulation of supplies and prices, in keeping with the Arab oil precedent, would be met, first, by CIA attempts to subvert non-cooperative anti-Western regimes and, if that was unsuccessful, by military intervention. But such intervention, of course, would involve grave risks once the producing countries begin to stockpile atomic weapons, which is certain to happen within a decade, or if the Soviet Union or China undertakes to act in their behalf.

Clearly this second option is acceptable only if the wealthy countries, in an effort to preserve their affluence, are willing to move toward authoritarianism at home and "resource imperialism" abroad, with all their attendant dangers.* If they are not willing to do so, the alternative is a policy that would allocate resources within and between nations not on the basis of ability to pay but in accordance with need. For the United States such a policy would require a reduced overall consumption of raw materials, particularly energy and mineral resources, and a shift of investment and employment from productive industry to public and private services.† Much capital and labor that are now either unemployed or engaged in production of consumer goods would be diverted to the rebuilding of cities, the construction of low-cost public housing, and the creation of such new public facilities as schools, hospitals, mass transportation systems, adult and child parks, playgrounds, entertainment areas, and centers for senior

---

*One wonders whether "resource imperialism" was what President Johnson had in mind when he declared in a speech delivered at Camp Stanley, South Korea, in November, 1966: "There are 3 billion people in the world and we have only 200 million of them. We are outnumbered 15 to 1. If might did make right they would sweep over the United States and take what we have. We have what they want. . . . We don't ask for much, but what we ask for we are going to get, we are going to keep, we are going to hold." (New York Times, November 2, 1966.)

†At present the United States, with about 7 percent of the world's population, uses 33 percent of the total energy. According to the United Nations Statistical Yearbook for 1973, American per capita consumption of energy is twice that of the United Kingdom, Australia, Sweden, and the Netherlands, three times that of France and twenty times that of China. Americans also consume approximately 25 percent of the world's steel production, almost a third of the supply of synthetic rubber, and more than a quarter of the supply of tin. Overall, Americans probably consume each year between a quarter and a third of the total world production of nonrenewable resources.

citizens. The ranks of the unemployed and underemployed could supply much of the manpower from which staffs to run these enterprises could be recruited and trained. Those who remained unemployed or who were unemployable would be provided with an income well above present welfare levels, under a guaranteed-annual-income plan or some form of the "negative income tax."

The full integration of blacks and other minorities, however, requires more than their being provided with an adequate income. Nor would a massive aid program, or "Marshall Plan for Blacks," as has been suggested, accomplish very much unless there were careful and perhaps unwelcome controls imposed on how and where the money was spent. Raising black living standards is essential, to be sure, but it will not in and of itself produce rapid integration. What is needed, in addition, are a variety of incentives for integration to which the white population will immediately respond, that is, incentives that will encourage whites to share housing, schools, recreational and other facilities with blacks and minorities. Since we know that money incentives are powerful inducements to changes of attitude and behavior, we should consider whether monetary rewards in the form of rent rebates and other subsidies could be used to promote white movement into black neighborhoods and white acceptance of black movement into white areas. Businessmen, teachers, medical professionals and paraprofessionals, lawyers, and others from the white community could be paid more for living and working in the ghetto. Only then will blacks begin to be integrated culturally as well as economically and socially and the present black orientation toward so-called Afro-American culture and its ghetto-based derivatives give way to an interest in Judaic-Christian Western culture. Ultimately, one hopes, Americans will not require "combat pay" as a reward for integrating, but that time is several score years away.

A more equitable distribution of consumer goods, the total supply of which was held constant or reduced in an effort to conserve resources and alleviate worldwide poverty, would necessitate limits on the number and variety of products well-off families were permitted to own. There is no evidence that any American family would suffer severely if it were not permitted to possess more than one house or apartment (or were required to share its weekend and vacation dwelling with another family), one car, one televison set, one radio, and one each of the major appliances used in the kitchen and home laundry (i.e., dishwasher, refrigerator, etc.). Considering the size of the typical family, one bathroom should suffice. (Of course, exceptions in all categories could be made for families whose members included handicapped persons, invalids, and those confined to their beds because of infirmity or chronic illness.) Certain types of household goods and wearing apparel, especially furnishings and garments made of scarce fabrics or materials such as the skins of wild animals, could be eliminated altogether without adversely affecting the sum of happiness and perhaps without doing injury to one's "average expectable" narcissism.*

In fact, most consumption changes would have positive and beneficial effects on health and longevity. A reduction in food consumption and a shift away from animal fats, meat, sugar, and high-calorie foods probably would reduce the incidence of cardiovascular and other diseases in America and Western Europe and at the same time increase the supply of grains to countries whose people suffer from chronic hunger.† Lower room temperatures

---

*Affluent-level consumption may relate more to anxiety than to narcissism. As psychoanalyst Karl Abraham observed many years ago, patients with extreme dependency needs and those whose libido is fixed or inhibited in a parental attachment tend to become extremely anxious in situations that call for a transfer of libido onto others. By spending money in a more or less random fashion—for example, by buying unnecessary and useless items—they symbolically gratify the repressed desire to transfer libido onto a variety of objects that is the source of the anxiety; in effect, they find it easier to love things than to love persons. (Karl Abraham, "The Spending of Money in Anxiety States" (1917), in *Selected Papers of Karl Abraham* [New York: Basic Books, 1968], pp. 299–302.) Perhaps in America anxieties of all sorts are relieved by compulsive spending on gadgets and products for which there is no real need and in which, after a short time, there is no further interest.

† 1972 American per capita meat consumption was 254 pounds per year, compared with 212 pounds for the French, 192 for the West Germans, 171 for the British, 112 for the Swedes, and 51 for the Japanese. The average grain consumption of each American was 2,200 pounds, of which only 7 percent was consumed directly in the form of bread, cereal, baked goods, etc. The rest of the grain was fed to cattle, swine, and poultry. Since other people's direct consumption of grain is much higher than that of Americans (the Chinese eat 360 pounds of the total 400 pounds consumed annually per capita), even a small reduction of meat consumption would release millions of tons of grain for the relief of famine in parts of Asia and Africa. According to Lester Brown of the Overseas Development Council, a meat reduction by Americans of only 10 percent would produce

in the United States—Americans are notorious for overheating their homes—would not only conserve fuel, it would also, physicians believe, reduce the frequency of winter colds and related respiratory distress. Limiting families in the number of cars and household appliances would further reduce fuel needs and, insofar as it led to more physical activity, be beneficial to health as well. Compulsory recycling of used products and the elimination of unnecessary waste would contribute to the preservation of the natural environment as well as add to the total quantity of goods available for distribution.

But even if Americans choose not to consume less in behalf of a more egalitarian world and just society, many decisions that now are made privately will in the future be subject to social control. Just as the businessman today accepts regulations that fifty years ago he would have denounced as both un-American and unthinkable, so the American of the twenty-first century is likely to take for granted restrictions on his freedom of action that he would regard, if they were imposed today, as outrageous. The vital questions for the future are not whether there are to be restrictions, but by what methods these restrictions are to be decided upon and to whom and in what manner they will be applied. The choice, in particular, is between a policy of fairness that will improve the quality of life for all Americans and a policy of arbitrary selections and discriminatons that will benefit only certain groups in the population.

Whatever the policy, there can be little doubt that procreation in the future will not be left to personal whim or chance and that the overall growth of the national population will be adjusted to economic and social requirements, including the availability of jobs. Marriage licenses will be easily obtainable, but not licenses to have children; the latter are likely to be limited to those, married or unmarried, who can meet certain standards or pass certain tests demonstrating their fitness to be parents. Sexual relations, on the other hand, will be even less restricted than at present, reflecting not only the changes in morality that were discussed in an earlier chapter but new concepts of equality. Assuming that women continue to outlive men and that the disproportions be-

---

at least 12,000,000 tons of grain, or enough to feed 60,000,000 grain eaters for an entire year. (Sources: *Organic Gardening,* September, 1974; *The Futurist,* August, 1974; New York *Times,* October 25, 1974.)

come greater, a frequent living arrangement in the future will consist of one man living with two or perhaps three women.[20] If present trends hold for the future, sexual life will begin earlier and end later for most Americans, and practices that are now regarded as deviant or "kinky" will become commonplace.*

The choice of education, employment, and residential locality will be subject to regulation, again in accordance with social needs. When there are too few physicians and too many lawyers, for instance, the medical schools will expand and the law schools contract; the question of who goes to college and what courses he or she takes will be socially determined rather than left to students and their parents. Nor will the campuses continue to function as institutions in which young people spend their "prolonged adolescence," that is, as pleasant places that accommodate those among the young who are too young to be adults engaged in full-time work and too old to be children engaged in full-time play. The colleges and universities will sort themselves out as to major purpose, with some, perhaps most, primarily training students for service occupations and office employment and others mainly educating the young people who are destined for the graduate schools and ultimately the professions and upper-echelon managerial jobs. The probability is that all high school graduates and college students will be required to spend three or four years in a National Service Youth Corps working at jobs ranging from street cleaning and conservation projects to teaching in prisons and providing companionship for the elderly who live alone.

Undoubtedly the growth and size of cities will be regulated and efforts made to create cities within cities by decentralizing city governments and establishing a number of separate mini-municipalities within a given urban area. (Perhaps recourse should be had, again, to the power of money: families and individuals could be paid to leave overcrowded areas and settle in the new cities being created in underpopulated areas of the West.)

---

*One can imagine a good deal of sexual freedom even in an authoritarian America. The pursuit of sexual pleasure, if compulsive enough, tends to promote indifference to the loss of freedom in other areas, and to that extent it can perform diversionary and escapist functions in a society beset by severe problems. In America at the present time there is much evidence that sex, not religion, serves as the "opiate of the people."

Movement within cities, especially movement by private cars, will be restricted, with some streets reserved for pedestrian traffic, some for bicycles, and some for buses and taxis. The trolley car is likely to be revived as a favored means of city transportation, perhaps in conjunction with a monorail system. Truck movements in cities, including their loading and unloading, will be confined to nighttime hours—a step, incidentally that would have the desirable side effect of making streets safer and nightlife possible in areas that now are totally deserted after dark.

These changes in the practices and routines of everyday life will go far toward making life in America more livable and workable. There can be no certainty, however, that such changes can take place within the framework of what is essentially a free society. Each of them now is opposed by powerful business, union, religious, or consumer groups—not infrequently all four—and restrictions on freedom of choice in areas that traditionally have been private and unregulated by public agencies would be unpopular with a majority of citizens. The odds, therefore, are *against* the necessary changes being effected without recourse to authoritarian government.

Nor is the likelihood greater that the United States will willingly relinquish its position as the world's foremost military power and self-proclaimed guardian of the so-called Free World. The viability of the American economy requires, as a minimum, a high level of defense expenditures, and even if this were not the case, any large-scale retreat from our guardian role in international affairs would be opposed by influential networks of interlocking military and corporate interests. While thus far both have accepted the principle of civilian control of foreign and military policy, they may not be prepared to accept the principle at any price, especially if that price is, in their view, the abandonment of the free-enterprise system, military impotence, and American capitulation to the Soviet Union and China.* America's multinational corpora-

*That the military is increasingly restive under civilian control can hardly be denied. Despite presidential directives abolishing the use of the Attorney General's list of subversive organizations in connection with security investigations, the Army in late 1974 was still relying on the list in establishing grounds for discharge of personnel. The extent of its intelligence activities within the United States is unknown, but it is known that from 1967 to 1970, and perhaps into the present, the Army has conducted systematic surveillance of civilian officeholders

tions, with 30 percent of their profits derived from overseas operations, tend to be expansionist, not contractionist, with regard to our international commitments.

Any retreat abroad may also encounter psychological resistance that is in some ways similar to that aroused by reform. For in the "Free World" mythology that is the major justification for our international position, one can detect still another national equivalent of the private myths and fantasies that screen us from the realities of evil and death.[21] Just as we imagine, in accordance with some treasured family legend but contrary to the truth, that our ancestors were liberty-loving stalwarts who arrived on the *Mayflower* or that they enjoyed a higher social status than was, in fact, the case, so we make moral supermen of the Pilgrims and Founding Fathers or celebrate the superiority of American motives to European motives, thereby conveniently repressing the materialism and self-interest of the first years of our national history. American nationalism, with its earlier dreams of independence and statehood and later one of empire, is also suggestive of the immortality fantasies of private mental life, those fantasies of self-permanence that encourage us to achieve something that will, in the words of Stendhal's Lucien Leuwen, "leave a scar on the landscape." Unfortunately for the place in history of the United States, the scars America has left on the landscape in recent years have been literal ones.

But however difficult the effort may be to overcome the legends and fantasies that are rooted in the nation's psyche, the effort nevertheless must be made. While the resistance to reform and

---

and civic organizations totally unrelated to military affairs. While there are few published expressions of opinion like that of retired General Thomas A. Lane in 1971 to the effect that "we know what it takes to defeat a war of liberation but we don't have political leaders who will do what must be done" (New York *Times,* August 1, 1971), on at least one occasion in the final days preceding President Nixon's resignation Defense Secretary James R. Schlesinger thought it necessary to issue instructions that there be no troop movements without his approval, even if such movements were ordered by the White House. On August 25, 1974, Bernard Gwertzman reported in the New York *Times* that there were "two major areas of concern" to Schlesinger. "The first was that in some 'improbable' situation, Mr. Nixon or one of his aides might get in touch with some military units directly. . . and order that some action be taken to block the 'constitutional process.' The second was that a genuine national emergency might develop. . . ."

change, a kind of national neurosis, cannot be completely undone, with courageous leadership and the mobilization of conscience it can be restrained enough to permit meaningful changes
to take place. Surely the time has come to relinquish the myths
that we are a selfless people whose principal function in world
affairs is to advance the cause of freedom and right of self-deter-
mination. Our interventions in Chile, Greece, Guatemala, Vietnam, Italy, and countless other countries, and our eagerness to
render economic and military aid to police states whose dungeons
bulge with political prisoners, establish beyond any doubt that we
are as interested in power and the national advantage as the British were in the nineteenth century or the French and Spanish before them. Nor is there much point in imagining, as conservatives
and liberals of goodwill are wont to imagine, that our statesmen
and diplomats can be persuaded to tell the truth or that the CIA
can be "controlled" without a major disengagement from our self-
proclaimed missionary "Free World" role. So long as we remain
committed to such a role, we will continue to subvert regimes we
do not like by methods both open and concealed, and subversion
by whatever method does not permit the truth to be told or the
CIA to be "controlled." The whole justification for clandestine
warfare is that in today's world it is no longer feasible, at least not
without grave risks, to entrust gunboats and troops with the task
of overthrowing a government hostile to the United States. Because now we cannot send in the Marines, we send in the CIA, the
effectiveness of which depends on secrecy, deception, and lies, depends, in short, on the absence of "control." To demand that the
CIA be accountable to Congress, the members of which in substantial number may or may not support its goals and techniques
of operation in certain instances, is a bit like demanding that the
Mafia be accountable to the police.*

*Asked in 1964 whether the FBI and CIA would truthfully answer questions
about whether Lee Harvey Oswald had ever worked for these agencies, Allen W.
Dulles, former director of the CIA, is reported to have said: "I think under any
circumstances, I think Mr. [J. Edgar] Hoover would say certainly he didn't have
anything to do with this fellow." Queried whether the CIA would give a similar
reply, Dulles responded: "Exactly." He also is reported to have said of himself: "I
would tell the President of the United States anything, yes, I am under his control. I wouldn't necessarily tell anybody else, unless the President authorized me
to do it." (Quoted from Harold Weisberg, *Whitewash IV* [Maryland: Weisberg,

Americans, unfortunately, do not always realize that much of what they like very much and do not wish to give up cannot be separated from that part they dislike and want to be rid of. Just as the United States, if it wishes to be the Godfather of the "Free World," must tolerate CIA subversion, so American society if it wishes to remain democratic must restructure its institutions and habits and move toward social equality. For if past experience is any guide, freedom and stability in the public sphere will not be compatible for long with inequality and disorder in the private domain. In any contest between democracy and anarchy, and there have been many in history, the inevitable tendency of the latter is to destroy the former.

A movement in this direction, in fact, can already be seen in America with respect to increasing rates of crime and violence. In addition to curtailing freedom of movement and inspiring much racism, the incidence of crime and violence has generated efforts not to abolish inequality but to detect crimes and violent acts before they are committed or are in the process of being committed. The result has been innumerable invasions of privacy about which it is futile to complain, and no doubt the cameras and hidden detection devices in stores, offices, banks, employee washrooms, and other places, the mail searches and monitoring of telephone calls, the television cameras on street lampposts focused on pedestrian movement, the airport screening of passengers and their luggage—no doubt these techniques of citizen surveillance are only at an early stage of development. For if crime and violence increase, spying technologies not yet invented will be in routine use, and little then will be left of the right to privacy.*

1974], in New York *Times*, November 23, 1974.) In view of these statements, there was no way of determining, in 1975, the truth of CIA denials that it engaged in assassination; according to its top officials, the agency only discussed such possibilities. Earlier there had been denials that the CIA involved itself in domestic intelligence activities, activities that clearly violated its charter, and these denials proved false.

*The erosion of liberties and rights is discernible in such newspaper stories as: "City Judge Denies Bail in Bomb Case" (New York *Times*, March 11, 1970); "Spartans [Industries] to Share List of U.S. Shoplifters" (New York *Times*, June 12, 1970); "Federal Computers Amass Files on Suspect Citizens" (New York *Times*, June 28, 1970); "Electronic Gadgets Making Security a Big Business" (New York *Times*, May 27, 1971); "Wiretaps in U.S. Up 37% in Year" (New York *Times*, May 6, 1972); and "Unions Say Some Stores Here Use Two-Way Mirrors in Dressing Rooms to Curb Rise in Shoplifting" (New York *Times*, July 4, 1974).

Nor is privacy the only basic right that is threatened. The time is almost at hand when it will be possible to control human behavior by a variety of means including chemicals or drugs, surgical modifications of the brain, the implantation of minute radio receivers in the brain that receive messages from computers, and other devices. Behavior-control experiments with animals suggest that violence and a variety of anti-social acts, such as sexual abuse, drunkenness, drug addiction, and theft, can probably be eliminated or significantly reduced by altering the nature of messages received and processed by the brain. In numerous experiments cats have been "programmed," for example, not to attack mice, and charging bulls brought to a halt. The investigations of Dr. José M. R. Delgado of Yale University Medical School, a leading figure in brain research, suggest that happiness itself or at least a tranquil state of mind can be "programmed" and that in a relatively short time scientists will know enough about the brain to produce any type of behavior society may desire.

Such knowledge and control of the mind will make it possible to eliminate much suffering, most serious forms of mental illness, and ultimately many types of brain disturbance and malfunction. But in addition mankind will possess for the first time in history the means of regulating collective behavior without recourse to force or the threat of force. If, for example, the future rulers of a society wish to make war, a chemical substance added to the food or water or the transmission of a certain electrical message to brains that at birth were "programmed" to receive these messages will produce an aggressive warlike state in the population. Alternatively, chemicals and electrical messages will be used to promote obedience and docility in a social group that is prone to crime and violence or contemplating rebellion. Given certain refinements in the technology of behavior control, eventually it will be possible to do away with discontent regardless of source and all forms of alienation, protest, and dissent except those officially permitted.

Because, then, the cruelties that men have inflicted upon each other in the past will no longer be necessary, and prisons, concentration camps, torture, and executions will be abolished, there is much to be said for this ultimate state of behavior control. But the ultimate state is identical with the perfect totalitarian state, perfect in the sense that its leaders do not rule through terror and coercion but through the infusion of contentment in the populace. For surely the perfect totalitarian society would not be a society like that of Nazi Germany or Soviet Russia, but one in which, although the schools, newspapers, and libraries were completely free, it never occurred to a single citizen that anything was wrong.

The totalitarian society of the future, insofar as it embraced the principle of economic and social equality, would be a decent society but not a free one; it would approximate the condition that Bertram Gross has called "Benevolent Fascism." The question facing Americans and, for that matter, many Europeans is whether Western free society is also capable of decency, a decency based on equality, respect for others, self-discipline, and a refusal to play the role in the world of either God or Godfather. Because if it is not capable of decency it will not only cease to be free, it will lose those qualities of conscience, generosity, and compassion it already possesses and sink finally and irretrievably into barbarism. Liberties once lost can be regained, but civilized habits and customs of life that have been built up over centuries, once destroyed, can disappear forever.

Not all problems can be solved, to be sure. At present we seem not to know what to do about inflation, depression, and unemployment, much less how to go about eliminating war, hunger, and poverty in the world community. Every day brings fresh evidence that collective ignorance is overcoming collective wisdom, and it may be that the beast in man is in the process of finally triumphing over the saint. Just as Freud was not the first to discover that man is not by nature good or peaceloving, Hitler will not be the last to put that discovery to supremely evil use. But while it is true, as Tocqueville observed, that "around every man a fatal circle is traced, beyond which he cannot pass," it is equally true that "within the wide verge of the circle he is powerful and free: as it is with man, so with communities. The nations of our time cannot prevent the conditions of men from becoming equal; but it depends upon themselves whether the principle of equality is to lead them to servitude or freedom, to knowledge or barbarism, to prosperity or wretchedness." [22]

Acknowledgments

For research grants and other assistance I am grateful to The City University of New York, especially former Chancellor Albert H. Bowker and President of the Graduate School Harold M. Proshansky. A sabbatical provided by The City University enabled me to spend the academic year 1972–1973 as a visiting professor at the Hebrew University of Jerusalem, certainly one of the most stimulating environments in which to teach and write. The officers, faculty, and students of Hebrew University were very generous in allowing me ample amounts of uninterrupted time for research and thought, and they also provided occasions during which I could think out loud, as it were, about some of the issues discussed in these pages. Many of them offered constructive criticisms of various themes and in other ways provoked me into rethinking propositions that I had long since come to regard as settled questions. I particularly wish to thank Yehezkel Dror, S. N. Eisenstadt, Saul Friedlander, Emanuel Gutmann, Jacob Landau, David Ricci, Dov Ronen, Martin Seliger, Ehud Sprinzak, and Jacob L. Talmon. Mrs. Naomi Meyuchass, secretary of the Department of Political Science, and her able assistants Drora Shoshani and Marsha Yossefian were unfailingly understanding and helpful. My debt to Lea Chesner, combination typist, translator, tour director, arranger, and above all expert shredder of red tape, is substantial.

I am particularly grateful to Joan Pyle Dufault, upon whom I have inflicted a variety of moods and temperaments during the past three years and who in ways more numerous as well as more personal than can be mentioned here has been indispensable to

331

both author and book. Some of the ideas discussed first took form in talk sessions that began a long time ago with my friend Albert Haas, Jr. I am deeply grateful to him for sharing with me his own broad knowledge and experience, some of which is reflected in chapters 3 and 9. Chapter 2 has benefited from critical readings by two other friends, Edward D. Joseph, MD, and Joseph M. Natterson, MD. While I absolve them from any responsibility for what appears, I hope they will agree that I have made good use of their comments and suggestions.

For inspiration and encouragement at various times, some of them crucial, I am grateful to many friends and colleagues. Patricia E. Rogow contributed much that can never be adequately acknowledged and which it will always be beyond my means to repay. Before and during the writing of the book I had occasion to engage in conversation and/or argument with the following individuals, to all of whom I am obligated for rewarding discussions: Gordon Adams, Eliot Asinof, Samuel Atkin, MD, Thomas Balogh, Margaret Bayldon, Viola Bernard, MD, Samuel Bloom, Ellen Boneparth, John H. Bunzel, John Butterfield, MD, Gerald and Florence Cohen, Peter and Beatrice Cookson, Robert H. and Susan Cremin, Joan S. Crowell, Virginia Currey, Lane Davis, William and Georgia Delano, Mary DiGangi, MD, Terry Dintenfass, Robert Dorn, MD, and Natalie Dorn, Stanley Duane, Julius C. C. Edelstein, Robert Engler, Heinz Eulau, Ralph and Janet Evans, Charles Fisher, MD, Oscar Forel, MD, Georgio Freddi, Edward Graham, Elinor Haas, Susan Haas, Andrew Hacker, Adolf F. Holl, Irving Howe, the late Don D. Jackson, MD, Donald Bruce Johnson, David Kairys, MD, and Eileen Kairys, K. S. Karol, Patricia Kendall, Robert Kwit, MD, Serge Lafaurie, Harold D. Lasswell, Paul F. Lazarsfeld, Hugh L'Etang, MD, Sandra Levinson, Peter Loewenberg, John H. Lynch, Jr., Norman and Jeanne MacKenzie, Alan Marcus, Judd Marmor, MD, Hubert and Rochelle Marshall, Marilyn Mikulsky, Graeme C. and Kathleen C. R. Moodie, Frank Montero, James N. Murray, Jr., Minna Post Peyser, A. Borden Polson, MD, and Jeanne Polson, Susanne T. Osterstrom, Leo Rangell, MD, Melvin Reder, Thomas Reilly, Donald H. and Leah Riddle, Paul Roazen, Janice Rule, Camille de Bellet Sauge, Herbert and Maggie Scarf, Robert Schwartz, Lenore Schwartz, Frederick Seiler, Petra T. Shattuck, Tuvia and Hagid Shlonsky, the Right Honorable Peter Shore, MP, and Elizabeth Shore, MD,

Michael Sigall, Richard and Yola Sigerson, Norman and Mary Doyle Springer, the late Harvey Swados and Bette Swados, the late Paul Tillett, Vernon and Dean Van Dyke, Helen Watt, Franz Weissenboeck, William H. Whyte, Jr., H. H. and Virginia T. Wilson, Suzanne Wolkenfeld, and Elliot Zupnick.

Once again I wish to express my gratitude to my editor at Putnam's, Harvey Ginsberg, and my agent, James Oliver Brown. In this venture as in others Harvey has been much more than an editor and Jim much more than an agent, and I trust it will always be so.

My thanks go also to Patricia Hughes White, secretary in chief, whose perseverance in handling office chores is equaled by her patience in dealing with difficult colleagues, disappointed graduate students, irate authors of articles and delinquent messenger boys. Somehow she found time in the midst of this chaos to type portions of the manuscript with skill and imagination. Other typists included Alene Egol (who expertly checked footnotes and bibliography), Annette Phillips, Minna Fyer, Myra Alperson, and Pamela Kokmotos. Research assistance was provided by Robert Danziger, Edna Fast, David Ferns, Donna Oglio Goldoff, Yael Gordon, Barbara Hochfield, Jane House, Mark Galanty, and John Staub.

ARNOLD A. ROGOW

New York, Jerusalem,
and Southfield
1972–1975

Notes

PREFACE

1. From Dickens' letter of April 1, 1842, to William C. Macready. By permission of the Pierpont Morgan Library. "I love and honor very many of the people here," Dickens added ". . . but 'the mass' (to use our monarchical terms) are miserably dependent in great things, and miserably independent in small ones."

2. J. H. Plumb has remarked, "No one in his senses would choose to have been born in a previous age unless he could be certain that he would have been born into a prosperous family, that he would have enjoyed extremely good health, and that he could have accepted stoically the death of the majority of his children." (Quoted by C. P. Snow in "The Two Cultures: A Second Look," *London Times Literary Supplement,* October 25, 1963.) Plumb was speaking of a time much earlier than the New Deal period, but his comment is also pertinent to an era that was characterized by large-scale unemployment, want, and approaching war.

3. John Maynard Keynes, *The Economic Consequences of the Peace* (New York: Harcourt, Brace and Howe, 1920), p. 4. Keynes was referring to the European wish after World War I to "return to the comforts of 1914. . . ." But perhaps, he added, "it is only in England (and America) that it is possible to be so unconscious [of the realities]."

4. From "Do Not Go Gentle into That Good Night" in *The Poems of Dylan Thomas.* Copyright 1952 by Dylan Thomas. Reprinted by permission of New Directions Corporation.

CHAPTER 1

1. Quoted in Edmund S. Morgan, *The Puritan Family* (New York: Harper & Row, 1966), pp. 1–2. As Morgan points out, "There was a type of man whom the

Puritans never tired of denouncing, a man who obeyed the laws, carried out his social obligations, never injured others . . . this paragon of social virtue, the Puritans said, was on his way to hell." See also John Demos, *A Little Commonwealth: Family Life in Plymouth Colony* (New York: Oxford, 1970).

2. George Francis Dow, *Everyday Life in the Massachusetts Bay Colony* (New York and London: Benjamin Blom, 1967), pp. 225–26.

3. Henry Bamford Parkes, *The American Experience* (New York: Vintage, 1959), pp. 5–6.

4. *Ibid.,* p. 7.

5. Quoted in J. C. Furnas, *The Americans: A Social History of the United States, 1587–1914* (New York: Putnam, 1969), p. 67.

6. Quoted from Lawrence's *Fifty Years* in Ralph Henry Gabriel, *The Course of American Democratic Thought* (New York: Ronald, 1940), pp. 149–50. "In the long run," Lawrence added, "it is only to the man of morality that wealth comes. We believe in the harmony of God's universe. We know that it is only by working along His laws natural and spiritual that we can work with efficiency. Only by working along the lines of right thinking and right living can the secrets and wealth of nature be revealed. . . . Material prosperity is helping to make the national character sweeter, more joyous, more unselfish, more Christlike. That is my answer to the question as to the relation of material prosperity to morality."

7. Abbott did not lack a social conscience, and he was sympathetic to the social gospel movement. See his *Christianity and Social Problems* (Boston: Houghton Mifflin, 1896), pp. 78–81.

8. Horace Greeley, *Recollections of a Busy Life* (New York: E. B. Treat, 1872), p. 542.

9. On the role of the churches in the late nineteenth century see Henry F. May, *Protestant Churches and Industrial America* (New York: Harper & Row, 1949); R. H. Johnson, "American Baptists in the Age of Big Business," *Journal of Religion*, Vol. II (1931), pp. 63–85; Charles E. Merriam, *American Political Ideas* (New York: Macmillan, 1926); William Wilson Manross, *A History of the American Episcopal Church* (New York: Morehouse, 1935); Agnes Rush Burr, *Russell H. Conwell and His Work* (Philadelphia: J. C. Winston, 1917).

10. Quoted in John C. Miller, *Origins of the American Revolution* (Boston: Little, Brown, 1943), p. 460.

11. Quoted in Parkes, *op. cit.,* p. 43.

12. Quoted from Crèvecoeur's *Letters from an American Farmer* (1782), in Merle Curti, *The Growth of American Thought* (New York: Harper & Row, 1943), p. 11.

13. Miller, *op. cit.,* pp. 408–11. The horrors attributed to both sides anticipate some of the later atrocities of Vietnam, but is it not clear how many of the horror stories reflect reality and how many were invented by propagandists, especially those on the American side. As Miller suggests, it is "significant that the [American] version of the battle, replete with British atrocities in all their gruesome detail, was the first to reach the people of England and America" (p. 409).

14. Irving Kristol, *The American Revolution as a Successful Revolution* (Washington, D.C.: American Enterprise Institute, 1973), p. 7.

15. Literature dealing with the Constitution is vast and, for the most part, of engaging interest since many of the issues involved illuminate matters of pres-

ent-day interest. The most important commentary on the Constitution itself is still *The Federalist,* regarded by many historians as the most original and important work in political theory written in America. But *The Federalist,* a series of newspaper articles that appeared in 1787–1788, was designed to influence public opinion toward ratification, and in places it suffers from an exhortatory style that is more pleading than persuasive. Several articles written by Hamilton are more important for what they do not reveal about Hamilton's hopes for the Constitution than for what they reveal of the pro-Constitution position. The best work on the period is associated with the names of Charles A. Beard, John Fiske, Max Farrand, Robert E. Brown, Merrill Jensen, Charles Warren, Allan Nevins, Richard Hofstadter, Robert L. Schuyler, and Carl Van Doren. The complexities of Hamilton's personality, which remains something of an enigma, are dealt with in Nathan Schachner, *Alexander Hamilton* (New York: Appleton-Century, 1946), and Jonathan Daniels, *Ordeal of Ambition: Jefferson, Hamilton and Burr* (New York: Doubleday, 1970); the definitive biography of James Madison is that of Irving Brant. See especially his *James Madison: Nationalist, 1780–1787* (Indianapolis: Bobbs-Merrill, 1948) and *James Madison: Father of the Constitution, 1787–1800* (Indianapolis: Bobbs-Merrill, 1950).

16. Richard Hofstadter, *The American Political Tradition and the Men Who Made It* (New York: Knopf, 1948), p. 10. See also his *America at 1750: A Social Portrait* (New York: Knopf, 1971).

17. See Alpheus Thomas Mason, "The Federalist—A Split Personality," *American Historical Review,* Vol. 57, No. 3 (April, 1952), pp. 625–43.

18. C. E. Vaughan has noted that while it is "quite true that [Locke] uses the word 'property' to include the 'life, health and liberty' as well as the 'outward possessions' of the individual . . . it is clear that it is property in land and commodities which he has primarily in view . . . he had set himself to prove that property, in the usual and narrower sense, had already taken full shape under the convenient 'law of nature': that it was, therefore, one of the inalienable rights which man brought with him from the natural to the civil state. . . . And whatever the intention of Locke, the inevitable effect of it all is to set up a tyranny of the individual . . . the tyranny of the economically strong over the economically weak, of the rich over the poor." *(Studies in the History of Politcal Philosophy Before and After Rousseau,* Vol. 1, *From Hobbes to Hume,* [Manchester, Eng.: Manchester University Press, 1939], p. 168).

19. The effects of abundance on American history and character are explored in David Potter, *People of Plenty* (Chicago: University of Chicago Press, 1954). The contrast between high levels of spending on private consumption and low levels of expenditure on public services is dealt with in John K. Galbraith, *The Affluent Society* (Boston: Houghton Mifflin, 1958). Both books should be read in conjunction with Michael Harrington, *The Other America* (New York: Macmillan, 1962), in which the stress is on the magnitude and persistence of poverty in the United States.

20. Quoted in Parkes, *op. cit.,* p. 43.

CHAPTER 2

1. New York *Times*, August 31, 1972.
2. *New York Review of Books*, October 21, 1971.
3. Quoted by Peter Lefcourt in *Village Voice*, February 29, 1968.
4. Quoted from a Theater of Ideas discussion by Lillian Gordon in "Beyond the Reality Principle: Illusion or New Reality?", a paper presented at the October 16, 1969, meeting of the Institute for Psychoanalytic Training and Research. I am indebted to Ms. Gordon for the Fiedler statement and several of the quotations that follow.
5. Quoted in *New York Times Magazine*, October 5, 1968.
6. Quoted in *Saturday Review*, February 15, 1969.
7. New York *Times*, December 16, 1973.
8. New York *Times* of July 15, 1972, reported that virtually all witnesses testifying before the House Select Committee on Crime "agreed that a drug epidemic was engulfing the New York City [public] schools."
9. New York *Times*, November 18, 1970.
10. New York *Times*, December 3, 1971.
11. *New Yorker* magazine, January 8, February 5, 1972. Ms. Kael was referring to *Straw Dogs* and *Clockwork Orange*.
12. Many of these themes and the mood and life-style of the counterculture are almost perfectly captured in a letter sent by Bryan McDonald, a counterculture organizer in New Zealand and a coordinator for Peace Festivals, Inc., of Auckland. The handwritten letter, undated but sent sometime in 1971, is as follows:

SALUTATIONS,

Beautiful to hear from you. We have received many good vibes from the U.S. since the thing in Rolling Stone.

We have had to postpone the festival until next summer which will be late Jan. 1972. We lost our 2 sites at the last moment.

We are corresponding with some heavy people in Frisco in an effort to build up a much bigger festival for next summer. We have had some good offers and are sure we can get it together.

We are working on an idea of holding a world festival of the brotherhood of man. If our brothers on the West Coast get behind it, it should evolve beautifully. One of the guys is ex-road manager of Quicksilver, another is in Studio Ten—did all Janis's takes, now working with Dead, Airplane, etc. Third brother helps with festivals, because he digs them—works with Ken Kesey and Pranksters et al.

As you see, contacts are O.K.—wow this writing is getting uneven—all the typing people are in the country, beaches, islands, etc. for a holiday.

About N.Z.—it's too beautiful—good beaches, lakes, rivers, bush, mountains, etc. More heads per population than most places. Most people are beginning to really turn on to what's here.—Becoming part of the road to Katmandu—get quite a few people in their Wooden Ships en route to the East.

There's still plenty of land around as the total population is only 2 1/2 mill.

Counterculture is growing—cops don't have guns yet so there are very few violent trips around, apart from the odd brawl or fight—as straight N.Z.ers are very sport conscious and some are inclined to get on ego trips about physique etc.—but N.Z. is peaceful relative to the world.

Things are getting a bit more repressive—more busts etc. but if you are reasonably cool, you can survive. Trend now is to turn on or trip in the country, or beaches etc., away from city paranoia.

If you intend coming here, let us know as we have a strong brotherhood around the whole country who can arrange free places for you to stay and show your things etc.

Re—land availability, some friends and I intend buying some land when we get enough bread, as it is still possible to get a place by the sea—which is rich with seafoods etc. In places it's as cheap as $5 per acre in large blocks, but this is mainly very rough bush. However, land away from the cities is still really cheap—you can get farmland bordering on the sea with bush on it et al.

We are part of a lot of people who are in a movement called Serenity who put on concerts, provide places for people to crash, do community work etc.

P.F. Inc. is a non-profit group—in fact we have to work to earn enough to eat—but food's pretty cheap and you can get fruit, shellfish etc. for nothing if you have contacts.

If you have any ideas, contacts or would like to get involved with the festival—called Pacifica—let us know.

Sorry about long time in replying but we were in the country for New Year etc when your letter arrived.

> Love & Serenity,
> BRYAN McDONALD

13. T. E. D. Klein in New York *Times*, March 28, 1972.

14. Theodore Roszak, *Sources: An Anthology of Contemporary Materials Useful for Preserving Personal Sanity While Braving the Great Technology Wilderness* (New York: Harper & Row, 1972.), pp. xxii–xxiii. See also his *The Making of a Counter Culture* (New York: Doubleday, 1969) and *Where the Wasteland Ends: Politics and Transcendence in Postindustrial Society* (New York: Doubleday, 1972).

15. Letter from Dr. Paul Williamson of McComb, Mississippi, reprinted from the medical newsletter *Practice* in New York *Times*, November 12, 1970.

16. *Science*, March 27, 1970, p. 1691.

17. Writings of the late Paul Goodman, who made no secret of his homosexuality and who, on occasion, was a critic of counterculture behavior, are an excep-

tion. For what turned out to be his final personal summing up, see his *New Reformation: Notes of a Neolithic Conservative* (New York: Vintage, 1971).

18. The best work on both alienated and radical youth in America, utilizing the approaches of both psychology and sociology, is that of Kenneth Kenniston. His major books are *The Uncommitted: Alienated Youth in American Society* (New York: Delta Books, 1965) and *Young Radicals: Notes on Committed Youth* (New York: Harvest Books, 1968). Activism on the Berkeley campus is dealt with in S. M. Lipset and S. Wolin, *The Berkeley Student Revolt* (Garden City, N.Y.: Doubleday Anchor, 1965). The psychoanalytic literature, mainly in the form of articles and monographs, is extensive. See especially Martin Wangh, "Some Unconscious Factors in the Psychogenesis of Recent Student Uprisings," *Psychoanalytic Quarterly*, Vol. 41, No. 2 (1972), pp. 207–23. The view that such uprisings are almost wholly neurotic in origin is presented in the writings of Bruno Bettelheim, of which his *Obsolete Youth* (San Francisco: San Francisco Press, 1970; reprinted from *Encounter*) is a summary statement. Psychoanalytic interpretations relevant to both activism and adolescent rebellion in general are found in Adelaide M. Johnson, "Sanctions for Superego Lacunae of Adolescents," in K. R. Eissler, ed., *Searchlights on Delinquency* (New York: International Universities Press, 1949); and Adelaide M. Johnson and S. A. Szurek, "The Genesis of Antisocial Acting Out in Children and Adults," *Psychoanalytic Quarterly*, Vol. 21, No. 2 (1952), pp. 323–43. Peter Blos *et al.*, "A New Adolescent?," *Psychosocial Process*, Vol. 2, No. 1 (1971), is a useful contribution. See also Erik H. Erickson, "Reflections on the Dissent of Contemporary Youth," *International Journal of Psychoanalysis*, Vol. 51 (1970), pp. 11–22; Henry and Yela Lowenfeld, "Our Permissive Society and the Superego," *Psychoanalytic Quarterly*, Vol. 39 (1970), pp. 590–608; and James L. Titchener, "The Day of a Psychoanalyst at Woodstock," in Warner Muensterberger, ed., *The Psychoanalytic Study of Society*, Vol. 5 (New York: International Universities Press, 1972).

19. Quoted in Irving Howe, *Politics and the Novel* (New York: Fawcett, 1957), p. 27. The word "collapsible" was underlined by James.

20. *International Herald Tribune*, March 7, 1973. A Pentagon spokesman commented: "These people had their feet on the ground while in prison" and declared that there would be no objection to the proposed corporation.

21. For an account of the controversy about whether or not Igor Stravinsky had in fact said and written words attributed to him by Robert Craft—and also whether Stravinsky had or had not eaten live crayfish in Strasbourg—see Donald Henahan's "But Was It Stravinsky?" in New York *Times*, May 7, 1972. Craft's rejoinder to Lillian Libman, another close associate of the late composer, and her reply to him may be found in the pages of *New York Review of Books*.

22. New York *Times*, December 4, 1972. The *Times* reporters, while persuaded that those and others named in the article had received injections of some type from Dr. Max Jacobson, added, "It cannot be said with certainty that the Kennedys or, with a few exceptions, any other specific patient received amphetamine. It is known, however, that Dr. Jacobson . . . buys amphetamine at the rate of 80 grams a month. This is enough to make 100 fairly strong doses of 25 milligrams every day."

23. The government's role as lawbreaker is examined in Jethro K. Lieberman's *How the Government Breaks the Law* (New York: Stein and Day, 1972.) The extent to which the government has compelled individuals to violate their own consciences merits a book in itself.

24. New York *Times*, February 18, 1972.

25. Ti-Grace Atkinson, quoted in New York *Times*, May 29, 1970.

26. Rev. J. Lawrence Yenches, DD, of the Church by the Sea, Bal Harbour, Florida, at the Florida League of Cities banquet, quoted in New York *Times*, December 9, 1972.

27. Sonya Kovalevsky, "Her Recollections of Childhood" (1895), quoted in *New Yorker*, June 27, 1970.

28. Urie Bronfenbrenner, *Two Worlds of Childhood: U.S. and U.S.S.R.* (New York: Russell Sage Foundation, 1970). See also New York *Times*, April 14, 1970, and *Science*, March 13, 1970.

29. Sigmund Freud, *Civilization and Its Discontents* (London: Hogarth, 1930), p. 93.

CHAPTER 3

1. Quoted in Richard Hofstadter, *The American Political Tradition and the Men Who Made It* (New York: Knopf, 1948) p. 56.

2. Charles A. Beard, *An Economic Interpretation of the Constitution of the United States* (New York: Macmillan, 1913), p. 149. For a critical view of Beard's findings see Richard Hofstadter, *The Progressive Historians* (New York: Knopf, 1968); and Robert E. Brown, *Charles Beard and the Constitution: A Critical Analysis of an Economic Interpretation of the Constitution* (Princeton: Princeton University Press, 1956).

3. Beard, *op. cit.*, p. 324.

4. Quoted by Robert Sherrill in *New York Times Book Review*, March 4, 1973.

5. Quoted by C. L. Sulzberger, New York *Times*, March 23, 1973. Nakasone confided to Sulzberger that "what shocks us most is that the United States has become so weak we find not only that the dollar is flabby but, more basically, there is inflation, reduction in your labor productivity, a marked decline in work hours and in the quality of the goods we buy from you." Not long after, the Japanese were to experience major economic difficulties.

6. Ronald Steel in a review of Richard J. Barnet, *Roots of War* (New York: Atheneum, 1972), *New York Times Book Review*, June 11, 1972.

7. Senator Frank Church quoted in New York *Times*, February 1, 1974. According to Church, the agreements were the "brainchild" of the National Security Council and, while not precisely illegal, were nevertheless "made in secret session" and "never legislated." The most incisive account of oil-industry operations in the United States and abroad is Robert Engler, *The Politics of Oil* (New York: Macmillan, 1961; rev. ed. 1975).

8. Quoted by Simon Lazurus and Leonard Ross in *New York Review of Books*,

June 28, 1973. As a number of critics of the regulatory approach have noted, the ICC and other regulatory agencies have served their industrial clients by substituting cartel arrangements for competition and permitting consumers to be exploited by monopolistic price structures and services. Relevant literature includes Gabriel Kolko, *Railroads and Regulations: 1877–1916* (Princeton: Princeton University Press, 1965); and Paul McAvoy, *The Economic Effects of Regulation* (Cambridge: Massachusetts Institute of Technology Press, 1965).

9. Mark J. Green, ed., *The Monopoly Makers.* (New York: Grossman, 1973). See also Green *et al.*, *The Closed Enterprise System* (New York: Grossman, 1972); Robert J. Heilbroner *et al.*, *In the Name of Profit* (New York: Doubleday, 1972); Ralph Nader and Mark J. Green, eds., *Corporate Power in America* (New York: Grossman, 1972).

10. New York *Times*, December 24, 1971, and January 29, 1972. In 1974 the FTC appropriation was $32,500,000.

11. Harrison Wellford, *Sowing the Wind* (New York: Grossman, 1973).

12. Quoted in New York *Times*, April 1, 1974. The expression "business-as-usual considerations" in reference to the background of the DC-10 crash is from a New York *Times* editorial of March 23, 1974. See also John Godson, *The Rise and Fall of the DC-10* (New York: McKay, 1975).

13. Quoted in Green *et al.*, *The Closed Enterprise System, op. cit.*, p. 148.

14. Quoted from *International Herald Tribune*, May 23, 1973.

15. Edwin H. Sutherland, *White Collar Crime* (New York: Holt, Rinehart and Winston, 1949).

16. Robert L. Heilbroner *et al.*, *In the Name of Profit* (New York: Doubleday, 1972). Heilbroner's "Profiles in Corporate Irresponsibility" deals with Dow Chemical, B. F. Goodrich (rubber), General Motors, Susquehanna Corporation (conglomerate), Richardson-Merrell (pharmaceuticals), and Colonial Pipeline.

17. Quoted in Sutherland, *op. cit.*, p. 10.

18. Richard Armstrong, "The Passion That Rules Ralph Nader," *Fortune*, May, 1971, p. 228.

19. Source: Council of Economic Advisors, Department of Commerce, Bureau of Labor Statistics. See also Eileen Shanahan, "Income Distribution Found Little Changed Since War," New York *Times*, February 2, 1974.

20. Quoted from a *Monthly Labor Review* article (Labor Department) by Peter Henle, senior specialist on labor for the Library of Congress, in New York *Times*, December 27, 1972.

21. New York *Times*, March 25, 1974.

22. Dennis C. Pirages and Paul R. Erlich, *Ark II: Social Response to Environmental Imperatives* (San Francisco: W. H. Freeman, 1974), p. 85.

23. New York *Times*, March 25, 1974. I am grateful to Robert Danziger for calculating the percentage increase.

24. New York *Times*, July 22, 1972.

25. Gresham Sykes, *The Society of Captives* (Princeton: Princeton University Press, 1958).

26. M. H. Brenner, "Fetal, Infant, and Maternal Mortality During Periods of Economic Instability," *International Journal of Health Services*, Vol. 3, No. 2 (1973), pp. 145–59.

27. Quoted from a study by Morey J. Wantman and D. G. Hay reported in *Medical Tribune*, March 19, 1970.

28. Brenner, "Economic Changes and Heart Disease Mortality," *American Journal of Public Health*, Vol. 61, No. 3 (March, 1971), pp. 606–11; "Patterns of Psychiatric Hospitalization Among Different Socioeconomic Groups in Response to Economic Stress," *Journal of Nervous and Mental Disease*, Vol. 148, No. 1 (1969), pp. 31–38; "Economic Change and Mental Hospitalization: New York State, 1910–1960," *Social Psychiatry*, Vol. 2, No. 4 (1967), pp. 180–88.

29. Study by the Citizens' Board of Inquiry into Hunger and Malnutrition, summarized in *International Herald Tribune*, October 28–29, 1972. See also New York *Times*, October 27, 1972, which carried a fuller report of the study.

30. New York *Times*, April 28, 1970.

31. Science editor Albert Rosenfeld in *Saturday Review World*, March 23, 1974, p. 59. Italics in original.

32. *Ibid.* A New York study based on 445 autopsies on stillborn and newborn infants showed that the infants of poor mothers were 15 percent smaller than those of nonpoor mothers. The thymus, spleen, liver, and adrenal glands, all involved in growth processes, were affected more than the brain, kidneys, heart, and skeletal bones. *Science*, Vol. 166 (November 21, 1969), p. 1026.

33. The quoted portion is from the classic work on political theory by Thomas Hobbes, *The Leviathan* (1651). As may be guessed, Hobbes was not a young man when he wrote these words but, at age sixty-three, almost a "senior citizen." Despite his pessimism, he lived to be ninety-one.

34. Editorial in *Science*, September 8, 1972.

35. New York *Times*, March 31, 1974.

36. New York *Times*, May 28, 1974.

37. New York *Times*, November 27, 1972.

38. The metaphor was frequently used by de Gaulle, who, politically active until shortly before his death in 1970 at age seventy-nine, was never visibly "shipwrecked." France himself lived to be eighty. Simone de Beauvoir, whose book *The Coming of Age* (New York: Putnam, 1972) is the best book to date on the subject of aging, was sixty-four when she wrote that old age was a "parody" of life. Does this suggest that even the most productive and vigorous of the aged cannot avoid feelings of pessimism and defeatism that are rooted in the aging process itself?

39. Ralph Nader and Kate Blackwell, *You and Your Pension* (New York: Grossman, 1973). See also Fred J. Cook, "The Case of the Disappearing Pension," *New York Times Magazine*, March 19, 1972. Reasons include: the loss of a job before a minimum period of time has elapsed, for whatever reason; changing jobs or changing unions; disability; employer bankruptcy; and other causes. According to Robert Sherrill, at Du Pont a pension can be terminated if the pensioner engages in any activity "which is harmful to the interest of the company." (New York *Times*, March 4, 1973.)

40. Mary Adelaide Mendelson, *Tender Loving Greed* (New York: Knopf, 1974); Donn Pearce, *Dying in the Sun* (New York: Charterhouse, 1974). See also Susan Jacoby, "Waiting for the End: On Nursing Homes," *New York Times Magazine*, March 31, 1974.

41. Margaret Kenrick, MD, in *Medical Tribune*, August 9, 1972. Although elderly and handicapped persons may have trouble dealing with stairs and escalators, many of the newer airport and rapid-transit facilities lack elevators. The effect is to make travel difficult or impossible for those who use crutches or are confined to wheelchairs.

42. New York *Times*, July 26, July 27, July 30, 1972; August 8, 1972.

43. New York *Times*, November 25, 1971. The Nader report on nursing homes contains numerous instances of cruel treatment deliberately inflicted on elderly and helpless persons, such as making them remain naked for long periods of time and otherwise dealing with them as if they were animals. See, for example, Claire Townsend, *Old Age: The Last Segregation* (New York: Bantam, 1971.).

44. New York *Times*, September 24, 1972. The carnival worker, who had been dead sixty-one years, was displayed in the garage of a funeral home in Laurinburg, North Carolina. Apparently his father had made a down payment on his funeral in 1911 but never returned to complete the transaction. Following complaints from prominent Italian-Americans and others in 1972, the owner of the funeral home agreed to bury the body, but only after storage and funeral costs had been paid.

45. Gunnar Myrdal, *An American Dilemma* (New York: Harper & Row, 1962). The preceding paragraph and much of what follows is drawn from my "The Revolt Against Social Equality," *Dissent* (Autumn, 1957), pp. 365- 71.

46. *Democracy in America* (New York: Harper & Row, 1966), p. 47.

47. New York *Times*, April 27, 1969. An accompanying picture showed a female customer of the bank driving up in one of her three Rolls-Royces, of which the chauffeur was black. In 1974 the bank's future was uncertain as the result of large losses in its foreign-exchange trading department, and on October 8 it was declared insolvent and taken over by the European-American Bank and Trust Company, a consortium organized by six European banks.

CHAPTER 4

1. George Orwell, *1984* (New York: Harcourt, 1971).

2. New Haven: Yale University Press, 1939, pp. 98, 100, 109.

3. Suzanne K. Langer, "The Social Influence of Design," *University: A Princeton Quarterly* (Summer, 1965), pp. 11–12. Langer's point is that these dolls are based on the "half-baked psychological theory" that children identify with teenagers.

4. Rollo May in *Saturday Review*, March 26, 1966.

5. *Sexual Behavior in the Human Male* and *Sexual Behavior in the Human Female* (Philadelphia: Saunders, 1948 and 1953).

6. *Human Sexual Response* (Boston: Little, Brown, 1966). In their more recent *The Pleasure Bond: A New Look at Sexuality and Commitment* (Boston: Little,

Brown, 1974), Masters and Johnson deal with sexual behavior in a less impersonal or mechanistic fashion. The major point stressed is that true sexuality involves commitment and not merely physical manipulation, but they also emphasize that a fulfilling relationship between a man and a woman is not possible without mutual sexual satisfaction.

7. Boston: Little, Brown, 1970.

8. New York *Times*, December 17, 1957.

9. From a book review by Broyard in *International Herald Tribune*, February 8, 1973.

10. *New York Review of Books*, December 9, 1965.

11. "Three Contributions to the Theory of Sex," in *The Basic Writings of Sigmund Freud* (New York: Modern Library, 1938), p. 563.

12. Emile Durkheim, *Suicide* (Glencoe, Ill.: The Free Press, 1951), p. 270.

13. The origins, history, usages in many languages and cultures, and persistence of the word "fuck" is explored at length in Leo Stone, MD, "On the Principle of Obscene Words of the English Language," *International Journal of Psychoanalysis*, Vol. 35, Part I (1954), pp. 1–27. See also Sigmund Freud, "The Antithetical Meaning of Primal Words" (1910), *Standard Edition*, Vol. 11 (London: Hogarth, 1957; reprinted 1968), pp. 153–61.

14. *Contributions to the Psychology of Love: The Most Prevalent Form of Degradation in Erotic Life,* in *Collected Papers*, Vol. 4 (London: Hogarth, 1949; first published in 1912), p. 214.

CHAPTER 5

1. In 1970 New York, with a five-borough population of 7,895,000, was the third largest city in the world. Shanghai was first, with 10,820,000 persons, followed by Tokyo, with 8,841,000. Of the top ten most-populated cities, only two, London and Moscow, were in Europe, and only New York of American cities made the list. (*United Nations Demographic Yearbook*, 1972.)

2. New York *Times*, December 6, 1970.

3. Lady Haire of Whiteabbey in New York *Times,* January 11, 1972.

4. New York *Times,* July 19, 1971.

5. *New York Review of Books*, December 14, 1972.

6. Letter to the Editor from George W. English, Jr., in the travel section of New York *Times*, March 1, 1970. "I shall advise my friends," Mr. English concluded his letter, "both at home and in Europe, to visit Spain or perhaps one or another of the emerging nations in Africa this summer."

7. Lee Rainwater, "Poverty, Race and Urban Housing," in *The Social Impact of Urban Design* (Chicago: The University of Chicago Center for Policy Study, 1971), p. 19.

8. New York *Times*, March 15, 1970.

9. New York *Times*, July 9, 1969.

10. New York *Times*, June 19, 1970.

11. New York *Times,* June 27, 1971.

12. New York *Times,* April 7, 1972.

13. New York *Times,* March 5, 1973.

14. Oscar Newman, *Defensible Space* (New York: Macmillan, 1972).

15. William H. Whyte, Jr., "The Case for Crowding," *The Last Landscape* (New York: Doubleday, 1968). Reprinted in John Kramer, ed., *North American Suburbs* (Berkeley, Calif.: Glendessary Press, 1972), pp. 306–21. Whyte points out that the New York City Housing Authority has used only 16 percent of a 2,000-acre site for buildings.

16. Newman, *op. cit.* Newman suggests that the high-rise buildings for the elderly work best when they are "located at the periphery of the project, immediately adjacent to surrounding streets, and if possible, physically separated from the buildings housing children and play areas."

17. Whyte, "Please, Just a Nice Place to Sit," *New York Times Magazine,* December 3, 1972.

CHAPTER 6

1. The report by the heads of criminological institutes in fourteen countries was summarized in New York *Times,* December 5, 1971.

2. Unless otherwise noted, the source for all criminal statistics is the *American Almanac for 1974 (The Statistical Abstract of the United States)* or the FBI's *Uniform Crime Reports.* According to the latter, the number of serious crimes (murder, assault, rape, robbery, burglary, larceny, and auto theft) rose from 8,100,000 in 1972 to 8,600,000 in 1973. Since 1960 serious crime has increased 120 percent. (New York *Times,* September 6, 1974.) Note should be taken, however, that crime statistics regardless of source are notoriously unreliable and should be evaluated with care. Reporting agencies, such as police departments, differ in skill and methods for collecting data, and for obvious reasons crime statistics are subject to a good deal of manipulation.

3. New York *Times,* March 17, 1970. Anthony Lewis in *Times* of April 2, 1973, quoted one estimate from an unidentified source that "when a burglar does a good job, the odds are 50 to 1 against being convicted for it."

4. According to the FBI report as summarized in New York *Times,* August 29, 1972, blacks in 1971 accounted for 66 percent of robbery arrests, 62 percent of murder arrests, and 50 percent of forcible-rape arrests. The overall percentage of black violent-crime arrests was 54.8, an increase of 1.5 percent over the previous year.

5. The study by three University of Pennsylvania sociologists was reported in New York *Times,* October 19, 1972. Of the total of 9,945 boys studied, 3,475, or 35 percent, were involved with the police to the extent that "an official recording of the act resulted." Of the 10,214 juvenile crimes committed that year, 627 boys, or 6 percent of the 9,945, accounted for 53 percent.

6. *American Almanac,* p. 150.

7. Dotson Rader, "The Sexual Nature of Violence," New York *Times*, October 22, 1973. See also his *Blood Dues* (New York: Knopf, 1973). Rader's principal point is that acts of violence by young men "are long-delayed reactions against authority, against powerlessness before authority, authority usually presented to males in boyhood in the person of the dominant woman, the matriarch and teacher." Unfortunately for this thesis, matriarchal societies are less prone to violence than societies dominated by males. Assertions that Americans and America are oriented toward violence do not prove much, either. For example, H. Rap Brown's statement that "violence is as American as cherry pie" does not say anything about the causes of American violence or, for that matter, why cherry pie is so American. (Isn't cherry pie as popular or almost as popular in some other countries?)

8. Studies supporting these hypotheses are summarized in *Psychiatric News*, August 2, 1972; New York *Times*, December 27, 1970; December 9, 1971; and December 29, 1971. Research on primate behavior, especially the work of Harlow at Wisconsin, Deets at Pittsburgh, and Hamburg at Stanford, throws much light on the origins and control of violence in monkeys and other animals. For an account of brain research related to sources of violent behavior, see the summary by Harold M. Schmeck, Jr., in New York *Times*, December 27, 1970.

9. New York *Times*, May 18, 1969. See also Omer R. Galle, Walter R. Gove, and J. Miller McPherson, "Population Density and Pathology," *Science*, April 7, 1972, pp. 23–30; New York *Times*, October 26, 1972; and Ada Louise Huxtable in *Times*, November 5, 1972.

10. New York *Times*, January 27, 1972. The British Broadcasting Corporation report on television violence found that "twice as many 'good' American as 'good' British characters were victims of violence and the American characters were more likely to die violent deaths . . . half the American 'bad' characters met with a violent death, compared with 1 in 10 of the British 'bad' characters."

11. Monica D. Blumenthal, "Predicting Attitudes Toward Violence," *Science*, June 23, 1972, pp. 1296–1303. See also New York *Times*, May 26, 1971. The study in 1969 was based on a sample of 1,374 men "selected to represent all men in the United States between the ages of 16 and 54, and to represent all races, religions, economic and social classes." It was conducted by the University of Michigan's Institute for Social Research.

12. I have developed this interpretation at length in "Edmund Burke and the American Liberal Tradition," *Antioch Review*, Vol. 17, No. 2 (Summer, 1957), p. 255. Reprinted in *The Burke-Paine Controversy: Texts and Criticisms* (New York: Harcourt, 1963).

13. "Violence in America: Historical and Comparative Perspectives," *National Commission on the Causes and Prevention of Violence* (Washington, D.C.: Government Printing Office, 1969).

14. New York *Times*, April 14, 1974.

15. Quoted in Chicago *Tribune*, January 15, 1971.

16. Quoted in New York *Times*, December 29, 1971.

17. Albert J. Reiss as quoted in New York *Times*, January 28, 1972.

18. The report was summarized in New York *Times*, July 20, 1974.

19. In an editorial of May, 1967, The National Rifle Association publication, *The American Rifleman*, lamented the tendency of "some courts to pamper criminals," the lawbreaking and mob violence, and pointed out that "the armed citizen represents a potential community stabilizer. His support of law and order, whether as a civilian member of the posse comitatus or as one of the unorganized militia, defined as the 'whole body of able-bodied male citizens,' could prove essential. . . . If the U.S. civilian population were generally disarmed . . . how many policemen would the nation need?" In 1973 a Baltimore group calling itself Black October claimed in a leaflet that it had killed two heroin dealers and would kill others in the future. (New York *Times*, August 27, 1973.)

20. One of the best recent books on prison is Jessica Mitford, *Kind and Unusual Punishment: The Prison Business* (New York: Knopf, 1973). On Soledad and the California prison system, see Robert J. Minton, Jr., *Inside* (New York: Random House, 1971); Eve Pell *et al.*, eds., *Maximum Security: Letters from California's Prisons* (New York: Dutton, 1972); and Steven V. Roberts in New York *Times*, February 7, 1971. On Attica: New York State Commission on Attica, *Attica* (New York: Bantam, 1972); and Herman Badillo and Milton Haynes, *A Bill of No Rights* (New York: Outerbridge and Lazard, 1972). On New Jersey's Trenton State Penitentiary: Gresham Sykes, *The Society of Captives* (Princeton, N.J.: Princeton University Press, 1958). On parole and its problems: Tom Wicker in New York *Times*, July 27, 1972, and March 8, 1974. See also Piri Thomas, *Seven Long Times* (New York: Praeger, 1974).

21. This example of judicial inequities was given by Ralph Nader in testimony before the Senate Subcommittee on Criminal Laws and Procedures and quoted in New York *Times*, July 20, 1974.

22. The suspect, Juan V. Corona, in 1971 was accused of murdering twenty-five men and burying their bodies in California orchards. Because he was denied bail and had a poor command of English, Mexican-American organizations alleged that his civil rights, including the guarantee of a fair trial, had been violated.

23. Jean-Paul Sartre, Preface to Frantz Fanon, *The Wretched of the Earth* (New York: Grove Press, 1966), p. 18. For other interpretations of violence and its role in the United States, see Hannah Arendt, *On Violence* (New York: Harcourt, 1972); Stephen Schafer, *The Political Criminal: The Problem of Morality and Crime* (New York: Free Press, 1973); Ted Robert Gurr, *Why Men Rebel* (Princeton, N.J.: Princeton University Press, 1970); Hugh Davis Graham and Ted Robert Gurr, *The History of Violence in America: Historical and Comparative Perspectives* (New York: Bantam, 1969); Richard E. Rubenstein, *Rebels in Eden: Mass Political Violence in the United States* (Boston: Little, Brown, 1971); David Abrahamsen, MD, *Our Violent Society* (New York: Funk & Wagnalls, 1970); Fred R. von der Mehden, *Comparative Political Violence* (Englewood Cliffs, N.J.: Prentice-Hall, 1973). The late historian Richard Hofstadter was typically insightful and persuasive in his Introduction to Hofstadter and Michael Wallace, eds., *American Violence: A Documentary Study* (New York: Knopf, 1970), a portion of which was reprinted as "The Future of American Violence," *Harper's* magazine, April, 1970, pp. 47–53.

Chapter 7

1. Elliott Liebow, "No Man Can Live with the Terrible Knowledge That He Is Not Needed," *New York Times Magazine,* December 22, 1972.

2. New York *Times,* May 15, 1971. According to most accounts of the shooting, the police fired without provocation. One student reported: "When they stopped firing, the first thing they did was reach down and pick up their shells." The phrase "killed some niggers" is reminiscent of the way duck hunters talk after a successful day in the blinds, e.g., "We sure killed us some ducks today. . . ."

3. New York *Times,* July 2, 1971.

4. For a suggestive psychoanalytic exploration of white attitudes toward the Indians, see Rogin's "Liberal Society and the Indian Question," *Politics and Society,* May, 1971, pp. 269–312. Whereas liberals in recent times have been more pro-civil rights than conservatives, there is little difference between them historically in the treatment of Indians. Thus in the early period few distinctions can be made between Washington and Adams, on the one hand, and Jefferson and Jackson, on the other. On this point see Wilbur R. Jacobs, *Dispossessing the American Indian* (New York: Scribner's, 1972); and Virgil J. Vogel, *This Country Was Ours* (New York: Harper & Row, 1972). Other useful reading on the so-called Indian Question includes Sar A. Levitan and Barbara Hetrick, *Big Brother's Indian Programs—With Reservations* (New York: McGraw-Hill, 1972); and Estelle Fuchs and Robert J. Havinghurst, *To Live on This Earth* (New York: Doubleday, 1972).

5. Psychiatrist Joel Kovel makes the point that during the anal stage of psychosexual development, which is roughly between the ages of one and three, the nuclear ideas of dirt and property take hold of the personality system, and they remain through life associatively linked with the idea of excrement. The child both hates and desires what comes from his body; later in life derivative negative feelings attach to dirt and excrement, and positive feelings attach to property and possessions. Thus racism, Kovel argues, since it incorporates themes concerning dirt, excrement, sexuality, and power, becomes invested with anal fantasies. *(White Racism: A Psychohistory* [New York: Vintage Books, 1970].)

6. Winthrop D. Jordan, *White Over Black* (Baltimore: Penguin, 1969), pp. 162–63.

7. New York *Times* , March 8, 1970.

8. For example, Robert W. Fogel and Stanley L. Engerman, *Time on the Cross,* two vols. (Boston: Little, Brown, 1974), especially Vol. 1, *The Economics of American Negro Slavery.* In *The White Man's Burden: Historical Origins of Racism in the United States* (New York: Oxford, 1973), a condensation of his earlier *White Over Black* (1969), Winthrop D. Jordan's interpretation of the psychosexual background of black-white relations is similar to the one advanced here, although he disagrees on the earliest history. While it is true, as he claims, that sixteenth-century Elizabethan Englishmen traveling in Africa brought back accounts of sexual excesses indulged in by Africans, these, in the main, must have been as imaginary as the accounts of African women having sexual congress with

apes. These reports, in other words, tell us more about Elizabethan Englishmen than about Africans.

9. According to a 1971 report of the Urban Institute, as quoted by Tom Wicker in New York *Times*, July 25, 1971.

10. New York *Times*, March 22, 1970; May 6, 1974.

11. New York *Times*, March 24, 1972.

12. David G. Gil, *Violence Against Children* (Cambridge: Harvard University Press, 1970).

13. Gene Gordon, MD, and Dale Meers, in a paper presented to the 27th Congress of the International Psychoanalytic Association, Vienna, as reported in New York *Times*, July 30, 1971.

14. The Moynihan memorandum was dated January 16, 1970, but was not released to the public until March 1. White House Press Secretary Ronald L. Ziegler declined to say what Nixon's reaction had been or explain the delay in making the memorandum a matter of public knowledge.

15. New York *Times*, December 12, 1972. Warren was referring to the election of 1876, in which Democrat Samuel J. Tilden captured the popular vote by more than 250,000, but lost the electoral vote to Rutherford B. Hayes. Hayes, in order to win the electoral votes of the South, withdrew the Army and, in effect, terminated Reconstruction. The year 1876, therefore, marks the beginning in the South of apartheid American style, the constitutionality of which was not seriously questioned until the *Brown* v. *Topeka Board of Education* case of 1954, perhaps the most important and certainly the proudest decision of the Warren Court.

16. According to New York *Times*-Yankelovich Survey, as reported by Jack Rosenthal in *Times*, November 6, 1972. The Yankelovich Survey is highly respected by professional pollsters and students of public opinion.

17. Anthony Lewis in *International Herald Tribune*, November 4, 1972.

18. The poll, taken for *Newsweek*, was too small for maximum reliability since it was based on telephone interviews with a national cross section of 548 adults. A Gallup Poll in March, 1970, found 86 percent opposed to busing.

19. David Rosenthal, head of the psychology laboratory at the National Institute of Mental Health, as quoted in *Medical Tribune*, February 21, 1973. Dr. Rosenthal added: "The implication of a genetic basis underlying some criminality does not mean that an individual harboring the genotype must at some time commit a crime. My own opinion is that most crime arises because of environmental and psychological influences, and that socio-cultural factors in modern society primarily underlie the great current crime wave." See also Arthur R. Jensen, *Educability and Group Educability and Group Differences* (New York: Harper & Row, 1973); and William Shockley, "Crime and Dysgenics," *Skeptic: The Forum for Contemporary History*, Special Issue No. 4 (n.d.), pp. 50–51.

20. S. E. Luria, "What Can Biologists Solve?," *New York Review of Books*, February 7, 1974.

21. William B. Provine, "Geneticists and the Biology of Race Crossing," *Science*, November 23, 1973, pp. 790–96.

22. Joint Center for Political Studies, *National Roster of Black Elected Officials*, Vol. 3, May, 1973.

CHAPTER 8

1. Quoted in New York *Times*, February 7, 1971.
2. Anne R. Somers in *Medical Opinion*, July 1972, p. 26.
3. *Medical Tribune*, August 9, 1972.
4. Quoted from an article by Dr. Harry A. Sultz in *American Journal of Public Health*, referred to in New York *Times*, April 25, 1970. Dr. Sultz, admitting it was "hard to tell" whether the increase was due to improved diagnosis or reflected an actual rise in the ulcer rate, nevertheless thought that "there has been a real increase, in addition to an increased medical awareness of it."
5. Philip Slater, *The Pursuit of Loneliness* (New York: Beacon, 1971), p. 68. He perceptively notes that a similar function is performed by "the laughing narration of the events of a particularly chaotic day, in which one minor disaster follows hard upon another, or several occur simultaneously (' . . . and there I was, the baby in one hand, the phone and doorbell both ringing . . . '). These sagas are enjoyed because they conceal the fundamental vacuity of the housewife's existence. Saying 'everything happened at once' is an antidote to the knowledge that nothing ever happens really."
6. All remarks quoted are from New York *Times*, October 1, 1969, and March 31, 1972.
7. New York *Times*, May 16, 1971.
8. From an advertisement in New York *Times* for Norma Skurka and Oberro Gill, *Underground Interiors* (New York: Quadrangle, 1972). The cover of *New York Times Magazine*'s home section of September 30, 1973, features the living room of a house in which the owners, turning their "backs on the city," have created a windowless "oasis . . . related to the theory of minimalistic art."
9. Their first study of Muncie, *Middletown*, was published in 1929. *Middletown in Transition* appeared in 1937.
10. Alden Whitman in New York *Times*, December 3, 1970.
11. Based on *Statistical Abstract of the United States*, issued September, 1972.
12. New York *Times*, August 22, 1972.

CHAPTER 9

1. J. David Singer and Melvin Small, *The Wages of War: 1816–1965* (New York: John Wiley, 1972). The study is summarized in New York *Times*, May 6, 1971.
2. Lewis Richardson, *Statistics of Deadly Quarrels* (London: Stevens, 1960). See also Derek Freeman, "Human Aggression in Anthropological Perspective," in J. D. Carthy and F. J. Ebling, eds., *The Natural History of Aggression* (London: Academic Press, 1964), pp. 109–19.
3. Quoted in Alonzo L. Hamby, *Beyond the New Deal: Harry S. Truman and*

American Liberalism (New York: Columbia University Press, 1973), pp. 115–17. As Hamby, who is sympathetic to Truman, perceptively observes, "His approach to diplomacy was all too American. He was convinced of American innocence and altruism. He saw international problems as moral problems, international relationships as matters that could be handled in the same way as personal relationships. It was natural for him to be outraged by the Russian presence in Eastern Europe . . ." (*Ibid.*, p. 115).

4. Already literature dealing with responsibility for the Cold War would fill a good-sized library. The more important books among those that hold the communist powers mainly responsible include: Dean Acheson, *Present at the Creation: My Years in the State Department* (New York: Norton, 1969); Charles E. Bohlen, *The Transformation of American Foreign Policy* (New York: Norton, 1969); Harry S Truman, *Memoirs: Year of Decisions,* (Garden City, N.Y.: Doubleday, 1955) and *Memoirs: Years of Trial and Hope* (Garden City, N.Y.: Doubleday, 1956); Eugene V. Rostow, *Peace in the Balance* (New York: Simon and Schuster, 1972); W. W. Rostow, *The Diffusion of Power* (New York: Macmillan, 1972); Lyndon B. Johnson, *The Vantage Point* (New York: Holt, 1971). Books critical of American policy and/or espousing the view that the United States bears the major responsibility for the Cold War include: Gabriel Kolko, *The Politics of War* (New York: Random House, 1968); Richard J. Barnet, *Roots of War* (New York: Atheneum, 1972); Gar Alperovitz, *Atomic Diplomacy: Hiroshima and Potsdam* (New York: Doubleday, 1965) and *Cold War Essays* (New York: Doubleday, 1970); William Appleman Williams, *The Tragedy of American Diplomacy* (New York: Dell, 1962); Richard J. Walton, *Cold War and Counter-Revolution: The Foreign Policy of John F. Kennedy* (New York: Viking, 1972); Louise FitzSimons, *The Kennedy Doctrine* (New York: Random House, 1972); Charles Yost, *The Conduct and Misconduct of Foreign Affairs* (New York: Random House, 1972); David Halberstam, *The Best and the Brightest* (New York: Random House, 1972). See also Townsend Hoopes, *The Limits of Intervention* (New York: McKay, 1969), and *The Devil and John Foster Dulles* (Boston: Atlantic, 1973); James F. Byrnes, *Speaking Frankly* (New York: Harper & Row, 1947); Desmond Donnelly, *Struggle for the World: The Cold War, 1917–1965* (New York: Harper & Row, 1965); D. F. Fleming, *The Cold War and Its Origins, 1917–1960,* 2 vols. (Garden City, N.Y.: Doubleday, 1961); Louis J. Halle, *The Cold War as History* (New York: Harper & Row, 1967); William D. Leahy, *I Was There* (New York: McGraw-Hill, 1950); Walter Millis, ed., *The Forrestal Diaries* (New York; Viking, 1951); Arnold A. Rogow, *James Forrestal: A Study of Personality, Politics and Policy* (New York: Macmillan, 1963); Elting E. Morrison, *Turmoil and Tradition: A Study of the Life and Times of Henry L. Stimson* (Boston: Houghton Mifflin, 1960); Henry L. Stimson and McGeorge Bundy, *On Active Service in Peace and War* (New York: Harper & Row, 1947). The single most important article on the subject is, of course, George F. Kennan ("Mr. X") "The Sources of Soviet Conduct," *Foreign Affairs,* Vol. 25 (July, 1947)., pp. 566–82. It is doubtful that any article in history has ever had such an influence on a nation's foreign policy.

5. John Lewis Gaddis, *The United States and the Origins of the Cold War, 1941–1947* (New York: Columbia University Press, 1972), pp. 316–17.

6. *Ibid.*

7. Fulbright, *op. cit.*

8. *The Pentagon Papers, op. cit.,* pp. 15, 50–53, 144, 158, 428–29. Although France, Britain, the U.S.S.R., and Communist China were in general satisfied with the agreements, the United States merely "took note" of the agreements; and in August, 1954, the National Security Council concluded that the agreements were a "disaster" that "completed a major forward stride of Communism which may lead to the loss of Southeast Asia." *(The Pentagon Papers,* p. 15.)

9. *The Pentagon Papers,* pp. 16–23. Lansdale was the model for Colonel Hilandale in Eugene Burdick and William Lederer, *The Ugly American* (New York: Norton, 1958), and it is widely believed that Pyle in Graham Greene's *The Quiet American* was largely based on Lansdale.

10. Detailed evidence on the extent and long-term consequences of defoliation may be found in: Seymour M. Hersh, *Chemical and Biological Warfare* (Indianapolis: Bobbs-Merrill, 1968); Major Frederick J. Brown, *Chemical Warfare* (Princeton, N.J.: Princeton University Press, 1960); Steven Rose, ed., *Chemical and Biological Warfare* (Boston: Beacon, 1968); Thomas Whiteside, *Defoliation* (New York: Ballantine, 1970); Stanford Biology Study Group, *The Destruction of Indochina* (Box 3724, Stanford, Calif.); Barry Weisberg, *Ecocide in Indochina* (New York: Canfield Press, 1970); and Robin Clarke, *The Silent Weapons* (New York: McKay, 1968).

11. Sources: Department of Defense, U.S. Senate Subcommittee on Refugees and Escapees, Agency for International Development.

12. The extensive literature dealing with atrocities in Vietnam includes: Daniel Lang, *Casualties of War* (New York: McGraw-Hill, 1969); Seymour M. Hersh, *My Lai 4: A Report on the Massacre and Its Aftermath* (New York: Random House, 1972); Richard Hammer, *One Morning in the War: The Tragedy at Son My* (New York: Coward-McCann, 1970); Telford Taylor, *Nuremberg and Vietnam: An American Tragedy* (New York: Quadrangle, 1970); Frank Harvey, *Air War— Vietnam* (New York: Bantam, 1970); Mark Lane, *Conversations with Americans* (New York: Simon & Schuster, 1970); Richard A. Falk *et al.*, eds., *Crimes of War* (New York: Random House, 1971); Edward S. Herman, *Atrocities in Vietnam* (Philadelphia: Pilgrim Press, 1970); Jonathan Schell, *The Village of Ben Suc* (New York: Knopf, 1967); John Duffet, ed., *Against the Crime of Silence* (New York: Simon & Schuster, 1970); Neil Sheehan, "Should We Have War Crime Trials?," *New York Times Book Review,* March 28, 1971; Noam Chomsky, *At War with Asia* (New York: Pantheon, 1970).

13. Testimony of several Vietnam veterans during the presentencing hearing of Harleton Lewis Armstrong, accused in the bombing of the University of Wisconsin Army Mathematics Research Center, New York *Times,* October 17, 1973.

14. *Ibid.*

15. Ron Perez, former combat medic, in New York *Times,* October 13, 1970.

16. Quoted by New York *Times* critic John Leonard from interviews with Vietnam veterans reported in Mark Lane, *Conversations with Americans* (New York: Simon & Schuster, 1970). New York *Times,* November 18, 1970.

17. Testimony of Scott Camile, "Michigan Winter Soldier Investigation," quoted in Frances Fitzgerald, *Fire in the Lake* (Boston: Atlantic Monthly, 1972), p. 466.

18. Kenneth B. Osborn, former Army intelligence agent attached to the Agency for International Development, in New York *Times*, October 17, 1970.

19. Quoted by John Leonard from Mark Lane, *op. cit.*, New York *Times*, October 17, 1973.

20. William Alan Curman, former airborne infantryman, in New York *Times*, October 17, 1973.

21. Mary McCarthy, *Vietnam* (Baltimore: Penguin, 1967), p. 14.

22. *Ibid.*, p. 16. In 1970 Ngo Cong Duc, Secretary General of the Socialist Opposition bloc in the National Assembly of South Vietnam, estimated that more than 400,000 Vietnamese woman were prostitutes, with the number "increasing daily." (New York *Times*, October 24, 1970.)

23. New York *Times*, January 27, 1974. At that time the United States was spending approximately $2 billion per year on arms, ammunition, and military fuel for Vietnam, Laos, and Cambodia. (Anthony Lewis, New York *Times*, February 7, 1974.)

24. Quoted by George Wald in New York *Times*, January 10, 1972.

25. *Wall Street Journal*, May 28, 1969.

26. For a perceptive appraisal of the profits side of the military-industrial complex see I. F. Stone's "In the Bowels of Behemoth," *New York Review of Books*, March 11, 1971. According to Col. and James A. Donovan, in 1970 some 2,072 retired senior military officers were employed by defense industries (Colonel James A. Donovan, *Militarism, U.S.A.* [New York: Scribners, 1970].) The argument that profits and efficiency are inversely related to each other in the defense industry is presented in detail in Leonard S. Rodberg and Derek Shearer, eds., *The Pentagon Watchers: Students Report on the National Security State* (New York, 1970); Richard F. Kaufman, *The War Profiteers* (New York: Bobbs-Merrill, 1970). See also Richard J. Barnet, *The Economy of Death* (New York: Atheneum, 1969).

27. Quoted in New York *Times*, July 4, 1971, from a thirty-one page computer printout of "civil disturbance" reports accumulated by the Army in connection with the first Vietnam moratorium on October 15, 1969. The Army, while not identifying the sources of its information, admitted in 1970 that it had conducted an extensive domestic surveillance program for three years.

28. *Ibid.* The computer printout listed the names of "political participants" in the moratorium, including Governor Francis W. Sargent of Massachusetts, Governor Kenneth M. Curtis of Maine, and Senators Edward M. Kennedy and George McGovern.

29. Major General Thomas A. Lane (ret.) in New York *Times*, January 11, 1971.

30. General Bruce K. Holloway testifying before a subcommittee of the House Appropriations Committee, March 23, 1971, quoted in New York *Times*, July 13, 1971.

31. Recent psychoanalytic literature concerned with aggression and war includes Leo Stone, "Reflections on the Psychoanalytic Concept of Aggression," *Psychoanalytic Quarterly*, Vol. 40, No. 2 (1971), pp. 195–244; Jacob A. Arlow, "Perspectives on Aggression in Human Adaptation," and Edward D. Joseph, "Aggression in Human Adaptation," and Edward D. Joseph, "Aggression Redefined—Its Adaptational Aspects," *Psychoanalytic Quarterly*, Vol. 42, No. 2

(1973), pp. 178–84, 197–213; Gregory Rochlin, *Man's Aggression: The Defense of the Self* (Boston: Gambit, 1973); Samuel Atkin, "Notes on Motivations for War: Toward a Psychoanalytic Social Psychology," *Psychoanalytic Quarterly*, Vol. 40, No. 4 (1971), pp. 549–93; Jacob A. Arlow *et al.*, Symposium on "The Role of Aggression in Human Adaptation," *Psychoanalytic Quarterly*, Vol. 42, No. 2 (1973), pp. 178–266.

32. Alexander Mitscherlich, *Society Without the Father* (New York: Harcourt, 1963). See also Paul Federn, "*Zur Psychologie der Revolution: Die vaterlose Gesellschaft,*" *Der österreichische Volkswirt*, Vol. 2 (1919), pp. 571 ff., 595 ff., quoted in Mitscherlich, pp. 299–300.

33. Mitscherlich, *op. cit.*, p. 301. Of interest in this connection is the finding of Peter Merkl that in a group of 582 Nazi Youth movement members, one-third had lost their fathers prior to reaching age eighteen. Merkl's unpublished research and related studies are explored in Peter Loewenberg, "The Psychohistorical Origins of the Nazi Youth Cohort," *American Historical Review*, Vol. 76, No. 5 (December, 1971), pp. 1457–1502.

34. Mitscherlich, *op. cit.*, p. 302.

35. This theme and others related to it are discussed in C. L. Sulzberger, *An Age of Mediocrity* (New York: Macmillan, 1973). See also Amaury de Riencourt, *The Coming Caesars* (London: Cape, 1958).

36. In his Stanford University address of 1906 James called for "the moral equivalent" of such martial virtues as "intrepidity, contempt of softness, surrender of private interest, obedience to command . . ."—virtues he felt should be preserved. The meaning of "moral equivalent" as used above is, therefore, somewhat different from that given to the phrase by James.

37. *The Complete Poems of Cavafy*, trans. with some notes by Rae Dalven (New York: Harcourt, 1961), pp. 18–19.

Chapter 10

1. Miller's comment appeared in New York *Times*, November 4, 1972. On Mailer, see his article in *Life* magazine, from which the statement is quoted, and the somewhat modified version of it in his *St. George and the Godfather* (New York: New American Library, 1972). The most thorough and incisive recent study of the Presidency is Arthur M. Schlesinger, Jr., *The Imperial Presidency* (Boston: Houghton Mifflin, 1973).

2. New York *Times*, July 28, 1974.

3. Sigmund Freud, *Group Psychology and the Analysis of the Ego* (New York: Liveright, 1949; first published 1922), p. 49.

4. The survey of between 1,700 and 1,800 adults aged twenty-one and over in a national cross section was conducted by Michigan's Institute for Social Research. It was reported in New York *Times*, November 5, 1971.

5. For a report of the 1,524-voter survey see *International Herald Tribune*, July 5, 1968.

6. See New York *Times*, December 3, 1973.

7. New York *Times*, March 7, 1971.

8. Isaac Asimov in *Psychology Today*, April 1969, p. 39.

9. Quoted from an unidentified commentator on the Pentagon Papers by R. W. Apple in *New Statesman*, June 18, 1971.

10. Relevant reading on these topics includes: Victor Marchetti and John D. Marks, *The CIA and the Cult of Intelligence* (New York: Knopf, 1974); and David Wise and Thomas B. Ross, *The Invisible Government* (New York: Random House, 1964).

11. Johnson, campaigning against Republican presidential candidate Barry Goldwater, told an audience in New Hampshire on September 28, 1964: "We are not going north and drop bombs at this stage of the game. . . ." But on September 7, according to the Pentagon Papers, Johnson and his advisers had concluded that bombing attacks on North Vietnam were essential if the war was to be won. Five months later, in February, 1965, the bombing began.

12. On Moynihan see New York *Times* November 6, 1970; on "birth signs" see New York *Times*, October 9, 1971; on Roosevelt, New York *Times*, January 16, 1971; on Reagan's friend, New York *Times*, September 27, 1970; on Chief Justice Burger, New York *Times*, September 19, 1971; on Justice Powell, New York *Times*, August 31, 1972; on Bernstein, New York *Times*, November 25, 1970.

13. New York *Times*, April 6, 1969. A later article in *New York* magazine reported that Peale, who, like Graham, is a close friend of Nixon's, drives a Cadillac (his wife owns a Mercedes), but "agonized over the purchase. . . ." (New York *Times*, May 20, 1974.)

14. *Time*, July 15, 1974.

15. The best accounts of the "Checkers" episode, among the many that have been published, is Gary Wills, *Nixon Agonistes* (New York: New American Library, 1969), pp. 93–114. See also Earl Mazo, *Nixon: A Political and Personal Portrait* (New York: Harper & Row, 1959); Bela Kronitzer, *The Real Nixon: An Intimate Biography* (Skokie, Ill.: Rand McNally, 1960); Rowland Evans, Jr., and Robert D. Novak, *Nixon in the White House: The Frustration of Power* (New York: Random House, 1972); Joe McGinniss, *The Selling of the President* (New York: Trident, 1968). John Osborne's several *Nixon Watch* books are insightful. Arthur Woodstone's *Nixon's Head* (New York: St. Martin's Press, 1973), which alleges to be a psychoanalytic study, is interesting but unreliable.

16. Wills, *op. cit.*, p. 97. There are several versions of the "Checkers" speech, some of them quite different from the one appearing in Nixon's *Six Crises* (New York: Doubleday, 1962).

17. Interview with Rabbi Baruch M. Korff, portions of which were published in New York *Times*, July 17 and 18, 1974.

18. New York *Times*, September 19 and 23, 1973.

19. The *Times* story was headed: "Justice Department's New Image: Nixon's Right Arm," December 25, 1969.

20. New York *Times*, April 12, 1970. The former commissioners, Mortimer M. Caplin and Sheldon S. Cohen, called for an investigation.

21. New York *Times*, June 11, 1970.

22. *Life* magazine, July 17, 1970.

23. New York *Times*, March 6, 1973. Frederic V. Malek, a Haldeman assistant, gave Hickel's staff only a few hours to vacate their offices.

24. The Senators included Edmund S. Muskie of Maine, Harrison A. Williams, Jr., of New Jersey, and Joseph M. Montoya of New Mexico. New York *Times*, November 16, 1970.

25. New York *Times*, February 16, 1971.

26. The statement to Korff was made during an interview on March 13, 1974, that was reported in New York *Times*, July 7, 1974. The "Farewell" speech was delivered August 9, 1974.

27. Interview with Garnett D. Herner of Washington *Star-News*, November 5, 1972, reprinted in New York *Times*, November 10, 1972.

28. *Ibid.*

29. Tape transcript, April 4, 1972.

30. *Ibid.*, June 23, 1972.

31. Wills, *op. cit.*, pp. 169–71.

32. *Ibid.*, p. 171.

33. Quoted in *ibid.*, p. 170.

34. Michael Rogin and John Lottier, "The Inner History of Richard Milhous Nixon," *Transaction*, November–December, 1971, p. 21.

35. Mazlish, *In Search of Nixon* (New York: Basic Books, 1972), p. 22.

36. Rockefeller's statement, made to a San Francisco audience, is quoted by columnist Shana Alexander in *Newsweek*, December 23, 1974.

CHAPTER 11

1. Quoted in Joseph A. Dowling, "Psychoanalysis and History: Problems and Applications," *Psychoanalytic Review*, Vol. 59, No. 3 (1972), p. 437. See also Hofstadter's *The Age of Reform* (New York: Knopf, 1966) and *The Paranoid Style in American Politics* (New York: Random House, 1965). Hofstadter's view of Populism as, in some respects, a reactionary movement prone to nativism and the conspiracy theory of history has been challenged by a number of historians, among whom one of the most influential is Norman Pollack. See his "Hofstadter on Populism: A Critique of the Age of Reform," *Journal of Southern History*, Vol. 26 (1961), pp. 478–500; and *Response to Industrialism* (Cambridge, Mass.: Harvard University Press, 1962).

2. E. H. Carr, *The Twenty Years Crisis* (New York: Harper & Row, 1964), p. 20.

3. Quoted from Borkenau's "The Communist International" in Arthur Koestler, *The Yogi and the Commissar* (New York: Macmillan, 1945), p. 67. See also Harold D. Lasswell, *Psychopathology and Politics* (New York: Viking Press, 1960; first published 1930); *World Politics and Personal Insecurity* (New York: Free Press, 1965; first published 1935); and *Power and Personality* (New York: Norton, 1948). Also relevant are E. Victor Wolfenstein, *The Revolutionary Personality*

(Princeton, N.J.: Princeton University Press, 1967); and Robert C. Tucker, *Stalin as Revolutionary* (New York: Norton, 1973).

4. As Freud never tired of pointing out, there is little evidence that altruism is innate in the human condition and much evidence that man is essentially *Homo homini lupus.* "The bit of truth behind all this—one so eagerly denied—is that men are not gentle, friendly creatures wishing for love, who simply defend themselves if they are attacked," he wrote in 1930 in *Civilization and Its Discontents,* "but that a powerful measure of desire for aggression has to be reckoned as part of their instinctual equipment. The result is that their neighbor is to them not only a possible helper or sexual object, but also a temptation to them to gratify their aggressiveness on him, to exploit his capacity for work without recompense, to use him sexually without his consent, to seize his possessions, to humiliate him, to cause him pain, to torture and to kill him." *(Civilization and Its Discontents* [London: Hogarth Press, 1949], p. 85.)

5. Koestler, *op. cit.,* p. 74.

6. See, for example, "The Liberals Love Barry Goldwater Now," *New York Times Magazine,* April 7, 1974.

7. New York *Times,* February 13, 1967.

8. New York *Times,* December 8, 1957. Muller's forecast was for the year 2057.

9. See, for example, the successive issues of *The Futurist* since it began publication in 1966. Its June, 1974, issue, "The World of 1994," is of special interest, since it contains the views of Glenn T. Seaborg and Margaret Mead, among others. *The Futurist,* which is, for the most part, hopeful about the future, is the official publication of World Future Society: An Association for the Study of Alternative Futures. See also the August 24, 1974, issue of *Saturday Review World,* "2024 A.D.: A Probe into the Future," with articles by Andrei Sakharov, Kurt Waldheim, Rene Dubos, and McGeorge Bundy among others.

10. New York *Times,* December 31, 1969.

11. New York *Times,* February 20, 1970.

12. Robert L. Heilbroner, *An Inquiry into the Human Prospect* (New York: Norton, 1974); Andrew Hacker, *The End of the American Era* (New York: Atheneum, 1970). See also Theodore J. Lowi, *The End of Liberalism* (New York: Norton, 1969); James MacGregor Burns, *Uncommon Sense* (New York: Harper & Row, 1972); Richard N. Goodwin, *The American Condition* (New York: Doubleday, 1974); Peter Schrag, *The End of the American Future* (New York: Simon & Schuster, 1974); Daniel J. Boorstin, *Democracy and Its Discontents* (New York: Random House, 1974).

13. *The Limits to Growth,* pp. 23, 44, 173–74.

14. Ronald G. Ridker, "To Grow or Not to Grow: That's Not the Relevant Question," *Science,* December 28, 1973, pp. 1315–18.

15. New York *Times,* February 25, 1973.

16. *The Limits to Growth,* pp. 174–75.

17. McGeorge Bundy, "After the Deluge, the Covenant," *Saturday Review World, op. cit.,* pp. 18–19.

18. See her editorial, "World Population, World Responsibility," in *Science,* September 27, 1974.

19. New York *Times,* October 16, 1974.

20. See, for example, Roger Revelle, "Avoiding a Population Catastrophe," *Current,* March, 1974, pp. 42–49; and "Sex in the Future," *Psychiatric Opinion* (Roche Laboratories), June, 1973.

21. On the use of myth as a screening device see Ernst Kris, "The Personal Myth: A Problem in Psychoanalytic Technique," *Journal of the American Psychoanalytic Association,* Vol. 4 (1956), pp. 653–81.

22. *Democracy in America,* Vol. 2 (New York: Schocken Books, 1972), p. 400.

Bibliography

BOOKS

Abrahamsen, David, MD. *Our Violent Society*. New York: Funk & Wagnalls, 1970.

Acheson, Dean. *Present at the Creation: My Years in the State Department*. New York: Norton, 1969.

Adams, Charles Francis. *Autobiography*. Boston: Houghton Mifflin, 1916.

Adler, Norman, and Charles Harrington. *The Learning of Political Behavior*. Glenview, Ill.: Scott, Foresman, 1970.

Alperovitz, Gar. *Atomic Diplomacy: Hiroshima and Potsdam*. New York: Doubleday, 1969.

———. *Cold War Essays*. New York: Doubleday, 1970.

Ambrose, Stephen E., and James Alden Barber, Jr. *The Military and American Society*. New York: The Free Press, 1972.

Anderson, Jack, and Carl Kalvelage. *American Government Like It Is*. New York: General Learning Press, 1972.

Arblaster, Anthony, and Steven Lukes. *The Good Society*. New York: Harper & Row, 1971.

Arendt, Hannah. *Crises of the Republic*. New York: Harcourt, 1972.

———. *On Violence*. New York: Harcourt, 1972.

———. *The Origins of Totalitarianism*. New York: Meridian, 1958.

Attica: The Official Report of the New York State Commission. New York: Bantam, 1972.

Bach, Richard. *Jonathan Livingston Seagull*. New York: Macmillan, 1973.

Badillo, Herman, and Milton Haynes. *Bill of No Rights: Attica and the American Prison System*. New York: Dutton, 1972.

Barnet, Richard J. *Economy of Death*. New York: Atheneum, 1969.

———. *The Roots of War*. New York: Atheneum, 1972.

——— and Ronald Muller. *Global Reach: The Power of the Multinational Corporations*. New York: Simon & Schuster, 1975.

Barone, Michael, Grant Ujifusa, and Douglas Matthews. *The Almanac of American Politics.* New York: Gambit, 1972.

Beard, Charles A. *An Economic Interpretation of the Constitution of the United States.* New York: Macmillan, 1913.

Bennis, Warren G., and Philip E. Slater. *The Temporary Society.* New York: Harper & Row, 1969 (1964).

Bettelheim, Bruno. *Obsolete Youth.* San Francisco: San Francisco Press, 1970.

Bohlen, Charles E. *The Transformation of American Foreign Policy.* New York: Norton, 1969.

Boorstin, Daniel J. *Democracy and Its Discontents.* New York: Random House, 1974.

Brenner, Charles. *An Elementary Textbook of Psychoanalysis.* Garden City, N.Y.: Doubleday, 1957.

Bronfenbrenner, Urie. *The Worlds of Childhood: U.S. and U.S.S.R.* New York: Russell Sage Foundation, 1970.

Brown, Dee. *Bury My Heart at Wounded Knee.* New York, Holt, 1971.

Brown, Major Frederick J. *Chemical Warfare.* Princeton, N.J.: Princeton University Press, 1960.

Brown, Robert E. *Charles Beard and the Constitution: A Critical Analysis of an Economic Interpretation of the Constitution.* Princeton, N.J.: Princeton University Press, 1956.

Brown, Stuart G. *Revolution, Confederation and Constitution.* New York: Macmillan, 1971.

Burgess, Anthony. *A Clockwork Orange.* New York: Ballantine Books, 1972 (1962).

The Burke-Paine Controversy: Texts and Criticisms. New York: Harcourt, 1963.

Burns, James MacGregor. *Uncommon Sense.* New York: Harper & Row, 1972.

Byrnes, James P. *Speaking Frankly.* New York: Harper & Row, 1947.

Calvert, Greg, and Carol Neiman. *A Disrupted History: The New Left and the New Capitalism.* New York: Random House, 1971.

Cantril, Albert H., and Charles W. Roll, Jr. *Hopes and Fears of the American People.* New York: Universe, 1971.

Carr, Edward H. *The Twenty Years Crisis.* New York: Harper & Row, 1964.

Carthy, J. D., and F. J. Ebling. *The Natural History of Aggression.* New York: Academic Press, 1968 (1964).

Center for Policy Study. *The Social Impact of Urban Design.* Chicago: University of Chicago Press, 1971.

Chamberlain, Wilt, and David Shaw. *Wilt.* New York: Macmillan, 1973.

Chomsky, Noam. *At War with Asia.* New York: Pantheon, 1970.

Clarke, Robin. *The Silent Weapons.* New York: McKay, 1968.

The Committee of Concerned Asian Scholars. *The Indochina Story.* New York: Pantheon, 1971.

The Complete Poems of Cavafy, trans. and with notes by Rae Dalven. New York: Harcourt, 1961.

Connell, Robert William. *The Child's Construction of Politics.* Melbourne: Melbourne University Press, 1971.

Connery, Robert H., and Demetrios Caraley. *Governing the City: Challenges and Options for New York*. New York: Praeger, 1969.

Crick, Bernard, and William A. Robson. *Protest and Discontent*. Baltimore: Penguin, 1970.

Davies, A. F. *Essays in Political Sociology*. Melbourne: Chesire, 1972.

———. *Private Politics*. Melbourne: Melbourne University Press, 1966.

Davis, David Brion. *The Fear of Conspiracy*. Ithaca, N.Y.: Cornell University Press, 1971.

De Beauvoir, Simone. *The Coming of Age*. New York: Putnam, 1972.

———. *Force of Circumstances*. New York: Putnam, 1964.

Delany, Sheila. *Counter-Tradition: The Literature of Dissent and Alternatives*. New York: Basic Books, 1971.

Dollard, John, Neal E. Miller, Leonard W. Doob, O. H. Mowrer, and Robert R. Sears. *Frustration and Aggression*. New Haven: Yale University Press, 1961 (1939).

Donleavy, James P. *The Onion Eaters*. Baltimore: Penguin, 1972.

———. *A Singular Man*. Baltimore: Penguin, 1966.

Donnelly, Desmond. *Struggle for the World: The Cold War, 1917–1965*. New York: Harper & Row, 1965.

Dror, Yehezkel. *Crazy States*. Lexington, Mass.: Heath, 1971.

Duffet, John, ed. *Against the Crime of Silence*. New York: Simon & Schuster, 1970.

Dulles, John Foster. *War, Peace and Change*. New York: Garland, 1960.

Dumont, Matthew, MD. *The Absurd Healer*. New York: Science House, 1968.

Durkheim, Emile. *Suicide*. New York: The Free Press, 1951.

Eissler, K. R., ed. *Searchlights on Delinquency*. New York; International Universities Press, 1949.

Ellul, Jacques. *Autopsy of Revolution*. New York: Knopf, 1971.

Engler, Robert. *The Politics of Oil*. New York: Macmillan, 1961.

Erickson, Erik H. *Identity, Youth and Crisis*. New York: Norton, 1968.

Esherick, Joseph W., ed. *Lost Chance in China: The World War Two Despatches of John S. Service*. New York: Random House, 1974.

Evans, Rowland, Jr., and Robert D. Novak. *Nixon in the White House: The Frustration of Power*. New York: Random House, 1972.

Falk, Richard A., *et al.*, eds. *Crimes of War*. New York: Random House, 1971.

Faltermayer, Edmund K. *Redoing America*. New York: Collier, 1969.

Firestone, Shulamith. *The Dialectic of Sex: The Case for Feminist Revolution*. New York: Bantam, 1972 (1970).

Fitzsimons, Louise. *The Kennedy Doctrine*. New York: Random House, 1972.

Fleming, D. F. *The Cold War and Its Origins, 1917–1960*. Garden City, N.Y.: Doubleday, 1961.

Fliess, Robert, ed. *The Psychoanalytic Reader*. New York: International Universities Press, 1967 (1948).

Fogel, Robert W., and Stanley L. Engerman. *Time on the Cross*. Boston: Little, Brown, 1974.

Forman, James. *The Making of Black Revolutionaries*. New York: Macmillan, 1972.

Forrester, Jay W. *World Dynamics*. Cambridge, Mass.: Wright-Allen Press, 1971.

Frank, Jerome D. *Sanity and Survival: Psychological Aspects of War and Peace*. New York: Vintage, 1968.

Frazier, Walk. *Rockin' Steady*. Englewood Cliffs, N.J.: Prentice-Hall, 1970.

Free, Lloyd, and Hadley Cantril. *The Political Beliefs of Americans: A Study of Public Opinion*. New York: Simon & Schuster, 1968.

Freud, Sigmund. *Civilization and Its Discontents*. London: Hogarth, 1949.

———. *Collected Papers*. 5 vols. London: Hogarth, 1925–1950.

———. *Group Psychology and the Analysis of the Ego*. New York: Liveright, 1949 (1922).

———. *An Outline of Psychoanalysis*. London: Hogarth, 1949.

———. *Standard Edition of the Complete Works of Sigmund Freud*. 24 vols. London: Hogarth, 1953–1975.

Friedrich, Carl J. *Totalitarianism*. New York: Grosset & Dunlap, 1954.

Fromm, Erich. *Escape from Freedom*. New York, Rinehart, 1941.

Fuchs, Estelle, and Robert Havinghurst. *To Live on This Earth*. New York: Doubleday, 1973.

Fuller, R. Buckminister, Erica A. Walker, and James R. Killian, Jr. *Approaching the Benign Environment*. New York: Collier, 1970.

Gaddis, John Lewis. *The United States and the Origins of the Cold War*. New York: Columbia University Press, 1972.

Gil, David G. *Violence Against Children*. Cambridge, Mass.: Harvard University Press, 1970.

Glazer, Nathan, and Daniel Patrick Moynihan. *Beyond the Melting Pot*. Cambridge, Mass.: MIT Press, 1970 (1963).

Goodman, P., ed., *Essays in American Colonial History*. New York, Holt, 1967.

Goodman, Paul. *New Reformation: Notes of a Neolithic Conservative*. New York: Vintage, 1971.

Goodwin, Richard N. *The American Condition*. New York: Doubleday, 1974.

Graham, George J., Jr., and George W. Carey. *The Post-Behavioral Era: Perspectives on Political Science*. New York: McKay, 1972.

Graham, Hugh Davis, and Ted Robert Gurr. *The History of Violence in America: Historical and Comparative Perspectives*. New York: Bantam, 1969.

Graham, James. *The Enemies of the Poor*. New York: Vintage, 1973.

Green, Mark J., ed. *The Monopoly Makers*. New York: Grossman, 1973.

——— et al. *The Closed Enterprise System*. New York: Grossman, 1972.

Green, Phillip, and Sanford Levinson. *Power and Community*. New York: Pantheon, 1969.

Greene, Graham. *The Quiet American*. New York: Viking Press, 1967.

Greenstein, Fred I. *Personality and Politics*. Chicago: Markham, 1969.

Gurr, Ted Robert. *Why Men Rebel*. Princeton, N.J.: Princeton University Press, 1970.

Hacker, Andrew. *The End of the American Era*. New York: Atheneum, 1970.

Halberstam, David. *The Best and the Brightest*. New York: Random House, 1973.

Halle, Louis J. *The Cold War as History*. New York: Harper & Row, 1967.

Hamby, Alonzo L. *Beyond the New Deal: Harry S. Truman and American Liberalism*. New York: Columbia University Press, 1973.

Hammer, Richard. *One Morning in the War: Tragedy at Son My.* New York: Coward-McCann, 1970.

Hancock, M. Donald, and Gideon Sjoberg. *Politics in the Post-Welfare State: Responses to the New Individualism.* New York: Columbia University Press, 1972.

Hardwick, Elizabeth. *Seduction and Betrayal: Women and Literature.* New York: Random House, 1974.

Harrington, Michael. *The Other America.* Baltimore: Penguin, 1966 (1963).

Harris, Thomas A., MD. *I'm OK—You're OK.* New York: Harper & Row, 1967.

Harvey, Frank. *Air War—Vietnam.* New York: Bantam, 1970.

Haskell, Molly. *From Reverence to Rape: The Treatment of Women in the Movies.* New York: Holt, 1974.

Hayden, Tom. *The Love of Possession Is a Disease with Them.* New York: Holt, 1972.

Heilbroner, Robert L. *An Inquiry into the Human Prospect.* New York: Norton, 1974.

——— et al., *In the Name of the Profit.* New York: Paperback Library, 1972.

Herman, Edward S. *Atrocities in Vietnam: Myths and Realities.* Philadelphia: Pilgrim Press, 1970.

Hersh, Seymour M. *Chemical and Biological Warfare.* Indianapolis: Bobbs-Merrill, 1968.

———. *Cover-Up: The Army's Secret Investigation of the Massacre at My Lai 4.* New York: Random House, 1972.

———. *My Lai 4: A Report of the Massacre and Its Aftermath.* New York: Random House, 1970.

Hobbes, Thomas. *The Leviathan* New York: Dutton, 1950 (1651).

Hockett, H. *Political and Social Growth of the American People.* New York: Macmillan, 1940.

Hofstadter, Richard. *The Age of Reform.* New York: Knopf, 1955.

———. *The American Political Tradition and the Men Who Made It.* New York: Knopf, 1948.

———. *The Paranoid Style in American Politics.* New York: Random House, 1965.

——— and Michael Wallace, eds. *American Violence: A Documentary Study.* New York: Knopf, 1970.

Hollander, Xaviera. *The Happy Hooker.* New York: Dell, 1972.

Hollingsworth, J. Rogers. *Nation and State Building in America.* Boston: Little, Brown, 1971.

Hoopes, Townsend. *The Devil and John Foster Dulles.* Boston: Atlantic Monthly Press, 1973.

———. *The Limits of Intervention.* New York: McKay, 1969.

Hornsby, Alton, Jr. *The Black Almanac.* Woodbury, N.Y.: Barron's Educational Series, 1972.

Horowitz, Irving Louis. *The Use and Abuse of Social Science: Behavioral Science and National Policy Making.* New Brunswick, N.J.: Transaction, 1971.

Hoult, Thomas Ford. *The March to the Right: A Case Study in Political Repression.* Cambridge, Mass.: Shenkman, 1972.

Howe, Irving. *Politics and the Novel.* New York: Fawcett, 1967 (1957).

Huxley, Aldous. *Brave New World and Brave New World Revisited*. New York: Harper & Row, 1965 (1932).

Jacobs, Wilbur R. *Dispossessing the American Indian*. New York: Scribner's, 1972.

Johnson, Lyndon Baines. *The Vantage Point*. New York: Holt, 1971.

Jordan, Winthrop D. *The White Man's Burden: Historical Origins of Racism in the United States*. New York: Oxford University Press, 1973.

———. *White Over Black*. Baltimore: Penguin, 1969.

Josephson, Eric and Mary. *Man Alone: Alienation in Modern Society*. New York: Dell, 1966 (1962).

Kahler, Erich. *The Tower and the Abyss*. New York: Braziller, 1957.

Kammen, Michael. *People of Paradox*. New York: Knopf, 1972.

Kaufman, Richard F. *The War Profiteers*. Indianapolis: Bobbs-Merrill, 1972.

Keniston, Kenneth. *The Uncommitted*. New York: Delta, 1967 (1960).

———. *Young Radicals*. New York: Harcourt, 1968.

Kinsey, Alfred E., *et al*. *Sexual Behavior in the Human Female*. Philadelphia: Saunders, 1953.

———. *Sexual Behavior in the Human Male*. Philadelphia: Saunders, 1948.

Knutson, Jeanne N. *The Human Basis of the Polity*. Chicago: Aldine, 1972.

Koestler, Arthur. *The Yogi and the Commissar*. New York: Macmillan, 1967.

Kolko, Gabriel. *The Politics of War*. New York: Random House, 1968.

———. *Railroads and Regulations: 1877–1916*. Princeton, N.J.: Princeton University Press, 1965.

Kovel, Joel. *White Racism: A Psychohistory*. New York: Pantheon, 1970.

Kramer, John. *North American Suburbs: Politics, Diversity and Change*. Berkeley, Calif.: Glendessary Press, 1972.

Kronitzer, Bela. *The Real Nixon: An Intimate Biography*. Skokie, Ill.: Rand McNally, 1960.

Laing, R. D. *The Divided Self*. Gretna, La.: Pelican, 1966 (1960).

———. *The Politics of Experience and the Bird of Paradise*. Baltimore: Penguin, 1967.

Landau, David. *Kissinger: The Uses of Power*. Boston: Houghton Mifflin, 1972.

Lane, Mark. *Conversations with Americans*. New York: Simon & Schuster, 1970.

Lane, Robert E. *Political Man*. New York: Free Press, 1972.

———. *Political Thinking and Consciousness*. Chicago: Markham, 1969.

Lang, Daniel. *Casualties of War*. New York: McGraw-Hill, 1969.

Lasswell, Harold. *Politics: Who Gets What, When, How*. New York: Meridian, 1958 (1936).

———. *Power and Personality*. New York: Norton, 1948.

———. *Psychopathology and Politics*. New York: Viking Press, 1960 (1930).

———. *World Politics and Personal Insecurity*. New York: Free Press, 1965 (1935).

Lederer, William, and Eugene Burdick. *The Ugly American*. New York: Norton, 1958.

Levin, Murray B. *Political Hysteria in America: The Democratic Capacity for Repression*. New York: Basic Books, 1971.

Levitan, Sar A., and Barbara Hetrick. *Big Brother's Indian Programs—with Reservations*. New York: McGraw-Hill, 1971.

Levitt, Karl. *Silent Surrender*. New York: Liveright, 1971.

Lieberman, Jethro K. *How the Government Breaks the Law*. Baltimore: Penguin, 1972.

Lipset, Seymour M. *Politics and the Social Sciences*. New York: Oxford University Press, 1969.

———— and S. Wolin. *The Berkeley Student Revolt*. New York: Harcourt, 1968.

Lowi, Theodore J. *The End of Liberalism*. New York: Norton, 1969.

Lynd, Robert S. *Knowledge for What? The Place of Social Science in American Culture*. Princeton, N.J.: Princeton University Press, 1970 (1939).

———— and Helen Lynd. *Middletown in Transition*. New York: Harcourt, 1937.

Mailer, Norman. *Saint George and the Godfather*. New York: New American Library, 1972.

Marchetti, Victor, and John D. Marks. *The CIA and the Cult of Intelligence*. New York: Knopf, 1974.

Marcuse, Herbert. *One-Dimensional Man*. Boston: Beacon, 1970 (1964).

Masters, William H., and Virginia E. Johnson. *Human Sexual Response*. Boston: Little, Brown, 1966.

————. *The Pleasure Bond: A New Look at Sexuality and Commitment*. Boston: Little, Brown, 1974.

Mazlish, Bruce. *In Search of Nixon*. New York: Basic Books, 1972.

Mazo, Earl. *Nixon: A Political and Personal Portrait*. New York: Harper & Row, 1959.

McAvoy, Paul. *The Economic Effects of Regulation*. Cambridge, Mass.: MIT Press, 1965.

McCarthy, Mary. *Medina*. New York: Harcourt, 1972.

————. *Vietnam*. Baltimore: Penguin, 1968.

McGinniss, Joe. *The Selling of the President*. New York: Trident, 1968.

Meadows, Donella H., Dennis L. Meadows, Jorgen Randers, William W. III Behren. *The Limits to Growth*. New York: Universe, 1972.

Mehden, Fred von der. *Comparative Political Violence*. Englewood Cliffs. N.J.: Prentice-Hall, 1973.

Melman, Seymour. *The Permanent War Economy: American Capitalism in Decline*. New York: Simon & Schuster, 1975.

Mendelson, Mary Adelaide. *Tender Loving Greed*. New York: Knopf, 1974.

Midura, Edmund M. *Why Aren't We Getting Through? The Urban Communication Crisis*. Washington, D.C.: Acropolis, 1971.

Miller, S. M., and Frank Riessman. *Social Class and Social Policy*. New York: Basic Books, 1968.

Millis, Walter, ed. *The Forrestal Diaries*. New York: Viking, 1951.

Mitford, Jessica. *Kind and Unusual Punishment; The Prison Business*. New York: Knopf, 1973.

Mitscherlich, Alexander. *Society Without the Father*. New York: Harcourt, 1969 (1963).

Moore, Burness E., and Bernard D. Fine. *A Glossary of Psychoanalytic Terms and Concepts*. New York: The American Psychoanalytic Association, 1968.

Morison, Etling E. *Turmoil and Tradition: A Study of the Life and Times of Henry L. Stimson*. Boston: Houghton-Mifflin, 1960.

Myrdal, Gunnar. *An American Dilemma*. New York: Harper & Row, 1962.

Nader, Ralph, and Kate Blackwell. *You and Your Pension.* New York: Grossman, 1973.

———— and Mark J. Green, eds. *Corporate Power in America.* New York: Grossman, 1972.

National Commission on the Causes and Prevention of Violence, 1969. *To Establish Justice, To Insure Domestic Tranquility.* Washington, D.C.: U.S. Government Printing Office, 1969.

National Roster of Black Elected Officials, Vol. 3, 1973. Washington, D.C.: Joint Center for Political Studies, May, 1973.

Nixon, Richard. *Six Crises.* New York: Doubleday, 1962.

Novak, Michael. *The Rise of the Unmeltable Ethnics.* New York: Macmillan, 1972.

Oglesby, Carl. *The New Left Reader.* New York: Grove Press, 1969.

Orwell, George. *1984.* New York: Harcourt, 1971.

Osborne, John. *The Third Year of the Nixon Watch.* New York: Liveright, 1972.

Parkes, Henry Bamford. *The American Experience.* New York: Vintage, 1959.

Pearce, Donn. *Dying in the Sun.* New York: Charterhouse, 1974.

Pell, Eve, ed. *Maximum Security: Letters from California's Prisons.* New York: Dutton, 1972.

The Pentagon Papers, ed. by Neil Sheehan and E. W. Kenworthy. New York; Quadrangle, 1971.

Perry, Huey. *"They'll Cut Off Your Project": A Mingo County Chronicle.* New York: Praeger, 1972.

Pirages, Dennis C., and Paul R. Erlich. *Ark II: Social Response to Environmental Imperatives.* San Francisco: W. H. Freeman, 1974.

Platt, Anthony M. *The Politics of Riot Commissions.* New York: Collier, 1971.

Pollack, Norman. *Response to Industrialism.* Cambridge, Mass.: Harvard University Press, 1962.

Rader, Dotson. *Blood Dues.* New York: Knopf, 1973.

Rank, Otto. *The Myth of the Birth of the Hero.* New York: Vintage, 1964 (1932).

Rapson, Richard L. *Major Interpretations of the American Past.* Des Moines: Meredith, 1971.

Raskin, Marcus G. *Being and Doing.* New York: Random House, 1971.

Reich, Wilhelm. *The Mass Psychology of Fascism,* trans. Vincent R. Carfagno. New York: Farrar, Straus, 1970.

Reiche, Reimut. *Sexuality and Class Struggle.* New York: Praeger, 1971.

Richardson, Lewis. *Statistics of Deadly Quarrels.* London: Stevens, 1960.

de Riencourt, Amaury. *Coming Caesars.* London: Cape, 1958.

Roazen, Paul *Freud: Political and Social Thought.* New York: Vintage, 1970 (1968).

Rochlin, Gregory. *Man's Aggression: The Defense of the Self.* Boston: Gambit, 1973.

Rodberg, Leonard S., and Derek Shearer, eds., *Pentagon Watchers: Students Report on the National Security State.* New York: Doubleday, 1970.

Rogow, Arnold A, *James Forrestal: A Study of Personality, Politics, and Policy.* New York: Macmillan, 1963.

————. *The Jew in a Gentile World.* New York: Macmillan, 1961.

————. *The Psychiatrists.* New York: Putnam, 1970.

Rose, Steven, ed. *Chemical and Biological Warfare.* Boston: Beacon Press, 1969.

Rostow, Eugene V. *Peace in the Balance.* New York: Simon & Schuster, 1972.

Roszak, Theodore, H. *The Making of a Counter Culture.* Garden City, N.Y.: Doubleday, 1969.

———. *Sources.* New York: Harper & Row, 1972.

———. *Where the Wasteland Ends: Politics and Transcendence in Post Industrial Society.* New York: Doubleday, 1972.

Rubenstein, Richard E. *Rebels in Eden: Mass Political Violence in the United States.* Boston: Little, Brown, 1971.

Ryan, William. *Blaming the Victim.* New York, Pantheon, 1971.

Sartre, Jean-Paul. *The Wretched of the Earth.* New York: Grove Press, 1966.

Schaar, John H. *Escape from Authority.* New York: Harper & Row, 1961.

Schafer, Stephen. *The Political Criminal: The Problem of Morality and Crime.* New York: Free Press, 1973.

Schell, Jonathan. *The Village of Ben Suc.* New York: Knopf, 1967.

Schlesinger, Arthur M., Jr. *The Imperial Presidency.* Boston: Houghton Mifflin, 1973.

Schrag, Peter. *The End of the American Future.* New York: Simon & Schuster, 1974.

Selected Papers of Karl Abraham. New York: Basic Books, 1968.

Sennett, Richard. *The Uses of Disorder, Personal Identity and City Life.* New York: Vintage, 1970.

Short, James F., Jr., and Marvin E. Wolfgang. *Collective Violence.* Chicago: Aldine, 1972.

Singer, J. David, and Melvin Small. *The Wages of War: 1816–1965.* New York: John Wiley, 1972.

Skurka, Norma, and Gil Oberro. *Underground Interiors.* New York: Quadrangle, 1972.

Slater, Philip. *The Pursuit of Loneliness.* Boston: Beacon, 1971.

Slomich, Sidney J. *The American Nightmare.* New York: Macmillan, 1971.

Smith, M. Brewster, Jerome S. Bruner, and Robert W. White. *Opinions & Personality.* New York: John Wiley, 1964 (1956).

Soble, Ronald, and Robert Dallas. *The Impossible Dream—The Equity Funding Story: The Fraud of the Century.* New York: Putnam, 1974.

Spengler, Oswald. *The Decline of the West.* New York: Knopf, 1962 (1922).

Sperlich, Peter W. *Conflict and Harmony in Human Affairs: A Study of Cross Pressures and Political Behavior.* Skokie, Ill.: Rand McNally, 1971.

Statistical Abstract of the United States, 1972, 1973, 1974.

Stavins, Ralph, Richard E. Barnet, and Marcus G. Raskin. *Washington Plans and Aggressive War.* New York: Vintage, 1971.

Steel, Ronald. *Imperialists and Other Heroes.* New York: Random House, 1971 (1964).

Stendhal. *The Private Diaries of Stendhal.* New York: Norton, 1962.

Stimson, Henry L. and McGeorge Bundy. *On Active Service in Peace and War.* New York: Harper & Row, 1947.

Stolz, Matthew. *Politics of the New Left.* Beverly Hills, Calif.: Glencoe, 1971.

Sullivan, Harry Stack. *Conceptions of Modern Psychiatry*. Washington, D.C.: William Alanson White Psychiatric Foundation, 1947.

Sulzberger, C. L. *An Age of Mediocrity*. New York: Macmillan, 1974.

Sutherland, Edwin H. *White Collar Crime*. New York: Holt, 1949.

Swomley, John M., Jr. *American Empire*. New York: Macmillan, 1970.

Sykes, Gresham. *The Society of Captives*. Princeton, N.J.: Princeton University Press, 1958.

Taylor, Telford. *Nuremberg and Vietnam: An American Tragedy*. New York: Quadrangle, 1970.

Thomas, Piri. *Seven Long Times*. New York: Praeger, 1974.

Tocqueville, Alexis de. *Democracy in America*. New York: Harper & Row, 1966 (1835).

Topping, Seymour. *Journey Between Two Chinas*. New York: Harper & Row, 1972.

Townsend, Claire. *Old Age: The Last Segregation*. New York: Bantam, 1971.

Truman, Harry S. *Memoirs: Year of Decisions*. Garden City, N.Y.: Doubleday, 1955.

———. *Memoirs: Years of Trial and Hope*. Garden City, N.Y.: Doubleday, 1956.

Tuchman, Barbara W. *Notes from China*. New York: Collier, 1972.

Uniform Crime Reports for the United States Federal Bureau of Investigation. Washington, D.C.: Government Printing Office.

United Nations Demographic Yearbook.

Vogel, Virgil J. *This Country Was Ours*. New York: Harper & Row, 1972.

Walton, Richard J. *Cold War and Counter-Revolution: The Foreign Policy of John F. Kennedy*. New York: Viking Press, 1972.

Weisberg, Harold. *Whitewash IV*. Maryland: Weisberg, 1974.

Weiss, Richard, and Gary B. Nash. *The Great Fear: Race in the Mind of America*. New York: Holt, 1970.

Wellford, Harrison. *Sowing the Wind*. New York: Grossman, 1973.

Whiteside, Thomas. *Defoliation*. New York: Ballantine, 1970.

Whyte, William H., Jr. *The Last Landscape*. New York: Doubleday, 1968.

Wicker, Tom. *A Time to Die*. New York: Quadrangle, 1975.

Williams, William Appleman. *The Tragedy of American Diplomacy*. New York: Dell, 1972.

Willner, Ann Ruth. *Charismatic Political Leadership*. Princeton, N.J.: Center of International Studies, Princeton University, 1968.

Wills, Garry. *Nixon Agonistes*. New York: New American Library, 1971. (1969).

Wolfenstein, E. Victor. *The Revolutionary Personality: Lenin, Trotsky, Gandhi*. Princeton, N.J.: Princeton University Press, 1967.

Wollheim, Richard. *Sigmund Freud*. New York: Viking Press, 1971.

Wolman, Benjamin B. *The Psychoanalytic Interpretation of History*. New York: Basic Books, 1971.

Yost, Charles. *The Conduct and Misconduct of Foreign Affairs*. New York: Random House, 1972.

Zinn, Howard. *The Politics of History*. Boston: Beacon, 1971.

Zwick, David. *Water Wasteland*. New York: Bantam, 1971.

Newspapers

Berkeley *Barb*
Chicago *Tribune*
Des Moines *Register*
The Guardian
International Herald Tribune
Le Monde
London *Times*
Los Angeles *Free Press*
Los Angeles *Times*
Miami *Herald*
National Observer

New York *Daily News*
New York *Times*
Philadelphia *Bulletin*
Princeton *Packet*
San Francisco *Chronicle*
Tri-Boro Post
Tuesday's Child
Wall Street Journal
Washington *Post & Times-Herald*
Washington *Star-News*

Magazines and Periodicals

American Historical Review
American Journal of Orthopsychiatry
American Journal of Public Health
The American Rifleman
Antioch Review
The Atlantic
Authors Guild Bulletin
Bulletin of the Atomic Scientists
Commentary
Congressional Quarterly
Cosmopolitan
Current
Dissent
Ebony
Eros
Esquire
Foreign Affairs
Fortune
The Futurist
Harper's
History of Childhood Quarterly
International Journal of Health Services
International Journal of Psychoanalysis
Journal of the American Psychoanalytic Association
Journal of Nervous and Mental Disorders
Life

Look
Medical Opinion
Medical Tribune
Monthly Labor Review
The Nation
New Republic
New Statesman
New York
New Yorker
New York Review of Books
Organic Gardening
Playboy
Playgirl
Politics and Society
Princeton magazine
Psychiatric Opinion
Psychoanalytic Quarterly
Psychosocial Process
Rolling Stone
Saturday Review World
Science
Scientific American
Social Psychiatry
Time
Transaction (Society)
Viva

Index

370

Ralston Purina, 82 n.
Randolph, Edmund, 36, 37
Rather, Dan, 288
Reagan, Ronald, 285
Reformers, psychology of, 306–9
Reformism, 317
Rembrandt van Rijn, 230 n.
Report on Manufactures (Hamilton), 40 n.
Republican Party, 182
"Resource imperialism," 320
Reston, James, 277
Revolutionaries, modern American, 182–85
Revolutionary Suicide (Newton), 216
Revolutionary War. *See* American Revolution
Rhode Island, defense contracts, 268 n.
Richardson, Lewis, 246
Ridenhour, Ronald Lee, 264
Riley, Clayton, 199 n.
Roberts, Steven V., 48–49
Rockefeller, David, 167
Rockefeller, John D., III, 286
Rockefeller, Nelson, 127, 282, 304
Rockin' Steady (Frazier/Berkow), 146 n.
Rogers, Carl, 48 n.
Rogin, Michael, 200, 301
Rolling Stone (magazine), 47
Rome, Italy, 142 n., 170
Roosevelt, Elliott, 285
Roosevelt, Franklin D., 12, 43, 44, 186 n., 214, 257, 275, 282, 286
Roosevelt, Theodore, 43, 186 n., 263 n., 302–3
Rosten, Leo, 146
Roszak, Theodore, 64, 66
Roth, Philip, 50 n.
Rousseau, Jean-Jaques, 103
Rousset, David, 9
Rubber Soul (Beatles), 73
Rubin, Jerry, 58 n., 64
Rumania, 253, 255
Runyon, Damon, 154

Sackler, Arthur M., 82 n.
Saigon, Americanization of, 265
St. Louis, Mo., 144, 149, 226 n.; black suburban population, 224 n.; and crime, 176 n.; job attrition, 151; Pruitt-Igloe public housing complex, 160–62; unemployment, 152; welfare percentage, 147 n.
St. Paul, Minn., 133, 138, 203
Sales tax, 99
San Diego, Calif., 158, 158 n.
San Francisco, Calif., 158, 242
San Francisco *Chronicle*, 116 n.
Santayana, George, 305

Sartre, Jean-Paul, 196
Satyricon (film), 74
Say and Seale, Lord, 29
Scandinavia, 319 n.
Schlesinger, Arthur M., 305 n.
Schlesinger, James R., 326 n.
Scholastic Aptitude Test scores, 55
Schonberg, Harold C., 141
Schrag, Peter, 54–55
Schutz, William, 63
Scotsman (train), 163
Seale, Bobby, 216
Sears, Roebuck Company, 150
Secondary process behavior, 50–51
Seize the Time (Seale), 216
Sensitivity training, 47
Select Committee of the New York State Assembly (1875), 306 n.
Seven Years War, 31
Sex: and fascism, 275; premarital, 113, 114 n., 116 n.; and racism, 201–4, 308–9; and violence, 136–37
Sex manuals, 123
Sex therapy clinics, 125–26
Sexual dysfunction, 119–20, 124–25
Sexual freedom, in future societies, 323–24, 324 n.
Sexual revolution, 72–73, 112–39; and adultery, 118–19; failure of, 131–33; and literature, 128–31; and politics, 138; and violence, 117, 118, 136–37
Shaffer, John H., 87
Shaft, 220
Shakespeare, William, 54, 55
Shannon, William V., 105
Shaw, David, 146 n.
Shays, Daniel, 35
Shays' Rebellion, 35 n.
Shell Oil Company, 110 n., 149
Shepard, Thomas, 19, 20, 24, 27, 39
Sherman, William Tecumseh, 261
Shockley, William, 216–17
Shoplifting, 56–57
Shopping center, suburban, 225–28
Shriver, Sargent, 258 n.
Shultz, George P., 298
Sinatra, Frank, 128, 228 n.
Sinclair, Upton, 92
Singular Man, A (Donleavy), 121 n.
Sitting Bull, 200
Six Crises (Nixon), 295
Slater, Philip, 236
Slavery, 34, 203–4
Smith, Jacob H., 263 n.
Smith Act, 283
Snowden, Lord, 127
Soble, Ronald L., 91 n.